"The rise of the biblical counseling movement is one of the most helpful and hopeful developments in the recent history of the Christian church. This movement has returned counseling where it belongs, in the church and in the Scriptures. In this massively important new book, some of the leading figures in the biblical counseling movement set forth a wealth of wisdom. We have needed this book for a long time."

—Dr. R. Albert Mohler Jr., president, the Southern Baptist Theological Seminary

"As a pastor I am constantly on the lookout for the kind of material that helps me in dealing with the care of my congregation. *Christ-Centered Biblical Counseling* is a wonderful compendium of godly wisdom that is a vital resource for a busy pastor. I commend it warmly."

—Alistair Begg, senior pastor, Parkside Church, Chagrin Falls, Ohio

"Those of us who are seeking to help needy, hurting people find hope in Christ owe a great debt of gratitude to those who contributed to this rich resource. It will make us more biblically grounded in our counsel and inspire us to believe that He really can transform lives!"

—Nancy Leigh DeMoss, author, Host of Revive Our Hearts Radio, Niles, Michigan

"There is a growing interest among Christians in using the Word of God to resolve serious troubles of the soul. And it is evident that the Bible is the final authority for all Christians. But does it contain the necessary theological sophistication to address these deep problems of the soul in a definitive way? *Christ-Centered Biblical Counseling* answers this question in an affirmative and robust manner. Readers will not be disappointed with the insights provided by the authors, who themselves are among the leaders in biblical counseling. The emphasis that is placed upon bringing counseling back to the local church is especially refreshing, for it is not the model used by the current psychotherapeutic world. Readers who have a high view of God's Word will find this book to be an invaluable read."

—Dr. John D. Street, president, National Association of Nouthetic Counselors, chair, MABC Graduate Program, The Master's College and Seminary

"This multiauthor handbook represents a new consensus that is emerging in biblical counseling. Solidly based in Scripture and written to help people to experience victory over sin, Christ and His gospel are pervasively put forward as God's primary means of soul healing, with an irenic spirit and nuance regarding the role of biology and relationships in spiritual problems and how to help."

—Eric L. Johnson, Lawrence and Charlotte Hoover Professor of Pastoral Care, The Southern Baptist Theological Seminary, Louisville, Kentucky

"If you love Jesus and want to be used by Him to help people through the personal ministry of the Word, *Christ-Centered Biblical Counseling* is an absolutely amazing resource."

—Mark Driscoll, founding and preaching pastor of Mars Hill Church, founder of Resurgence, cofounder of Acts 29

"*Christ-Centered Biblical Counseling* is more than a book about a topic. It represents new friendships that are forming around a common vision for discipleship and counseling permeated by the grace of the gospel, by the wisdom of Scripture, and by the centrality of the local church. This is a new development within our time, but its roots can be seen all through church history. This book captures a worldview. It maps deep truths that shape Christian care. It is a significant start and a reminder that we have much more work to do until the entire body of Christ is captivated by this common vision."

—Dr. Tim S. Lane, Christian Counseling & Education Foundation president and faculty, author of *How People Change*

"*Christ-Centered Biblical Counseling* is warm, personal, gentle, always wanting to listen and know the person, confident in the Spirit's working through the Word of Christ…Biblical counseling is in good hands as it moves to the next generation."

—Dr. Ed Welch, Christian Counseling & Education Foundation faculty, author of *Shame Interrupted*

CHRIST-CENTERED BIBLICAL COUNSELING

JAMES MACDONALD
GENERAL EDITOR

BOB KELLEMEN & STEVE VIARS
MANAGING EDITORS

HARVEST HOUSE PUBLISHERS
EUGENE, OREGON

Cover by Dugan Design Group, Bloomington, Minnesota

Cover photo © Viktor Gladkov / Shutterstock

Published in association with the literary agency of Wolgemuth & Associates, Inc.

In nearly all cases, people's names and details of their situations have been changed in order to protect their privacy. In the extremely few exceptions, permission has been granted to the publisher for the right to use their names and stories.

CHRIST-CENTERED BIBLICAL COUNSELING
Copyright © 2013 by Biblical Counseling Coalition
Published by Harvest House Publishers
Eugene, Oregon 97402
www.harvesthousepublishers.com

Library of Congress Cataloging-in-Publication Data

Christ-centered Biblical counseling/James MacDonald, Bob Kellemen, and Stephen Viars, general editors.
  p. cm.
Includes bibliographical references and index.
ISBN 978-0-7369-5145-6
  1. Counseling—Religious aspects—Christianity. 2. Bible—Psychology. I. MacDonald, James, II. Kellemen, Robert W. III. Viars, Stephen
  BR115.C69C47 2013
  253.5—dc23   2012027772

Printed in the United States of America

13 14 15 16 17 18 19 20 21 / LB-KBD / 10 9 8 7 6 5 4 3 2 1

Contents

Foreword

David Powlison

W̲hat kind of book are you picking up? *Christ-Centered Biblical Counseling* is like an architect's 1:12 scale model. A scale model intends to communicate "the concept" of a structure, not the myriad details of engineering, construction process, financing, and the like. Think of this book as a scale model of biblical counseling, delineating key theological underpinnings and sketching key methodological implications. There's enough detail to give you a feel for what the finished house will look like. But making the house your home will take work and prayer, further study and conversation, much putting into practice, and a lifetime of our maturing together.

Christ-Centered Biblical Counseling paints the broad strokes of counseling. Just for starters, those broad strokes revolutionize the meanings that our culture attaches to the word *counseling*. These chapters do not intend to cover all counseling problems or topics—or to probe particular problems or topics in great detail. However, the discussion and case studies will give you a solid feel for how the Word of life speaks into the lives of troubled and troublesome people who face a world of troubles.

This book affirms that a *good* counselor is many things simultaneously: tender and firm, responsive yet purposeful, candid and tactful, patient yet urgent, attentive and instructive, profound yet practical, prayerful and hardworking, comforting yet challenging, empathetic and objective, flexible yet committed, faithful to Jesus Christ and relevant to any person facing any trouble…along with many other good and desirable qualities. While the ingredients of deft conversation are hard to capture on paper, the tone and content of what you read will give you a feel for how godly wisdom carries on a compassionate and constructive conversation.

This book will not unpack the differing ways that, say, Deuteronomy or Ruth, a psalm or proverb, a scene in Luke, or a sentence from Ephesians come to life in the grit and grime of life lived. But you will gain a feel for the comprehensive relevance and adaptability of God's diverse self-revelation. The Word made flesh turns worlds upside down. The Christ who calls all nations, tribes, tongues, and peoples also speaks to each individual at the very points of deepest need.

As part of your reading strategy, approach this book as a scale model intending to communicate the concept of biblical counseling. All of us who counsel or desire to do so will better serve the welfare and well-being of others as we catch this vision, so that we can then work out the myriad details and implications.

It is no accident that this is the work of *many* contributors—a network, a coalition, a community of shared vision and mission. We are united in the conviction that the Christian faith speaks foundationally to the issues of counseling.

We are not clones, of course. We live and work within different ecclesiastical cultures and denominations. We serve in different organizations, pursuing different ministry objectives. We have different gifts, different strengths and weaknesses. But an underlying unity predominates. You will notice how consistently the common ground of Christian faith controls the discourse. Take careful notice of the common commitments that bring diverse Christians to work together.

As you read, you will note these pages represent a *development* upon the hard work of a previous generation. You will hear in the core commitments an essential continuity with the past. For example,

- Reality is God-centered and all human beings are worshippers, whether or not they are conscious of this reality and its implications.

- God our Father, Christ our Savior, and the Holy Spirit our Lifegiver is purposefully on-scene and actively working in people's lives.

- Scripture is comprehensively relevant to the things that concern, preoccupy, and trouble humankind.

- Counseling is an integral aspect of ministry and of church life.

Christ-Centered Biblical Counseling upholds these commitments and more. So come to listen. Learn. Ponder. Expect familiar Bible words, truths, metaphors, and passages to come at life and counseling from a fresh angle, and to generate fresh implications.

Then ask questions that carry your learning forward: How might I understand and handle this life problem or this theological reality with greater faithfulness and wisdom? How can I better conceptualize and practice this aspect of counseling? How can I grow truer to the mind-set and express purposes of Christ?

Ultimately the purpose of a scale model is to build the real thing. So read as if you are also part of the construction crew. As one who desires to counsel biblically, help to build a proper structure for faithful counseling ministry within the living body of Christ. Give yourself to the work of reading well, so that your response to this book contributes to this work-in-progress that God calls "my people." We grow up into the image of Jesus Christ by speaking truth in love, and that is the heart of a counseling model and methodology worth building.

David Powlison received his AB from Harvard College and worked four years in psychiatric hospitals before attending seminary. He graduated with an MDiv from Westminster Theological Seminary and began a career in biblical counseling. Along the way he received his PhD from the University of Pennsylvania in the history of science and medicine, with a focus in the history of psychiatry. David has been at the forefront of thinking and writing in biblical counseling for more than 30 years. He has written numerous articles on counseling and on the relationship between faith and psychology. His books include *Speaking Truth in Love, Seeing with New Eyes,* and *The Biblical Counseling Movement: History and Context.* David is the senior editor for the *Journal of Biblical Counseling.* He teaches as a faculty member for the Christian Counseling and Educational Foundation (CCEF) in Glenside, Pennsylvania, and also serves as a visiting professor at Westminster Theological Seminary.

In Christ Alone

Bob Kellemen and Steve Viars

What would motivate forty evangelical leaders to carve out the time from their active ministries to write a book together? What mission could possibly unite such a large number of Christian leaders?

The list of coauthors for *Christ-Centered Biblical Counseling* is long and varied. Some are senior pastors, while others lead biblical counseling, soul care, and discipleship ministries in churches. There are those who are relatively young, while others have over forty years of experience working with hurting people in our churches and communities. We are men and women with broadly diverse ethnic and cultural backgrounds. Many of our team members are accomplished authors, world-class speakers, and distinguished professors. So, what brought this divergent group of men and women together?

Are you ready for a surprise? It has nothing to do with money. None of the contributors to this book will be paid a dime. They knew from the beginning that any proceeds from this project would be given to advance the ministry of the Biblical Counseling Coalition.

That information changes the question, doesn't it? Why would forty leading evangelicals take time to write a book together and give all the proceeds to a new coalition of men and women committed to building stronger relationships and developing cutting-edge resources for the biblical counseling movement?

The Joy and Power of Unity

Here's the answer: because we want to promote authentic spiritual growth among God's people in ways that are grace-based and gospel-centered, relationally and theologically robust, grounded in the local church, and relevant to everyday life and ministry. Although we work in a variety of ministry settings, we are all deeply interested in the process of progressive sanctification—daily growth in Christ. We are less interested in the number of disciples and more interested in the quality of discipleship.

Some of us serve on the front lines in local churches desperately trying to help people in our congregations and communities draw closer to our Redeemer as we face the challenges of real life together. Others on our team are professors and authors seeking to mold and mentor the next generation of Christian leaders. We all want to be part of developing cutting-edge resources that bless those who are humble enough to acknowledge their need of counseling and equip those compassionate enough to counsel others in times of need.

We believe this task is so vast and vital that it is best accomplished as a unified group. It is a matter of creating greater synergy among people committed to biblical counseling who believe that together, we can accomplish more. We are persuaded that there is both joy and power in unity.

Important Foundations

As women and men who are passionate about God and His Word, we are guided by the comprehensive truths of Scripture. Three passages have especially directed our thinking:

- "I therefore, a prisoner for the Lord, urge you to walk in a manner worthy of the calling to which you have been called, with all humility and gentleness, with patience, bearing with one another in love, eager to maintain the unity of the Spirit in the bond of peace" (Ephesians 4:1-3).

- "Speaking the truth in love, we are to grow up in every way into him who is the head, into Christ, from whom the whole body, joined and held together by every joint with which it is equipped, when each part is working properly, makes the body grow so that it builds itself up in love" (Ephesians 4:15-16).

- "Grow in the grace and knowledge of our Lord and Savior Jesus Christ. To him be the glory both now and to the day of eternity. Amen" (2 Peter 3:18).

There are fresh winds blowing in the world of biblical counseling, pastoral care, soul care, one-another ministry, and discipleship among all those who long to speak the truth in love so that we grow up in Christ. Yes, we are thankful for the men and women in previous years who blazed a trail of counseling and discipleship that flowed from God's sufficient Word. Their impact on our lives and ministries is rich and strong. God, in His sovereignty, chose to bless many people who were involved in various expressions of biblical counseling in days gone by—pastors and churches, professors and schools, writers and publishing houses, executives and parachurch ministries.

However, somewhere along the line we were not as careful and proactive about working together. Silos of individual ministries became larger and—by administrative necessity—more isolated. We have not always been the greatest stewards of the resources and opportunities God has entrusted to us. Too frequently busyness and minor differences have prevented us from working together in a collegial fashion. And we have paid a price. Spending too much time in one's individual silo can produce pride, isolation, and a stagnated ministry. We have not always benefitted from the power of collaboration and the profit of collegial review and interaction.

All of that is changing, powerfully and rapidly. It really is a new day. We are seeking to break down the silos. We want to find ways to develop stronger and godlier relationships between leading men and women committed to biblical counseling in the United States and around the globe. We are willing to devote time and energy to make that happen.

We also believe the net effect of these friendships will be the production of cutting-edge resources to help people in Christ's church who are trying to counsel others in a variety of formats and forums. Whether you call it soul care, counseling, intensive discipleship, or spiritual growth, we hope that by working together a deeper, richer body of resource materials will be made available to God's people.

Speaking the Truth in Love

Through the book you hold in your hands, we want to model the very principles we espouse by working together to craft a description of *Christ-Centered Biblical Counseling*. As we unite to write this book, our purpose is to equip God's people to change lives with Christ's changeless truth. We want to grow together in learning how to *promote personal change centered on the person of Christ through the personal ministry of the Word.*

We're writing in response to God's command to work together to prepare His people for works of service. We desire that the body of Christ may be built up as we speak gospel truth in love to one another. We seek to listen carefully to how God may be using the strengths and emphases of our brothers and sisters to sharpen our thinking and enhance our beliefs and ministry practices. We invite you to join us on our journey.

In each chapter we focus on truth applied to life by blending theological wisdom and practical expertise. In Part 1—chapters 1 to 14—we emphasize a practical *theology* of biblical counseling. In Part 2—chapters 15 to 28—we highlight a practical *methodology* of biblical counseling.

A Robust and Relational Approach to Biblical Counseling

In the spirit of the words of Paul and Peter quoted above, here is the kind of ministry approach we hope to develop throughout *Christ-Centered Biblical Counseling*:

- grace-based and gospel-centered (Part 1)
- relationally and theologically robust (Part 1)
- grounded in the local church (Part 2)
- relevant to everyday life and ministry (Part 2)

Biblical Counseling Is Grace-Based and Gospel-Centered

It is our prayer that *Christ-Centered Biblical Counseling* will be dripping with grace and overflowing with the sweet savor of Jesus. We have all been deeply impacted with the awareness that Peter ended his great epistle with a pointed and powerful command: *grow in grace.*

Biblical counseling does not offer a system or a program, but rather it shares a person—*the* Person—Jesus Christ. *Christ-Centered Biblical Counseling* heralds a grace-based and gospel-centered foundation for all of life, all ministry, and all biblical counseling.

Biblical counseling strives above all else to bring glory to God. Counseling is ultimately not about the counselee or the counselor, but about the Divine Counselor. To that end, John Piper and Jack Delk lead the way by proposing how to keep the main thing the main thing in the midst of the suffering and sin that every counselor must address. They powerfully explain the purpose of our efforts and define our goal and passion as ministers of the gospel.

Ernie Baker and Jonathan Holmes build on this foundation by showing how we place our trust not in any human system of change, but in the transforming power of the Redeemer as the *only* hope to change people's hearts. Continuing this Trinitarian theme of counseling focused on the Father, Son, and Holy Spirit, Justin Holcomb and Mike Wilkerson demonstrate that biblical counseling is Spirit-dependent and prayer-saturated.

Grace-based biblical counseling is God-glorifying, Christ-centered, Spirit-dependent, *and* other-centered—because of its Trinitarian roots. Kevin Carson and Jeff Forrey develop this Trinitarian application by exploring what a model of counseling looks like that is built upon the relationship modeled within the Trinity. The answer to this core question obliterates the stereotype of biblical counseling—that it is aloof and solution-focused. Instead, it portrays wise counseling that models intimate involvement for the purpose of other-centered living.

Biblical Counseling Is Relationally and Theologically Robust

What makes biblical counseling truly biblical? *Christ-Centered Biblical Counseling* seeks to offer a positive and comprehensive answer to that question by communicating a robust, relational approach to biblical counseling. Our prayer is that this approach will increase your confidence in the sufficiency and relevancy of God's Word to address real-life issues.

We lay the foundation for this robust approach in chapters 1 to 4 through addressing life's first ultimate question: *Who is God and how can we know Him?* We build on that foundation in chapters 5 and 6 as we explore life's second ultimate question: *Where do we find answers—what is our source of truth for life?*

If we are to use the Bible effectively, then we must use it the way God wrote it—in narrative form. Our team rejects the notion that the Bible is simply an encyclopedia of disconnected Bible verses. God's Word is less like a cookbook and more like a novel. Thus, John Henderson vividly portrays the grand narrative of Scripture and its place in the process of progressive sanctification.

Next, Steve Viars and Rob Green address the issue of the sufficiency of Scripture. No issue has been more vital and more passionately discussed in biblical counseling. Pastors Viars and Green describe the theological essence of the concept and the practical implications of counseling from the sufficient Scriptures.

Chapters 7 and 8 then address life's third set of ultimate questions: *Who are we? How do we understand people—biblically?* Bob Kellemen and Sam Williams set the groundwork by conveying a comprehensive biblical understanding of God's original design of who we are and how we relate. They offer a theocentric understanding of the *imago Dei*—the image of God in humanity.

Who we are is not a question we can ask without also seeking to understand the context in which we live. Jeff Forrey and Jim Newheiser share a biblical understanding of the core influences that shape the responses of the human heart as they address a biblical perspective on the "nature/nurture" discussion.

Then the theological sky turns gray as we focus our attention on the nature of the problem. In chapter 9 we explore life's fourth set of ultimate questions: *What went wrong? Why do suffering and sin exist? What is the condition of fallen human nature?* In answer to these questions, Robert Jones and Brad Hambrick develop a working and workable theology of sin that assists the biblical counselor in diagnosing problems biblically.

Chapters 10 through 13 then speak to life's fifth set of ultimate questions: *Can people change? How do people change? What difference does the gospel make?* Pastor Robert Cheong initiates this section with a pointed discussion of the centrality of the gospel for Christian living and biblical ministry. Once we have laid the foundation of the beauty of God's grace and the perfection of God's Son, Stuart Scott addresses a nuanced perspective on the "balance" between what has become known as "the gospel indicatives and the gospel imperatives."

With this theological foundation of salvation and sanctification having been built, Lee Lewis and Michael Snetzer discuss the actual process of growing in Christlikeness. Then, Bob Kellemen and Dwayne Bond help us to face the facts—we are involved in a spiritual battle and we must understand the weapons of our spiritual warfare.

As the biblical narrative began before the beginning with the Trinity, so the Bible's grand narrative continues after the end with eternity. Nicolas Ellen and Jeremy Lelek answer life's sixth ultimate question: *What difference does our future destiny make in our present reality?*

Every approach to counseling and personal change must wrestle with these ultimate life questions. We believe God's Word alone provides the true and most compelling answers to these critical counseling issues.

If you've tracked with us thus far, and if you are a student of systematic theology, then likely you've "caught" how our chapters follow the classic doctrines covered in systematic theology:

- Chapter 1: Theology Proper—God the Father

- Chapter 2: Christology—God the Son

- Chapter 3: Pneumatology—God the Holy Spirit

- Chapter 4: Trinitarian Theology—God the Father, Son, and Holy Spirit

- Chapters 5 and 6: Bibliology—God's Word

- Chapters 7 and 8: Anthropology—Creation/Humanity

- Chapter 9: Hamartiology—Fall/Sin

- Chapters 10 through 13: Soteriology—Redemption/Salvation

- Chapter 14: Eschatology—Consummation/the Hope of Eternity

This theological foundation is no accident. We are convinced that God's Word has relevant answers for our real-life questions—that's why we call Part 1 "A Practical Theology of Biblical Counseling." We want to open God's Word to provide you with compelling, penetrating insights for Christian living.

Biblical Counseling Is Grounded in the Local Church

If you are versed in systematic theology, then you might be wondering, "But what about ecclesiology—the doctrine of the church?" In Part 2 of *Christ-Centered Biblical Counseling* we explore the place of Christ's church in the overall counseling process and the relevance of biblical counseling to everyday life. Building on the foundation of chapters 1 to 14, chapters 15 to 28 combine to address life's seventh set of ultimate questions: *How do we help? How do we care like Christ in the body of Christ?*

By saying that biblical counseling is grounded in the local church, we are not communicating that it is an insulated process isolated from the real world. We are saying quite the opposite—truly biblical counseling emphasizes a vision for the entire church impacting one another *and* the surrounding community.

Chapters 15 to 20 probe how we help—*congregationally*. These six chapters provide living-color answers to vital questions like, "What does biblical counseling look like in churches saturated with confidence in the sufficiency and relevancy of God's Word?" "What impact does this vision-in-action have on personal growth, church health, and community outreach?"

Pastors Steve Viars and Rob Green introduce the answers to these questions by demonstrating that God calls and equips the church to be not simply a place *with* biblical counseling, but a place *of* biblical counseling. Another best-practice pastoral team, pastors Mark Dever and Deepak Reju, describe why church health makes an enormous difference in a biblical counseling ministry.

While our culture distinguishes between preaching (the public ministry of the Word), counseling (the private ministry of the Word), and personal application (the personal ministry of the Word), the Bible considers the three holistically. Kevin Carson paints a portrait of what the public, private, and personal ministries of the Word look like in day-to-day ministry.

When we embed biblical counseling into the fabric of the church, it impacts and integrates into everything in the life of the church. Brad Bigney and Ken Long describe the seamless ways that biblical counseling and small group ministry unite to equip God's people to speak the truth in love.

Robust biblical counseling results in ongoing spiritual formation. Robert Cheong and Heath Lambert explore the intersections between biblical counseling and the spiritual disciplines.

In the final chapter in this "congregational section," Rod Mays and Charles Ware build upon the truth that for all eternity we will fellowship and worship together in multicultural diversity. Therefore, biblical counselors need to understand biblical principles of multicultural relating and counseling.

Biblical Counseling Is Relevant to Everyday Life and Ministry

With the underpinning of a healthy body growing together, the profound relevancy of biblical counseling for everyday life will be on display. In chapters 21 through 28, we investigate how to care like Christ from the vantage point of formal biblical counseling. Embedded corporately, we know how to become further equipped to minister *individually*.

Jeremy Pierre and Mark Shaw begin that process by illustrating the place of robust relationships in biblical counseling. Having established the necessity for the ongoing context of Christlike love, Randy Patten and Mark Dutton share the core principles of speaking the truth in love—the how-to elements of biblical counseling.

Of course, true and lasting change into the image of Christ is not a mechanical process, as Howard Eyrich and Elyse Fitzpatrick explain as they address issues of the heart. James MacDonald and Garrett Higbee build on this heart foundation by devoting two chapters to the development of the powerful issues of confession, repentance, and forgiveness.

The concluding three chapters emphasize issues that at times have been somewhat neglected in biblical counseling and personal discipleship—suffering, emotions, and the physical body. Bob Kellemen and Greg Cook describe how to help hurting people to find God's healing hope. Jeff Forrey outlines a robust biblical theology of emotions. And Laura Hendrickson probes the complex mind-body connection that is both majestic and deeply troubling to many.

To Him Be the Glory

When Peter counsels us to grow in the grace and knowledge of our Lord and Savior Jesus Christ, he does so with one ultimate goal: "To him be the glory both now and to the day of eternity. Amen." The last words—the last prayer—of the last sentence of Peter's last inspired letter serves as our prayer for *Christ-Centered Biblical Counseling*.

It's all about *Him*. As important as it is to develop collegial relationships that provide robust resources, if our focus is on us, then our focus is off base. Our prayer is that *Christ-Centered Biblical Counseling* will equip you to equip others also *so that* we bring Him glory through our individual and corporate growth in Christlikeness.

Part 1

A Practical Theology of Biblical Counseling

The Glory of God: The Goal of Biblical Counseling

John Piper and Jack Delk

John Piper

While preaching a sermon series at our church on the subject of eschatology, I taught from 1 Thessalonians 4:13-18 about Jesus' second coming. Paul begins and ends the passage in a way that allowed me to say to my people, "*This* is what you do with eschatology." Paul begins like this: "We do not want you to be uninformed, brothers, about those who are asleep, that you may not grieve as others do who have no hope." Then he closes, "Therefore encourage one another with these words." He begins and ends on a *pastoral* note. Eschatology is about how you suffer and how you help.

I stopped speaking, and we took some time for discussion. People only wanted to know whether the time frame was premillennial, postmillennial, or amillennial. I responded, "You're missing the point. Do you hear this? Paul doesn't want them to be ignorant of the fact that Jesus is alive. Jesus will come back. We will be with Him forever. Why? So they'll *grieve* a certain way. So they'll *encourage* (comfort) each other a certain way. Do you see what knowledge is about? It's about how to grieve. It's about how to counsel grieving friends. You speak knowledge into people's lives, and it impacts their grief. This is what your mouth is for: 'The mouth of the wise is a fountain of life.' Knowledge is so others can drink life-giving words. Doctrine is all about delight, all about how you live, all about how you counsel."

Defining Biblical Counseling

As a starting foundation, consider my definition of biblical counseling: Biblical counseling is God-centered, Bible-saturated, emotionally-in-touch use of language to help people become God-besotted, Christ-exalting, joyfully self-forgetting lovers of people. I'd like to unpack that definition in what follows, and ask, What is the relationship between delight and doctrine? What is the relationship between counseling and the church? What is the relationship between God's glory and His love for us?

Teaching Truth

Biblical counseling is God-centered, Bible-saturated, emotionally-in-touch use of language to help people become God-besotted, Christ-exalting, joyfully self-forgetting lovers of people. What does that mean? First, it means *teaching truth*. That 1 Thessalonians 4:14-18 passage bursts with truth:

> Since we believe that Jesus died and rose again, even so, through Jesus, God will bring with him those who have fallen asleep. For this we declare to you by a word from the Lord, that we who are alive, who are left until the coming of the Lord, will not precede those who have fallen asleep. For the Lord himself will descend from heaven with a cry of command, with the voice of an archangel, and with the sound of the trumpet of God. And the dead in Christ will rise first. Then we who are alive, who are left, will be caught up together with them in the clouds to meet the Lord in the air, and so we will always be with the Lord. Therefore encourage one another with these words.

Biblical counseling is nothing if it is not God-centered and Bible-saturated. R.C. Sproul said to me not long after James Boice died that in one of his last conversations with him, Dr. Boice said, "R.C., we are surrounded by pastoral wimps who say, 'People don't need teaching, they don't need knowledge: they need to be hugged, they need silence, they need stories, they need experiences shared.'" James Boice is absolutely right about the shrinking emphasis on teaching. People desperately need to be taught about the nature of God. They desperately need a biblical, God-centered perspective on everything. *Before* a calamity like September 11, we lay the foundations for our people of the granite sovereignty and glory of God so that they don't say, "Nonsense!" or don't shut their mouths with nothing to say. That's what biblical counseling is about—whether it is from the pulpit, in the office, or over the fence in the backyard. My take on the nature of counseling is that it has to do with knowledge, it has to do with our mouth, it has to do with doctrine, it has to do with the nature of God—communicated in ways that change hearers.

I get that from 1 Thessalonians 4:13-18, and, of course, it is all over the Bible. Consider Romans 15:4: "Whatever was written in former days was written for our instruction, that through endurance and through the encouragement of the Scriptures *we might have hope*" (emphasis added). Everything written is hope-giving. It all moves from written knowledge to heart-fearing. Or Psalm 19:7-8, "The law of the Lord is perfect, *reviving* the soul; the testimony of the Lord is sure, *making wise* the simple; the precepts of the Lord are right, *rejoicing* the heart." Teaching makes alive. Witness makes wise. Precepts produce joy. If they don't, something is wrong. You are doing something wrong!

Precepts produce change in emotions. Preaching goes to the emotions with doctrine. John 15:11 says, "These things I have spoken to you...*that your joy might be full.*" Speaking is about joy. Preaching is about joy. Counseling is about joy. You go from the head to the mouth to the head to the heart and produce joy, which transforms a person's life.

Restoring Counseling to the Church

Let me shift to my second concern—getting counseling into the church. Where else would it be, for goodness' sake? Can it be anywhere else and be true?

There are hindrances here. Let me point out and address just one. A lot of people reading this might respond, "It doesn't work," or "I've never seen anybody given to doctrine who is emotionally in touch!" There's one of the biggest obstacles. Here's my recommendation. Almost everything I do with my life is intended to solve this problem. If counseling, as I have laid it out, is to be restored to the church, *affection must be restored to reflection*. If counseling is to be restored to the church, *delight in God must be restored to doctrines about God*. Savoring Christ must be restored to seeing Christ. Tender contrition must be restored to tough conviction. Communion with God must be restored to contending for God.

I take that last one from John Owen. He said, "We have communion with God in the doctrines we contend for."[1] That is his measure of whether he is contending truly. "I must learn to commune with God in the doctrine." Isn't that an interesting phrase? Who talks like that today? You have to go back 300 years to find things so powerful on sin and communion with God. "Contending for and communing with God in a doctrine." Where is there a systematic theology class that helps students realize that when you unpack the incarnation or the nature of the Trinity or the two natures of Christ or the substitutionary atonement, you commune with the Lord as you defend and contend for the doctrine, or else you are not doing it right? No wonder people often don't want to be around doctrinally driven individuals! They aren't doing doctrine right. They aren't emotionally in touch with the truths they teach.

I believe we have a huge problem with this in the Reformed community. Reformed people are so afraid of emotion that they think I am talking about subjectivism. Pastors have a big job here, an impossible job. But we who are pastors have to do this. We have to consider our biblical mandate with regard to modeling for our people what is hindering the arrival of their being effective counselors to each other. I am more concerned about my people counseling each other than I am about my doing counseling myself. I counsel mainly from the pulpit *in order to create counselors*, a couple thousand of them.

Here is what it says about pastors and God's people in Hebrews 13:17: "Obey your leaders and submit to them, for they are keeping watch over your souls, as those who will have to give an account. Let them [the leaders, elders, pastors] do this with joy and not with groaning, for that would be of no advantage to you." This is an amazing mandate for pastors. Basically, it is saying that if pastors want to love their people and to be an advantage rather than a hindrance to them, they need to be happy. Is that a bad paraphrase? I'd go to the mat with any scholar over that paraphrase! It says, "Let them do this pastoral work—watching over your souls—with joy, not with groaning, because that would be of no advantage to you."

Pastors, Christian leaders, and biblical counselors, if you want to love and bless people, pursue your joy! If you become indifferent to the pursuit of your own joy, you become indifferent to love, and you can't equip the church to counsel. That is sin! You cannot love people if you are indifferent to your happiness in the Lord.

Now there are hosts of Reformed and other types who sin when they preach and talk about doctrine by denying in their whole demeanor the preciousness of what they are talking about. The people do not come away saying, "That was the sweetest thing I have ever heard." The pastor or biblical counselor doesn't look like he thinks it is sweet or precious. He doesn't look like he thinks it is life-changing or that it would make him happy. In fact, he seems to be talking in a way that indicates he's kind of afraid that it *will* make him happy.

Why would anyone want to come back to listen? We all want to be happy! That is exactly the way God made us. The desire to be happy is the same as the desire of being hungry. It is a God-given thing, written right on our hearts. God put Himself as the all-satisfying center of all joy. The reason you are not happy, if you are not, is because you have not gotten to the center yet. Joyful leaders, who commune with the truths they contend for, are crucial to restoring counseling to the church.

The Glory of God

Third, how does this relate to *the glory of God?* This restoring delight to doctrine, affection to reflection, savoring to seeing, communion to contending—how does that relate to the glory of God? The whole book of Hebrews moves toward big issues like hold fast to your confidence, be strong in your encouragement, be joyful in your assurance, be deep in your contentment (Hebrews 3:6; 6:18; 10:34; 13:5). These words—confidence, encouragement, assurance, contentment—are all emotion-laden. The book of Hebrews is all about your joy, persevering in it, and being radically ready to lay down your life to take the gospel where it hasn't gone.

Why? Because it is all about Christ. Everything in it is about the superiority of Christ's priesthood, sacrifice, covenant, and mediatorial work. That glorious, grand, Christ-exalting foundation in Hebrews aims to produce confidence and joy and assurance and contentment and the radical lifestyle that flows from it. That means that if you preach, teach, and counsel in a way that people begin to delight in this Christ, He gets all the glory. The book is structured so that the magnificence of Christ's superiority supports confidence, encouragement, and contentment. The pervasive presence of such positive, satisfying emotions in your church magnifies the foundation for them, Jesus Christ.

Jonathan Edwards said it this way:

> So, God glorifies Himself also toward the creatures in two ways: 1. By appearing to…their understanding. 2. In communicating Himself to their hearts, and in their rejoicing and delighting in, and enjoying, the manifestations which He makes of Himself… *God is glorified, not only by His glory's being seen [known, reflected upon], but by its being rejoiced in…* God made the world that He might communicate, and the creature receive, His glory and that it might [be] received both by the mind and the heart. He that testifies his idea of God's glory [doesn't] glorify God so much as he that testifies also his approbation of it and his delight in it.[2]

You see and understand Christ: doctrine. You trust and love Christ: joy.

On the one hand, you have some Reformed leaders who testify to their ideas about God by crossing every "t," dotting every "i," and getting the doctrines right, to which I say, "Absolutely, Amen! I am with you." On the other hand, you have some Charismatic leaders who are all emotion—get those hands up and clapping, and those feet stomping, and feel something, for goodness' sake, or God hasn't arrived! I'm also with them! I hate the cleavage between these two. I am going to do everything within my power while I breathe to help each of these folks see that, according to Edwards, they are giving God only half His glory. *Know Him truly and don't feel Him duly*—He gets half His glory. *Feel Him duly and don't know Him truly*—He gets half His glory. Let's give Him all of His glory, as Jonathan Edwards did.

That means, depending upon which of those "camps" we are in, we must join Paul in his apostolic goal. "Not that we lord it over your faith, but we work with you for your joy" (2 Corinthians 1:24). The apostolic goal: work with the church for its *joy!* Do you do that? Is that your mandate? Do you get up in the morning dreaming about how to work with the church for its joy? Maybe you think that was an isolated slip of Paul's pen, and that he meant to write "faith" there. That's what it sort of sounds like. "Not that we lord it over your faith, but we are workers together with you for your faith." But he said "joy" instead of "faith."

In Philippians 1, Paul is not sure whether he is going to live or die. He wants to die to go to be with Jesus, yet he knows he should stay. Why?

"Convinced of this, I know that I will remain and continue with you all, *for your progress and joy in the faith*" (Philippians 1:25, emphasis added). Isn't that amazing? The great writer of the doctrinally unsurpassed book of Romans says his whole life on planet earth is devoted to the joy of the saints. So pastors, Christian leaders, and biblical counselors better not think they have a more noble goal.

We talked about the nature of counseling, and how Word and knowledge have an impact on heart and feeling. Second, we talked about restoring counseling to the church by restoring affection to reflection. Third, we related that to the glory of God by arguing that God is most glorified in us when we are most satisfied in Him.

Therefore, if you're a pastor, if you want God to be most glorified in your people, you must satisfy them with God. The agenda that notion sets for how you preach and teach is wondrous. How will you be faithful to the Scripture and get God right? The heart-work can be done only by the Holy Spirit. Joy is His fruit. This goal makes you a desperate pastor (and biblical counselor) because you cannot make people happy in God by yourself. Yes, you can make them happy in church by telling stories, by making them laugh, so they're glad they came to your church. You can even grow a church without God and without the Holy Spirit. What you cannot do, though, is make people happy in God without God. The human soul is wired to be happy in everything else but God since the Fall. If your goal is to be a worker with and for their joy in God, you are desperately inadequate. This is why we are called to the Word and prayer. He performs; ask Him. We are desperate for His help.

To Love and Be Loved

Fourth, I want to speak concerning what it is to love and be loved. What is it for God to love and for us to be loved by Him? What is it for us to love God and love other people? This is right at the heart of biblical counseling, isn't it? A sense of being loved, helping people to become loving people, and understanding how God loves us—sinners that we are.

For many years I have been trying to figure out how God's pursuit of His glory relates to His love for you and me. What I find gets clearer every year, and in recent months has gotten even clearer. For example, a woman came up to me after church, weeping her eyes out in distress over the problems in her life. At one point in our conversation I asked her, "If you were in a place where you had your family, perfect health, all your favorite foods, and all your favorite recreation, and you didn't have to feel guilty, would you still want to be there if Jesus wasn't there?" She cried out, "Yes!" That is where a lot of professing Christians are. The gifts of Christ are what they feel good about, not Christ. Forgiveness feels good, getting rid of guilt feels good, staying out of hell feels good, having a marriage work feels good, having the kids stay off drugs feels good, and having the body made well feels good. Frankly, Jesus can take a vacation. Just give me these things.

But, I don't think there will be anyone in heaven who doesn't want to be around Jesus more than they want anything else. This is why I am serious about joy. If you do not have joy in Jesus, you won't go to heaven.

So, what does it mean to be loved by God? God's love is almost impossible for Americans to grasp after fifty years of being saturated with love interpreted as enhancing self-esteem. For most Americans, to be loved is *to feel made much of*. That's the very definition of love. If you do things and say things that make much of me, I feel loved by you. If you don't, I don't. That means the love of God is inconceivable and unfeelable by those people. God is not into making much of us. To the degree that we distort the cross into an affirmation of my diamond-in-the-rough value, we lose the love of God. The cross is all about vindicating the righteousness and the glory of God, who has been pleased to enable unworthy sinners to delight in Him.

Why would He treat us so kindly when we are sinners, forgiving all our sins so that we might enjoy making much of Him? I ask this question everywhere I go now, to see if people are American or Christian. I ask, "Do you feel more loved when God makes much of you or do you feel more loved when God, at the cost of His Son, enables you to enjoy making much of Him forever?" These are two profoundly different root sources of satisfaction. One is being made much of; the other is seeing and savoring God and making much of God. Where is the bottom of your satisfaction? Everything in our culture teaches you to make being made much of the bottom of your satisfaction, which is what the devil wants you to do. This has been the case for all of us ever since the Fall. That we might instead be so deeply and inwardly transformed that there might be a new root source to our joy is inconceivable to the natural man! This is why the cross is folly, God is folly, and the church is folly to the natural man. The spiritual man is fundamentally a person whose deepest root source of joy has been altered from self to God.

Consider John 11: "Now a certain man was sick, Lazarus of Bethany, the village of Mary and her sister Martha. It was the Mary who anointed the Lord with ointment, and wiped His feet with her hair, whose brother Lazarus was sick. So the sisters sent word to Him, saying, 'Lord, behold, he *whom You love* is sick'" (verses 1-3 NASB, emphasis added). Don't miss that word "love." Jesus loves Lazarus. Lazarus is sick. What does love mean? "But when Jesus heard this, He said, 'This sickness is not to end in death, but for the *glory of God*'" (verse 4 NASB).

There are two massive biblical realities here: love of people and the glory of God. The driving question in my life for the last twenty years has been, "How do they relate?" The passage goes on, "This sickness is not going to end in death, but for the glory of God, so that the Son of God may be glorified by it. Now Jesus *loved* Martha and her sister and Lazarus" (verses 4-5 NASB, emphasis added).

This is not a loveless thing going on here. *This is love.* This is a portrait of love, and a portrait of how God the Son will be glorified. Then comes the absolutely, unintelligible conjunction from the standpoint of the world: "When therefore He heard that he was sick, He then stayed two days longer in the place where He was" (verse 6 NASB).[3] The "therefore" carries a megaton of theology! Jesus loves Lazarus. Lazarus is sick and he is going to die. It's a hard thing to die, for someone to drown in his own pneumonia, or for his liver to be eaten away, or his kidneys or stomach to suffer with such horrific pain, and no morphine in those days. I don't know how Lazarus died, but he was dying, and it was slow. Are You just going to let him die? Why do You not love him? But Jesus says, "I love him. I love you, Martha, and I love you, Mary. I'm not going to fix this problem." Why? In order that the Son of God may be glorified.

How would you define love on the basis of this text? Here's my definition:

> Love is doing whatever you have to do at whatever cost to your-
> self in order to help another person stop finding pleasure in being
> made much of and help them get to the mature, God-exalting,

Christ-besotted, joyfully self-sacrificing, self-forgetting delight in making much of God for the sake of others.

Jesus was going to do what Lazarus, Mary, and Martha needed to be able to glorify Him. How can we help our people break free from the love affair of being made much of? How can we all forget this little thing called the ego, and be ravished by what we were made for—God? Nobody takes a trip to stand on the edge of the Grand Canyon in order to enhance his or her self-esteem. The reason people go to the Grand Canyon is that a whisper of common grace remaining in their lives tells them they were made for something great outside themselves that draws the soul out into the most healthy, glorious, self-forgetting experience of delight—call it worship—that the world can scarcely imagine. Love does what is needed to help others love God's glory in Christ. Counseling is one of the most crucial forms of love. Counseling does what is needed to help others love God's glory in Christ.[4]

Increased Satisfaction in Christ Jesus: The Role of the Biblical Counselor

Jack Delk

If biblical counseling is about the glory of God, and if God is most glorified in us when we are most satisfied in Him, then the role of the biblical counselor is to help increase satisfaction in Jesus Christ. How can we as counselors help those we counsel find their satisfaction in all that God is for us in Christ Jesus? It is a process; often slow, sometimes painstaking, but it is a process. It is a process that requires much patience, love, and often repetition. It is a process that may look like three steps forward and two steps back. But this is the path of the biblical counselor. If our counsel is to be Christ-centered counsel that leads our counselees to increased satisfaction in Jesus, I would suggest three steps toward that one result.

First, God needs to be a part of the story. After listening to a counselee unpack their story there is usually something, or rather someone, left out—namely God. In the midst of their trial, pain, or suffering, God is not mentioned; He is forgotten. As a counselor I ask, "Where is God? Where is He in your struggle? Does He know what you are experiencing, thinking, feeling, desiring?" I want them to see that God *is* part of their story and He's been there the whole time.

But bringing God into the story is just a first step. Next I want to help the counselee see that God is sovereign in their story and the goodness of His sovereign designs. I want my counselees to see God seated on His throne as the Lord of the universe.

To get there I ask another series of questions: "If God is in this story, if He is part of your story, could He have changed it? Could He change your situation, your circumstance right now?" Yes, He could, but He hasn't. The struggle remains, the pain is there, and the trial is hard.

More questions: "Do you believe that God is good? Is God good as He exercises His sovereignty? Does He want what is best for you?" I want the counselee to see that God is good in His sovereignty. Even in the hardest moments of life, God is good and is working good. "And we know that for those who love God all things work together for good, for those who are called according to his purpose. For those whom he foreknew he also predestined to be conformed to the image of his Son, in order that he might be the firstborn among many brothers" (Romans 8:28-29). As biblical counselors we can say with confidence that God will use their circumstances, their experiences, to conform them to the image of Jesus—that is the good He has promised. Bringing God into the story and affirming God's sovereignty in it puts God at the center where He belongs. The counselee's perspective is reoriented from self-focus to God-focus. The counselee sees that their story is not ultimately about them, it is about God; our counsel now becomes God-centered.

Third, I want to help the counselee see that their story is part of something much bigger than themselves; it is part of God's grand narrative of redemption. It is about God's glory and fame. Although their story may seem exceedingly small and insignificant compared to all that God is doing throughout time and history, it is important to God. God is concerned and intimately involved in their story because it is part of His story, part of what He is doing. Because the larger story is primarily about God and His glory, the counselee can be confident that God is over every minute detail because God is jealous for His own fame and reputation, about what the counselee's story says about Him.

As a biblical counselor I want to encourage my counselee that the Bible is relevant to their struggle. The Bible speaks to their experience. The Bible deals with life at both its best and its worst. The Bible talks about betrayal. The Bible talks about sin and its consequences. The Bible talks about conflict, suffering, and dysfunctional families. The Bible talks about illness and physical ailments. And the Bible is full of wonderfully encouraging, God-glorifying stories of redemption, restoration, healing, and reconciliation in the lives of imperfect, broken people, people just like them. The counselees' names may not be written in the pages of their Bible, but if they are in Christ, their story is part of God's grand narrative of redemption. And the climax of that narrative is found in the gospel of Jesus Christ, where all lasting joy is found.

We are all weak sinners in need of a Savior; Jesus Christ is that Savior. What's more, Jesus knows us. He has experienced our temptations and is familiar with our suffering.

> Since then we have a great high priest who has passed through the heavens, Jesus, the Son of God, let us hold fast our confession. For we do not have a high priest who is unable to sympathize with our weaknesses, but one who in every respect has been tempted as we are, yet without sin. Let us then with confidence draw near to the throne of grace, that we may receive mercy and find grace to help in time of need (Hebrews 4:14-16).

We have a Savior who will lead us to God without fear or shame. "For Christ also suffered once for sins, the righteousness for the unrighteous, that he might bring us to God" (1 Peter 3:18).

There is hope in the gospel. There is healing in the gospel. There is power in the gospel. "The saying is trustworthy and deserving of full acceptance, that Christ Jesus came into the world to save sinners, of whom I am the foremost" (1 Timothy 1:15). There is inexpressible joy in the gospel. "Oh, taste and see that the LORD is good!" (Psalm 34:8). Hearts are drawn to the heavens in worship. Together we are satisfied in all that God is for us in Christ Jesus. We lead our counselees to become God-besotted, Christ-exalting, joyfully self-forgetting lovers of people and lovers of God, no matter the struggles and crises they are in or encounter in the future. This doesn't mean that pain, suffering, or sin is insignificant; it is real. Pain hurts, struggles are hard, and sin flowing from us and coming at us is a reality of the human experience. But seeing God at the center, receiving the illuminating truth of His Word, experiencing God's grace in the gospel in the past gives hope for the present and the future. The earth may shake, dust may swirl all around us, but this we know: When the quaking stops and the dust settles, Jesus will still be on His throne, ruling, reigning, and interceding for His own.

The Power of the Redeemer

Ernie Baker and Jonathan Holmes

Desperate, oppressed, full of guilt and bitter—this was the state of Kelli's anguished soul before learning of the rich resources the Lord had provided through His person and Word. At age twelve, Kelli felt so dirty and guilty that she would repeatedly chant to herself, "Jesus I'm sorry, God forgive me; Jesus I'm sorry, God forgive me." At age sixteen, these dirty feelings developed into a sense that she was also physically dirty, thus leading to deep compulsions to be cleansed. She began picking at any impurities on her body. Any spot of acne became the enemy to be extracted. She describes it as a "sick ritual" that she practiced for hours.[1]

In her desperation, Kelli announced to her mom that she was demon-possessed. A few weeks later she found herself at a local obsessive-compulsive disorder center awaiting her first appointment. As she went through therapy she found temporary relief through cognitive-behavioral counseling. She was told that with the correct combination of medicine and cognitive-behavioral therapy, she would be able to live a normal life. She was assured that the only reason she was struggling was because they had not found the winning combination yet. Her therapist said that these difficulties were the product of a chemical imbalance that prevented her brain from functioning normally and that she would never change.[2]

Kelli faithfully took the medicines prescribed and continued to fight the desperation that was still growing inside. Despite all of this, she continued to feel guilty and picked at everything—still feeling miserable, dirty, and guilty. So, she turned to the only thing left for her to do: curse God. The hatred within turned into an intense, passionate loathing. It scared her at first, but then she just kept sinking deeper.

Could the Lord help someone like Kelli? Is there power in the person of Jesus Christ to release her from this oppression? Can the Lord use her understanding and practicing of biblical principles to help set her free? This is exactly what the Scriptures promise in Isaiah 61.

In Isaiah 61:1-2a, the Lord says of Himself,[3] "The Spirit of the Lord GOD is upon me, because the LORD has anointed me to bring good news to the poor, he has sent me to bind up the brokenhearted, to proclaim liberty to captives, and the opening of the prison to those who are bound; to proclaim the year of the LORD's favor...."

These verses are set in a context of future hope for God's people and against the backdrop of Isaiah's prophecy of impending captivity. The Anointed One promises that He would be sent for broken people who can be healed, set free, and accepted by the Lord. This amazing message was intended to give great hope for those experiencing the pain of exile and captivity, but as we will see, they were also fulfilled in our Lord's ministry and are still being fulfilled today.

Who is this amazing person who gives hope to people like Kelli? It will be easy to see in Isaiah 61 how this incredible *person*, with a definite *pattern* to His ministry, had a *purpose* for coming.

The Person

The Anointed One speaks and says He has been anointed by "the Spirit of the LORD." We know this is the Messiah, since the word translated "anointed" is *Mashach*,[4] which is the word from which *Messiah* originates. This is also the equivalent to the New Testament title *Christ*. This anointing by the Spirit is for a mission, since that is what this type of anointing represented in the Old Testament.

The New Testament clearly reveals who this person is when Jesus, while visiting His hometown synagogue, reads this passage from Isaiah and states, "Today this Scripture has been fulfilled in your hearing" (Luke 4:21).

The message of Isaiah is reinforced by Matthew because he tells us that Jesus had a tender heart for the needs of people. In Matthew 9:36, we are told that He "had compassion." This word translated "compassion" is not just a word that shows He loved people through His actions. It is a feeling word.[5] Jesus felt deeply the needs of others. So, if we are going to be Christlike counselors, we

too ought to be moved by the needs of people. Colossians 3:12 tells us that
we are to have this same type of heart toward others.[6] Brokenhearted people,
like Kelli, need this compassionate ministry.

The Pattern

Isaiah shows that the Messiah's pattern of ministry is not just a ministry
of words. His pattern of ministry was one in which poor, brokenhearted, and
captive people experienced freedom and purpose.

The Poor

These poor are the afflicted, the humbled, and the oppressed.[7] For the
people of Isaiah's time it would bring comfort to know that the Messiah cared
about their needs during the captivity. During our Lord's time on earth this
was demonstrated through His personal ministry to the poor, such as touching
lepers and caring for those overtaxed by Rome. Today, biblical counseling
desires to be used of the Lord with the afflicted. We desire to minister hope,
comfort, and healing to the oppressed, since this is the pattern of the Lord's
ministry (Isaiah 40:1).

The Brokenhearted

The Lord is promising to minister to those whose hearts have been shat-
tered. This type of ministry is necessary because of what sin has done to the
world. Isaiah 1:6 describes the people of Judah's hearts as having "no sound-
ness...but bruises and sores and raw wounds." Kelli can relate, and so can those
who have been rejected by family, suffered a broken relationship, or endured
some other result of living on a fallen planet—in a body impacted by the Fall.
We truly live in a Genesis 3 world and are suffering a "Genesis 3 hangover."[8]

Liberty to Captives

Our enemy loves to see people oppressed and hates to see people set
free. We minister regularly to those in bondage to drugs, alcohol, and sexual
sin, but our Lord promises, through the power of the gospel, to set them free.

Opening of the Prison to the Bound

The imagery here seems to be of those bound in prison not having seen "the light of day" for a long time. Scripture repeatedly uses this imagery to describe the Lord's power, what happens at salvation, and what He does in a person's life afterwards.[9] Colossians 1:13-14 makes it very clear that "He has delivered us from the domain of darkness and transferred us to the kingdom of his beloved Son, in whom we have redemption, the forgiveness of sins."

The Lord desires to open blinded eyes. He helps people see things they haven't seen before. Light bulbs go on, lies are revealed, and truth is understood. The alcoholic realizes the bottle is actually idolatry and that what he believed to be an adequate refuge to deal with the pressures of life has been a lie. The sexually abused girl who has believed she has no worth and is full of shame realizes her true identity is in Christ and that she has a wonderful, merciful Savior who can understand being abused and shamed.

The Purpose

It is clear from Isaiah 61 that our Lord was on a mission. He was sent with a message.[10]

Good News

One of the most exciting things is that our Lord came with "good news"[11] for people being beaten up by life. The gospel is about a person who transforms lives now as someone becomes His follower. Inherent in the gospel message is the promise to change lives. Speaking evangelistically the Lord said, "Come to me, all who labor and are heavy laden, and I will give you rest. Take my yoke upon you, and learn from me, for I am gentle and lowly in heart, and you will find rest for your souls" (Matthew 11:28-29). *The gospel is not just a message to believe; it is a person to follow.* Isn't this what the Great Commission (Matthew 28:18-20) is about? We are sent on a mission to "make disciples," not just to proclaim a message.[12]

Bind Up

Christ came to "comfort and heal the wounded,"[13] and this is the character of the whole Trinity. Psalm 147:2-3 says, "The LORD...heals the brokenhearted and binds up their wounds." It is this message which gives so much hope to our counselees because ultimately it is founded and based on the character of our God.

Of course, the Lord did this physically. He touched lepers and the blind, but His ministry was also one of "binding the brokenhearted" as He restored a dead son to a mother or raised a much-loved friend from the dead. But He also did this for the emotions. Isn't that what "brokenhearted" implies? Think of the mother whose son was raised and how this ministered healing to her soul.

One of the ways of defining biblical counseling is "broken people helping other broken people find healing through the power of the gospel and in the power of the Spirit as they apply the living principles of Scripture (Hebrews 4:12) to life." Ultimately this is possible because a broken Messiah ministers to broken people.

Liberty and Opening of the Prison

Our Lord came to break enslavements to sin and to help people come out into the light of day and truly deal with sin (Ephesians 5:11). It is hard to imagine a more appropriate description of what happens when an alcoholic becomes free from his enslavement or when one addicted to pornography has his eyes opened, repents, and starts viewing relationships in a more healthy way.

To Proclaim the Year of the Lord's Favor

Those who were in captivity and experiencing the consequences of sin can experience the favor instead of displeasure of the Lord. What wonderful good news if we dare to believe it! They can now do what is pleasing to the Lord because they have now been accepted by Him. In New Testament terminology we are now "in Christ."[14] We are now "accepted in the Beloved" (Ephesians 1:6 NKJV).

To Grow "Oaks of Righteousness"

Isaiah 61 describes a true rags-to-riches story. Here are people who start out as brokenhearted and in captivity and end up as "oaks of righteousness" (verse 3). Titus 3:3-7 presents the same pattern: "For we ourselves were once foolish, disobedient, led astray, slaves to various passions and pleasures...But when the goodness and loving kindness of God our Savior appeared, he saved us...through Jesus Christ our Savior, so that being justified by his grace we might become heirs."

Biblical counseling seeks to help people who have repented and turned to Christ realize their new position in Him and that they were saved by grace through faith to grow by grace through faith. God is up to something big in their lives as He helps them grow to be like His Son, helping them to put their past in its place.

The prophet Isaiah, in soaring words and pictures, proclaims a Messiah who has the power to effect great change for those who will come to Him. As we flip through the pages of Scripture, we get to see glimpses of this redemptive work happening in real time. Specifically in John 4, we get to see the Christ of Isaiah brought into full view. The gospel accounts allow us to see the Wonderful Counselor of Isaiah in high definition. We see Him bringing good news to the poor, binding up the brokenhearted, proclaiming liberty to the captives, and opening the prison to those who are bound. Fulfilling the rich prophecies of Isaiah 61, we see Jesus in human flesh bringing reality to these precious promises as He encounters the infamous Samaritan woman at the well.

It's important to remember that as biblical counselors, it is never our goal to bring our own pithy advice, conventional how-to's, or recycled anecdotes. We seek to give a counsel that is living and active. The focus of our counseling model is unlike any other: Jesus Himself. Paul Tripp writes:

> In confronting people with truth, we confront them with Christ. This is quite radical, for it says that truth, in its most basic form, is not a system, a theology, or a philosophy. It is a *person* whose name is Jesus. Living a godly life means trusting him, following him, and living like him. Personal ministry weaves the threads of grace and truth through every part of a person's life. In that it is truly incarnational, because grace and truth will always lead people to Christ.[15]

God not only wants to bring us to Himself, He desires to make us into the image of His Son.[16] What a difference from systems of therapy, which seek to help people become an improved version of themselves.

So it is in John 4, that we see Him as the Wonderful Counselor blending thoughtful questions coupled with robust theological directives. Following the pattern laid out in Isaiah 61, here we see a real-life case study where Jesus' *pattern, person,* and *purpose* all culminate in a life-changing testimony.

The Pattern of Christ

Whenever we see Jesus in action, we should want to stop and pause. We should want to learn about what He is doing. We should want to see how He interacts with people. We should want to eavesdrop on the counseling session. How does He draw people out? What kinds of questions does He ask? How does He know when to stop, pause, and love? How does He balance grace and truth? In John 4, we see a pattern of Jesus being *intentional, interactive, insightful,* and *illustrative.*

Intentional

There is an intentionality about Jesus' interactions that is unmistakable. Every conversation has a purpose and every question probes for an answer. Before the conversation with the Samaritan woman even begins there's a sense of intention and purpose in Jesus' journey.

John records for the reader specific details in verses 1-6 to help set the stage for this life-changing encounter. Everything from Jesus' journey to Galilee, His travel through Samaria, His sitting at the well in the middle of the day, the "holy geography"[17] of the location—all of it culminates in His initiation in conversation with the woman. Examples abound in the Gospels where Jesus makes intentional decisions to go to particular places, speak with particular people, and not speak with others. H.A. Ironside wrote, "There are so many different records of those with whom the Lord Jesus Christ had conversations that we get a marvelous unfolding of His wonderful wisdom in opening up the Word of God to needy souls."[18]

Interactive

Jesus' intentionality obviously leads to interaction. Jesus asks questions, engages, listens, and offers wise counsel. The same should be said of Christ-centered counseling. Commentary pages have been devoted to all the gender, social, ethnic, and religious barriers Christ crossed to interact with the Samaritan woman from a race despised by Jesus' Jewish countrymen.[19] Yet that doesn't stop Him. He sees a woman in need and begins to speak with her. It might seem obvious, but John in this short exchange will use the word "said" and "answered" twelve times. Jean-Marc Chappuis notes, "The most common-place communication may expand to become suddenly firm and substantial. That clearly is what happens in the meeting between Jesus and the Samaritan woman."[20]

To borrow a well-used phrase, Jesus reclaims and sanctifies the common here.[21] He interacts with the woman at the entry point of normal conversation. However, the reader is aware something inherently deeper is at stake. Jesus is seeking to take this conversation and expand it into something life-imparting.

Illustrative

Jesus' ministry with the Samaritan woman is intentional and interactive; it's also rich in illustration. Jesus makes good use of what is around Him as He evangelizes and counsels with the Samaritan woman. Using an everyday, pedestrian topic such as water opens the floodgates of Old Testament imagery.[22] Discussing the topic of water provides a door for Him to enter into a deep, spiritual conversation about a thirst which never can be quenched.

This shouldn't surprise us—after all, Jesus is a master teacher and model counselor of Scripture (He is the culmination of it, cf. John 5:39; Luke 24:27). He draws on a well of Old Testament imagery to have a theological conversation with the woman. Jesus begins to build bridges with the Isaiah who Himself had a vision for the people to "draw water from the wells of salvation" in the last days (Isaiah 12:3). Jewish tradition held that the provision of water was closely associated with the coming of Messiah, the Wonderful Counselor.[23] Isaiah himself had a vision of people who, in the future age, would not hunger or thirst (Isaiah 44:3; 49:10; 55:1). On a hot and dusty day, Jesus takes what is available and uses a simple need to dig deep into the heart of this woman.

Insightful

There's insight and discernment on the part of Jesus that pushes for more than just an earthly, temporal resolution to the Samaritan woman's problem.

He knows there is something greater at stake than just matters of water,[24] well location, and who worships where. Jesus' goal is for the Samaritan woman to become a worshipper in spirit and in truth. G. Campbell Morgan observed how Jesus uses this door into her heart: "In effect He said, I hear the cry of your soul for this water. I have this water to give, but there is something in your life that has first to be set right."[25]

Jesus insightfully and skillfully says that the thing which needs to be set right is the disposition of the heart to seek out love and acceptance in someone or something other than ourselves. For so long this woman has been looking for meaning and significance in all the wrong places. The men she had known and the past relationships they represent are really just empty cisterns which can never truly satisfy her heart desires. Yet, here before her is the Man, Jesus Himself, living water incarnate.

The Person of Christ

At the end of the day, Jesus Himself was the answer the woman was seeking. Goals that do not have as their end the counselee's complete and total worship of God provide less-than-biblical outcomes. Jesus is not content to just leave people where they are. Meeting Jesus is intended to be transformational.

As counselors we have the great privilege of incarnating and imaging God the Son in this way. One must note here, too, that one can have a conversation that is *intentional, interactive, insightful,* and *illustrative* but still not offer that which can truly effect biblical change. Jesus *is* the power for change. That's why He came to earth: to seek and save a people for Himself who would worship Him in spirit and truth. Imagine the woman's surprise when He reveals in John 4:26, "I who speak to you am he"! Being confronted for the first time with the realization that she is speaking to Messiah Himself must have been a truly remarkable experience.

The Purpose of Christ

The trajectory of this narrative serves an unmistakable purpose. This is no mere mid-afternoon water cooler talk. Jesus is after more than just mere life-improvement. While not ignoring the woman's concerns, He realizes that one aim must have preeminence of purpose. Kevin Huggins writes, "Jesus used the concern that was of most interest to the Samaritan woman at the time (worship) to help her discover something about her own heart she desperately needed to change."[26] Between verses 20-24, a form of the Greek verb *proskuneo* (to worship) is used ten different times. Distilling the woman's concerns regarding worship and the location of such, Jesus says, "The hour is coming, and is now here, when the true worshippers will worship the Father in spirit and truth, for the Father is seeking such people to worship him. God is spirit, and those who worship him must worship in spirit and truth" (John 4:23-24).

While certainly not all of the conversation is recorded for us by John, the elements of importance are there. Jesus enters into the world of the Samaritan woman with an unmistakable goal. He desires that this woman become a true worshipper of God, to restore her back to what she was truly designed for.

Could He have offered counsel regarding the woman's current living arrangements? Absolutely. Could He have counseled her on ways to deal with shame and the reproach of her countrymen? Certainly. However, Jesus knew what this woman needed. Jesus realized something of eternal significance was at stake. Her desire for other men, illicit lovers, all point to a woman searching for love and acceptance in things which ultimately will disappoint. As Augustine notes, God made us for Himself and for His great glory—therefore, "our hearts find no peace until they rest in you."[27] Pascal, echoing Augustine's point, wrote:

> What else does this craving, and this helplessness, proclaim but
> that there was once in man a true happiness, of which all that now
> remains is the empty print and trace? This he tries in vain to fill with
> everything around him, seeking in things that are not there the help
> he cannot find in those that are, though none can help, since this
> infinite abyss can be filled only with an infinite and unchangeable
> object; in other words by God himself.[28]

Jesus comes to the woman with an invitation of something which will not only satisfy her greatest yearnings and desires, but also transform her at her very core. It's an offer of a new life and a new heart; it's an offer of *shalom* and forgiveness. He calls to her to forsake those things which she has clung to for meaning and significance and embrace life in Him. This call to change is something which the biblical counselor extends to the counselee—forsake your empty cisterns and idols and come to the One who offers living water.

As biblical counselors, if we are seeking to distinguish what makes our counsel unique, it is that all conversations will inevitably lead to Jesus Christ. No other approach to life offers the person of Jesus Christ revealed in Scripture. It is His pattern, purpose, and person which as counselors we seek to demonstrate, advocate, and incarnate. These three characteristics are what truly distinguish Christ-centered counseling from other models. Christ-centered biblical counseling is aimed at more than offering an empathetic ear or pragmatic solutions. Jesus offers Himself as living water which answers our greatest need for forgiveness and oneness. Jean-Marc Chappuis observes astutely:

> Jesus would have been a bad Rogerian…the gospel conversations, in fact, notably those reported by John and even more especially those with Nicodemus and the Samaritan woman, testify that he accomplishes only two-thirds of Rogers' program. He practices empathy. He perceives and respects the internal frame of reference of those to whom he is speaking. On the other hand, he does not submit to Roger's third precept, which is that of non-directedness. On the contrary, he does direct the attention of his interlocutors authoritatively towards a new horizon of their existence, towards a possibility offered them to live differently.[29]

A Christ-Empowered Transformation

As Kelli began to read through the Gospel accounts, she discovered that Jesus could heal any disease or illness, and that when He did, He always healed in totality. This same Jesus was the Lord that she was crying out to so desperately to heal or "fix" her. Was He not capable of doing so? Kelli began to learn the importance of living out the truths she read in the pages of her Bible.

What had been missing in her sessions of cognitive-behavioral therapy? Why was she left unsatisfied and empty? Kelli writes:

> I had not turned to the only One who was able to truly heal and save. Trying to remedy my hopelessness through behavioral therapy was like trying to fix a car without tools. While the techniques practiced in therapy had great potential to be helpful, they lacked the

substance that was able to make the program effective. Only Jesus, through the power of His Word, was able to break down my walls and help me cope with the difficulties and trials I thought insurmountable.

It is through biblical, Christ-centered counseling that young women like Kelli are able to be truly transformed within, freed from their internal slavery and idolatry, and become true worshippers of Jesus. And as counselors, it is our joy to be a part of people's journeys of personal transformation into the image of Jesus Christ.

The Ministry of the Holy Spirit

Justin Holcomb and Mike Wilkerson

Life is a mess of sin and suffering. When people find themselves in over their heads, they come to us, the counselors, and quickly, *we're* in over *our* heads with them. What do they want? Often they want relief from the pain or practical advice for how to break sin patterns. Sometimes they're aware that there's more to it, something deeper.

What do we want for them? If we're thinking biblically, then we'll want to provide some immediate, practical help. But we also know that the roots of their problems are likely deeper than they are aware, and that God is often up to something greater than merely cleaning up the messes as we see them and in the ways that we would clean them.

We know that biblical counseling will involve prayer and Scripture—we can't go far without those. Yet if we're not careful, even prayer and Scripture can be deployed in the counseling process as mere techniques—the technologies of biblical counseling—rather than as means of engaging with the living God who alone is sufficient for the needs at hand.

Case Study: A Young Married Couple

Suppose a young married couple comes to you seeking help. Let's call them John and Emily. Since their wedding night, they've found intimacy difficult. And the trouble is not just in the bedroom; it's in every room of the house.

Emily is terrified of sex. She's also defensive and resistant to talking about certain issues in her past. John is disappointed and tempted to push for what he wants. After all, he reasons, marriage is supposed to include sex, right? In their hurt, fear, and anger, they've said words to each other they can never take back. Clearly, these matters will take time and patience to resolve. You commit to working with them over a period of months.

One day, Emily hints at something painful about her relationship with her stepfather. She's beginning to trust you, so you delicately invite her to say more. What spills out is a tear-filled story of a childhood spoiled and traumatized by a stepfather who would visit her bedroom at night to touch her in ways she was too young to understand, but that made her feel dirty nonetheless. You're horrified as you hear about this helpless girl overpowered by a selfish and deceitful man.

Later, John's secret comes out. He thought marriage would fix it, but it hasn't, especially given their sexual difficulties. It's getting worse, in fact. Pornography.

He's beginning to trust you, too. So, he confesses, eyes always to the floor. He admits to his despair after years of failure, even at times entertaining thoughts of suicide. He's overwhelmed by what he now knows about his wife's past. He knows that his sin multiplies her pain. This increases his shame and the distance between them.

What Do You Want?

Surely you long for Emily to know the love and affection of a gracious heavenly Father. But you know this might be hard for her to grasp. You long for her to see that, in Christ, God calls her clean and holy, not contaminated. But she's felt broken, defiled, and ashamed for as long as she can remember. So this, too, will be hard for her to grasp.

You want John to know freedom from this bondage—to assure him that there's hope, and that it doesn't all ride on his summoning his long-lost willpower to stop it. You'll want him to see how what Jesus has already provided for him is better than what he seeks in pornography. You want him to be convicted of his sin, not just regretful for the consequences. You want him to repent from the heart, and to walk faithfully in freedom. You know the process will probably require identifying the sin beneath the sins, the idolatry that fuels his behavior. This undoubtedly lies darkened beneath layers of slippery self-deception. In the end, you want him to rest in Christ's work for him—complete forgiveness and cleansing from sin's shame.

What Does the Holy Spirit Want?

This is only the tip of the iceberg, of course. There's much more going on in John and Emily and between them, and much more help that you hope to offer.

Scripture should help, right? Let's assume that you're well-versed. As they talk, you can think of plenty of relevant passages. But will those verses connect and make a difference?

Thankfully, biblical counselors are becoming aware of the naiveté and malpractice in the prescription "take two verses and call me in the morning." So, let's suppose you're more sophisticated, more compassionate, more engaging, and more nuanced. You can weave their stories into God's story. Will that help?

Yes, but there's more. You see, what you want for them—the truths you hope they will see, the love of God you long for them to embrace and extend to others—the reason you want those things is because there is One who wants John and Emily to have those things even more than you do. The Holy Spirit.

In fact, *rather than asking about the role of the Holy Spirit in counseling, we should be asking about the counselor's role in the Holy Spirit's counseling!* Yes, there will be Scripture. Yes, there will be prayer. Yet, it is good for us to focus on the Holy Spirit's personal presence, agency, and efficacy. We should not reduce *Him* to the topic of "prayer in counseling," nor to "Scripture in counseling."

By taking this more personal approach, we'll be reminded that prayer is not just a technique of spirituality; it is conversation with our Redeemer, a person. Further, the Spirit is at work even before we pray and in ways for which we may not even know how to pray. He does more than we ask or think (Ephesians 3:20). We'll also be reminded that the Scriptures are not magical formulae that work apart from our understanding; they are meaningful communications from a personal God about Himself that we might know Him. It is the Spirit who opens our hearts and minds to know God through the Scriptures.

Counseling that lacks this dependence on the Holy Spirit ceases to be Christian. Jay Adams is emphatic here:

> Ignoring the Holy Spirit or avoiding the use of Scriptures in counseling is tantamount to an act of autonomous rebellion. Christians may not counsel apart from the Holy Spirit and His Word without grievously sinning against Him and the counselee.[1]

Siang-Yang Tan agrees:

> The role of the Holy Spirit in counseling is therefore a crucial one. He is the ultimate source of all true healing and wholeness. All true Christian counseling needs to be done in the Spirit, by the Spirit's power, truth, and love, under the Lordship of Christ, and to the glory of God.[2]

Biblical Counseling Is a Trialogue

If the Holy Spirit is the primary counselor, then biblical counseling is not merely a dialogue between a counselor and a counselee. Rather, it is a trialogue in which a counselor participates in the Spirit's work already underway with the counselee.[3] The Spirit is actively engaged in counseling, working directly on the counselor and the counselee, and through each to help the other. Consider the following trialogue diagram and some conclusions we may draw from it.[4]

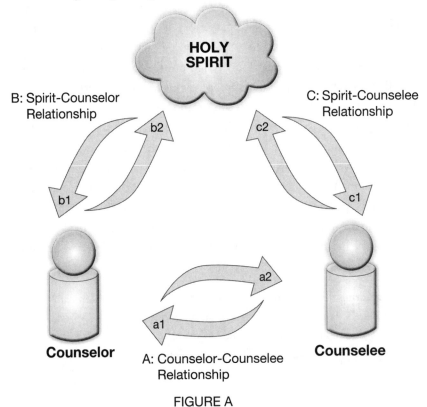

FIGURE A

God-Centered

First, the diagram reminds us to remain God-centered in our counseling. Our ultimate goal is to help counselees to know and love God. You might even say that the goal of biblical counseling is *to promote communication between the Spirit and the counselee* (C1 and C2 in Figure A). All of the change and growth in Christlikeness that we'd wish to see as a fruit of our counseling will happen in the context of one's relationship with Him, as the counselee learns to receive His grace in its many forms (forgiveness, comfort, guidance from God's Word, and much more), and respond in faith in its many out-workings (love of God and neighbor, repentance, obedience). As Paul Tripp says, the difference between biblical counseling and any non-Christian form of counseling is that our ultimate hope for change does not rest in a system but in a personal Redeemer.[5]

The Spirit at Work Through the Word

Second, the Spirit is at work on the counselee. We now turn our attention to two more lines in Figure A: from Spirit to counselee (C1), and from counselor to counselee (A2). It's hard to capture everything you might want to say in a single diagram, but if we could add red for the work of the Spirit and blue for the work of the counselor, then the line from counselor to counselee (A2) would be purple, or perhaps a red-and-blue braid.

The questions we now face are: Is it the counselor's words, knowledge, skill, and compassion that make the difference? Or is it the Spirit? Or, if it's both, then how might that be? And how can we as counselors be intentional about that participation? It will help us to answer such questions if we take a step back and observe the relationships between the Spirit's work, our words of counsel, and God's Word.

God works through words. He created everything by speaking, and sustains it always by His powerful word (Hebrews 1:3; 11:3). He also ordained that language would be a primary means of revealing Himself to us, resulting in Scripture. His ultimate self-revelation, however, came in the *person* of Jesus Christ. Now the gospel is a proclamation—words—about that person and His work. These are not merely descriptive words, however, for the Spirit causes them to bring about life and faith in the hearts of believers.[6] It is the Spirit

alone who opens the eyes of our hearts to the revelation of God, and it is He
who accomplishes something in us by this revelation. John Calvin made essentially the same point:

> The simple and external demonstration of the Word of God ought,
> indeed, to suffice fully for the production of faith, did not our blind-
> ness and perversity interfere. But such is the propensity of our minds
> to vanity that they can never adhere to the truth of God, and such
> is their dullness that they are always blind even to his light. Hence,
> without the illumination of the Holy Spirit the Word has no effect.[7]

The more we receive God's Word by faith, the more effect it has upon
us, and the more we are transformed.[8] In other words, to be counseled biblically—or to be discipled in general, really—is to receive God's Word more
and more deeply as the Spirit drives it deeper into the heart. The Spirit works
through the Word to change us; He acts upon us and *accomplishes* something.

The way human speech works bears some similarity to the way God's
speech works. It does more than string together words: it conveys intent, and
it can also accomplish things.[9] Consider as an analogy the words spoken by a
minister at a wedding: "I now pronounce you husband and wife." These words
do not merely *describe* the couple as married; they *make* the couple married.
The same words could be written in a letter by the husband to his wife on their
first anniversary: "I remember how I felt when the minister said, 'I now pronounce you husband and wife.'" In that case, the very same words are spoken in
a different context with a different intent. In the wedding, the minister's intent
is to pronounce the couple married; in the anniversary letter, the husband's
intent is to remind his wife of that special moment. What is *accomplished* by
those words in each case? In the wedding, the minister's words result in a new
marriage; in the letter, the same words result in the enjoyment of a memory.

It matters what words counselors say, why they say them, and what they
hope to accomplish by speaking. As biblical counselors we want to intend what
the Spirit intends and to participate in what the Spirit means to accomplish.
The kinds of things biblical counselors hope will happen in their counselees
are the very things the Spirit *does* to them through the Word.

This is not to say that, if the Spirit works through the Word, then biblical
counseling should consist in merely reading Scripture as if it were magical.

Quite the contrary, this insight moves us away from a merely magical-propositional orientation to the Word, and into a relational orientation. Merely hearing the syllables of Scripture will not suffice for change, nor will a mere understanding of its concepts. Rather, the Spirit illuminates the Word for believers so that they might understand it spiritually, leading to a knowledge of God and to Christ dwelling in their hearts through faith (1 Corinthians 2:13; Ephesians 3:16-17).

The Spirit works to drive the seed that is God's Word deep into the heart, where it will take root and produce life (Luke 8:11; 1 Peter 1:23). Therefore, every method a counselor uses that helps a counselee to receive the Word more deeply turns out to be an expression of the Spirit's own agenda.

How We Pray: Client-to-Spirit, Counselor-to-Spirit

Ed Welch says that all counseling is a variation on a single theme: knowing and praying for the counselee. Of all the questions the counselor might ask, then, the central guiding question in the counselor's mind is, "How can I pray for you?"[10] Our prayers will be informed by knowing (1) the Spirit's person and work, and (2) what we need. We ask Him to do that which He loves to do, that for which we are so needy. We turn our attention now to the arrows going up from counselor and counselee in Figure A.

Let's return to John and Emily from our opening case study. Recall: Emily has shared with you through tears that she was violated many times by her stepfather. One thing you might want for Emily is for her to know God's comfort amidst her terrible suffering. He is, after all, "the Father of mercies and God of all comfort, who comforts us in all our affliction" (2 Corinthians 1:3).

Does the Spirit want to comfort Emily? Certainly. Among the many good things He has for her, comfort is one. Is this what He wants to minister *now*, though? This is an opportunity for prayer: *What do You want for Emily now?*

Suppose you conclude that comforting Emily in this moment is what you want and probably what the Spirit wants, too. You now know, when you speak, what your intent will be—to comfort—and as clearly as you can prayerfully discern, it is the Spirit's intent as well.

Now, what do you say? What words should you choose? You may mention, read, or have Emily read 2 Corinthians 1:3: "Blessed be the God and

Father of our Lord Jesus Christ, the Father of mercies and God of all comfort." You may expound it by helping her to understand Paul's situation and how it relates to her own. You may ask her questions about the passage that deepen her reflections upon it. You may tell stories of how God has saved His people from trouble in the past: rescue from Egypt in the Exodus, restoration after captivity in Babylon. You may "let the redeemed of the Lord say so," sharing how He has comforted you. By any means available—Bible, story, metaphor, illustration, crying with her—you attempt to help her know this God of all comfort.

The question is, will Emily finally receive God's comfort by all of this? Will your labor bear its fruit? Will your message accomplish what you intend? If only you select the right passages of Scripture, if only you expound them correctly, skillfully and personally—will she get it? If you identify and deconstruct lies and distortions in her view of God along the way, hoping to clear her vision—will this suffice?

In the end, what we want for Emily is not merely cognitive nor conceptual. We do expect the Spirit will work through Emily's cognitions, so we should strive to communicate skillfully so that she may understand. *But we want more.* We want a personal God to act personally upon Emily in this moment, deeply assuring her of His love for her and stirring her affections for Him.

At some point, no doubt, it will be time for John to be convicted of his sin with pornography.[11] He may already be convicted before he comes to see you. Or, he may only be confessing the most superficial awareness of the sin while lacking conviction about the deeper sins of the heart that underlie his behavior. Following a similar pattern as you did with Emily, you identify this goal prayerfully, concluding that this is the work the Spirit has in mind for John now.

You may choose words to help him face the gravity of his sin, to help him count the cost of his sin against Emily and against God—the betrayal, broken trust, spiritual adultery, idolatry. Since your goal is not to preach, but to help John see what he's not seeing about God and his own sin, you might choose words in the form of questions. You may help him to see the dark reality that he has probably in some way supported the sexual slave trade and human trafficking that have likely been involved in producing the images he's seen. You may help him to see the consequences he is bringing to his own body and brain.

Your intent in all of this is that John would experience a deep conviction that drives repentance from the heart, resulting in a forsaking of this sin. But your words have limits. You can convict him in the external, objective sense of presenting the case against his sin, like a trial lawyer. But you can't do the work deep in John's heart that must be done to spark the necessary change. That is a work of the Spirit (John 16:8). Your work is to speak as the Spirit leads and to pray that He convicts. It is not simply that you "get out of God's way" and let Him convict. It is, rather, that you participate in His work while recognizing that He is the one who gives your words their force and effect to accomplish what He intends.

Much of the prayer that we've suggested so far would go unnoticed by a video camera in the counseling room. It has been more like continuous communication, remaining in tune and attentive to the Spirit, not consuming any real time in the counseling session. It's all happening as quickly and fluidly as a musician might play along while reading sheet music. For the practiced musician, the time between seeing what next notes to play and playing them with appropriate feel is usually unnoticeable.

In addition to the counselor's prayer throughout, he may also look for opportunities to invite the counselee to pray. Remember that, ultimately, we want to nurture the counselee's relationship with God (Relationship C in Figure A). At key moments in the conversation, it may be appropriate to pause and ask, for example, "Have you confessed this to God? Would you like to take a moment to do that now?"[12]

Or, we may pause and ask the Spirit to help us see what He wants us to see in that moment—*Holy Spirit, what would You like us to see now?*—and then wait quietly, listening for a few moments. While we should pray like this with confidence and expectation that the Spirit will help us, we should be somewhat tentative about concluding exactly what He has said and how to apply it. We are not here trying to bypass the human thought process to get to some other-worldly and authoritative "Thus saith the Lord." Rather, we ask that the Spirit would work through our thoughts and emotions to illuminate.[13] After praying, we might ask, "Does anything come to mind?" If so, we discuss it, and we receive and apply whatever we might normally affirm. Sometimes this will lead us down unexpected paths. Yet if it bears fruit that is Christ-exalting and biblical—like we'd hope for any of our methods—then we trust that the Spirit has helped us, and we're thankful.

The Counselor's Skill and Method

If the Holy Spirit is the primary counselor, then of what importance is the skill and training of the human counselor? Our attention turns now to the relationship between counselor and counselee (Relationship A in Figure A). We discussed this in part already when we pointed out above that the Spirit works through God's Word and the words spoken by the counselor.

The familiar notion of "getting out of God's way" is helpful as a reminder that the Spirit is primary in counseling, but if we're not careful with that idea, it can also lead to some distortion in our understanding of the relationship between the Spirit's work and the counselor's. A dualism is when two ideas or principles that truly belong together as a unified whole are separated and then pitted against each other. What then happens is that some affirm the first idea to the exclusion of the second, while others affirm the second to the exclusion of the first.

In this case, we have two ideas that belong together: (1) the Spirit is at work and is the primary counselor, and (2) the counselor is at work and his skill is important. If these two ideas are pitted against one another and one is taken to the exclusion of the other, we end up with one of two distortions—the counselor is reduced to either a medium or a mechanic.

A medium is a passive conduit for some other spirit's communications. Biblical counselors make this mistake when they overestimate the authority of their own words or when they underestimate the amount of interpretation that is involved in communicating God's Word or any of the promptings that the Spirit may bring to mind.

A mechanic fixes cars with his own hands. He may consult a manual, but his are the only hands at work. Counselors make this mistake when they overestimate the efficacy of their skills and methods. Biblical counselors err in this way when they treat the Bible like a car manual and people like machines.

As much as we may need to remember to get *out* of God's way, we must also remember to get *in* His way—meaning, we should prayerfully seek to understand the Spirit's "way" in any situation and go there, following His lead.

Jay Adams harmonizes these two ideas well:

> The Holy Spirit ordinarily effects his characterological work in the lives of believers through the means of grace. He uses the ministry of

the Word, the sacraments, prayer and the fellowship of God's people as the principal vehicles through which he brings about such changes…Methodology and technique, skill and exercise of gifts are all consonant with the work of the Spirit. What makes the difference is one's attitude and inner motivation: does he do what he does in reliance upon his own efforts, in dependence upon methods and techniques, or does he acknowledge his own inability and ask the Spirit to use his gifts and methods?[14]

If it's true that the Spirit produces new life through the seed that is God's Word, then the counselor's skill in handling that seed is important, just as for a farmer planting seed in hopes of a good crop (Luke 8:11-15). Understanding it and applying it well will matter. Understanding the environment will matter. Choosing good timing and planting seed in fertile, cultivated soil will matter. Protecting seeds from being choked out by weeds or thorns that threaten to choke out the life in those seeds will matter.

Yet all of these "farming skills" are used in dependence on the Spirit, who ultimately is the one who causes growth (1 Corinthians 3:6-7). Siang-Yang Tan summarizes: "Training and competence in counseling or therapy skills are still needed, but such skills are used in dependence on the Holy Spirit."[15]

The Spirit Empowers the Counselor (and the Counselee)

We turn now to the Spirit's empowerment of the counselor (B1 in Figure A). One place in Scripture where human skill and the Spirit's empowerment come together is in the appointment of Bezalel to construct the tabernacle. "I have filled him with the Spirit of God, with ability and intelligence, with knowledge and all craftsmanship" (Exodus 31:3). Bezalel was no doubt a skilled, talented artisan already.[16] God, in His own creativity and wisdom, had designed and prepared one such as Bezalel for this task. Still, Bezalel's skill would need to be empowered by the Spirit of God. This filling of the Spirit would not replace his ability, intelligence, and craftsmanship; rather, it would empower and extend them to do far more than Bezalel could ever do in his merely human, albeit God-designed, capacity. *The result was not Spirit-filled-instead-of-skillful; it was Spirit-filled-skill.*

The language used to describe Bezalel's endowment is worthy of closer examination. The Hebrew word *hokmah*, which the ESV translates "ability," is "essentially a high degree of knowledge and skill in any domain…The nearest English equivalent that encompasses its semantic range is 'expertise.'"[17] This word, along with the others used here (*tebunah*: practical, applied competence; *da'at*: knowledge in the broadest sense), picks up many layers of meaning in Proverbs, where the sage demonstrates deep understanding—theoretical, practical, and ethical—in many areas of life. His way of life and his way of knowing are grounded in the fear of the Lord, which is the beginning of wisdom, knowledge, insight, knowledge of God, spiritual vitality, confidence, hatred of evil, and the love of good (Proverbs 1:7; 2:5; 8:13; 9:10; 10:27; 14:27; 19:23).

Isaiah brings together the same ideas in his prophecy about the Messiah in Isaiah 11:2: "The Spirit of the LORD shall rest upon him, the Spirit of wisdom and understanding, the Spirit of counsel and might, the Spirit of knowledge and the fear of the LORD."[18]

Here again, we have "wisdom" (*hokmah*), "understanding" (*binah*: intellect, intelligence, problem-solving, and conceptual thinking),[19] "counsel and might" (a single idea in two words, referring to a king's ability to "gather data for decision making and the forcefulness to make decisions," especially military ones),[20] and "knowledge" (*da'at*), all grounded in the fear of the Lord. The phrase "the Spirit of wisdom and understanding," especially in the Greek translation of the Old Testament, is very similar to that found in Exodus 31:3 for Bezalel.

What is Isaiah saying about the Messiah? That he would be a wise king like Solomon, powerful like David, yet peaceful and ushering in peace for the people. He would return God's people to shalom. He was to be unlike any human king on the scene at the time, most of whom in Israel had either been "craven, cynical, pompous [and] spiritually bankrupt," or arrogant and oppressive like the Assyrian kings.[21] Reading through the rest of Isaiah 11, you find that the Messiah's rule of Israel's returning exiles results in a veritable heaven on earth. So grand is that vision as to lead Bible commentator John Oswalt to conclude:

> This picture cannot be applied to any human king. It is either an unattainable ideal or the figure envisioned is somehow superhuman. That it is the latter is supported by the vision of the return which is

linked to the Messiah's reign (vv. 10-16). That return is not merely an ideal, nor is the Messiah. He is a reality, but a superhuman one.[22]

What would distinguish this king from the others? What would mark Him as the Messiah? "The Spirit of the LORD shall rest upon him." So it's mind-blowing that in Ephesians, Paul would be so bold as to adopt the language of Isaiah 11:2 and pray that God would give to the average Joe Ephesian "a spirit of wisdom and of revelation in the knowledge of him" (Ephesians 1:17).[23] He prays similarly for the Colossians: "We have not ceased to pray for you, asking that you may be filled with the knowledge of his will in all *spiritual wisdom and understanding*" (Colossians 1:9, emphasis added).

Notice here that Paul is not just praying for their counseling toolboxes to be filled with such apparatuses as "wisdom" and "knowledge" and "revelation." He is praying that they would receive the great gift of the Holy Spirit. *He* is the Spirit of wisdom and revelation.[24]

But notice, too, that he's not just praying for the counselors among those Ephesians and Colossians. He's praying for all of them. Every Christian has received the great gift of the Holy Spirit (Luke 11:13; Matthew 7:11). The Spirit helps us to walk in His ways, to know God, to see the glory of God in the face of Jesus Christ, and to be transformed as we behold Him (Galatians 5:16-17; 2 Corinthians 3:17-18; 4:6).

We have every reason—with the Spirit thus empowering both the biblical counselor and the Christian counselee—to pray fervently and expectantly with Paul:

> ...that according to the riches of his glory he may grant you to be strengthened with power through his Spirit in your inner being, so that Christ may dwell in your hearts through faith—that you, being rooted and grounded in love, may have strength to comprehend with all the saints what is the breadth and length and height and depth, and to know the love of Christ that surpasses knowledge, that you may be filled with all the fullness of God. Now to him who is able to do far more abundantly than all that we ask or think, according to the power at work within us, to him be glory in the church and in Christ Jesus throughout all generations, forever and ever. Amen (Ephesians 3:16-21).

The Unity of the Trinity

Kevin Carson and Jeff Forrey

A distinctive characteristic of biblical counseling is the role played by theology in shaping its theory and practice. In this chapter we explore how one element of theology—the doctrine of the Trinity—affects both the goals and the practice of counseling Christians. The connection between the Bible's teaching about God's triune existence and its teaching about counseling might not be immediately obvious, but the connection has to do with "making disciples." Any counseling based on Scripture must be a form of discipleship, because building and strengthening the relationship of people with God was the purpose of the writers of the Bible. When Jesus gives the Great Commission to "make disciples," He does so with a focus on the Trinity.

The Great Commission:
Discipleship in the Name of the Triune God

Jesus' Great Commission places discipleship at the heart of His purpose for the church: "All authority in heaven and on earth has been given to me. Go therefore and *make disciples* of all nations, baptizing them in the name of the Father and of the Son and of the Holy Spirit, teaching them to observe all that I have commanded you. And behold, I am with you always, to the end of the age" (Matthew 28:18-20, emphasis added). There are three important points Jesus makes in these comments that will be relevant for our purposes in this chapter.

First, Jesus was given *all* authority from His heavenly Father.[1] The extent of Jesus' authority (encompassing both heaven and earth) testifies to His divinity, and it clearly gives the reason why His disciples must follow through with the commission—no human authority has the right to contradict what Jesus says.[2]

Second, Jesus promises to be *present with His disciples* as they carry out His commission. Jesus' presence encourages His disciples to move outside their comfort zones and to boldly explain the gospel to others—who may or may not be receptive to it. His promise to be present "to the end of the age" indicates that the Great Commission is not limited to just the disciples who saw the risen Lord when He spoke these words. He is present with all of His disciples as they make disciples until He returns, which hints at the Spirit's role in the work of Christ's followers (which receives greater attention in the Gospel of John and in Acts).

Third, Jesus clarifies that making disciples will involve *going, baptizing,* and *teaching. Going* refers to taking the initiative in sharing the message of Christ with "all nations"—not restricting it to Israel, as Jesus had instructed His disciples in Matthew 10:5-6; 15:24.[3]

Baptizing occurs when new converts respond favorably to the gospel; it symbolizes their cleansing of sin and their identification with their new Master, Jesus. Jesus says the baptisms of new converts are done "in the name of the Father and of the Son and of the Holy Spirit." We will examine the significance of this specification below, drawing especially from the teachings of John and Paul. But already it is clear that the believer's new life as a disciple of Jesus Christ *means having a relationship with the Triune God.*

Teaching is necessary for discipleship, because having a relationship with the Lord also means adopting a different lifestyle—one directed by the commandments of Jesus. New converts need to be taught *how* to obey Jesus' teaching. Making disciples is not accomplished by merely giving information about Jesus, but by enabling people to conform their lives to the example of Jesus. Disciples obey Jesus' teaching instead of merely hearing it (James 1:22-25); they conform their lives to it rather than trying it out and discarding it (John 8:31-32; 15:1-8).

The content of the teaching is "all" Jesus "commanded"—that is, everything that Jesus *intended to affect the lives of His disciples.* This would include not only His verbal instructions but also His behavioral example.[4] Jesus Himself taught, "A disciple is not above his teacher, but everyone when he is fully trained will be like his teacher" (Luke 6:40). The life-transforming nature of a close relationship with Jesus was evident in the lives of the apostles— ordinary, "uneducated" men who "astonished" the Jewish religious leaders with their passionate proclamation of the gospel of Christ (Acts 4:8-14). Still later, Paul would challenge the Corinthians, "Follow my example, as I follow the example of Christ" (1 Corinthians 11:1 NIV).

There are numerous implications for biblical counseling derived from the Great Commission. Counseling done "in the name of…the Son" must submit to His supreme authority; biblical counselors do not have any authority to deviate from Jesus' purposes for the work of the church. Consequently, counseling done within the church must include an invitation to have a relationship with Jesus through the gospel for anyone who is not a Christian.

Moreover, counseling among Christians in the church involves teaching people *how to obey* what Jesus taught as it touches upon their concerns. It focuses on the practical application of biblical principles in people's lives. As biblical counselors conform their goals in counseling to Jesus' Great Commission, they can be assured of their Savior's presence. Finally, the ministry of biblical counseling should be conducted in order to foster and nurture a close relationship with the Triune God.

A Glimpse into the Father/Son/Spirit Relationship and Its Reflection in the Church

Out of all the Gospels, John does the most to develop the relationship of God the Father, God the Son, and God the Spirit and to show how their relationship should affect the lives of Christians. God's plan of redemption is guaranteed to be fruitful by the planning of the Father, the sacrifice of the Son, and the indwelling presence of the Spirit. The life and ministry of a disciple of Christ should be modeled after the Son's relationship to the Father and the Spirit. John's explanation of these dynamics amplifies what is significant about "baptizing [converts] in the name of the Father *and* of the Son *and* of the Holy Spirit, [*and*] teaching them to observe all that I have commanded" (Matthew 28:19-20, emphasis added).

The Relationship of the Father and the Son

In John 1, we are introduced to Jesus as the unique divine Son, although in a somewhat unexpected manner: "In the beginning was the Word, and the Word was with God, and the Word was God. He was in the beginning with

God" (John 1:1-2). John 1:14-17 clarifies that the "Word" is Jesus Christ. The title "Word" and the allusions to Genesis 1 in John 1 point us to the divinity of Christ, since no one else could be the Creator and source of life.[5] In addition, John introduces the relationship between Jesus and God the Father that will receive significant attention throughout the rest of the Gospel.

Jesus was sent by the Father and bears the Father's authority for His ministry. "'For this reason the Father loves me, because I lay down my life that I may take it up again. No one takes it from me, but I lay it down of my own accord. I have authority to lay it down, and I have authority to take it up again. This charge I have received from my Father...The works that I do in my Father's name bear witness about me'" (John 10:17-18,25).[6]

Jesus taught only what He had heard from the Father. "'I have not spoken on my own authority, but the Father who sent me has himself given me a commandment—what to say and what to speak. And I know that his commandment is eternal life. What I say, therefore, I say as the Father has told me'" (John 12:49-50).[7]

Jesus did only the works that the Father gave Him to do. "Jesus answered them, 'My Father is working until now, and I am working.' This was why the Jews were seeking all the more to kill him, because not only was he breaking the Sabbath, but he was even calling God his own Father, making himself equal with God. So Jesus said to them, 'Truly, truly, I say to you, the Son can do nothing of his own accord, but only what he sees the Father doing. For whatever the Father does, that the Son does likewise'" (John 5:17-19).[8]

The association of the Son and the Father is so close that one is said to be "in" the other (John 10:37-38; 14:9-11). Jesus says He and the Father are "one" (John 10:30), even referring to Himself by God's covenant name (John 8:58). Seeing Jesus means seeing the Father (John 1:18; 12:45; 17:6); loving Jesus means loving the Father (John 8:42).[9]

The Relationship of the Spirit to the Father and the Son

Especially in the second portion of the Gospel, John presents how the Spirit functions in relation to the Son and the Father in the plan of redemption. Initially, the Son "utters the words of God," and can do so because He "gives the Spirit without measure" (John 3:34). Later, the Spirit is sent by the

Father and the Son in order to guide and empower the disciples as they began the work that Christ left for them to do (John 14:16,26; 15:26-27; 16:7-11). The Spirit's role is to pass on what He received from Jesus, who had received it from the Father (John 16:12-15). In this way, the Spirit seeks to glorify the Son just as the Son seeks to glorify the Father.

The Relationship of Believers to the Father, Son, and Spirit

It is striking how the relationship of the Father, Son, and Spirit is used to set expectations for believers' lives in the Gospel of John. No one enters the kingdom of God apart from being born of the Spirit and believing in the name of the Son (John 3:5-18). Believing in Jesus is a reality for those who have experienced birth by the Spirit as granted by the Father (John 6:63-65). Those who have believed in the Son glorify Him (John 17:10), and if the Son is glorified, then so is the Father (John 13:31-32).

Jesus used the occasion of washing His apostles' feet to point out how they ought to serve others as He had served them:

> He said to them, "Do you understand what I have done to you?…If I then, your Lord and Teacher, have washed your feet, you also ought to wash one another's feet. For I have given you an example, that you also should do just as I have done to you. Truly, truly, I say to you, a servant is not greater than his master, nor is a messenger greater than the one who sent him" (John 13:12-16).

Jesus' instruction to the apostles parallels His teaching about doing only what the Father wanted Him to do.

Jesus also told His apostles that their love for one another would be evidence of having been loved by Him: "A new commandment I give to you, that you love one another: just as I have loved you, you also are to love one another. By this all people will know that you are my disciples, if you have love for one another" (John 13:34-35). This parallels how the Son shares the love shown to Him by the Father: "As the Father has loved me, so have I loved you" (John 15:9).

Jesus described the relationship of the apostles to Himself using the language of being "in" one another; this too parallels what is true of Him and His

Father. "Yet a little while and the world will see me no more, but you will see me. Because I live, you also will live. In that day you will know that I am in my Father, and you in me, and I in you" (John 14:19-20).

Jesus tells His apostles that obeying His commandments is the way to abide in Him, just as He does the same in relation to His Father: "If you keep my commandments, you will abide in my love, just as I have kept my Father's commandments and abide in his love" (John 15:10).

Unity between the Father and Son is the model (and precondition) for unity among believers (John 17:22). Jesus prays for His disciples, "I am no longer in the world, but they are in the world, and I am coming to you. Holy Father, keep them in your name, which you have given me, that they may be one, even as we are one. While I was with them, I kept them in your name, which you have given me" (John 17:11-12). Jesus wanted the apostles to be kept in the Father's name so that they may be one (that is, be unified in purpose), just like Him and His Father.

When Jesus prays for those who will come to faith in the future, He anticipates that future disciple-making would have the same effect as His ministry on earth had had. "I do not ask for these only, but also for those who will believe in me through their word, that they may all be one, just as you, Father, are in me, and I in you, that they also may be in us, so that the world may believe that you have sent me" (John 17:20-21).

Receiving the Spirit for ministry is contingent upon believing in the Son (John 7:39). Just before His ascension, the resurrected Christ appears to His apostles and tells them to continue the ministry they had begun together. But in order for them to carry out the will of the Father in His name, they would need the Spirit's empowerment: "'Peace be with you. As the Father has sent me, even so I am sending you.' And when he had said this, he breathed on them and said to them, 'Receive the Holy Spirit'" (John 20:21-22).[10]

In order for Jesus' disciples—then or now—to fulfill the Great Commission, they need to understand how their task is to mirror the task Jesus had during His earthly ministry. When they go and make disciples, they do so in the "name" of Jesus, who had received the "name" of the Father. Furthermore, the only way they can succeed in their task is through the Holy Spirit, who has been sent by the Father and the Son.

The relationship exhibited by the Triune God becomes the standard for unity, intimacy, perfect fellowship, harmony, and oneness among Christians. The believers' love and friendship with one another should intentionally reflect the relationships within the Trinity. These relationships within the church demonstrate the glory of God in love, kindness, graciousness, enjoyment, hope, and unity.

The Unity of the Trinity and the Necessary Effect upon Christians and Their Ministries

Throughout Ephesians, Paul explores how the work of the Trinity affects the lives of Christians. He not only helps Christians understand better the functional unity of the Trinity, but also helps them effectively minister to each other with a Trinitarian focus.

The Functional Unity of the Trinity

Paul begins Ephesians differently than most of the other letters he wrote, opening the book with an extended anthem of praise (Ephesians 1:3-14).[11] This anthem helps us understand the unity of the Trinity in that each person of the Godhead performs a different function in the plan of redemption but shares the same agenda and purposes. Paul begins by expressing thanks to God for all spiritual blessings in Christ (verse 3), and follows this proclamation with individual praise for each person of the Trinity.

Regarding God the Father, Paul identifies Him as the creator and initiator of the plan of redemption, including adoption as sons (verses 4-6). Paul also states God's agenda—that the believer is to live holy and blameless before Him (the process we call progressive sanctification). Furthermore, Paul helps us understand the Father's motivation as the pleasure of His good will, and he concludes with God's purpose: "to the praise of his glorious grace" (verse 6). The Father, then, creates and initiates a plan of redemption in which the believer is to live a holy life for the praise of God's glory.

Paul then shifts his praise to Jesus Christ as the Son of God (verses 7-12). Jesus is the one who enacted the plan of redemption, providing forgiveness of sins through the payment of His own blood. God's agenda in Christ is to bring everything (including our counselees) under the headship of Christ. Paul also provides the motivation and purpose, "according to the purpose of him who works all things according to the counsel of his will, so that we who were the first to hope in Christ might be to the praise of his glory" (verses 11-12). In other words, in Christ the Father is uniting all things under the one head, Christ, for the purpose of living to the praise of His glory.

Paul concludes his anthem of praise with reference to God the Holy Spirit (verses 13-14). The Holy Spirit marks the believer as God's own through His sealing, and He is the guarantee of the believer's inheritance—the conclusion of the redemption plan. The agenda is to guarantee God's work in the believer until the believer acquires possession of the inheritance in eternity. Once again, the purpose is to the praise of His glory. So the Holy Spirit works in and with individual believers, guaranteeing the work God initiated and that Christ secured for the praise of God's glory.

The implications for life and ministry of this functional unity in the Trinity are numerous. The Trinity worked *in unity* to plan, provide, and protect the plan of redemption. Furthermore, the Trinity worked in unity *for* the believer. When the believer was dead in trespasses and sins (2:1), God moved toward the sinner in mercy, motivated by love, and demonstrating His grace (2:4-7). Likewise, the Trinity works in unity *in* the believer. God has an agenda for each believer, from the point of salvation to ultimate glorification, to live a lifestyle that is emblematic of a follower of Jesus Christ.

This functional unity of the Trinity, as demonstrated in perfect harmony and fellowship as God, challenges all of us who try to help others in the disciple-making process. As counseling takes place, we must look past the sin to see the person for whom Christ died and paid the ransom price. Accordingly, we must demonstrate the same kind of mercy, love, and grace demonstrated by God toward the sinner. God chose to provide for the sinner's salvation by grace, to adopt sinners as children, bringing all things under the headship of Christ and guaranteeing the process of redemption for those who trust in Him—all according to the riches of His grace, for the praise of His grace so that believers might live for the praise of His glory. We must adopt God's agenda and walk alongside counselees to help them grow as disciples of Jesus Christ.

The Trinity Provides Unity for Believers

Believers not only discover the functional unity of the Trinity in Ephesians, they also learn how the Trinity provides unity *for* believers with God and others (2:11-22). Paul tells believers to remember who they were before Christ and redemption (2:11-12). Believers once were known only as "Gentiles"—without Christ, without citizenship in Israel, without covenants of promise, without hope, and without God. Jews called them the "uncircumcision" in order to highlight the fact that they were on the outside looking in, excluded instead of included, and not part of God's people. However, Christ changed that when He shed His own blood to bring them into a relationship with Himself (2:13). They went from being outcasts and people-less to being citizens and family members together in the body of Christ. Furthermore, Paul reminded them that God is joining them together into a holy temple in Christ; they are being built into a home for God by the Spirit (2:19-22).[12] So, for the believer, everything has changed relationally.

Christ brought about this change for believers (2:14-18). Referring to Christ, Paul simply states, "He himself is our peace" (2:14). By the blood of Christ, God created a new group made up of both Jews and Gentiles and broke down the wall separating them, the law of commandments. With the hostility eliminated between the groups, peace and unity are the result. Paul also declares that through the cross Christ reconciled this new group to God. So Christ provides peace and unity between neighbors (horizontally) and between God and believers (vertically). Interestingly, Paul refers to the work of the Trinity to summarize the peace and unity that Christ provides: "Through him [Christ] we both have access in one Spirit to the Father" (verse 18).

For the counselor this understanding is critical. Initially, the fact that Christ has broken down all barriers for those in Him compels the biblical counselor not to view the counselee as a "project" or the relationship as merely professional. Instead, both the counselor and counselee share an intimate fellowship in Christ. The attitudes, values, and conversation must flow from an awareness of the unity shared between family members in God's household—which of course should reflect the unity of the Trinity. In addition, the effort to help this counselee see progress and change ought to reflect the price paid by Christ, God's work in building a holy temple, and an awareness of the Holy Spirit's presence for, with, and in this counselee.

The Work of the Trinity Impacts the Counseling Process

Paul challenges the believer to live consistently with the wonderful salvation God has provided. "I therefore, a prisoner for the Lord, urge you to walk in a manner worthy of the calling to which you have been called" (4:1). Paul wants the redeemed person to live harmoniously with his position in Christ. He describes how: "with all humility and gentleness, with patience, bearing with one another in love, eager to maintain the unity of the Spirit in the bond of peace" (4:2-3). Paul is saying that the attitude of believers toward one another should promote the unity made possible by the indwelling Spirit. We as counselors must notice how he says to be "eager to maintain" the unity. Counselors should fervently preserve this unity, recognizing how it reflects the unity of the Trinity and cost Christ everything.

Paul does not stop here though. "There is one body and one Spirit—just as you were called to the one hope that belongs to your call—one Lord, one faith, one baptism, one God and Father of all, who is over all and through all and in all" (4:4-6). In this list, Paul uses the term *one* seven different times, which emphasizes his sense of urgency for unity.[13] There is one body—the new body created in Christ and reconciled with God. There is one Spirit—the Spirit who makes His home in the believer and provides access to the Father. There is one hope of your calling—the believer lives in the one hope of completed redemption in which God graciously saved the believer through faith and is God's workmanship in Christ. There is one Lord—Jesus Christ—in whom God is building a holy temple through His shed blood, providing the forgiveness of sin. There is one faith—the content of what a person believes, and that which the pastor-teacher uses to build unity in the church (4:11-13). There is one baptism—one sign of believers' unity with Christ and His death as well as their unity with other believers.[14] There is one God and Father of all—Paul concludes his list by stressing the sovereignty, authority, omnipotence, and omnipresence of God. Considered all together, Paul wants the believer to understand the necessity of eagerly protecting the unity provided by Christ between believers and between God and His children. It is this unity that we must also consider as we work with our counselees.

Paul offers much more to counselors as they consider the rest of the book of Ephesians. Essentially, all the believer's relationships should reflect this greater understanding of the unity we share in Christ. To be models for Christ-centered relationships, counselors should be that much more aware and affected by the unity of the Trinity and their unity with counselees. Paul includes exhortations regarding how we speak to one another and how we live in general. He challenges us to speak the truth in love for the purpose of growing people in Christ (4:15,25). We are to build each other up (4:26,29-30) by speaking words that reflect the grace we have received from God in Christ (4:31-32). In regard to how we live, he urges us to live together in light of our relationship to God the Father, Son, and Spirit.[15] The end result is that we should serve our counselees from the rich foundation of our relationship with the Triune God.

So how does this play out in the daily work of counseling? We do the work of counseling first *as disciples*. Thus, we need to be living examples of a deep-rooted relationship with the Triune God for our counselees. From this foundation, we help our counselees see a life consistent with God's agenda. This takes place only as we understand the counseling process as a process that is life to life, brother/sister to brother/sister, member to member, living stone to living stone. We share a precious relationship together that reflects the perfect, harmonious relationship of the Godhead. Our counseling then must engender and protect the unity of the body as demonstrated in the Trinity as we offer meaningful, practical counsel to counselees.

The Difference a Trinitarian Focus Makes in Counseling

A clear grasp of the relational model exhibited in the Triune God and its effects upon unity among believers directly impacts the purpose, practice, and priorities of the biblical counselor. Regarding purpose, the counselor focuses on both the vertical and horizontal relationships of the counselee. The counselor cannot settle for adaptive emotions, helpful behavior, or satisfying relationships as defined by societal norms. The goal cannot be personal happiness for the counselee without specific regard for others and one's own character development in Christ. Instead, the purpose of counseling is to help the counselee view life and trials in the light of a personal relationship with the Triune God. As the counselee understands this primary relationship in all areas of life, the counselee grows in horizontal relationship with others as well.

Furthermore, understanding the Trinity also affects counseling practice. When the process of counseling flows out of a Trinitarian model, the counselor and counselee share a rich, deep-rooted, tender, and united relationship with each other in Christ. All forms of detached, professional, solution-oriented, aloof therapy fail to satisfy the depth, intimacy, and energy demanded by the unity of the Trinity and unity among believers. The counselor-counselee relationship emanates from a shared relationship in Christ. Therefore, the counseling relationship resembles the rapport of family members, the bond of living stones in the same building, the affiliation of fellow citizens, and the unity of members of the same body. This relationship flexibly moves with the ups and downs, joys and disappointments, blessings and struggles of image-bearers of Christ characteristic of progressive sanctification. The counselor is not primarily a doctor, professional, or technician; the counselor is a friend, brother/sister, and companion in Christ amid suffering and sin.

Likewise, the priority of counseling changes as well. Regardless of the kind of circumstance—suffering or sin—the Trinitarian model forces the counselor and counselee to view life in total dependency on God. Jesus lived on earth in complete awareness of the desires of the Father and the stewardship of the glory of God. The Spirit indwells the believer and ministers in total regard for the plan of God and the believer's conformity to the image of Christ. The idea of living life or counseling about life where God is in absentia is foreign to a Trinitarian focus. Instead, the counselor and counselee carefully, humbly, honestly, vulnerably, and consciously move forward together toward Christlikeness, relating to one another in ways similar to the Triune God and provided for in the Father's plan through Jesus Christ by the Holy Spirit.

The Grand Narrative of the Bible

John Henderson

If we intend to counsel from the Scripture well, we must resolve to see and apply it within the form God wrote it—as a narrative. Remedying the "one-problem-one-verse-one-solution" approach to ministry means we comprehend the Bible's grand narrative and connect it with wisdom to our daily lives. The redemptive movement of the Bible provides a context within which and from which we offer wise biblical counsel.

How can the central message of Scripture influence, shape, and instruct the ministry of counseling? What better way to answer this question than through a narrative.

The Greenhill

In a scenic corner of North Carolina you can find a narrow gravel road winding northward into a range of ruddy foothills, just outside the town of Rutherfordton. At the end of the road, nestled against a modest hill, sits a sizable and comfortable lodge surrounded by oaks and elms and walnut trees. The rustling of the wind in the treetops, if steady enough, can enchant the human senses and entice the mind to forget almost anything. Locals refer to the lodge as The Greenhill.

The summer months are extremely busy with hikers, bikers, and tourists. Once the days become cold and wet, the trails leading in and out of the foothills settle down and the visitors to the lodge start to fade like the morning mist. By late October a great many guestrooms in the lodge lay empty.

If you were at The Greenhill on this one particular evening in October then you would find the owner, Mr. Kindren, sitting at his usual table beside the great fireplace in the dining hall, trying to read a newspaper. While his astute and serious eyes focused on the pages, his ears were far more attentive to Fred, his cook and barkeeper, who was at the moment lecturing the one and only member of the wait staff, Mia, about the art of brewing lattes and mixing cocktails. He believed many problems in the world could be solved if everyone had the proper drink at the proper time.

Between his comments regarding the perfect consistency for cappuccino froth, Mia interjected a detail or two about the latest trends in music and film, or the newest gadget available for enhancing connectivity in a global society. Mia had hundreds of friends, most of whom she had never actually met. Visitors were amazed by how much she knew about people she had never seen. Living fully for oneself, Mia thought, was the order of the day. Solid commitments and restraints were things of the past.

Beneath the sound of their voices, and just above the crackling of the fire, you could make out the melody of a song. Reggie, the inn's janitor, was whistling the tune of some ancient hymn. This was his custom whenever he mopped the floor or washed the dishes, or almost anytime he was occupied in work. If you had been often to a church, then you would probably recognize the melody. All those hymns of Christian faith, Reggie believed, "belonged in the atmosphere."

Three Travelers

Given the lull in tourists, every member of The Greenhill staff expected to finish their work within the hour and retire to their residences, which is why they were so surprised to hear the front door swing open and footsteps in the foyer. They knew what it meant: Guests! Excited at the prospect of paying customers, Mr. Kindren hurried to greet them.

The bustle of human voices, bodies, and baggage moved upstairs into some of the bedrooms. Mr. Kindren scrambled back into the dining hall and ordered his staff to prepare refreshments. After a few moments the three travelers returned downstairs and found a table in the middle of the room—close enough to the fire to enjoy its warmth, yet far enough away to avoid the little tufts of smoke escaping from the hearth. Their bodies sagged with weariness.

The young woman, named Maggie, looked on the brink of tears. Two days ago and a hundred miles away, she had abandoned her husband and two small children. "I can't take this anymore," she told friends and family. The pressures of caring for a home, dealing with stubborn kids, and supporting a difficult husband created, in her words, "a miserable place without hope." People at her church said she was dreadfully depressed. She simply felt crazy—tired, ashamed, and finished. Running away was the only thing she knew to do. Seared into her memory was the image of her five-year-old son weeping at her feet, pulling on her jeans and begging her to stay. She didn't.

On her way out of town Maggie met Kirk. He was also weary and frustrated with life, but for different reasons. Kirk went wherever he pleased. He did whatever he wanted. Life bored and burdened him. People, he believed, were to blame. Others had let him down. His ex-wife and twenty-three-year-old son were total disappointments. The impeccable moral principles he carried had been violated so often that he was about finished with human beings altogether.

The third traveler, a young and quiet man named Wilson, was new to the group. Kirk and Maggie found him several days ago in a town fifty miles to the west. They had never known a man so shy and reserved. They pitied Wilson. He was the youngest of the group and, from their point of view, the most fragile. Any wrong or careless word, they suspected, might crush Wilson's spirit beyond repair.

The Pursuit

"What brings you to the area?" Mr. Kindren asked them while placing a basket of crackers on the table.

Kirk and Maggie looked up. "Happiness," they responded in chorus. Kirk added, "We are each in search of happiness."

Now the response may sound peculiar to you, but it was not at all strange to Mr. Kindren, or to anyone else in the room. People were constantly seeking happiness in those days. Guest after guest came through The Greenhill trying to find some kind of joy or peace or hope or pleasure or freedom or whatever they considered essential to their personal "happiness."

"Well, you have come to the right place," Mr. Kindren announced. "We have strong opinions and clear convictions about happiness at The Greenhill.

This lodge exists to help people discover true happiness. All of us have looked into it and have a sense of how and where to find it."

"Really!" Maggie replied.

"Oh yes," Mr. Kindren declared. "We're all Christians here. And we have the Bible, the Word of God that gives us all the answers to our problems."

Maggie tensed up. "Oh! Never mind. I have read the Bible. I know what it says. It can't help me right now."

Mr. Kindren retorted, "Nonsense! Tell me your problem, and I will find you a solution from the Bible." He pulled up a chair and sat eager to hear her story.

There was a long pause. Maggie was not eager to share, but to her own surprise she spoke out. "How could it hurt?" she muttered, "I'm at the end of my rope." She began to share her story—the varied joys and sorrows of her childhood, her parents and hometown, and her many plans for life. Jesus "saved her" as a teenager. She was "a good girl," eager to please and do the right thing. College was exciting—full of hopes and dreams. Then somewhere, somehow, Maggie "lost herself." Life stopped unfolding the way she wanted. Marriage and children took her down an unexpected, dreary road. "Everything got heavy and exhausting," she added. "I don't *feel* anything anymore, nothing good at least. I feel trapped in my own home. Suffocated. I keep waiting for it to change, for the kids to grow up, for some space and peace, for more *life* in my life." Maggie looked down at her wedding ring. "I don't know what else to say."

Competing Stories

Maggie's words and countenance hung heavily in the air like a fog. The pause in the conversation, from Fred's point of view, was the perfect opportunity to lighten Maggie's load and the somber atmosphere in the room by serving a few drinks. "Here's what you all need. Drink up! Tomorrow has enough trouble of its own God tells us,[1] so don't worry about it. Pain is unbearable only if you can feel it."

The drink sounded good to Maggie. She was, in fact, quite thirsty. But she was not convinced a cocktail would improve reality.

"Thank you, but I'm not sure a drink will make my life any better," Maggie remarked.

"But it will make you *feel* better," Fred replied, "which *makes* life better. I'm pretty sure the good apostle Paul knew what he was talking about when it came to being happy. 'Let us eat and drink, for tomorrow we die,'[2] he once said."

Kirk raised his glass. "Well said!"

A subtle groan could be heard across the room. Reggie, while mopping a little section of floor under a table, overheard Fred's counsel and couldn't contain himself. "Fred, I think you're missing Paul's point by a mile or two. No doubt Maggie needs something from Scripture, even that portion of Scripture, which holds a key to our troubles and our happiness."

Mia chimed in from a stool at the bar. "Honey, I say you just charge forward and find whatever makes you happy. It's what God wants for you. I think you're on the right track. It doesn't sound like you and your man are compatible. Maybe family life isn't for you—God may not have wired you for it. You can't love anyone else if you don't look after yourself first."

For a moment, Maggie lightened up a bit. The idea of charging forward under Mia's banner gave her an initial jolt of validation, even courage. She liked the distraction from the turmoil in her soul. It relieved a little pressure, but not for long. She couldn't shake the looming sense that something was terribly wrong. Mia's words rang a bell of freedom from the shackles she bore, but the after-tones, if she listened carefully, simply offered slavery of a different kind.

With the determination of a soldier, Mr. Kindren stood, walked to a bookshelf on the other side of the room, and returned to the table with a stack of Bibles. He addressed Maggie with a gentle yet serious tone. "Don't listen to them, my dear. God has better answers for you."

Turning to Paul's letter to the Corinthians, Mr. Kindren read a single sentence: "To the married I give this charge (not I, but the Lord): the wife should not separate from her husband (but if she does, she should remain unmarried or else be reconciled to her husband), and the husband should not divorce his wife."[3] Mr. Kindren looked up. "I love how wonderfully simple the Scripture makes our lives. I think you have your answer. You're miserable because you're disobeying God's Word. If you obey, life will be well and you will probably feel a lot better too. Are there other questions on your mind we can answer?"

Maggie frowned. "But I was miserable before I left my husband. I've been miserable ever since I had a husband. I've tried to do the right thing, and I've been terribly unhappy."

Mr. Kindren replied as one who had heard such an argument before, "Ah, but God doesn't intend for you to be happy—only pure and submitted before Him. Jesus said, 'If anyone would come after me, let him deny himself and take up his cross daily and follow me.'⁴ You must learn to do the right thing even if you hate it."

The Story

No one knew quite what to say. Maggie stared at the fire. She didn't have the energy to argue. Reggie stepped forward and spoke with a look of concern, "Mr. Kindren, sir, I'm not so sure that's exactly how those scriptures best apply, or that they address what Maggie needs right now from the Book."

"Whatever are you talking about?" Mr. Kindren muttered, clearly annoyed.

"I mean, those are wondrous verses and all, but they may not make a lot a sense if she doesn't get *the Story* behind the verses." Reggie paused, then added, "The story of the Bible shows how fiercely the Lord works for people's true happiness. Purity, submission, and happiness, from God's point of view, can't be rightly separated. I mean no offense, and I'm guessing you're trying to get her downriver to a good place. I just can't figure how you'll help her along by standing at the banks, drawing out buckets of water, and throwing them on her feet. They're good buckets of water and all, but they have no current by themselves. Just like the rest of us, Maggie needs to be swept *into* the river."

An uncomfortable silence followed. Everyone stared at Reggie, who began to wonder if he had just crossed the line.

He kept talking: "I think the Word gives all kinds of remedies full of grace and truth, but not so often in the form Maggie just received. God wrote it more like a storybook than an encyclopedia. It gives a bunch of great answers to big questions, it's true, but *always connected* to the Lord's bigger plan—a bigger plan, mind you, certain to bring about the true happiness of His people, which is wonderfully kind of Him, since almost all people refuse to understand what happiness actually is and where it may be found."

Mr. Kindren rolled his eyes and retorted, "Whatever are you talking about now, Reggie?"

"I know I may not be making any sense, but it seems to me like the Word acts like a mass symphony of instruments working in harmony and building to something grand more than a phone book of musical soloists up for hire. All the stories and poems and letters and oracles and wisdom verses of God's Word, like individual instruments in a great orchestra, serve *the whole story*. You served Mrs. Maggie a beautiful but single note from a single instrument in the orchestra. No doubt there are solos and duos all around, and each of these comfort and convict us in their way and time, but they aren't strumming and blowing on their own. In His time, I think the Lord wants us to hear and appreciate the way they harmonize."

"Why do you call it *the* Story?" Kirk asked suspiciously.

"Let me see," Reggie reflected. "I guess to set it off from all *the other stories* being thrown around in the world. People are always coming up with stories to explain the universe and their lives and what's wrong and how to make it right. Evolution, for instance, gives us a storybook version of how the world and people came into being. All the psychologies and sociologies of the human race try to tell us why people think, feel, and live the way they do and how they're best improved. God's revelation is *the Story* meant to help us see clearly and interpret everything else. His account carries all the say-so. God Himself gives life and power, so His story delivers life and power.[5] Man's versions promise life and power while bringing death and futility, just like the serpent's story brought death and futility.[6] God's version confronts, reshapes, and even redeems or condemns all the other stories."[7]

Maggie's interest was piqued by now. "What story?" she asked.

Reggie grinned—nothing smug or clumsy, but that sort of look you see on a man's face when he's talking about his favorite things, those things meaningful, serious, and precious to his soul.

Reggie pulled up a chair.

"Whew! That'll take a bit of time to tell. I could try to sum it up, but then it can't really be summed up easily. It's why there aren't too many quick and easy answers in changing people. In a nutshell, the Bible shares the Story of God's careful work in creating, loving, judging, and saving a world that He made good and beautiful, but plunged into evil and ugly. The good news of His Story *announces* and *offers* a way for people like us to be made new again, to be forgiven and given eternal life with Him, in this life and the next.[8] It helps us know who God is and how He is acting in human history and in our lives here and now."[9]

Who It's About, and Why

Maggie looked curious. "Why do you say *His* story?"

"I suppose because *He* authored it and *He's* the middle of it, not us. Through this Book the Lord has chosen to express and fulfill *His* mission in the universe. It's not man's idea. It's not man's power and purpose that matters most. God created everything, and man rebelled and creation sunk into pitch-black darkness and death. Then God went to saving it and bringing it back to life, *like He planned all along*, to show off His incredible power and mercy. It was *His* mission to rescue those *He* prepared to rescue[10] in order for the whole universe to see and enjoy and worship *Him*.[11] The Bible gives us God's explanation of *His* mission to love and rescue *His* people for *His* name's sake."[12]

"I don't think we have time for all that right now, Reggie," Mr. Kindren answered. "They are in trouble. They need answers from God now!"

Reggie looked thoughtful. "Yes, I suppose so, Mr. Kindren. They're in trouble, just like we're all in trouble, in different ways of course. And the Bible's narrative shows how we got into trouble, and how the Lord is fixing the trouble in our lives and the whole universe. Everything Maggie's carrying and feeling and facing in her life, here and now, right down in the bottom of her soul, is *basically* what the Bible is about, and *basically* the same as everything the people of the Bible—who are the real, living stories—felt and faced there and then."

Maggie looked puzzled. "I thought the Bible was a book of rules to keep or I'd be punished, and suggestions to follow so God would love me."

"God gives us ideas and rules in the Scripture for sure, but all *as part of* Him revealing Himself, a personal and holy Creator who never changes, as part of convicting us and reconciling us to Him. God uses His Word to draw us to Him. God uses it to feed and change us.[13] God gives us what truly matters to human life through a true knowledge of Him.[14] Scripture, like a pair of corrective lenses, helps us see rightly.[15] The Story of Scripture *interprets* and *speaks into* the story of your life. Just like all of us, you need someone to show you the connection. You need the Spirit of God to help you see and cherish the connection."

Maggie sighed and stared back into the fire. "I still don't know where that leaves me. I mean, what does God's Story have to say to me?"

"I think that's a wonderful question," Reggie replied. "How should the overall message of the Bible shape the way you think and feel about God, yourself, and marriage? If you were to live consistent with the Story of the Scripture, then how would you live today? What would change? Or even, what story does God want to tell *through* your life and marriage? I think these are other ways of asking the same question."

The Movement of God's Story

Maggie began to understand what Reggie was talking about. "I realize those are questions I need to ask. But how do I answer them? It will take the rest of my life poring over God's Word to 'get downriver,' but where do I start?"

"In the beginning,"[16] Reggie replied, "where God chose to begin His story. Why not start there?" Reggie began to talk about Creation. The way Reggie described the little details of God's earth-forming handiwork made the whole scene come alive. "It's like God formed His own big theatre, like some master play writer putting together His stage,"[17] Reggie explained. "Just out of nothing. He spoke all into being, and then He made Man in *His* image, just from dust, and a woman from him, 'cause God wanted to show Himself and share Himself and enjoy Himself and all His glory through all He made."

No one at the table had ever heard marriage talked about the way Reggie talked about it from the Genesis story. "You see" Reggie explained, "God has always existed as Father, Son, and Holy Spirit. From eternity He had *others* of His nature to lean toward in love and happiness. Occupying and giving Himself in happy service to others is woven into His nature. So, after He made man and saw he was alone, the Lord said in a sense, 'That isn't good. That isn't like Me. He's got nobody of his nature to love and serve and give himself over to.' The man needed a helper to show God off in a beautiful way and do what God wanted him doing in blessing the whole world He made."

"I don't buy it," Kirk said smugly. "God made women and marriage to meet a man's need for respect, companionship, and other stuff."

"More like to make women their slaves and depressed," Mia snapped.

Reggie slowly shook his head. "Neither one of you are seeing marriage within God's plan. The Lord may very well use our marriages to bring many gifts, joys, and pains into our lives, but He firstly made it to help tell the Story, to show off the beauty of His redeeming love, and to help us live out His plan.

The true reason for marriage has God in the middle."

Maggie's eyebrows furrowed. Kirk squirmed a little in his chair. Mia chuckled, not because of anything Reggie said, but because she had just read an amusing text message on her phone. For the first time in a while since Reggie starting speaking, Mr. Kindren looked up from his cup of coffee.

Reggie continued, "Throughout the story of the Bible, God often spoke of His relationship to His covenant people Israel as a marriage.[18] The relationship between Christ and the church, from God's point of view, is a marriage. When He saved us through Jesus Christ, we became the bride of Jesus Christ.[19] Earthly marriage exists to help portray and enjoy the invisible union between Christ and His church."[20]

Mia re-entered the conversation: "Maggie's husband doesn't deserve to be compared to Jesus, that's for sure."

"None of us do," Reggie reflected, "and none of deserve to be married to Him. We're in covenant with Him because of grace. Maggie, God hasn't called you to honor and respect your husband because your husband deserves it, or simply to make your life work the way you want, but because Christ deserves it, because you can help tell the amazing story of Christ and the church in your attitude and affection toward your husband. God designed your marriage to serve an end far greater than itself."

"Those are hard words to bear," Maggie added. "I wish it didn't hurt so much."

"Yes, marriage can be painful. It can be hard to bear—that's part of the story too. There's agony and difficulty in marriage because we're sinners. We're married to sinners. Not long after God created marriage, sin and brokenness and death entered marriage."[21]

Reggie recounted the rebellion of Adam and Eve. He recounted the effects of their sin in their union with God and one another, and the effects for people today. "All the suffering we see and know in the world happens because evil happened and everything got cursed. It sounds like you experience these effects in your life and home."

There was a pause before Maggie replied, "Sadly, yes, and many you didn't mention."

"I think the whole account of Scripture can be encouraging for you. God explains your suffering and sin through His Word and the many true stories within. And He doesn't leave you there to rot. There's far more to the Story. Just when you thought God would strike everything away and start over in Genesis 3, He promised *re-creation*. He promised to send us a Savior who would rescue us from His wrath and make us His own people.[22] God promised to pour out His Spirit into our hearts for salvation.[23] All the songs and prophets of the Old Testament point to the Redeemer who would come and undo what we had done. Account after account sees *Him* coming. The Redeemer would restore and reconcile us back to the Father.[24] The New Testament explains how all this was accomplished in Jesus Christ, and why this matters to us, and to your marriage."

Before Reggie could resume speaking again, another voice arose. It wasn't quite as frail as everyone would have expected. "My home life was a train wreck," Wilson let out with a sigh. "My dad was gone before I knew it. Stepdads were in and out. They were cruel at best. It's hard for me to imagine a God that's different from men, or a good God who exists in the middle of my life. It's hard for me to imagine a Father altogether lovelier and purer than fathers. Never had I felt an attraction to the word *father*."

Until that moment Wilson had seemed only shy and insecure. Now everyone could see anger in him, and strength, and resolve. Wilson shared more of his story. Abuse. Despair. Night after night lying awake in his bed, praying to die.

Fred couldn't think of a drink to heal those wounds. Mia searched for ways to bring the conversation back to a happier note, but to no avail. No snide comments came to Kirk's mind. No verses of Scripture immediately came to mind for Mr. Kindren to quote as solutions to Wilson's troubles. What could anyone say? The group sat silently under a strong sense of discomfort.

"I'm so sorry, Wilson," Maggie eventually spoke out. "I don't know what to say, or what God would say to you right now."

"I do," Wilson replied. "I think He would say He loves me, and that no father on earth compares to Him. No father deserves to be compared to Him. He gave His Son to suffer and die in my place. He calls and strengthens me to endure suffering, too.[25] When I think about all those stories of the Bible, I remember how He never leaves or forsakes His children. He's never left me. The work He has begun in me He will complete, just as He completes His work in Scripture. All that He has promised to do, He will do. He has proved

Himself over and over. If I have Him, then I have everything. That's not just a verse or two, but constant themes throughout God's Story. He says and shows it a thousand different ways."

Wilson looked to the ceiling for a moment, then continued: "He wants me to believe it. And He wants *faith* working itself through *love* in my life. That's what Joseph and David and Daniel and Peter and Paul and John would all tell me. They lived it too."

Everyone sat shocked. What had happened to Wilson? How could they explain all this sudden courage and clarity? Maggie realized that nobody had actually paid any careful attention to him before now.

"The Lord Jesus is coming back," Wilson added. "The Story isn't over. A way of salvation has been provided, but we're not home yet. All I know is I want to be ready. I'm a new creation. Why spend my life living for myself? Why spend my life under self-centered fears and frustrations? Why would I want my life to be about me when it could be about Him, trusting Him and loving Him and loving people the way He loves people? That's happiness, according to His story—knowing Him and loving Him and being made like Him, a happiness dependent upon His grace."

The Rest of the Story

Wilson's words hung in the air. The minutes seemed like hours. Thoughts were unfolding. Affections were re-orienting. Whole books could be written about what was taking place and what would soon take place in everyone's hearts. Maggie left the table without a word. The others watched her bound up the stairs and collect her things. They heard a "Good-bye!" and "God bless!" trail off as she passed through the lobby and out the front door. She hadn't said where she was going. She didn't need to.

Wilson arose with a smile. "Good night each of you!"

"Good night, Wilson," Reggie replied. He then stood up, took his mop in hand, and returned to the patch of floor he had been working before he joined the conversation.

Mia glanced up and mumbled, but quickly re-engaged herself with the several strings of text messages alive and active on her phone. Fred downed his nightly shot of whisky before retiring to bed. Kirk, irritated as ever, went outside to smoke a cigarette and reflect on, from his perspective, the disappointments from the evening.

What Now?

Left alone sitting beside the fireplace, Mr. Kindren stared at the Bible in his hands. *What just happened?* he thought to himself. Scripture remained as truthful and powerful as ever before, but jumbled in his mind, as if he had to relearn the way he used it, as if the Lord was trying to reorient his approach to helping people. He was unsettled, humbled, needful of God. A new awe for the breadth and depth of Scripture was setting in—a new determination to dive into the gospel more deeply so he could convey it more fully. He sensed a desire to express more patience with the daily struggles of people and was struck by how "slowly" God may work upon human souls. All these thoughts somehow made him feel as though he were gaining a clearer focus on the immense power of Scripture.

"What now?" he prayed.

6

The Sufficiency of Scripture

Steve Viars and Rob Green

Imagine this. You wake up to the same odor you've smelled every day for the last nineteen years. Urine. It may not be very polite to mention in public, and certainly not in a book—but it is what it is. Your adoptive parents tell you the doctors said you were born with a deformed pituitary gland that doesn't secrete antidiuretic hormone to your kidneys. Whatever. All you know is that you receive a synthetic hormone several times each day. That at least keeps you alive, but it obviously doesn't work very well. Thus, you experience the daily wake-up call that pierces your nostrils, again. Good morning to you.

You wonder if it's going to be sunny today. Of course you have no way of knowing because you're blind. The specialists theorize that on your twenty-sixth day of development, even before your birth mother knew she was pregnant, a series of anomalies occurred. As a result, your optic nerves are severely underdeveloped and you have never seen anything but the faintest shadows. Someone else will have to give you the weather report.

When your feet hit the floor, they hurt. Badly. You have always experienced terrible pain in your feet. Your therapists like to say that you have texture issues. You just know that every step you take, it feels as though you are walking on bits of glass.

Still, it's time for you to make your way upstairs to the main floor of your house because you have to start getting ready for another day of school. That's no picnic either. You think about how your teacher attempted to teach you a simple math problem yesterday. You tried as hard as you could to understand, but you just couldn't. You even pounded on your head several times, but the answer just wouldn't come out. No wonder some people make fun of you and your classmates. That hurts too—a lot worse than your feet.

9

But something is happening as you near the top of the stairs. What is that noise? Are you...singing? Is that the song you learned in youth group last Sunday, the one about God lifting you up and giving you strength? And what is that on your face? Are you smiling? Something very amazing is happening here.

Is the Bible Sufficient for People with Physical Problems?

You can stop imagining. And it is okay to be relieved that this story is not really about you. But it will probably come as no surprise to learn that the vignette above is anything but a fairy tale. It is the true story of Steve's special-needs son Andrew (Drew), who has a long list of proven physical challenges and disorders. Over the years he has been to dozens of doctors, specialists, therapists, and consultants. Even recently, a neurologist determined after an extended EEG that Drew has been having multiple seizures each day, probably ever since he was born.

Why does this matter?

Drew's story is relevant in a book on biblical counseling because it raises a very important issue. Is God's Word sufficient for people who have proven physical problems? What about individuals in whom there has been no confirmed diagnosis but there is a strong suspicion that something is amiss physiologically? What is the relationship between the doctrine of the sufficiency of Scripture and men and women whose physical malfunctions seem to be contributing to their behavioral choices?

This is not just an academic question for counseling theorists to leisurely contemplate in an impersonal fashion. It involves real people like Drew, whose body is complicating the equation in all sorts of ways. If our counseling model is truly biblical, there will be a profound sensitivity to the way we think about and treat men and women suffering from physical symptoms we may never fully understand.

What About People Who Suffer?

So far we have been talking about what counseling theorists refer to as nature, the condition of the physical bodies our counselees possess. But there's more. The other side of the equation is the question of nurture, or environment.

Does our belief in the sufficiency of Scripture lead us to conclude that shaping influences in days gone by or instances of present suffering are unimportant?

A Painful Past

What do we do with a woman who comes in and shares a story of terrible abuse in her childhood? Or a man who describes an unstable home life in which his divorced mother dragged him to the address of whatever lover she was shacking up with at the time? Do we tell them to ignore their pasts and simply learn to obey God in the present? Or, do we focus on the past and assume such a person cannot live victoriously today?

Present Suffering

For other counselees, the issue has more to do with some episode of abuse or disappointment in the present. There are reasons why we buy boxes of Kleenex by the case at our counseling center. The stories that men and women bring into our offices about their current environments are truly heartbreaking.

The purpose of this chapter is to begin a discussion about how the doctrine of the sufficiency of Scripture relates to both nature and nurture. You won't counsel people for long before your position on this issue will be tested. Wise is the person who has considered this matter well.

What Is the Sufficiency of Scripture?

In his *Systematic Theology*, Louis Berkhof explains that the doctrine of the sufficiency of Scripture was an important product of the Protestant Reformation. In the 1500s, the Church of Rome believed that the Bible was terribly obscure and therefore required certain church leaders to interpret its deep mysteries. Some concluded that the Pope was infallible in matters of faith and practice when speaking *ex cathedra*. Even if his position was not found in the pages of Scripture, his addition was necessary truth for church life.

The Reformers thought otherwise. In regards to this subject, they argued for three essential doctrines. First was the perspicuity, or fundamental clarity, of the Word of God. That is not to suggest that they believed all passages in the Bible are easy to understand. But, as Berkhof explains:

Their contention was simply that the knowledge necessary unto salvation, though not equally clear on every page of Scripture, is yet conveyed to man throughout the Bible in such a simple and comprehensible form that one who is earnestly seeking salvation can, under the guidance of the Holy Spirit, by reading and studying the Bible, easily obtain for himself the necessary knowledge, and does not need the aid and guidance of the Church or of a separate priesthood.[1]

Second, the Reformers taught the principle of the analogy of faith, or *interpretation secundum analogium fidei*. Because of the perspicuity of Scripture, the Word of God interprets itself. This is why the Westminster Confession of Faith later emphasized that "the infallible rule of interpretation of Scripture is the Scripture itself: and therefore, when there is a question about the true and full sense of any Scripture (which is not manifold, but one), it must be searched and known by other places that speak more clearly."[2]

These two principles led to the emphasis on the *perficio* or *sufficientia* of God's Word. In contrast to the belief that Scripture is obscure and in need of human interpretation and addition, the Reformers believed that by and large the Bible is simple and understandable in its core teachings and therefore contains all the truth necessary to know and serve God.

As Wayne Grudem explains, "the sufficiency of Scripture means that Scripture contained all the words of God he intended his people to have at each stage of redemptive history, and that it now contains everything we need God to tell us for salvation, for trusting him perfectly, and for obeying him perfectly."[3]

Scripture's Claims to Sufficiency

My (Steve) wife Kris and I had a critical decision to make after we learned that Drew had abnormalities in the development of his brain. Does God's Word have anything to offer us as we try to raise our special-needs son? There is no question that Andrew had diminished capacity—we have the objective brain tests to prove it. But is there a difference between diminished capacity and no capacity?

People dealing with less certain diagnoses are faced with a similar question. What are we supposed to do with all the psychological labels that are based on something other than objective medical tests? Suppose for a moment that there is at least a suspicion that something may be going on in someone's brain, even if at this point it is unproven or improvable?

Queries like this are a healthy part of the conversation because they drive us back to our Bibles with a fresh, expectant gaze. What kinds of claims does God's Word make about sufficiency?

The Bible Has All We Need to Draw Us to Christ

In 2 Timothy, Paul wrote about the difficult conditions of the end times with Timothy, his "son in the faith." After listing in chapter 3 a number of challenges that go with living in a sin-cursed culture, Paul turned this young pastor's attention to all the resources available in Scripture:

> You, however, continue in the things you have learned and become convinced of, knowing from whom you have learned them, and that from childhood you have known the sacred writings which are able to give you the wisdom that leads to salvation through faith which is in Christ Jesus (2 Timothy 3:14-15 NASB).

Biblical counselors would be wise to think carefully about the logical progression of this chapter. Paul could have pointed Timothy to any number of possible sources of truth as he taught him about what effective pastoral ministry looked like in challenging times. But Paul's essential point was, "Never forget the centrality of the biblical gospel." It doesn't matter if we have helped a person feel better emotionally or improved some aspect of their situation if they are no closer to Christ when the process is concluded.

God's Word claims to be sufficient enough that even in trying circumstances; it can "give you the wisdom that leads to salvation." Kris and I were very careful not to press Drew into making a decision to repent of his sin and place his faith and trust in Jesus as Lord and Savior until he was truly ready. One evening when Andrew was 16 years old, we were fishing together when, without any prompting from me, Drew said, "Dad, I would like to become a Christian. Can you show me how?" We discussed verses he had learned at home and at Sunday school, and then he told me he was ready to make his decision for Christ. Right there on the banks of that pond, he placed his faith in Jesus.

I tell you that story to encourage you never to neglect proclaiming the gospel to those the Lord brings across your path. Sometimes we get so caught up in the debate about nature or nurture that we forget there is something even more fundamental to the human existence—the condition of one's soul. "Without faith it is impossible to please Him" (Hebrews 11:6 NASB). Thank God that He has entrusted us with a sufficient Bible, because "faith comes from hearing, and hearing by the word of Christ" (Romans 10:17 NASB).

The Bible Has All We Need to Help Us Order Our Affections

After Drew came to Christ, he still had the same cluster of physical problems and life circumstances as before. But now the power of God's Word had made his soul alive. He was united with Christ in His death, burial, and resurrection. The most important element of his existence—his heart—was now able to be cultivated to respond to the challenges of both his nature and his nurture in an entirely fresh way.

One of Drew's greatest responsibilities was examining and adjusting the nature of his desires. Would he find his joy only in eyes that saw, kidneys that worked, or feet that moved? If so, he was setting himself up for discouragement and depression.

This is another place where God's Word has served him so well. Consider these beautiful words from Psalm 1:

> How blessed is the man who does not walk in the counsel of the wicked, nor stand in the path of sinners, nor sit in the seat of scoffers! But his delight is in the law of the LORD, and in His law he meditates day and night. He will be like a tree firmly planted by streams of water, which yields its fruit in its season and its leaf does not wither; and in whatever he does, he prospers (Psalm 1:1-3 NASB).

Drew, like all of us, has to make a decision every day about the object of his greatest delight. Scripture points him to something beyond the challenges of his body and life situation. He has a Savior and God who is marvelous beyond comparison. "Delight yourself in the LORD" (Psalm 37:4 NASB). This is why Drew is able to sing as he walks up the stairs in the morning. Yes, he has a body that is seriously broken and his daily circumstances are challenging, to say the least. But he is learning each day that hard is not necessarily bad. A soul that is happy in the things of God can overcome tremendous obstacles.

The same is true for any counselee God may bring across your path. You may be working with someone who has physical problems as obvious as Drew's. Or, perhaps God has brought someone to you whose diagnosis is either inconclusive or focused more on behavioral criteria than objective medical tests and analyses. Equally challenging may be a person who is suffering from either past abuses or present turmoil. I want to say this as gently as I can, but at some point all of that is not the most relevant aspect of your counselee's story. This man or woman has a heart, a soul, an inner person and can therefore choose to love and adore Jesus in a way that transcends everything else that could be placed on the table.

The Bible Has All We Need to Explain Our Identity in Jesus

Every counselee has to decide who they are. We all select an identity and then make choices in the inner and outer man based on that fundamental belief.

I (Steve) often ask counselees to summarize their life story in ten words or less. I also frequently ask them to complete the sentence "I am _____." The answers to questions like this provide a marvelous and powerful window to the heart.

Scripture provides followers of Jesus with a rich tapestry of gospel indicative, explanations of who we are in Christ. The most important thing about Drew is not that he is blind—it's that he is a child of the living God. He's been forgiven through the precious blood of the Lamb. He has been redeemed by the power of God. He has been adopted into the family of the eternal Father. He has been united with Christ's death, burial, and resurrection. He has access to a living hope and a future inheritance. The list goes on and on, and each truth has a way of making Drew's physical ailments a less significant part of the story.

This is why wise counselors spend large amounts of time discussing the practical implications of the gospel indicatives. We are so prone to move into all the *dos* and *don'ts* of the Christian life that we miss the rich blessings that attend meditation on what God's sufficient Word tells us about our new identity in our Savior.

The Bible Has All We Need to Reveal the Motivations of Our Hearts

Discussions that focus exclusively on nature or nurture often leave counselees thinking about themselves as passive victims:

- I am who I am because of what other people have done to me.

- I am who I am because of forces inside my body outside of my control.

- I am who I am because of the way I am being treated today.

God's Word drives us to consider more personal, comprehensive explanations of the choices we make. Scripture challenges us to face the hard reality that we are active worshippers who continually reveal the identity of our functional god(s) by the ways we think, speak, and behave. Here is just a sample of how the Bible emphasizes the centrality of our hearts:

- "May my heart be blameless in Your statutes, so that I will not be ashamed" (Psalm 119:80 NASB).

- "Watch over your heart with all diligence, for from it flow the springs of life" (Proverbs 4:23 NASB).

- "Jesus said, 'Are you still lacking in understanding also? Do you not understand that everything that goes into the mouth passes into the stomach, and is eliminated? But the things that proceed out of the mouth come from the heart, and those defile the man. For out of the heart come evil thoughts, murders, adulteries, fornications, thefts, false witness, slanders. These are the things which defile the man; but to eat with unwashed hands does not defile the man'" (Matthew 15:16-20 NASB).

- "Each tree is known by its own fruit. For men do not gather figs from thorns, nor do they pick grapes from a briar bush. The good man out of the good treasure of his heart brings forth what is good; and the evil *man* out of the evil *treasure* brings forth what is evil; for his mouth speaks from that which fills his heart" (Luke 6:44-45 NASB, emphasis added).

- "Each one is tempted when he is carried away and enticed by his own lust. Then when lust has conceived, it gives birth to sin; and when sin is accomplished, it brings forth death" (James 1:14-15 NASB).

Understanding what God's Word says about the gospel indicatives prepares us to also invite Scripture to expose the nuances of our hearts. That is why Paul was able to be so authentic with the Christians in Rome about his struggles over doing the things he did not want to do while simultaneously failing to do the things he knew he should (Romans 7). He could be honest about what was happening inside of him because of his settled confidence in what God had taught him about who he was in Christ (Romans 6).

The Bible Has All We Need to Change into the Image of Christ

Jesus, in His high priestly prayer, made a profound request for those who would place their faith and trust in Him. "Sanctify them in the truth; Your word is truth" (John 17:17 NASB). The Holy Spirit takes the Word and helps us magnify God's Son as we progressively change into His image (Romans 8:28-29). No wonder Peter said that in Scripture's marvelous promises, we have "everything pertaining to life and godliness" (2 Peter 1:3 NASB). Paul echoed that sentiment when he told Timothy that God's Word makes His servants "equipped for every good work" (2 Timothy 3:17 NASB). Even the psalmist said that "the law of the LORD is perfect, restoring the soul" (Psalm 19:7 NASB).

It has been exciting for Kris and me to watch Drew become more and more like Christ. God's Word is powerful enough to pierce physical weakness and disease and help followers of Christ become more like their Savior whom they love.

The Bible Has All We Need to Find Our Hope in Eternity

The hard truth is that for many of our counselees, the weaknesses of their body or the pain of their circumstances may never change in this life. While the Bible never minimizes the pain, it does help us put the challenges of life in proper perspective:

> In this you greatly rejoice, even though now for a little while, if necessary, you have been distressed by various trials, so that the proof of

your faith, being more precious than gold which is perishable, even though tested by fire, may be found to result in praise and glory and honor at the revelation of Jesus Christ (1 Peter 1:6-7 NASB).

So why is a handicapped young man able to smile as he walks up the steps? It is not because we will ever fully understand all the aspects of his physical condition. We will never be able to protect him from a ridiculing world or even the struggles he has in his own heart. But God has given him and us a Bible that is sufficient. He truly offers all we need for life and godliness.

Letting the Sufficient Scripture Assign Nature and Nurture Their Appropriate Roles

It is undeniable that our bodies impact us in all sorts of ways. Drew's story illustrates that in a rather dramatic fashion. Other people at least suspect that something physiologically may be awry, but at this point in the development of medical science, there is no way of knowing for sure. We all live in a body that is cursed by sin and impacts our choices on a daily basis.

Our challenges are greatly magnified when we consider the power of our environment—the people and circumstances around us in both the past and present. Bible writers repeatedly encourage us to approach such challenges with authenticity and candor, acknowledging our past hurts and present suffering.

Secular counseling systems have historically gravitated back and forth between emphasizing nature or nurture, or a hybrid of the two. What is consistently missed is the centrality of the human heart. We are active worshippers and we reveal the identity of our functional God by the way we use our bodies and respond to our environment.

The beauty of this position is that God's Word is especially suited to directing those who want to focus primarily on the nature and direction of their own hearts.

- "Watch over your heart with all diligence, for from it flow the springs of life" (Proverbs 4:23 NASB, emphasis added).

- "The word of God is living and active and sharper than any two-edged sword, and piercing as far as the division of soul and spirit, of both joints and marrow, and able to judge the thoughts and intentions of the heart" (Hebrews 4:12 NASB).

Scripture helps us understand that as we grow in our love for Christ at the level of our hearts, we can use our bodies—even when struggling with diminished capacity—as "instruments of righteousness" (Romans 6:13) and respond to our circumstances in ways that conform us to the image of Christ (Romans 8:28-29).

Is the Bible's Sufficiency Active or Passive?

Some would agree with much of this discussion, but then would turn to secular disciplines to flesh out the content and emphases of their models. Championing the phrase "all truth is God's truth," these persons who seek to integrate psychology and God's Word at times end up with approaches that are long on secular ideas and short on biblical truth.

An Important Theological Reminder

Careful theologians always keep the concept of the noetic effect of sin near at hand. From the Greek word *nous*, this term refers to sin's effect on our ability to think and reason. Yes it is true that God's Word allows us to interpret the data around us and make (hopefully) wise observations. But we must never confuse the value of our observations with the plain truth of Scripture.

But Isn't All Truth God's Truth?

Sloganeering can lead to all sorts of error when it comes to the process of building a model of counseling. There is no question about ownership—yes, God owns the truth. The issue is our ability to derive truth apart from God's sufficient Word. The more a theorist understands the significance of the noetic effect of sin, the closer he or she will stay to the text of Scripture.

Should We Only Use Words from the Bible?

Church historians tell us that answering this question incorrectly has resulted in significant heresies throughout the generations. For example, the Arian controversy had to do with those who sought to deny the Trinity because the word *Trinity* is never found in Scripture. In commenting on this, John Piper said, "The heretics demanded 'no creed but the Bible' precisely so that they could use biblical language to evade biblical truth…to my surprise one form of the doctrine of the 'sufficiency of Scripture' was used to undermine Scripture's truth."[4]

Doesn't That Leave Us with Biblicism?

I am not arguing for a shallow approach to counseling that uses isolated proof-texts from Scripture apart from their context and intended meaning. However, if I am going to make a mistake in the counseling room, I would prefer that it be the result of staying too close to the Bible as opposed to being too far away. As John Frame said:

> For all this attention to contexts both scriptural and extra scriptural, *sola Scriptura* also demands that theological proposals be account-able to Scripture in some way. It is not enough for theologians to claim that an idea is biblical; they must be prepared to show in Scripture where that idea can be found. The idea may be based on a general principle rather than a specific text; but a principle is not general unless it is first particular, unless that principle can be shown to be exemplified in particular texts. So a theology worth its salt must always be prepared to show specifically where in Scripture its ideas come from. And showing that always boils down in the final analysis to citation of particular texts. This is why, for all that can be said about the abuses of proof-texting, proof-texts have played a large role in the history of Protestant thought. And there is some-thing very right about that.[5]

Does Psychology Play a Role?

The word *psychology* can refer to many different things, from hard data derived from behavioral tests to a personality theory that makes no attempt to prove its validity. In his *Cure of Souls*, David Powlison posed the unusual acronyms VITEX and COMPIN to guide his discussion. Those who hold to VITEX believe secular psychologies "must make a vital external contribution in the construction of a Christian model of personality, change, and counseling." Conversely, theorists who subscribe to COMPIN believe "the Christian faith contains comprehensive internal resources to enable us to construct" a counseling model. Powlison went on to argue for a COMPIN approach that learns from other models, but only "in a tertiary" fashion by saying:

> This is God's world, so everything, even if it intends to efface God, bears witness to God—understood and reinterpreted through biblical eyeglasses. The Bible freely traffics in the extra-biblical, in the creation, in fallen cultural products, in the terminology of the very contemporary falsehoods that God is attacking. But God always interprets and reinterprets. He is imperial. Biblical truth is a corrective gaze.[6]

A Final Word of Caution

Those who deny or minimize the sufficiency of Scripture or view the Bible as more of a passive screen should always remember that the other supposed sources of truth for building an approach to counseling are suspect. This has become even more apparent as secularists argue amongst themselves as they try to assemble the latest version of the Diagnostic and Statistical Manual of Mental Disorders-V. Two theorists from the University of Nevada School of Medicine recently commented on those who are stirring up "a vigorous discussion about the weaknesses of psychiatric diagnostic classification as well as troubling elements related to the DSM in general." They went on to list three troubling observations:

> First, our diagnostic system has not led to the identification of any biomarkers or biological causes for mental disorders; second, the diagnostic categories are heterogeneous within categories and often overlap with each other as well as with normalcy; third, diagnoses can cause real harm, not just to a few people, but to millions.[7]

Conclusions like this from leaders in the secular world should give biblical counselors even stronger reason to rejoice that God has given us in His Word all that we need for life and godliness.

Creating a Model Based on God's Sufficient Word

Putting these concepts together results in an approach to model building where God's sufficient Word produces gospel-centered, heart-focused counsel that allows both nurture and nature to function as informers to our theology work.

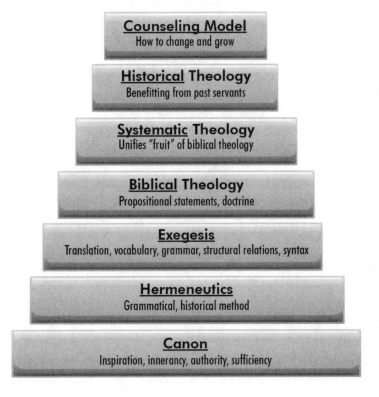

The process begins on the foundation of the Word of God. The counseling theorist uses appropriate principles of hermeneutics (Bible study) and exegesis to generate a biblical theology—propositional statements about God and His Word. That information is then organized into systematic theology, an organized approach to all that God has revealed to us in His Word. We then turn to historic theology to glean what we can from the godly men and women who have gone before us. From this study emerges an approach to change and growth that impacts the practical areas of everyday life.

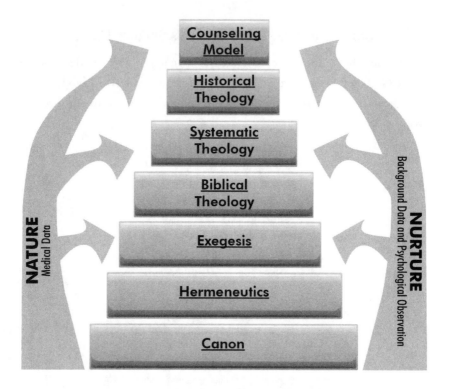

As this pyramid continues to develop, biblical counselors are constantly on the lookout for advances in our understanding of the human body. We encourage our counselees to receive regular medical workups, especially if any of their behaviors are uncharacteristic or give evidence of sudden change. Some biblical counselors even recommend that some of their counselees seek a physician's help for a possible prescription for a psychotropic medication not because it will necessarily address the cause of the problem, but because it may alleviate certain distressing symptoms. In any event, this pyramid leads the counselor to place central attention on what God's Word says about changes that need to take place at the level of the heart.

Biblical counselors also spend significant amounts of time gathering data about past hurts and present suffering. We also give some level of attention to psychological findings because we allow such information to fuel our theology work. God's Word helps us interpret and understand everything within our gaze.

It is likely that Kris and I will have the privilege of parenting Drew for many more years to come. Are there aspects of that which are frightening? Of course. But the same sufficient Bible that pointed young Timothy to the risen Savior directs us in a similar fashion. The sufficient Word points us to a sufficient Savior. He is, and will always be, everything Drew and his parents need for life and godliness.

The Spiritual Anatomy
of the Soul

Bob Kellemen and Sam Williams

To care for people biblically, we must know God personally—knowing the Creator of the soul—our great Trinitarian Soul Physician (which we addressed in chapters 1-4). Knowing the living Word drives us to the written Word as we use God's Word relationally in personal ministry (covered in chapters 5-6). With this foundation built, we can now begin to *understand people* biblically—examining the spiritual anatomy of the soul. We can learn our Creator's answer to the question, "Who am I?" (our focal point in chapters 7-8).

Pursuing God's Target:
The Image of God—God's Design of the Soul

In developing a biblical understanding of people, we must begin at the beginning, not at the Fall. Life as we now find it is not the way it was supposed to be.

In the film *Grand Canyon*, an attorney attempts to bypass a traffic jam. His route takes him along streets that become progressively gloomier and more deserted. His expensive car stalls on a secluded street patrolled by a local gang. The attorney manages to phone for a tow truck, but before it arrives three young thugs surround his disabled car and threaten his life. Then, just in the nick of time, the tow truck driver arrives. Savvy enough to understand what is about to go down, the driver takes the leader of the group aside to introduce him to metaphysics.

"Man," he says, "the world ain't supposed to work like this. Maybe you don't know that, but this ain't the way it's supposed to be. I'm supposed to be able to do my job without askin' you if I can. And that dude is supposed to be able to wait with his car without you rippin' him off. Everything's supposed to be different than what it is here."

The creation narrative teaches us how things were *supposed to be*—including how we were meant to live life with God and each other. It also teaches us God's *original* design for the soul—the nature of human nature as bearers of God's image (the *imago Dei*). It enables us to answer the questions, "What is health? What does a healthy image bearer look like?"

There are three central reasons why we must understand people biblically. First, the world has over 250 different models of the human personality. Human reason has attempted to understand the *creature through the creature*. The Bible, by contrast, provides us with the inspired understanding of the nature of human beings. Through God's revelation we come to understand the *creature through the Creator*.

Second, even within Scripture-based approaches to counseling, there is a tendency to emphasize one aspect of the human personality over others. We suggest an approach that offers a *comprehensive* understanding leading to people-helping that helps the *whole person to become a whole person in Christ*.

Third, knowing who God designed us to be provides us with our target in counseling and our purpose in life. The end goal of biblical counseling is *our inner life increasingly reflecting the inner life of Christ*. Our goal is not simply symptom relief, but Christlikeness. We are not solution-focused; we are *soul-u-tion-focused*.

For us to move others toward this goal or target, we must grasp God's comprehensive original design for the human personality. We are:

- Relational Beings: Loving with Passion—Affections

  - Spiritual Beings: Communion/Worship

  - Social Beings: Community/Fellowship

  - Self-Aware Beings: Conscience/Shalom

- Rational Beings: Thinking with Wisdom—Mindsets

- Volitional Beings: Choosing with Courage—Purposes

- Emotional Beings: Experiencing with Depth—Mood States

- Embodied Beings: Living with Power—Embodied Personality

- Embedded Beings: Engaging Our World—Embedded Socially

- Eternal Beings: Created by, Like, and for God—*Coram Deo* Existence[1]

Figure A helps to capture the essence of our comprehensive nature. Notice that the innermost *core* of our being is our spirituality—our capacity for relationship with God. Note also that the entire *circumference* of our existence is God-focused—we are *coram Deo* beings created by, like, and for God.

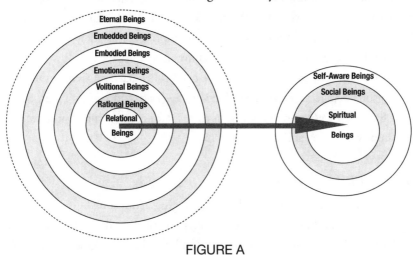

FIGURE A

In seeking to understand people biblically, we work our way "from the inside out." We'll trace the relational movement from our spiritual relationship with God outward toward our social, self-aware, rational, volitional, and emotional capacities. We'll then explore how we interact with our world as embodied beings and embedded beings. After that, we'll explore the significance for counseling of the reality that we are eternal beings.

We Are Relational Beings: Created to Love with Passionately/Sacrificially—Affections/Longings

Created in the image of our loving, Trinitarian God who eternally relates in the unity and diversity of Father, Son, and Holy Spirit, we are *relational* beings.

God designed us as *spiritual* beings who relate to Him, *social* beings who relate to others, and *self-aware* beings who relate to our own selves.

As relational beings, God designed us to love passionately. By passion, we do not mean romantic passion, but passion as in Passion Week and the Paschal Lamb. God made us to love sacrificially, to put others first. As God is a God of *agape* love, which initiates love for the benefit of another, so in our original design we are initiators of sacrificial love. God created us to love Him wholeheartedly and to care intimately about and to connect deeply with others.

According to Jesus, loving is the core of our being and our central calling: to love God and to love others (Matthew 22:35-40). Biblically and in church history our relational affections have been emphasized as a key component, even *the* key component, that makes us human.[2]

If we are to counsel powerfully, we need to understand that in the very core of our being, we have deep *affections, longings,* and *desires* (Psalm 62:5; 63:1,8; 84:2; 143:6). God designed us to *thirst* for relationship. Without relationships we shrivel, shrink, and dry up.

Spiritual Relational Beings

In Psalm 42:1-6, we see the threefold longing of our soul. Verses 1-2 highlight our *spiritual* longing: "As a deer pants for flowing streams, so pants my soul for you, O God. My soul thirsts for God, for the living God. When shall I come and appear before God?" David pictures a deer panting with thirst for the flowing stream of refreshing water. The word for "pant" indicates a strong, audible breathing, gasping, and panting caused by a prevailing draught. As the deer's throat thirsts for water, so David's soul thirsts for communion with God. His soul, designed by God and for God, is parched, empty, thirsty—desperate for God.

God designed us as *spiritual* beings to worship and commune with Him. The "Holy of Holies" of our soul is our capacity to love and worship God. As a deer pants for water, so we thirst and long for God. That's our target, our GPS, our measuring rod. We help counselees to address the questions, "How well am I worshipping God? Do I thirst after God with all my soul?"

Social Relational Beings

David mingles his spiritual thirst with his *social* thirst in verses 3-4: "My tears have been my food day and night, while they say to me all the day long, 'Where is your God?' These things I remember, as I pour out my soul: how I would go with the throng and lead them in procession to the house of God with glad shouts and songs of praise, a multitude keeping festival." Whereas David once joined with others in worship, now others mock him. Whereas he once was a leader of people, now he flees from the people he led. It is not good for David to be alone. He hungers for fellowship with the festive throng.

God designed us both for worship and for fellowship—to hunger for communion with Him and connection with one another. The God who created us for relationship with Himself also said that it was not good to be alone (Genesis 2:18). We are *social* beings created for community—to love our neighbor as ourselves. We help counselees to evaluate how well they are loving others. That's our counseling target: "How's your love life?"

Self-Aware Relational Beings

David's hunger includes a third dish: "Why are you cast down, O my soul, and why are you in turmoil within me? Hope in God; for I shall again praise him, my salvation and my God" (Psalm 42:5-6). David has *self-aware* longings. He speaks to himself, to his soul. He is self-aware. Disturbed and downcast, he longs for inner peace—he's thirsty for his original design. Human beings are unique among God's creation in their ability to reflect upon their inner experience.

God designed us with the capacity to relate to ourselves: We are *self-aware* beings. We are not computers or androids with artificial intelligence. We are not animals living on instincts. We can reflect on our own existence. In fact, Romans 12:3 commands us to reflect on ourselves accurately according to who we are in Christ. Our target with our counselees is a deep self-awareness of who they are in Christ.

We Are Rational Beings: Created to Think Wisely—Mindsets

Created in the image of our all-knowing, wise God, we are *rational* beings.

We think in words (beliefs) and pictures (images) as Adam did when he gave each animal a creative name that expressed and portrayed that animal's unique nature (Genesis 2:18-20). God designed us with minds that can perceive His world and advance His kingdom. In that original design, God empowered us to think wisely—to think God's thoughts after Him, to understand life from God's perspective.

We can summarize our rational capacity with the concept of *mindsets*. In counseling, we don't simply help people to change one thought; we help people to understand the *pattern* of their thinking—their mindsets. This is what Paul emphasizes in Romans 12:1-2 when he commands us to renew our minds— our deeply held and characteristic ways of thinking about God, self, and others.

"Spiritual eyes" is an image we can use to capture our original rational nature. We are not to look at life with "eyeballs only," but with 20/20 spiritual vision (2 Corinthians 10:3-7). God designed us to use our imagination (Isaiah 26:3), our spiritual vision to see our world, our relationships, our situations, our past, present, and future from God's perspective (2 Corinthians 4:16-18). We are to be visionaries dreaming big dreams for God's kingdom and God's people (Ephesians 3:20-21).

Our goal as counselors and counselees is to interpret life through eternal lenses with spiritual eyes. We pursue and target wisdom: rational maturity, which God defines as being transformed by the renewing of our minds as we look at life from an eternal perspective (Psalm 1).

We Are Volitional Beings: Created to Choose Courageously—Pathways/Purposes

Created in the image of our all-powerful God who creates out of nothing and whose purposes no one can ever thwart, we are *volitional* beings who act purposefully. God created us not as robots, but as sons and daughters with a will to choose His will. We are not animals who react on instinct, nor are we computers who act on input. We are human beings with a motivational capacity to act on the basis of our beliefs about what quenches our relational thirsts (Genesis 3:6).

God designed us to relate, to think, and also to choose. We have a will to set and pursue goals (Proverbs 20:5). We are motivated by what we believe will satisfy the deepest thirsts in our soul. So, in counseling, we don't only encourage people to change their behavior; we empower people through Christ to make changes at the level of deep heart motivation (Proverbs 16:2).

As originally designed by God, we are capable of choosing courageously instead of selfishly or cowardly. Like William Wallace in *Braveheart* when he was being tortured, our will shouts, "Freedom!" We bravely fight to free others.

Just as we can summarize our longings with affections, and thoughts with mind-sets, so we can summarize our ability to choose with the words *pathways* or *purposes*. We tread a path in our actions as we habitually train ourselves either toward righteousness or toward evil. Joshua recognized our capacity to choose a certain life direction when he exhorted God's people to "choose this day whom you will serve" (Joshua 24:15).

In Paradise, God gave humanity dominion (Genesis 1:26-28). Adam and Eve were to subdue the planet, expanding the reign of Paradise until all was Edenic. They were to be faithful stewards serving their Creator by being co-creators, vice-regents, and under-shepherds. Satan came to heist their reign, our reign. In our fallen state we declare, "My will be done! My kingdom come!" We are still willful, but stubbornly and rebelliously so. Christ came to restore us to our original state. In our redemption we can say, "Not my will, but Yours be done."

Thus, we have our next target. We are called to be a part of the amazing process of helping one another to pursue the purpose of courageously and unselfishly loving others for God's glory.

We Are Emotional Beings: Created to Experience Deeply—Mood States

Created in the image of our passionate and compassionate God, we are *emotional* beings who experience life deeply and internally. God created us to feel. Though the Christian world sometimes makes emotions "the black sheep of the image-bearing family," God loves emotions. Jesus wept, and so do we. The Spirit grieves, as we do. The Father rejoices, like we do. We have the emotional capacity to respond to our outer world based upon our inner actions, choices, goals, beliefs, images, longings, and desires.

Like God, we relate, think, choose, and feel. We experience life deeply, responding and reacting to our external situations based upon our internal affections, mind-sets, and pathways.

We can summarize our emotional capacity with the phrase *mood states*. In helping a hurting person, we don't simply try to address one emotion; instead, we work with people to manage their moods—to grow in their ability to handle painful, messy, complex feelings in a godly way—to soothe their soul in their Savior.

Like a gospel choir, or the composers of the spirituals, we are built to sing—to express our deeply felt emotions, both positive and negative. Like the psalmists, God designed us to express our inner feelings both with complaining psalms of lament and with joyful psalms of thanks.

Therefore our next counseling target is to help people to assess how well they are managing their moods. Are they maturely taking all their feelings before God and handling their emotions in a God-honoring way that helps others instead of bringing them harm?

We Are Embodied Beings: Created to Live Fully—Embodied Personalities

In chapter 8, Jeff Forrey and Jim Newheiser discuss the relationship between the heart and two arenas of influence: the body (we are embodied beings) and our social environment (we are embedded beings). Because of their in-depth examination, we will only briefly introduce the concept of embodied and embedded beings.

God, who is spirit, created us as embodied beings. He is infinite; we are finite. He is divinity; we are dust and divinity (Genesis 2:7). He is noncontingent; we are contingent. He is needless; we are needy. He is independent; we are dependent. He is without limits; we are limited.

God created us to entrust ourselves, body and soul, to His care, to enjoy embodied existence, to appreciate thankfully every good and perfect gift, and to use the members of our bodies as servants of righteousness (Romans 6:12-13). The body, the flesh, our skin and bones, is God's great gift to us.

We are one holistic being with physical (body) and metaphysical (soul) capacities. The Bible clearly highlights the complex interworking of body and soul, brain and mind. We are physical beings designed by God to live fully—

to express our personhood through our physical body. God gave us a physical body and a physical brain so that we could discipline ourselves to righteousness, as Paul explains in Romans 6—offering the parts of our body as instruments of righteousness. Like Samson, we can choose to surrender our physical body to lusts of the flesh or to works of righteousness.

In biblical counseling, we must take into account this complex inter-working and connection of the mind and body.[3] We must relate to people as holistic relational, rational, volitional, emotional, and physical beings. We are embodied persons.

We Are Embedded Beings: Created to Engage Our World—Embedded Socially

Who we are is not a question we can ask without also seeking to understand the context in which we live. Biblical counselors seek to understand the influences that shape the responses of the human heart.

As biblical counselors we seek to recognize the complexity of the connection between people and their social environment. Thus, we seek to remain sensitive to the impact of suffering and of the great variety of significant social-cultural factors (1 Peter 3:8-22) people have experienced. In our desire to help comprehensively, we seek to apply God's Word to people's lives amid both positive and negative social experiences—both now and in their past.

We Are Eternal Beings: Created by, Like, and for God—*Coram Deo* Existence

We have come full circle. We began with the core of our being, the "Holy of Holies" of the soul—we are spiritual beings designed to enjoy and exalt the God of the universe. We commence with the circumference of the embodied soul—we are *eternal* beings. We are *coram Deo* (in the presence of God) beings created by, like, and for God. As Ed Welch notes, properly comprehending the image of God leads "naturally to seeing that people are, at their very root, people-who-live-*before*-God and people-who-are-to-live-*for*-God."[4]

In Psalm 8, when David ponders the nature of human nature, his perspective is thoroughly theocentric. We live in-relationship-to-Deity. "You are mindful of him…you care for him…you have made him…and crowned him…

you have given him...O LORD, our Lord, how majestic is your name in all the earth!" Our lives are pervasively theological. We are *coram Deo* beings living face-to-face with God in Christ.

Pursuing God:
The Design of Life and Goal of Biblical Counseling

To be made in the image and likeness of God is to be made for relationship with Him and others, and to represent this magnificent God on earth. Creation is a theater in which God has chosen to project His glory in manifold ways. God intended that one particular part of the created order—His image bearers—would play a central role in reflecting and representing Him. Central to the essence and nature of humanity, of what it means to be human, is to be created by, like, and for this God.

Created *by* God

Every person we counsel is created *by God*. Genesis 1–2 is structured to highlight two points: (1) God is the creator of everything; (2) people are the apex of God's workmanship, uniquely handcrafted to display His glory (Genesis 1:26-28; 2:7-8; Psalm 139:13-14; Ephesians 2:10).

Genesis 1:26 contains a noteworthy transition as it describes how God created people. The Creator's approach is distinctively personal, as there is a shift in the description of His creative work from the previously typical mode of "let there be" (an impersonal metaphysical decree) to "let us make" (a much more personal and relational statement not unlike you might say to your spouse, "Let's make this together").

Genesis 2:7 again notes a change in God's creative method, as "the LORD God formed the man...and breathed into his nostrils the breath of life." God's personal touch is manifested in the making of this particular species, this particular part of His creation.

Furthermore, all of Genesis 1–2 emphasize that the whole earth, the atmosphere, the emerging land and the boundaries of the seas, the plants, and the animals are all formed and fitted, tailor-made just right—for us. The name of our earthly home, Eden, carries in the original Hebrew text the connotation of a pleasant place of delight. Even the trees and food are designed in such a way that they are "pleasant to the sight and good for food" (Genesis 2:9).

Like a good father designs a home for the children whom he loves, God pays special attention not only to how He made us, but also the place in which we were to reside. Scientists have recognized this remarkable congruence between people and the earthly home in which we dwell. Sometimes called the anthropic principle, it is plain for all to see that every aspect of this planet—from its atmosphere, to the motions of the sun and moon, to the geology and weather, to the composition of plants and animals—is fine-tuned just right to support human life.

In addition, this unique creation of humanity by God is not confined to the original creation of our forefathers, but instead is continued every time a baby is conceived, then develops inside, and then outside of the mother's womb, by God's providential hand. "You formed my inward parts; you knitted me together in my mother's womb. I praise you, for I am fearfully and wonderfully made. Wonderful are your works; my soul knows it very well" (Psalm 139:13-14).

That we are created *by* God has critical implications for biblical counseling. First, it means that the people we counsel do not exist as the result of an impersonal, unguided evolutionary process, but instead are specially designed by an intelligent (to say the least), holy, loving personal Being. There are no chance human beings. As we counsel, do we realize who designed the person who sits before us? The honor and dignity with which they are crowned calls us to respect them and listen well. This person, their problems, and their situation are as unique as their fingerprints. This is why we are to be quick to listen, slow to speak, and slow to arrive at final conclusions. This is the reason we ask open questions that leave room for richer, more personal responses. This is what motivates us to hear their whole story.

For the past twenty years, one of the rising explanatory stars in modern psychology has been evolutionary psychology. According to this theory, the explanation for human thought, behavior, and emotion is that we do, think, and feel what we feel because it increases our reproductive fitness and improves our capacity to survive. So, the evolutionary plot goes like this: "The chief end of man is mere existence and genetic perpetuation." Not a very meaningful story, is it? Such explanations for human behavior are deeply unsatisfying, not just aesthetically but also intellectually. If this is the point of life, empathy in counseling is reduced to just another evolutionary strategy.

According to biblical counseling, however, every counselee exists because of God's intelligent and purposive design. They are beautiful but broken, contingent beings put here by Someone else and for that Someone's purposes. Their worth or value is not trumped up or self-generated, but instead is derivative, dependent on the One who made them. And, the functionality and the fitness of their lives are contingent upon their fulfillment of the purposes for which they exist—to love, worship, and glorify God. Whether they realize it or not, and often we must help them remember, their lives are pregnant with purpose. It is God's mission that they are created for, and where they can find as much fulfillment as is possible on this planet.

Created *Like* God

It is rather impressive that we are made *by* God, in such a personal fashion, which confers great value upon us. Like pricey designer purses and watches whose value goes way beyond their functionality, our value comes from the One who designed and made us.

But perhaps the most amazing, and nearly incredible, words the Bible has to say about people is not that they are created *by* God, for that does not in itself set us apart from the rest of creation, but instead that we are designed in the very image and likeness *of* God Himself. This is reiterated three times in the creation account, and in several other places in Scripture. Genesis 9:6 and James 3:9-10 explain that the reason we should not murder a person or even curse one is that to do so is to deface the image of God (Job 31:13-15; Proverbs 14:31).

Most people would take offense if they saw someone burning their country's flag, because that flag is more than a piece of cloth; it represents something much greater and more important. To disrespect a person made in the image and likeness of God is a lot worse than desecrating a flag. We should be offended and repulsed in the same way when God's image bearers are desecrated—abused, beaten, neglected, discriminated against, and not loved and taken care of as they should be.

To be human means to be made, not just by, but even *like* God. Every man, woman, and child who requires counsel is a reflector and in some way a representative of God. You have been chosen by God to serve them, to love them, to speak His truth into the broken and wrong places in their lives. The image of God in us may be effaced, but it cannot be erased. They are sufferers and sinners, and may be saints, but they are also similar to God, even though that may not be so obvious because of the devastating and distorting effects of sin in their life.

Theologians refer to this similarity, this likeness, as the *imago Dei*, and have debated what it actually means to be created in the image and likeness of God, and especially what constitutes the image. Some theologians anchor the image in the human mind—that we are rational, intelligent, self-aware beings. Others locate the *imago* in the human conscience—that we are moral/ethical beings capable of discerning and choosing right and wrong, good and bad. Still others believe the *imago Dei* consists in that we, like God, have the capacity to exercise a type of dominion, control, stewardship over this delightful planet. We represent God as subcreators of culture—fulfilling the cultural mandate (Genesis 1–2).

Some theologians believe that the essence of the *imago Dei* is relational— that we, like God, are relational beings capable of communication and personal connection and loving and receiving love. We are like God in that we are not solo acts, but instead are pervasively relational beings, designed and destined to be properly connected with one another and with God.

The *imago Dei* is what separates every person from the animals and plants and the rest of creation. The unique dignity and sanctity of every human life, regardless of age, color, race, gender, or economic status in life is rooted here. This is the basis for a radical equality of worth and value among all persons.

In *The Weight of Glory*, C.S. Lewis points out how knowing the eternal significance of every person we meet should change how we treat (and counsel) others:

> It is a serious thing to live in a society of possible gods and god-
> desses, to remember that the dullest and most uninteresting person
> you can talk to may one day be a creature which, if you saw it now,

you would be strongly tempted to worship, or else a horror and a corruption such as you now meet, if at all, only in a nightmare... There are no ordinary people. You have never talked to a mere mortal. Nations, cultures, arts, civilizations—these are mortal, and their life is to ours as the life of a gnat. But it is immortals whom we joke with, work with, marry, snub, and exploit—immortal horrors or everlasting splendors.[5]

Learning to see each human as an *imago Dei* should sanctify our view of those we counsel and dignify our relationships with them.

Created *for* God

One of the central components, perhaps the essence, of the *imago Dei* is the capacity for a particular type of relationship with God, characterized by love, worship, and obedience. The Bible's take on mental health and mental disorder is theocentric. We are not just responsible for ourselves—we are responsible to Someone.

Every thought, desire, emotion, action, and impulse of each counselee is known by God and evaluated by God. "The LORD looks down from heaven; he sees all the children of man; from where he sits enthroned he looks out on all the inhabitants of the earth, he who fashions the hearts of them all and observes all their deeds" (Psalm 33:13-15). People are not the center of this mental health system. God is the only star in the system and our counselees are like moons, intended to revolve around this Son-God and to reflect His light. As John Piper writes:

> People are not important because they breathe. They are important because they have the capacity to honor God with their hearts and minds and bodies long after they stop breathing—forever. The most important thing about people is that, unlike animals and trees, they live forever in heaven glorifying God, or in hell defying God.[6]

A direct implication of this theocentricity in counseling is that "the chief end of man is to glorify God and enjoy Him forever" should be not only part of our confessions and catechisms, but also a crucial part of our take on counseling. Worship is central to the counseling project. Every counselee is a worshiper, and at the end of the day (and session), their problems are in fact a function of what or whom and how they worship.

Counselees are responsible for themselves—and, even more importantly, they and their counselors are responsible to Another. Every person is morally obligated and accountable to God. To counsel persons made by, like, and for God means that there are no God-free zones in the counselee's life or in counseling.

Christlike Counsel

If our counseling is truly Christ-centered, then our counseling must be Christlike. This includes our character as a counselor and our compassion as we counsel. But it does not stop there. It must also involve understanding people the way Jesus understands them.

In John 2:24-25, John informs us that Jesus "knew all people" and "knew what was in man." What occurs next in John's Gospel is fascinating. Jesus counsels two of the most different people anyone could ever imagine. First, He ministers to the male, religious, self-righteous, Jewish Pharisee—Nicodemus. Next, Jesus counsels the female, irreligious, immoral Samaritan—the nameless woman at the well.

As Jesus spoke truth in love to each of these individuals, He understood their *universal* identity as image bearers and He interacted with a focus on their *unique* identities. He took into account their social setting and their physical needs as He comprehensively and compassionately enlightened each of them to their deepest spiritual longing and ultimate spiritual need—Himself.

As the living Word, Jesus understood His creation. Christ-centered and Christlike counselors cling to the written Word to understand people comprehensively so they can minister to them compassionately.

The Influences on the Human Heart

Jeff Forrey and Jim Newheiser

Connie, now in her mid-forties, came from a family in which both parents were alcoholics. She started partying and drinking when she was in her early teens. She professed faith in Christ while in her mid-twenties and married a Christian man with whom she had three children. Over the past several years, she has gone on periodic drinking binges. When her husband took away her money and credit cards, she pawned the silver so that she could get alcohol.

Why is Connie this way? Was it the bad influence of her alcoholic parents (what has been called the "nurture" influence)? Does she have a genetic predisposition to alcoholism (what has been called the "nature" influence)? Is she helplessly under the control of alcohol?

Setting the Stage: Nature, Nurture, and the Biblical Counselor

The nature vs. nurture debate has been around for a very long time. Although the debate was most famously raised by Charles Darwin's cousin, Francis Galton, in nineteenth-century England, recorded questions about biological and nonbiological influences on our psychological development predate him by at least 600 years. On the nature side of the debate is the effect of genes, the nervous system, and the hormonal system on our behaviors and personality traits. On the nurture side of the debate is the effect of past and present relationships on our behaviors and personality traits.

Nature: To What Extent Does the Body Affect Our Behavior?

Today, we are hearing more about genetic "roots" to a wide variety of behaviors and personality traits. Such claims provoke a concern, especially among Christians, about *genetic determinism*—the idea that our genes inevitably produce certain behaviors and personality traits apart from our active choices. Even beyond consideration of genetic influences on behavior and personality, there are also questions about the roles played by the nervous system and the hormonal system—both in terms of their normal functioning and their dysfunction due to injury or illness.[1]

Nurture: To What Extent Do Relationships Affect Our Behavior?

The influence of other people on our behaviors, attitudes, and values occurs in both obvious and subtle ways. Without much forethought, we can say or do something that later prompts the realization, "That's just what mom would have done!" The tenacity of troubling behavior patterns and personality quirks creates frustration in some people seeking change in their lives because it seems like these patterns and quirks are "just the way I am"—leading to what we might call *social determinism.* For someone like Connie, the relative contribution of both parenting influences *and* bodily influences are pressing concerns. How can a biblical counselor help her make sense of her experience and help her to change?

A Biblical Counselor's Testimony

Because biblical counselors focus on addressing matters of faith and obedience in one's relationship to God and others, they might react against secular counselors who overemphasize the influence of Connie's body or relationships on her current struggles. Or, they might react by underestimating these potential influences on her current struggles. Either extreme will fail to account for the complexity of God's design. Jim's own early experience as a biblical counselor illustrates the potential imbalance.

When I (Jim) first began to learn about biblical counseling, I was very attracted to the truth that the Scriptures are sufficient to help people with their spiritual (soul/heart[2]) problems (2 Timothy 3:16-17; Hebrews 4:12). I appreciated that biblical counselors held people responsible for their actions and did not excuse sinful behaviors (such as drunkenness, outbursts of abusive anger, and sex crimes against children[3]). I was taught that people either have physical illnesses that may require a doctor's attention, or they have spiritual (sin) issues for which they need pastoral counsel from Scripture. I had a great skepticism about any diagnosis of mental illness, assuming that most such cases were actually soul problems rather than body problems. I also appreciated that biblical counselors didn't immediately revert to psychotropic drugs to address spiritual problems.

One of my earliest cases seemed to confirm my thinking. A man named Harry came into our counseling center. Harry was semiretired and in his late sixties. He was suffering from severe depression. He had little energy and no motivation. He was sometimes sleeping sixteen hours a day and had recently fallen asleep while driving his car, thankfully without harming himself or others.

Harry was under the care of a psychiatrist who had put him on large doses of a strong antidepressant medication that he would have to take for the rest of his life. In addition, Harry had been drinking excessively and was told that he was an alcoholic and would have to attend Alcoholics Anonymous meetings for the rest of his life. Harry's family had recently had him committed for several days, against his will, to an inpatient program at a local psychiatric hospital. Up until the past several months, Harry had not had a history of severe depression or substance abuse.

In the course of my counseling with Harry, I uncovered spiritual problems (sins) which were the source of his depression. As we read Psalm 32, in which David describes the way God's chastisement left him drained "as by the heat of summer" (verse 4), Harry exclaimed, "My problem isn't that I am sick or that I am an alcoholic. My problem is that I am a sinner!" Harry identified his sin as being that of spiritual laziness. After spending many years diligently working to serve his family and serving the Lord in his church, he had been spending his retirement years living the good life, with lots of parties and travel, while neglecting his own soul and his duty to serve the Lord.

When Harry repented of this sin, his life changed dramatically. He voraciously studied the Bible and other Christian books. He began to get more involved in his church. He made the decision to quit going to the AA meet-ings, even though his sponsor warned him that he would soon become a drunk again. He also went to his psychiatrist and asked for help getting off the psycho-tropic drugs. The psychiatrist was very upset, warning Harry that he couldn't be responsible if Harry were to do harm to himself or others after he went off the medication. Harry had to sign a release form and the psychiatrist dropped him as a patient after Harry stopped taking the medications. By God's grace, Harry never did go back to his drunkenness or his depression. Instead, he has spent the last fifteen years serving God and his family. He has gone on numerous mission trips to Latin America. He has served as an elder in his church. He became certified as a biblical counselor and served in a jail ministry.

While my experience in those early years of counseling was encouraging, for a time my view was imbalanced because I did not adequately take into account the influence the body can have on the soul/heart. The Lord saw fit to bring other cases into my life that forced me to come to a more accurate and comprehensive view of how the body's functioning can influence how someone acts. And not all the cases were as positive and dramatic as Harry's.

I saw people who were hearing voices telling them to do irrational things. While I could tell such counselees not to believe the voices, to put their faith first in God's Word, and then to trust those who love them, I didn't have any text in Scripture which would make the voices go away. I learned from people who have a medical background[4] that hearing voices or other irrational thinking often has physical causes. For example, some counselees have damaged their brains through excessive drug use. Others, through sinful responses to trouble or pressure (worry, obsessive desire for control, sleeplessness, etc.), seemed to have harmed their brains so that they were incapable of rational thought. I could tell them to repent, but it seemed that they were unable to comprehend their situation or what I was saying to them.

I also came across several cases in which biblical counselors or their family members suffered from severe depression or other disorders and required medications in order to stabilize them. This was humbling, in light of my tendency to reject medications. What these experiences exposed was not any deficiency in the Bible, but *my lack of understanding of how the body can influ-ence the soul/heart.*

Just as I have sometimes failed to adequately take into account the influence of the body on the heart/soul, I have sometimes failed to fully grasp how significantly the counselee's past and present relationships may be influencing the inner person. I have concluded that sometimes biblical counselors may not do an adequate investigation of counselees' social histories, wanting instead to jump to immediate biblical answers for the counselee's presenting problem. Biblical counselors might be reacting legitimately against the tendency of some counselors to spend many hours delving into a client's past, seeking to heal "painful memories" or "damaged emotions." Nevertheless, practices such as these should not deter biblical counselors from investigating how counselees have been and are being influenced by the relationships in their lives.[5]

God's Design: People Are Psychosomatic Creatures

Our bodies are part of our identity as human beings. God created humans as *psychosomatic* creatures. The immaterial heart/soul is the initiator of lifestyle choices; the body is the instrument it uses to carry out its desires.

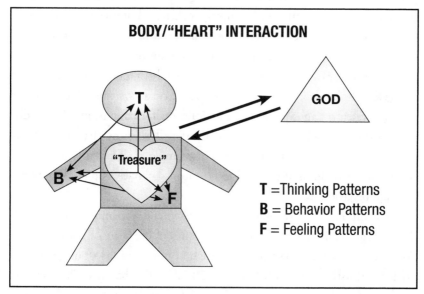

BODY/"HEART" INTERACTION

GOD

"Treasure"

B

T

F

T = Thinking Patterns
B = Behavior Patterns
F = Feeling Patterns

In Scripture, both Jesus and Paul present this understanding of human experience. In Luke 6:43-44, Jesus says that "good" trees produce "good" fruit and "bad" trees produce "bad" fruit. Each tree produces distinct fruit that identifies where it came from: "figs are not gathered from thornbushes, nor are grapes picked from a bramble bush" (verse 44). Then He draws a parallel to humans: "The good person out of the good treasure of his heart produces good, and the evil person out of his evil treasure produces evil, *for out of the abundance of the heart his mouth speaks*" (verse 45, emphasis added). The heart is the initiator of speech, and the mouth is the instrument used for expressing the values in the heart.

In Romans 6, Paul asserts, "We know that our old self was crucified with him in order that the body of sin might be brought to nothing, so that we would no longer be enslaved to sin" (verse 6). The "old self" is an expression that is equivalent to "darkened heart," "hardened heart," "heart of stone," etc., and all these expressions point to the values, standards, and desires of people seeking to live independently of God. Paul's emphasis in Romans 6, however, is on the Christian's freedom from sin's power. "So you also must consider yourselves dead to sin and alive to God in Christ Jesus. Let not sin therefore reign in your mortal body, to make you obey its passions. Do not present your [bodily] members to sin as instruments for unrighteousness, but present yourselves to God as those who have been brought from death to life, and your members to God as instruments for righteousness" (Romans 6:11-13).

In this age, prior to the second coming of Christ, our bodies are affected by the Fall (Romans 6:23; 8:20-23). The body's organ systems—including the nervous system—can experience limitations, malformations, injuries, or diseases (collectively called "weaknesses" in the New Testament) that can have various effects on the heart/inner person. For example, malfunctions of the sense organs or the brain itself can lead to erroneous analyses, confused thinking, and odd behavior.

In addition, the body's vulnerabilities (whether due to injury or congenital[6] defects) will set limitations on how the desires of the heart can be expressed. Some weaknesses may be temporary, such as physical exhaustion (Matthew 26:40) or thirst and hunger (Matthew 6:28-32). Other bodily weaknesses may last for years or a lifetime (e.g., John 5:1-5; 9:1). Though the body and the soul/spirit may be temporarily separated at death, they will be reunited at the resurrection when we will received glorified bodies like that of Jesus (Luke 23:39-43; 1 Corinthians 15:35-54; Philippians 1:21-23; James 2:26).[7]

The Bible Steers Us Away from Genetic (And All Types of Biological) Determinism

Since the heart is the initiator of lifestyle choices, it is both the *locus of moral responsibility* and the *focus of God's judgment*. God is able to administer perfect justice because He alone can assess the dictates of the heart (Jeremiah 17:10; Ecclesiastes 12:14; Romans 2:5-29; Hebrews 4:12-13). Therefore, the heart is the sufficient cause of sin, not the body.[8]

Although the heart/soul is the locus of moral responsibility according to the Bible, people often report struggles with sinful patterns such that it seems to them that the body is causing the sinful behaviors. Summaries of modern behavioral genetic research add to the impression that the *body* is the culprit in producing behavior patterns when we hear about the "gay gene," the "divorce gene,"[9] the "alcoholism gene," etc. The implication is that if a person has a certain genetic makeup, he or she can expect to see the associated behavior pattern. The problems for which genetic links have been identified *are* very difficult to address. However, it is important to realize that even with evidence of genetic influence, the question of what ultimately "causes" behavior takes us beyond the genes.

Genes do not "produce" behavior; they provide the blueprints for the processes involved in constructing proteins within cells. Those proteins might be necessary for a person eventually to exhibit certain behavioral traits, but they are not sufficient by their mere presence to cause the behavioral traits in question. From a biblical perspective, genes, as part of the body, only create the conditions within which a person might be capable of exhibiting behaviors. Thus, certain genes might even be necessary for people to be *vulnerable* to certain problematic behavior patterns. Nevertheless, behaviors are chosen and enacted by *persons,* not proteins or genes.[10] To say that *persons* choose and enact behaviors is to return to the heart as the necessary and sufficient cause of behaviors, because the heart is the control center of the person.

Encouraging People Who Struggle with Bodily Weaknesses

Several scriptural principles are helpful as we interact with people who struggle with bodily weaknesses.

1. People are *always* "fearfully and wonderfully made" (Psalm 139:13-16), even if there are genetic or congenital issues to contend with. In other words, God is sovereign over all the circumstances in our lives, including bodily trials (Job 2:1-8; John 9:3).[11]

2. What happens in the body (e.g., neurological disease, hormonal problems, chronic pain, etc.) can affect us spiritually (e.g., Job 2:4-6) and what happens in the soul (hopelessness, worry, anger, etc.) can affect us physically (e.g., Psalm 32:3-4; 38:1-8). Sometimes counselors will not be able to discern with certainty the relative contributions of bodily weakness and soul/heart issues to a counselee's presenting problem. In such cases they should have the counselee receive a physical exam *and* help the counselee understand the importance of assessing the heart issues as well. Counselors need to be willing to modify their handling of such cases as needed if medical problems are discovered by the physician. Any ambiguities in such cases call for giving counselees the benefit of the doubt (cf. 1 Corinthians 13:7).[12]

3. Bodily weaknesses do not have to hold us back from spiritual growth and are often used by God to help us to grow spiritually (2 Corinthians 12:7-10). Counselors can gently guide their counselees in reconsidering how their bodily weaknesses might serve God's larger purposes, in which His strength is shown through their weaknesses.

4. God will not allow us to be tempted through our bodily weaknesses beyond what we are able to handle for His glory, in the power of His Spirit (1 Corinthians 10:13).

5. Through Christ we can do all things to which God has called us, in spite of our weaknesses and limitations (Philippians 4:13; cf. Exodus 4:10-12; Proverbs 20:12). We are not judged for our physical limitations—only for our efforts to honor God within those limitations.

The Bible Steers Us Away from Social Determinism

Just as the soul/heart operates in the context of the body, the entire person (body and soul/heart) operates in a network of personal relationships situated within a society. People are *socially embedded* psychosomatic creatures.

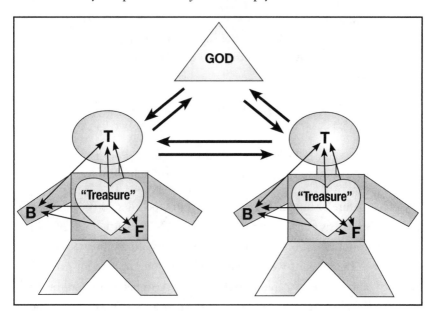

For this reason, it is not uncommon to hear in the media about people who come from abusive families becoming abusive in their own relationships later in life, or depressed people having parents who also struggled with depression, or children adopting the mannerisms of their parents and peers. The influence of other people on our lifestyle choices is clearly recognized by the biblical authors as well:

> When the LORD your God brings you into the land that you are entering to take possession of it, and clears away many nations before you, the Hittites, the Girgashites, the Amorites, the Canaanites, the Perizzites, the Hivites, and the Jebusites...You shall not intermarry with them, giving your daughters to their sons or taking their daughters for your sons, for they would turn away your sons from following me, to serve other gods (Deuteronomy 7:1-4).

> Whoever walks with the wise becomes wise, but the companion of fools will suffer harm (Proverbs 13:20).

> A disciple is not above his teacher, but everyone when he is fully trained will be like his teacher (Luke 6:40).

> Now when they [the Jewish leaders] saw the boldness of Peter and John, and perceived that they were uneducated, common men, they were astonished. And they recognized that they had been with Jesus (Acts 4:13).

> Do not be deceived: "Bad company ruins good morals" (1 Corinthians 15:33).

> Brothers, join in imitating me, and keep your eyes on those who walk according to the example you have in us (Philippians 3:17).

The social nature of human beings is rooted in God's design (Genesis 2:18), and it is tied to His purposes for us (Genesis 1:27-28; Matthew 22:36-40).

Furthermore, relationships and cultural norms often influence people in subtle ways. The Israelites were told by God to go into the land He had promised them and completely eradicate all traces of the inhabitants and their culture: "You shall make no covenant with them and show no mercy to them. You shall not intermarry with them" (Deuteronomy 7:2-3). Of particular concern were the objects associated with pagan worship:

> The carved images of their gods you shall burn with fire. You shall not covet the silver or the gold that is on them or take it for yourselves, lest you be ensnared by it, for it is an abomination to the LORD your God. And you shall not bring an abominable thing into your house and become devoted to destruction like it. You shall utterly detest and abhor it, for it is devoted to destruction (Deuteronomy 7:25-26).

It is important to note that *not* utterly detesting and abhorring what God detests would lead God to evaluate a person *in the same way as He evaluates the object of worship.*

The strength of relational influence is tied to the perceived closeness and similarity between the people. So strong is the possibility of being affected by one's family's values that God also told the Israelites in the Ten Commandments: "You shall not bow down to them [carved images of false gods] or serve them; for I the LORD your God am a jealous God, visiting the iniquity of the fathers on the children to the third and fourth generation of those who hate me, but showing steadfast love to thousands of those who love me and keep my commandments" (Deuteronomy 5:9-10). Some have misunderstood the elaboration on this commandment to say that generational sins are *inevitable* or that God capriciously makes subsequent generations suffer for the sins of the forefathers. However, God is clear: Those who are punished to the third and fourth generation are those who hate Him just as their forefathers had. Those who receive God's steadfast love are those who love Him.

Misunderstanding the generational implications of the second commandment is not just a recent phenomenon. The Jews also entertained this wrong view in response to the exile, and both Jeremiah and Ezekiel address it. Ezekiel's treatment of the subject is more detailed, as he describes three generations: (1) A righteous father has a wicked son who does not follow in his ways. (2) The wicked son himself has a righteous son. (3) This righteous son chooses to turn from his father's evil ways:

> If a man is righteous and does what is just and right— if he does not eat upon the mountains or lift up his eyes to the idols of the house of Israel, does not defile his neighbor's wife or approach a woman in her time of menstrual impurity, does not oppress anyone, but restores to the debtor his pledge, commits no robbery, gives his bread to the hungry and covers the naked with a garment, does not lend at interest or take any profit, withholds his hand from injustice, executes true justice between man and man, walks in my statutes, and keeps my rules by acting faithfully—he is righteous; he shall surely live, declares the Lord GOD.
>
> If he fathers a son who is violent, a shedder of blood, who does any of these things (though he himself did none of these things), who even eats upon the mountains, defiles his neighbor's wife, oppresses the poor and needy, commits robbery, does not restore the pledge, lifts up his eyes to the idols, commits abomination, lends at interest, and takes profit; shall he then live? He shall not live. He has done all these abominations; he shall surely die; his blood shall be upon himself (Ezekiel 18:5-13).

In cultures that stress the importance of family honor, such as those in biblical times, to stray from family beliefs is very frightening. The pull to maintain the family's values could seem insurmountable. Jesus, however, presents a different perspective on family values:

> So everyone who acknowledges me before men, I also will acknowledge before my Father who is in heaven, but whoever denies me before men, I also will deny before my Father who is in heaven. Do not think that I have come to bring peace to the earth. I have not come to bring peace, but a sword. For I have come to set a man against his father, and a daughter against her mother, and a daughter-in-law against her mother-in-law. And a person's enemies will be those of his own household. Whoever loves father or mother more than me is not worthy of me, and whoever loves son or daughter more than me is not worthy of me (Matthew 10:32-37).

Peter extends his Master's teaching to his largely Gentile audience:

> As obedient children, do not be conformed to the passions of your former ignorance, but as he who called you is holy, you also be holy in all your conduct, since it is written, "You shall be holy, for I am holy." And if you call on him as Father who judges impartially according to each one's deeds, conduct yourselves with fear throughout the time of your exile, knowing that you were ransomed from the futile ways inherited from your forefathers, not with perishable things such as silver or gold, but with the precious blood of Christ, like that of a lamb without blemish or spot (1 Peter 1:14-19).

Peter encouraged his readers by calling them "obedient children" (of God). The "passions of your former ignorance" refers to the desires that directed and energized their lives before becoming children of God by faith in Christ (cf. Ephesians 4:18). In order for his readers to be part of God's family, they had to be "ransomed from the futile ways inherited from [their] forefathers." The "futile [pointless, meaningless] ways inherited from [their] forefathers" refers to the godless lifestyle and values they had been taught by their parents. Through faith in Christ, they were freed from that bondage—freed to live a new lifestyle of holiness reflecting their relationship with their Father in heaven.

Family and peer influences, though they can be strong and subtle, need to be no more determinative in believers' lives than their genes. Social influences and bodily influences are both *subject to the condition of a person's heart*. Neither genetic nor social determinism accurately describes the realities of human experience in God's world.

Counseling People Dealing with Difficult Relationship Influences

From the preceding theological study, we can derive several biblical counseling principles for helping people who are dealing with difficult relationship influences.

1. Counselees' relational experiences should not be ignored. Counselors need to understand how counselees' experiences differ from their own and how those experiences may influence their hearts. Counselees will need assistance in looking at these relationships differently. They should be encouraged to show honor to others where honor is due. They should be taught how to say no to people when that serves God's purposes better (Proverbs 25:28).

2. Because the social environment is not determinative, no outside influence can force us to sin (cf. 1 Corinthians 10:13; 1 Peter 1:14-19). Counselees should not be allowed to use their social environment as an excuse for sinful behavior. The connections between negative relationships and sin—and between sin and the negative consequences in the person's life—should be identified.

3. Just as each of us has a body which is affected by the Fall, our social environment is greatly affected by human sinfulness. In a sense, each of us is from a dysfunctional (sinful) family and is growing up in a sick society (1 John 5:19)—some worse than others. That reality should help counselors be firm *yet compassionate* in responding to the struggles of their counselees who are being affected negatively by relationships. Counselors should be good listeners (Proverbs 18:2,13,15; 20:5) and should show compassion to those who have been hurt by past relationships (Romans 12:15). People's

relationship with God must be the primary influence in their lives. Those who lean upon other sinners too much will become like wilting bushes in the desert, but those who trust God will become like trees planted by a stream of water. They will flourish even during times of external trial (Jeremiah 17:5-8).

4. Counselors need to bring specific biblical truth to people who face temptation from their social experiences. It is beyond the scope of this chapter to do this in detail, but some examples might include helping the victim of abuse learn from Joseph's example (Genesis 37–50, especially 50:17-21) or helping estranged friends learn from Paul's counsel to Philemon.

5. Christians must never forget the resources they have in their relationship with the living God who will never fail or forsake them (Psalm 27:10; Hebrews 13:5). Furthermore, they are part of a community of believers bound together by the Holy Spirit and are gifted to serve and help one another (1 Corinthians 12; Ephesians 2:19-22; 4:3).

Do Not Lose Heart

Biblical counselors address the heart/soul using the Word of God. While they reject both social determinism and genetic determinism, they recognize that the Bible teaches that both one's body and social environment are influential on the inner person (heart/soul). In order to effectively counsel from the Word, they need to try to understand counselees' unique physical and social situations.

Everyone will experience temptations from bodily weakness and social influences, but the good news of the gospel is that in Christ, they can be overcome. Paul acknowledges this in 2 Corinthians:

> We have this treasure in jars of clay, to show that the surpassing power belongs to God and not to us. We are afflicted in every way, but not crushed; perplexed, but not driven to despair; persecuted, but not forsaken; struck down, but not destroyed; always carrying in

the body the death of Jesus, so that the life of Jesus may also be manifested in our bodies...

So we do not lose heart. Though our outer self is wasting away,
our inner self is being renewed day by day. For this light momentary affliction is preparing for us an eternal weight of glory beyond
all comparison, as we look not to the things that are seen but to the
things that are unseen. For the things that are seen are transient, but
the things that are unseen are eternal (4:7-10,16-18).

The Problem of Sin

Robert Jones and Brad Hambrick

In any field, accurate treatment requires accurate diagnosis, and accurate diagnosis requires knowing what to look for and why. Physicians know what tests to order for their patients because they understand how the body malfunctions and deteriorates. Similarly, counselors must understand the nature and origin of human problems to know what questions to ask and what answers to listen for.

What is the nature and origin of human problems? This lies at the foundation of every question a counselor must answer. Competing theories about the causes of counseling problems abound. The nature vs. nurture debate surfaces here in all of its complexity. Nature: are there inborn factors that make us do, feel, and think bad things? Nurture: are human problems produced by corrupted social forces, abuse, traumas, and the like? As we will see, both social and biological factors can influence human behavior. But counseling theories that assign causation to nature and/or to nurture fail to see how the soul permeates and governs both.[1]

For the biblical counselor, accurately understanding people and their problems begins with assessing them through the lens of God's Word. The Bible's answer is simple yet profound: the root cause is sin. Adam and Eve's disobedience at the Fall in Genesis 3 set in motion a deadly dynamic that has produced immeasurable personal, social, and natural devastation. Life after Eden is "not the way it's supposed to be":[2]

- "The LORD saw that the wickedness of man was great in the earth, and that every intention of the thoughts of his heart was only evil continually" (Genesis 6:5).

- "Surely there is not a righteous man on earth who does good and never sins" (Ecclesiastes 7:20).

- "[Jesus] said, 'What comes out of a person is what defiles him. For from within, out of the heart of man, come evil thoughts, sexual immorality, theft, murder, adultery, coveting, wickedness, deceit, sensuality, envy, slander, pride, foolishness. All these evil things come from within, and they defile a person'" (Mark 7:20-23).

What do we mean by sin? Perhaps the 1674 Westminster Shorter Cate-chism supplies the most famous historical definition: "Sin is any want [lack] of conformity unto, or transgression of, the law of God."[3] Evangelical theolo-gians concur. "Sin," writes Millard Erickson, "is any lack of conformity, active or passive, to the moral law of God. This may be a matter of act, of thought, or of inner disposition or state."[4] Sin can take many forms: transgressing imposed limits, falling short of or not fulfilling God's standards, or even doing the right thing with wrong motives.[5] Sin is a failure to measure up, in some way, to God's character as revealed in God's law.

If sin against God is the core human problem, how should we apply this truth to the countless personal and interpersonal issues our counselees face? How does a robust biblical view of sin's presence, influence, and corrosive effects help us as counselors? And how do these wide-ranging descriptions of sin point us to Christ as our ultimate source of hope? Obviously, a simplistic "sin is the bad things we do" will not suffice. To decipher the full breadth of life's struggles, we need something deeper than an elementary view of sin. Thus, we present for your consideration eight functional distinctions about sin that will help us wisely minister to people.

The Personal Sin We Commit and the Suffering We Experience Due to External Sin

Sin's influence is much broader than the direct consequence of personal sin. We not only sin; we suffer the consequences of sin.[6] Consider three ways. *First, we are part of a fallen, cursed creation.* Adam and Eve's sin brought God's judg-ment on them, on all their descendants, and on the entire creation, resulting in human suffering. The entire creation now groans (Romans 8:22-27).

Here we can think of various natural disasters and physiological problems, including neurological diseases, brain impairments, and cognitive decline as a result of aging. While these do not cause us to sin, they create diverse life disruptions that are hard to process, making faith and obedience more difficult.[7] In cases like these, wise biblical counselors eagerly work in tandem with wise physicians and other professionals with expertise to help alleviate suffering.

Second, we are sinned against by others. In one of the most chilling verses in the Bible, Paul describes the nature of the fallen human community apart from God's grace: "At one time we too were foolish, disobedient, deceived, and enslaved by all kinds of passions and pleasures. We lived in malice and envy, being hated and hating one another" (Titus 3:3 NIV).

No small part of counseling is helping people handle past and present mistreatment by others. Even when counseling focuses on the effects of living in a sin-bent social context, the counselor needs to understand sin and its remedy.

In this category of suffering we might consider pastoral neglect, various types of abuse, and dysfunctional family-of-origin influences. This category also includes societal and corporate sins, which vary by culture and time period.

Third, we reap the consequences of our own sin. Maybe it's the man who faces undesired singleness after sinfully divorcing his spouse, the alcoholic whose drinking led to his job loss, or the lonely woman whose abrasive tongue has driven away friends. The prolonged effects of personal sin are a form of suffering.

When we categorize suffering under the effects of sin, we confirm our thesis: *the* central problem that *every* counselee *always* faces is sin. Counseling involves more than merely calling people to repent of specific sins and providing accountability and practical guidance for godly living. It includes ministering the gospel's full redemptive impact to the personal, social, physical, and cultural effects of sin. To accomplish this biblical counseling mission, we need the whole church's ministry: preaching, small groups, mercy ministries, individual members exerting Christian influence in their professional and political settings, etc. The isolated work of a "pastor of counseling" meeting with individuals or couples will never be enough to combat sin's pervasive influence.

One advantage to this diagnostic approach is that it leads us to long for Christ's return. We "are waiting for new heavens and a new earth in which righteousness dwells" (2 Peter 3:13; see also Revelation 21–22), where there will be no more sin, sickness, pain, or tears. Biblical counseling doesn't pretend to hold out simplistic (the weakness of one-size-fits-all methodologies) or merely temporal (the weakness of eclectic counseling approaches answers); we know that ultimately, only King Jesus' return will make all things right.[8]

Sin as Our Inborn Condition and Sin as Our Behavior

In viewing sin as the root human problem, we must not assume that all sin results from deliberate choices for known evil over known good. A fuller understanding of our fallen nature recognizes sin as an inner disposition or state, not just an act or thought. The apostle John draws this distinction between condition and behavior: "If we say we *have no sin* [condition], we deceive ourselves, and the truth is not in us...If we say we *have not sinned* [behavior], we make him a liar, and his word is not in us" (1 John 1:8,10, emphasis added). John recognizes that sin is deeper than what we say or do; it includes who we are, our congenital depravity. In Psalm 51:3-5, David self-describes both his actual sinful behavior and his sinful prenatal depravity: "I know my transgressions, and my sin is ever before me. Against you, you only, have I sinned and done what is evil in your sight...Behold, I was brought forth in iniquity, and in sin did my mother conceive me."

In other words, sin is an inborn condition, not merely a behavior. Theologians call this "original sin," referring to every human's inborn sinful bent. This truth counters counseling theories built upon the premise that people are inherently good and do bad things only because of outside influences. According to Erickson, the Bible views the human race now as in "an abnormal condition...In a very real sense, the only true human beings were Adam and Eve before the Fall, and Jesus. All the others are twisted, distorted, corrupted samples of humanity."[9] When people rightly see sin as more than bad behaviors, observes Louis Berkhof, "they become conscious of the fact that they have been merely fighting the symptoms of *some deep-seated malady*, and that they are confronted, not merely with the problem of sins, that is, of separate sinful deeds, but with the much greater and deeper problem of sin, of *an evil that is inherent in human nature*" (emphasis added).[10]

While sin includes willed moral decisions, it is more pervasive than periodic self-destructive choices. Our problem runs deeper. David Powlison observes, "In truth, our core sin patterns rarely arise only from our conscious decisions. Which of us ever initially *decided* to be proud, people-pleasing, or perverse in our sexual longings?...Sinners sin instinctively."[11] Surely Lucy van Pelt's diagnosis applies to us all: "Discouraged again, eh, Charlie Brown? Do you know what your trouble is? The whole trouble with you is that you're you!"

How does sin-as-condition *and* sin-as-choice affect our counseling? It means we must speak, as Scripture does, both to who people are in Christ (gospel indicatives) and what people should do (gospel imperatives). Counseling sin requires both personal training (1 Timothy 4:8) and identity transformation (Ephesians 5:1-2). Counselors who minimize sin-as-condition may become unduly harsh or impatient with counselees who continue in sin or who react sinfully to provoking pressures—resulting in simplistic, moralistic approaches (like Bob Newhart's infamous "Stop it!" parody[12]) that neglect the progressiveness of sanctification. Or consider the parent who condescendingly scolds his child: "How hard is it not to hit your brother? Just do nothing and everything will be fine." That parent forgets that the child's primary battle lies with his six-year-old sin nature and how it expresses itself. (The child could just as easily say, "How hard is it not to yell at me? Just say nothing and you wouldn't sin.") Sin is a progressive, age-adaptive condition.

On the other hand, counselors who favor approaches summarized by "let go and let God" or "the problem is that you are trying to live the Christian life instead of letting Jesus live it for you" risk ignoring the countless Bible commands to put off sinful behavior and put on godly words and actions. The transformation that sin-as-condition requires is "worked out" through incremental, intentional changes (countering sin-as-choice) that are possible only because of the power of the gospel (Philippians 2:12-15; Paul's case study is grumbling).

Consider the complex problem of same-sex attraction. Many biblical counselors, including the authors of this chapter, believe that some people might have same-sex attraction against their will and choices. Having noted that biological factors might "shape or influence" but not "irresistibly compel" us, Welch observes:

Our sinful hearts express themselves in behavior via hundreds of factors, biology being one. A person whose sinful heart acts out in murder may have been influenced by unjust treatment, by parents who allowed him to vent his rage on siblings, and by Satan's incessant suggestions to kill. But none of these influences remove his personal responsibility for his intentions or actions. The ultimate cause of sin is always the sinful heart.[13]

Biblical counseling sees the suffering that comes with being cursed with a fallen nature. Because of this, we minister with compassion and humility, and we recognize that our ultimate hope is not in a superior theory and practice of biblical counseling, but in the restoration of all things which was secured by Christ's first coming and now awaits His second coming. Only this will ultimately rectify same-sex attraction and our other sin-as-condition struggles.

Sin as Unbelief and Sin as Rebellion

Theologians have long discussed whether Adam and Eve's sin was chiefly unbelief or chiefly rebellion. Some assert that they ate the forbidden fruit because they doubted God's Word, questioned God's goodness, did not believe God's promises, etc. Others argue that they rejected God's rule over their lives; they wanted to do their own thing despite God's clear words to them. Regardless of what motivated Adam and Eve, sin can emerge from motives of rebellion, doubt, or some combination of the two.

As counselors we must be careful not to classify sins but to get to know sinners. We might generically assume, for example, that anxiety and fear arise from unbelief, whereas adultery indicates rebellion. Yet even these examples are not so simple. An anxious man might worry because he doubts God's ability to protect and provide for him. But his anxiety might also arise from a rebellious heart that demands to be in control of situations and refuses to trust God to guide his life. Similarly, an adulterous wife might pursue an immoral relationship because she rebelliously wants to do what she wants, despite God's command for moral purity and marital fidelity. But she also might wrongly believe that her marriage should have provided a kind of ultimate fulfillment, and since it has not, she is looking for another relationship, failing to believe the gospel promise that true fulfillment comes only in relationship to God. Wise counselors must get to know each counselee rather than relying upon "common sense" or textbook knowledge about a given sin or diagnosis.

We see this kind of discriminating wisdom evident in a passage like 1 Thessalonians 5:14: "We urge you, brothers, admonish the idle, encourage the fainthearted, help the weak, be patient with them all." The question becomes this: How should we counsel various people who struggle with the same sin but from different motives, or the same person who fluctuates in the attitude that accompanies his sin?

Consider the husband-father who fails to lead his family in Bible reading and prayer. Why does he fail? Perhaps he is idle or unruly. If so, then he needs to be warned and called to repent. But the same failure could instead arise from timidity or fearfulness. The man might be afraid to lead his family. These fears can vary: that his inaccurate understanding of the Bible will mislead his family, that his wife (who may know her Bible better) might correct him, or that he might start and then stop again (like the smoker who says, "It's easy to quit smoking; I've done it thirty-seven times"). A third kind of husband-father, one who is "weak," might be a man who is illiterate, inexperienced, disadvantaged (e.g., raised by a father who mocked the Bible), or in some way disabled (e.g., dyslexia or a speech impediment).

Sin as Desiring Forbidden Objects and Sin as Desiring Good Things Too Much

There are forbidden items in God's law. God does not allow us to take someone else's property, to sleep with a person who is not our spouse, or to engage in criminal behavior. But most counseling does not involve forbidden things. Rarely does a wife say in marriage counseling, "I am angry with my husband because, amid our financial struggles, he refuses to rob the bank." Instead, she might say, "I am angry with my husband because he doesn't spend enough time with me." There is a difference between a wife wanting her husband to rob a bank and a wife wanting her husband to listen to her. The first is forbidden; it's a wrong desire because it's aimed at an immoral action. The second can begin as a good desire, but it can swiftly become a controlling desire that crowds out more important things or replaces God as the basis of our security. In both cases, these desires are or become sinful. We must put to death forbidden desires and submit ruling desires (even for good things) to God's priorities.

We see this second dynamic in James 4:1-2: "What causes fights and quarrels among you? Don't they come from your desires that battle within you?... You covet but you cannot get what you want, so you quarrel and fight. You do not have because you do not ask God" (NIV). While James does not tell us what his readers wanted, in holding out the possibility that God might give them their desired items, he implies that the items were not inherently evil. They were good things that had become inordinate, controlling desires.[14]

In our experience, most counseling cases today involve good desires that have become overgrown. In these cases the most relevant passages of Scripture may not be those that rebut particular manifestations of sin, but those that remind us to love God with all of our hearts. Our "overgrown desires" are modern synonyms for idolatry, and our aim in counseling is to encourage right worship, and not just eliminate bad behavior.

Sin as Internal (Concealed) and Sin as External (Revealed)

Looks can be deceiving. A person's outward behavior may appear godly, but inwardly she or he may be seething with sin. Recall Jesus' stinging rebukes to the religious leaders of His day:

> You clean the outside of the cup and the plate, but inside they are full of greed and self-indulgence...You are like whitewashed tombs, which outwardly appear beautiful, but within are full of dead people's bones and all uncleanness. So you also outwardly appear righteous to others, but within you are full of hypocrisy and lawlessness (Matthew 23:25-28).

Elsewhere, Jesus distinguishes between the outward sin of murder and the inward sin of anger, and between the external sin of physical adultery and the internal sin of lustful looking (Matthew 5:22,27-28).

This distinction brings at least two benefits. First, counselors will not be content with mere outward behavioral change. We will assess attitudes and intentions consistent with behavioral changes. "Turning the other cheek" should be accompanied by a willingness to pray for the abuser's ultimate good while still unvengefully allowing the law to play its role. (Notice how the heart attitudes of Romans 12:14-21 lead directly into the practical response of legal involvement in Romans 13:1-7.)

Second, counselors will distinguish the different types of replacement steps needed for internal and external sins. Putting off internal sins calls us to put on *Christ-centered attitudes* by repenting in private prayer. Putting off external sins calls us to put on *Christ-centered actions* by repenting in private prayer and then confessing to those we have sinned against.

Sin as Commission and Sin as Omission

Sins of commission involve words or actions which *should not* have been said or done. Sins of omission involve words or actions which *should* have been said or done but were not. First John 3:4 describes the first: "Sin is lawlessness." James 4:17 warns against the second: "So whoever knows the right thing to do and fails to do it, for him it is sin." Whether we transgress God's law (commission) or fail to conform to God's law (omission), we sin. This same commission-omission dynamic often appears in worship liturgies, like this famous confession from the *Book of Common Prayer*: "Most merciful God, we confess that we have sinned against you in thought, word, and deed, by what we have done, and by what we have left undone."[15]

The following chart pictures these possibilities in four quadrants, including both words and actions that a spouse might sinfully commit or omit:

	Commission	Omission
W o r d s	A husband yells at his wife	A husband fails to ask his wife how her day has been going
A c t i o n s	A husband hits his wife	A husband forgets to give his wife a birthday gift

While both perspectives are vital in counseling, we sometimes unwisely focus on commission sins and forget about omission sins, the ones that can often hurt even more deeply. While most married couples don't punch each other (commission), they often offend each other by various omission sins: "He doesn't spend time with me." "She doesn't respect me." This also guides our ministry agenda: It's one thing to help a counselee curb his cussing tongue; it's another thing to help him replace it with gracious words. It's one thing to help a man not throw a frying pan at his wife; it's another thing to help him wash that pan after a meal.

One of the most frequent sins of omission is the failure to get adequate rest. This sin of omission is most often paired with stealth sins of inordinate "good" desires such as ambition at work, giving children every opportunity, or a highly desired hobby. Without a complete view of sin, people can burn out in their pursuit of pleasure. Afterward they commit sins of commission, chasing forbidden desires. But they are never warned of their impending danger; they are merely reprimanded for the "big" sins commonly associated with burnout (e.g., adultery, addiction, or spending themselves into bankruptcy).

Sin as Rational and Sin as Irrational

One of the goals of counseling is to make sense of human struggles. Counselees want to understand the whys behind wrong behavior: "Why did my spouse have an affair?" "What would drive someone to _____?" We presuppose that rational explanations can always capture human struggles. Yet a robust view of sin poses a problem to this assumption. As Wayne Grudem reminds us, "All sin is ultimately irrational...Though people persuade themselves that they have good reasons for sinning, when examined in the cold light of truth on the last day, it will be seen in every case that sin ultimately just does not make sense."[16]

This is what theologians call "the noetic effect of sin," that aspect of our total depravity involving the moral corruption of our thinking. (The word *noetic* comes from the Greek New Testament word *nous*, meaning "mind".) As we sin, we change from rational creatures making decisions based upon principle and forethought to base creatures driven by desire and impulse. Sin, in one sense, is insane. Ecclesiastes 9:3 captures this: "The hearts of the children of man are full of evil, and madness is in their hearts while they live." Romans 1:28 carries the same idea: "Since they did not see fit to acknowledge God, God gave them up to a debased mind to do what ought not to be done." It's no wonder that in Luke 15:17 Jesus describes the prodigal son's repentance in this way: "he came to his senses" (NIV).

How can recognizing both the irrational and rational nature of sin help counselors? First, it protects the counselor from any obligation—and temptation—to have to explain all behavior. Sometimes the best explanation a counselee can give is that "I believed the lie that _____, and the more I believed it, the more my foolishness made sense to me." There are many sins for which an attempt to give a more rational explanation only results in excuse-making or blame-shifting.

Second, it allows the counselor to give effective, sober warnings at sin's earliest stages. A counselor might say to someone whose anger is escalating, "Six months ago you would have considered it wrong to swear at your wife; now you're defending taking her car keys, yelling obscenities, and not letting her move freely in the house. All of this is based on you believing the lie that she will have an affair just because her best friend did. Your every controlling action strains your marriage and reinforces your fear. Can you see how your sin makes your thinking more irrational and your controlling behavior more pervasive?"

Third, seeing sin as both rational and irrational reminds the counselor that change requires more than just accurate information, even divinely inspired biblical information. No problems come solely from a person's raw cognitions, and no one's growth will come from mere cognitive therapy. Thorough change demands heart transformation. And that requires the work of the Holy Spirit. We are entirely dependent on the Lord Himself, by His Spirit, to transform our heart—not only our thinking but also our desires, motives, affections, attitudes, etc. (2 Corinthians 3:18; Ephesians 4:17-19; Hebrews 4:12; 1 Peter 2:11). Counselees not only need God's Word; they need to commune directly with a person (Jesus) in conversation (prayer) about that Word, and they need God's Spirit to inwardly and progressively turn their entire being from sin toward God.

Sin as Degenerative and Sin as Self-Contained

Too often we think of sin as self-contained, point-in-time bad choices with no interconnection or momentum. But sin refuses to remain contained in the moment it is conceived. Scripture describes sin as "crouching at the door" with a "desire for you" (Genesis 4:7). Sin's author, the devil, "prowls around like a roaring lion, seeking someone to devour" (1 Peter 5:8). Sin is a predator with a progressive strategy for destruction. Sin gives Satan an "opportunity" to gain influence in our lives (Ephesians 4:27). Romans 6 personifies sin as a taskmaster that seeks to enslave us. Galatians 5 reminds us that the Christian's internal civil war is active and bilateral: while not only does the Holy Spirit battle against our remaining sin, our remaining sin vigorously battles back (Galatians 5:17). Scripture also uses the image of "hardening of the heart" to describe sin's deteriorating effect upon us. Hebrews 3:12-15 warns all Christians to guard against any sin that could harden their heart.

Based on this degenerative nature of sin, Welch observes how seeing sin's enslaving power captures more profoundly one aspect of popular culture's disease-model approach to addictions:

> Sin is more than a conscious choice. Like a cruel taskmaster sin victimizes and controls us (John 8:34). It captures and overtakes… (Galatians 6:1). In other words, sin feels exactly like a disease. It feels as if something outside ourselves has taken over. In fact, one of Scripture's images for sin is disease (e.g., Isaiah 1:5-6).[17]

This conception of sin can help our counselees see that the whole impact of their sin is greater than the sum of its parts. A neglectful parent may look at each choice that put self before family and not think that it adds up to a lifelong estranged relationship. The addict is often surprised at the subtle entrapment of substance abuse. Counseling must warn people that their sin does not remain a contented servant; it seeks to seize and master its participants. Passivity on the part of the counselor or the counselee will produce further degeneration. Sin must be killed, not merely kept in check.

A Solution Larger Than Ourselves

These eight distinctions provide an introduction to how essential and practical a biblical understanding of sin is for counseling. While each merits more attention, and additional distinctions could be explored (e.g., the social dynamics of sin or how personality relates to sin), we have seen enough to concur that "sin is the deepest explanation, not just one more problem begging for different and 'deeper' reasons."[18] No counseling diagnosis runs deeper than a detailed grasp of sin.

We can draw at least three implications from this examination of sin. First, our view of human problems determines who is qualified to speak to them. If sin is the primary human problem, then those with theological and practical expertise in dealing with sin—in its varied and complex forms—should lead the way in the field of people-helping. Unless we have an accurate and robust conception of sin, the church will concede much of its work to outside professionals and be ill-equipped to cooperate with them when needed. The best counselors to bring Jesus' help to struggling people are skilled, case-wise, theologically trained counselors.

Second, our expansive view of sin requires equally expansive methods of ministry. We saw in 1 Thessalonians 5:14 that wise people-helping involves flexibility in diagnosis and in treatment: "admonish the idle, encourage the fainthearted, help the weak, be patient with them all." As Powlison suggests, "Differing diagnoses of the human condition inevitably demand different 'words' of cure, contain different implications, and construct different responses. They call forth different kinds of missionary-pastors."[19] A biblical grasp of sin requires greater counseling dexterity.

Third, the biblical approach to sin allows us to relate more compassionately to those we counsel. Counselors wrestle against the same eightfold sin problems that our counselees face; we are not diagnostically different. "Psychiatric diagnoses are considered to be technical and bounded; you are either in or out," notes Welch. "In contrast, a biblical perspective puts many interpersonal differences on a continuum: people may have more or less of something. This is relevant to sins, spiritual gifts, weaknesses, and character qualities."[20] Both we and those we counsel share a common struggle against sin.

As Paul Tripp reminds us, biblical counselors are "people in need of change helping people in need of change."[21] And because biblical counselors personally experience the same dynamics of sin, they can lead counselees to the same Redeemer who both forgives and empowers.

To close on the high note of hope, a biblical view of sin makes us long for a solution larger than ourselves. It causes us to cling to Christ, the only one more powerful than the cause of human problems. "Human sin is stubborn," notes Plantinga, "but not as stubborn as the grace of God and not half so persistent, not half so ready to suffer to win its way."[22] Jesus offers true relief from the guilt and power of sin: "Truly, truly, I say to you, everyone who practices sin is a slave to sin...So if the Son sets you free, you will be free indeed" (John 8:34,36). Sin enslaves, Jesus liberates. In light of our Redeemer's work, we heed God's gracious invitation in Hebrews 12:1-2:

> Let us also lay aside every weight, and sin which clings so closely, and let us run with endurance the race that is set before us, looking to Jesus, the founder and perfecter of our faith, who for the joy that was set before him endured the cross, despising the shame, and is seated at the right hand of the throne of God.

The Centrality of the Gospel

Robert Cheong

We are living in an exciting time in history as God is renewing His church through a resurgence of gospel-centered preaching, community, missions, and counseling. From the pioneering days of Jay Adams, whom God used to help bring counseling back to its biblical roots, to the present day, in which an increasing number of churches have taken back their God-appointed responsibility to care for one another, we are witnessing how the gospel changes hearts and lives.

The Need to Understand the Gospel

Even though we will never fully understand the infinite power and beauty of our Redeemer and His gospel on this side of heaven, we must never stop our quest to experience "the surpassing worth of knowing Christ Jesus [our] Lord... and [to] be found in him" (Philippians 3:8-9). Why? Because the meaning of life and the purpose for living are found in Christ and are lived out through our relationship with Him (John 10:10; 14:6; Galatians 2:20). In fact, God's double-love command calls us to love Him with our whole lives while loving others in a way that reflects Him and His love for us (Romans 12:1; Matthew 22:37-40). It is through such love that God builds up His church (Ephesians 4:16) and advances His kingdom in this world (Matthew 28:18-20). In other words, God grows us, His church, as we grow in the love of Christ and experience His glory through our intimate and never-ending relationship with Him. Consequently, God receives glory as we grow in maturity and conformity to Christ through the redemptive work of His Spirit (2 Corinthians 3:18).

In spite of the church's growing application of the gospel within its various corporate functions while participating in God's mission to spread the good news to the ends of the earth, there is still a need to bring further clarity to our understanding of the gospel. The term *gospel* is being used frequently, as evidenced by the number of books being published with the term *gospel* in the title. Correspondingly, there are a growing number of books written to define the term more clearly from a biblical perspective, to defend it vigorously so that the term won't be diluted and distorted, and to showcase it honestly so that we might see the necessity of the gospel for everyday life.[1] The same concerns holds true when the gospel is referenced within biblical counseling circles.

There are several important questions we need to ask so that we can understand the fullness of how the gospel applies to the details and difficulties of life while experiencing the fullness of its power and grace when we care for others. For starters, are there any differences in how we counsel unbelievers and believers with the gospel? Next, given our understanding of the gospel, what should be our goal when we counsel others? Then, how should we respond to those in our church who are struggling with suffering and sin? And last, how should we live out the gospel with one another, even with those whom we are counseling?

We will address these broad questions *conceptually* as we establish a gospel framework from the Scriptures and *concretely* as we care for John, a church member who has battled lust for years and is seeking relief in the gospel. But before we take a look at why the gospel must be central in our approach to counseling, we need to understand what is meant by the term *gospel.*

What Is the Gospel All About?

If we misunderstand the gospel, whether it be approaching and applying it too broadly or narrowly, we might be guilty of misleading people along the spectrum of two extremes—proclaiming a *false* gospel and proclaiming a *powerless* gospel. A false gospel offers false hope and false salvation. A powerless gospel runs the gambit, from offering a lot of love and community that leads to no lasting change, to offering a lot of demands and guilt that play right into our legalistic tendencies.

Our first step in our quest to understand the gospel more fully will be to look at God's story of redemption that is showcased from cover to cover in the Bible. Then we will look at the connection between God's story and the gospel narratives found at the beginning of the New Testament. Finally, we will look at three key themes found in the gospel story.

God's Story of Redemption

The Bible is the greatest story ever told. But it is not just any story. The Bible is not like a factual documentary, or folklore, or even a script where the names have been changed to protect the innocent and enhanced with special effects to keep the audience's attention. All of Scripture, from Genesis to Revelation, is God's story of redemption, in which the passages and plot line point to the Redeemer, Jesus Christ (Luke 24:27).

God's incomparable story starts with the creation of the first man and woman in the Garden of Eden, where God created a relationship with those He made in His own image. The story takes a quick twist when the first man and woman fall from grace as they sinned by rejecting God and His word. As a result, God banished them from the Garden. Despite ongoing suffering and sin, God continued to hear and respond to the cries of His people while remaining faithful to them through His presence and promises. Then after over 400 years of silence, God sent His only Son, Jesus, to redeem His people from sin and restore His love relationship with them. Even though the cross of Christ accomplished our redemption, God is still working out His redemptive purposes in our everyday mess as we live in the grace of Christ. This amazing story of redemption culminates with the "consummation" of the marriage between Jesus and His bride, the church, where we, as God's people, will dwell in perfect oneness with our Redeemer for eternity. Now that we understand God's story of redemption as revealed through the Scriptures, let's take a look at how the gospel flows from this epic story.

God's Story and the Gospel

When we hear the term *gospel*, we quickly think about the first four books of the New Testament, which provide an up-close and personal account of the life, death, and resurrection of Jesus Christ. Certainly the gospel, or the good news of Jesus Christ, is found explicitly in these books written by Matthew, Mark, Luke, and John. But we can also see God's redeeming love from the beginning to the end of His grand story as revealed throughout the Scriptures. We can connect the dots between God's story of redemption and the gospel narratives when we remember that all of Scripture points to Jesus our Redeemer. In order to better understand this inseparable link between the story of God and the gospel of God, let's take a look at three prominent themes of the gospel found in God's story—kingdom, cross, and grace.[2]

The Gospel Story—Kingdom, Cross, and Grace

In order to understand the gospel more fully, we need to look at the breadth, width, height, and depth of the love of Christ (Ephesians 3:17-19), displayed not only 2000 years ago at Calvary, but also from creation to the cross, along with the ongoing work of the kingdom, cross, and grace of God through Jesus.

First, throughout the Scriptures we see God's sovereign rule over both heaven and earth. However, in this fallen world, we see His people rebelling against Him and fighting to establish their own kingdoms. But God's kingship is most fully revealed and most uniquely displayed as Jesus, our Savior King, ushered in the kingdom of God when He came down from heaven to earth. As a result of the death and resurrection of Christ, God established His kingdom, where His people would live in His world under the "redemptive rule" of Jesus.[3]

Next, throughout the story of redemption, we see God pour out His wrath against His sinful enemies while pouring out His grace upon His sinful people. God's redemptive work was marked throughout the Old Testament by sacrifice: God covered the shameful nakedness of Adam and Eve with the carcass of an animal in the Garden (Genesis 3:21); God passed over His people whose doorposts were covered with the blood of lambs as He killed the firstborn Egyptians, forcing Pharaoh to let God's people go (Exodus 12); and God provided Moses and Aaron with an elaborate sacrificial system within the tabernacle to atone for the sins of His people (Leviticus). But God's redemption through sacrifice is most fully revealed and most completely accomplished through the cross of Christ. Jesus served as the perfect sacrifice, satisfying the righteous wrath of God while displaying the redeeming love of God. Jesus restored the relationship between God and His people through His finished work on the cross so that they would be adopted into His family as the body of Christ (Romans 8:14-17; 12:5; 1 Corinthians 12:12-31).

Last, because Christ ushered in the kingdom of God and finished His saving work on the cross, our Redeemer calls us, as His people, to join Him in His radical mission of redemption through His grace. But what exactly is this grace in which we live? Grace is not some mystical vapor that we inhale and exhale. Rather, grace is found and experienced through our intimate relationship with Jesus (Romans 5:17; 1 Corinthians 1:4; Titus 2:11). Soul-nourishing, soul-renewing grace flows from our union with Christ as He is the vine and we are His branches (John 15) and He is the head and we are His body (1 Corinthians 12:27). Grace ultimately points to Jesus and is all about Him. Michael Horton makes this same point: "In grace, God gives nothing less than Himself. Grace, then, is not a third thing or substance mediating between God and sinners, but is Jesus Christ in redeeming action."[4]

Now that we have seen how the gospel of Jesus Christ is the climax of God's story of redemption and can be summarized by God's kingdom, cross, and grace, we are ready to look at some of the practical ways the gospel drives biblical counseling. We will start with an overview of John's chronic struggle with lust.

Desperate for Relief

John's first encounter with pornographic images at the age of twelve opened up a whole new world filled with overwhelming desires and unimaginable sensations. What seemed like the ultimate high in his early years of endless sexual fantasies and pleasure slowly morphed into obsession that eventually turned into enslavement. John never realized how his years of sexual struggles had shaped everything about him—his rituals at work and at home, his identity, how he looked at women, and how it hindered his relationship with God and his wife.

By the time John seeks counsel, he is haggard and hopeless. He confesses he doesn't know who he is anymore. He questions if he is even a Christian, convinced that God will never love or forgive him based on his years of perversion. He is also sure he has lost his wife, since he finally spilled his whole history out to her for the first time last week.

A million thoughts and emotions can flood our minds as we try to process all that John just shared. Where do we start? How will we begin to address his doubts, questions, and fears? We need some orientation as to where to begin. The only thought that bobs to the surface of our sea of confusion is that we all need Jesus and His gospel.

The Same Gospel for Everyone

Whether we are dealing with a lust-driven heart, pride-infused slander, or bitterness-laced division, we need the same gospel. Whether we are counseling an unbelieving neighbor, a newly baptized believer, or a grandmother who has been walking with Jesus for decades, everyone needs the same gospel.

Why is it helpful for us to know that the same gospel is needed regardless of the struggle or the struggler? Broadly speaking, we tend to think we need a different set of skills and know-how for each type of personal issue and person. Without being overly simplistic, by knowing that the gospel addresses every circumstance and every sufferer and sinner, we, as God's people, can bear each other's burdens with confidence knowing that regardless of the particulars, we will strive for the same goal, deal with the same sin, pursue the same love, fight for the same faith, and pray for the same repentance so that we can all rest in Jesus, by the grace and power of His Spirit.

The Same Goal

What is our goal as we journey with John or anyone else? The goal can be summarized by God's double-love command—to love God wholeheartedly and to love others in a way that reflects the gospel (cf. Matthew 22:37-40; Romans 12:9-21). But we all know that we can't love God and others like this on our own without the grace found in Christ.

As Christians, even though we have already been saved by grace (Ephesians 2:5), we have not yet experienced the fullness of God's redemption. That won't happen until we receive our resurrected bodies (1 Corinthians 15:35-49). If we are honest with ourselves, we are all too familiar with this "already but not yet" reality as we struggle deeply and continually with sin, as evidenced by our angry thoughts, fearful emotions, self-glorifying desires, wayward affections, and rebellious actions. Our relentless struggle with sin points to our desperate need for the continual redemptive work of Jesus in our hearts and lives.

The Same Sin that Warrants Death

Every sin is heinous before our holy God and separates us from Him. God described our sin condition in stark terms: "Your hurt is incurable, and your wound is grievous. There is…no medicine for your wound, no healing for you…Your pain is incurable. Because your guilt is great, because your sins are flagrant…" (Jeremiah 30:12-13,15). The sin described here is the same wicked sin that Christ nailed to the cross (Colossians 2:14) and the same evil sin that we still struggle with on this side of heaven.

In God's radical gospel, instead of pouring out His wrath upon us and killing us because of our sins against Him, He poured out His wrath upon His Son and killed Him in our place so that He could reconcile us to Himself through Christ (2 Corinthians 5:18) while disarming, shaming, and triumphing over the kingdom of evil (Colossians 2:15). What's more, God dealt with our sins not out of duty, the way a general stoically and aggressively carries out a battle plan, but out of love, the way a father compassionately and mercifully carries out his rescue plan.

The Same Love that Redeems

Despite being deeply sinned against by His rebellious people, God responded with redeeming love and declared His covenantal relationship with us: "I will restore health to you, and your wounds I will heal, declares the LORD…And you shall be my people, and I will be your God" (Jeremiah 30:17,22). God not only declared His identity (our God) but also our identity (His people). God demonstrated His love as He healed and restored us through the saving and substitutionary death of Jesus on the cross (1 John 4:9-10). If this wasn't enough, God poured out His love into our hearts through His Spirit (Romans 5:5) and promised that nothing, even our ongoing sinfulness, will be able to separate us from His love (Romans 8:35-39). God's radical love doesn't depend on who we are or what we have done, but on who Jesus is and what He has done.

God knows that we are prone to wander from Him and His perfect love. But because we live in His kingdom under the redemptive rule of Jesus and dwell within His abiding grace, God enables us to live a life of faith and repentance.

The Same Faith and Repentance That Draws Us to Christ

Too often we seem to equate faith and repentance with unbelievers. But as we have seen, we as believers are called to live by faith (Galatians 2:20) and to repent continually in the midst of the relentless battles that rage in our hearts (cf. James 4:1-10). The gospel shows us that the same faith and repentance that initially saved us is the same faith and repentance that the Spirit uses to sanctify us.

Since our rebellion against God, even as believers, is fueled by the toxic fumes of unbelief, God calls us to fight the good fight of faith (1 Timothy 6:12; 2 Timothy 4:7) and hold fast to our confidence in Jesus to the very end (Hebrews 3:6,14), knowing that all of what God has promised us is fulfilled in Jesus (2 Corinthians 1:18-20). God makes it clear that it is impossible to please Him apart from faith (Hebrews 11:6), since putting our trust in anything or anyone else amounts to adultery against God, who is our first love (cf. Revelation 2:4). But the freeing reality of the gospel is that even when we are faithless, God is faithful (2 Timothy 2:13) as He calls us to return to Him to receive abundant compassion and pardon (Isaiah 55:6-7).

There is an inseparable link between our faith and repentance. Repentance is necessary in our faithlessness, and faith is necessary for our repentance. The good news is that God enables both (Ephesian 2:8; 2 Timothy 2:25). Realizing that our natural bent is to turn away from the living God (Hebrews 3:12), God's gracious work in enabling our faith and repentance reflects His constant invitation for us to turn back to Him and abide in His love so that we can behold His glory in the face of Christ and experience the fullness of his joy and pleasure.[5] Repentance is shockingly beautiful when we see it not as "I sinned again, I need to repent," but as "I sinned against my God again, but He is calling me back so He can lavish me with His love and forgiveness." Given this gospel reality, we are foolish when we refuse to repent. Therefore, an abundant life in Christ requires that we abide in Christ through abundant faith and repentance.

Reflecting the Gospel in Our Response

Having seen that everyone needs the same gospel, regardless of the struggle and the struggler, how should we respond to John's suffering and sin? Our approach in caring for others is directly related to our personal understanding and experience in living out the gospel.

Why is this the case? If we have not been humbled by the gospel, we will not minister it with grace. If we have not experienced our deep sinfulness and Jesus' deep forgiveness through the cross, we will not love others well in the midst of their struggles. If we do not see the beauty and glory of God in our own redemption, we will not be able to offer a compelling redemptive vision for those who are hopeless and who doubt God's love for them. Based on knowing that everyone needs the same gospel, we can sit with John knowing that we deal with the same sinfulness, we need the same love, and we are called to the same life of faith and repentance.

Without Surprise

As we listen to the details of John's sexual struggles, we should neither be shocked nor surprised. Despite the deeply intense and pervasive nature of sexual sins, we can rest in knowing that Jesus redeemed us and is redeeming us from our chronic sinfulness. If we wrongly see John's enduring battle with sexual lust as one of the ultimate sins, then we can exalt his sin struggle more than the Redeemer, focus on changing neural pathways more than changing the affections of his heart, and think that only a professional or one who is "a recovering sex addict" can help him more than those men in his small group. If we place John in a separate category of Christians who have less faith or even as an unbeliever, and we assume "no Christian can struggle for years with porn," then we may be blind to our own lustful hearts.

We are no different than John in one sense. Sure, we may not struggle explicitly with porn like John, but our lustful hearts may be just as aggressive but more stealth as we strive for praise in the workplace, as we obsess over the next purchase, and we spend countless hours thinking about the next morsel we will devour, which vacation spot can bring the most rest, or the balance of our investment portfolio before we feel secure about our future. As we remember that we are just as sinful as John, we will respond to his seemingly hopeless condition with patience and grace.

With Patience and Grace

As we look at God's story of redemption, we see that He deals with His wayward people with long-suffering, mercy, and love. God makes it clear that since He created us in His image (Genesis 1:27) and redeemed us by His grace, He calls us to be like Him (Leviticus 19:2; 1 Peter 1:15-16). What does this mean practically? In one particular sense, God calls us to love others in the same way He loves us. Consequently, our counseling should reflect God and His redemptive ways.

Why is it crucial that we care for John in ways that reflect God's care for us? Simply put, if we do not relate to others as God relates to us, we will be hypocrites and our lives and counsel will contradict His gospel message and mission.

What are some ways that our response to John might fail to reflect the gospel? If we focus merely on his sexual sin, we can end up identifying him according to his particular sin struggle and give lip service to his God-ordained identity in Christ. If we focus on correcting his apparent sinfulness by telling him he is disobeying God's commandments and he simply needs to put off such sin and put on righteousness, we can end up relying on the law to bring about change and forget that only the love of Christ compels us to no longer live for ourselves but to live for Him (1 Corinthians 5:14-15). If John is "not getting it" or "not changing fast enough," we can become impatient and harsh with him and not remember that God is patient and gracious with us in our own ongoing battle with sin. We may resonate with John's relentless sexual struggles and may be totally empathetic towards his situation, but we may lack confidence in our ability to help him in his time of need.

With Confidence

There is nothing within us that makes us competent to help John. Rather, "our competence comes from God. He has made us competent as ministers of a new covenant…" (2 Corinthians 3:5-6 NIV). Our confidence comes from God, knowing that God will complete the work that He began in John (Philippians 1:6). Given God's ongoing work, we must believe that God's sanctifying Spirit can overcome John's lust-driven heart. Why wouldn't we believe this, knowing that God turned John's heart of stone into a heart of flesh (Ezekiel 36:26; 2 Corinthians 3:3)? We also have to believe that God, who designed and created us as sexual beings with sexual desires, is able to satisfy us more than anything in this world.

But we can also be confident that the God who supplies the faith needed to believe in the goodness of the gospel in our daily struggles is the same God who supplies the grace to turn from everything that draws our hearts away from Jesus. We have to be confident that the kindness of God will bring John to repentance (Romans 2:4). We have to be confident that God will lead John to the knowledge of the truth so that he might come to his senses and "escape from the snare of the devil, after being captured by him to do his will" (2 Timothy 2:26).

We will grow in confidence in the gospel as we shift our focus away from John's sexual sin and gaze more upon the grace found in Christ. Such grace makes John more aware of his lustful thoughts in every aspect of life, causes him to experience his sinfulness in deeper ways, and compels him to seek the throne of grace during his times of need (Hebrews 4:16). In addition, we need to remind John to look for evidence of God's grace in every aspect of his life, since God's redemptive work does not focus solely on his struggle with lust. We have to be confident that where sin abounds, God's grace abounds even more (Romans 5:20).

God does the work of supplying faith and repentance. But He has called each of us to step into the work of fighting the good fight of faith with one another so that we can point each other back to Christ as our only hope.

Living Out the Gospel in Community

God calls us to bear one another's burdens, and by doing so we fulfill the law of Christ (Galatians 6:2). God did not create us to live alone. He called us to live out the gospel within community, knowing that we need to encourage one another so that together we can fight the good fight of faith, hope, and love (Hebrews 10:19-25). We yearn for such community, but there are many reasons why we don't experience such intentional, redemptive relationships. Shyness, pride, shame, bitterness, self-absorption, fear of getting hurt, suspicion, or simply not having experienced such relationships are a few reasons that keep us from such community.

Dual Relationships

The counseling world draws a clear line between counselor and counselee. The counselor will probe without bounds into the life of the counselee, but reciprocation is discouraged. A code of ethics also limits the relationship to the counseling office and prohibits a deepening friendship outside of the formal counseling interactions. Such an approach flies in the face of what God has called us, as His church, to be and to do. How should we approach our relationship with John?

One Relationship

God's people are unique in that we are one in Christ. We are "one body and one Spirit… called to the one hope that belongs to [our] call—one Lord, one faith, one baptism, one God and Father of all, who is over all and through all and in all" (Ephesians 4:4-6). Therefore, God envisions one relationship for all situations, since He established this unique and enduring bond with Himself and His people. God designed His body to have a seamless life where we can work together, laugh and cry together, serve together, and care for one another. In other words, there is no separate relationship for caring for John and a separate relationship for enjoying life with John. Why would we need separate relationships knowing that we need the same gospel as we struggle with the same sinfulness, need the same love, and are called to the same life of faith and repentance?

The Beauty of Gospel Community

Aside from the reality of being in the same family and needing the same grace, there is an indescribable beauty that emerges from living life with others. In God's kingdom, every experience impacts every person as His redeeming love works in multidimensional ways. What does this mean? Simply put, God designed us to learn from and with others.

In the short time we have been journeying with John, the Holy Spirit has already made connections in our own minds as John expressed his insecurities as a man and as a husband. The Lord has given us insights into our own hearts and convicted us as John shared his discontentment with his life and how he escapes through fantasy, where he is king of his world and everything goes his way. But God has also deeply encouraged us as we sat and listened to John testify to God's goodness and faithfulness in the midst of his struggles.

Not only is God growing and changing us as we journey with John, but also he is growing as a direct result of loving us in intentional ways. This didn't happen from the start, but once John was convinced that his ability to pursue us with loving truth wasn't conditioned on him getting everything right, he began to encourage and challenge us with the gospel. He shared that as he ministered God's Word to us; he began to believe it for himself more and more.

But there is more. As the men in the group experienced the life-giving nature of gospel community, several men developed deep friendships with John outside of the weekly small group time. As a result, John spent less time in what others might consider "formal counseling" through his redemptive relationships with God and others. Also, more men have been involved in carrying John's burdens because everyone in the group is sharing and carrying their burdens as they live life together. Only God could design and enable such a beautiful community.

The Never-Changing Gospel

The gospel that saved us by grace through Jesus' finished work on the cross is the same gospel that is changing us by grace through His Spirit's enduring work in us. This never-changing gospel is all we have and all we need as we counsel one another, regardless of the struggle or struggler as we live under the redemptive rule of Jesus. Therefore, in our ongoing battle with sin, God calls us into a never-ending life of faith and repentance so that we can draw near to Jesus and be changed by His redeeming love. What good news!

The Gospel in Balance

Stuart Scott

Whether we are engaged in the private ministry of the Word of God as pastors, missionaries, counselors, or just a concerned brother or sister in Christ, it is important to answer the question, "What is thorough, biblical help?" Surely, the answer to that question begins with our faithfulness to study and apply the Scriptures accurately to our own lives and our own counseling ministries for God's glory.

Even though we grow in our understanding and, from time to time, need to adjust the picture of our counsel to that of God's, we know many unchangeable truths about how to help people in need. We must strive to know fully the person and situation in front of us (Proverbs 18:13,15,17; 20:5). We must humbly help them as a compassionate fellow-sinner and sufferer (Acts 20:18-19,31; 2 Corinthians 1:3-7; 1 Timothy 1:15). We must give them Christ and His truth (John 17:17; 1 Corinthians 1:23; 1 Timothy 4:2,13). We must encourage a true repentance from their sins and futile pursuits (2 Corinthians 7:10-11; 1 Thessalonians 1:9-10; 1 Timothy 6:2-12). We must guide them to a personal knowledge of their God that impacts their heart and the matters of life daily (2 Corinthians 3:18; Colossians 3:10; 2 Peter 3:18). We must practically assist them in their trials and weaknesses (2 Corinthians 4:1-18; 1 Thessalonians 5:14; 1 John 4:16-18). We must encourage them to be immersed and serving in the community of saints (1 Corinthians 12:4-26; Hebrews 10:24-25; 1 Peter 4:8-11). And surely, we must teach them to live for the glory of God (1 Corinthians 10:31; 2 Peter 3:18).

With these things in view, from the Word of God, what can we determine about the working emphases of our counsel in which these important goals must operate? Is it singular or plural?

At the heart of God's answer to these questions is the key to life itself: the gospel of Jesus Christ. It is foundational. It is motivational. It must be pivotal and applicable in every aspect of the counsel we give to those who are not, for one reason or another, living joyfully to the glory of God. It is, of course, pointless to move forward with this gospel application if the issue of salvation has not first been carefully explored and established to the best of our ability (1 Corinthians 2:7-14; 2 Corinthians 5:14-21; Titus 2:11-14).[1]

Though Christ and this gospel must be the very heart of what we do, if we take a step back in our view of *God's* counsel, we can see at least three clear and crucial emphases in His working content: Gospel Truth Applied (Titus 2:11-14), Heart/Worship Issues (Matthew 22:37-40), and Active Elements of Change (Romans 12–16; Ephesians 4–6; Colossians 3–4).

- Past, Suffering, Sin and Guilt
- Old Worship/Life Agendas
- Valuing God/Christ Supremely
- Pursuing God/Christ Alone
- Content in, Hoping in God/ Christ Alone
- Serving God/Christ Alone
- Abiding in Christ
- Humility vs. Pride
- Repentance with Faith (attitude)

- Dependent Work (exercise unto godliness)
- Put-off/Put-on
- Renewing the Mind
- No Provision for the Flesh
- The Spiritual Disciplines
- Involvement of the Body of Christ (one anothers)
- Loving and Serving in the Body and the World
- Active Repentance with Faith (fruitfulness)

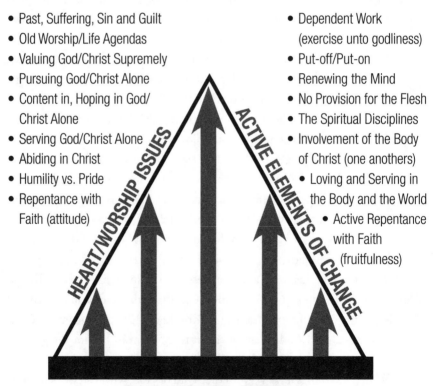

HEART/WORSHIP ISSUES

ACTIVE ELEMENTS OF CHANGE

Gospel Truths Applied
Who God Really Is, What He Deserves
Salvation, All that Christ Is, and Our Identity In Christ with
Its Privileges, and Its Obligations

No matter what issue brings a person to counseling, if we as counselors do not affirm the importance of all three of these emphases, devote significant session time to them, and assist those we help in ways to proliferate them, our help is incomplete and less effective than it could be. In this case, the struggling person is the one who suffers. Counselees are hindered in their victory, their growth, their ability to bring glory to God, and their usefulness in God's kingdom.

From the diagram on the previous page, we can see that the latter two emphases mentioned are not only vitally connected to the gospel of Jesus Christ, but that the two must be affected by the many realities and obligations inherent in it. This means that it is surely our job as biblical counselors to integrate key gospel truths into all aspects of the help we offer. If this is not the case, then our counseling is not truly gospel or Christ-centered, and therefore, it is not biblical counseling in the truest sense.

The Gospel in Focus

This gospel that we must encourage our counselees to appropriate is not just a collection of doctrinal truths or personal benefits. It is not a magical buzzword that must be dropped incessantly in our conversation and counseling. It is all about the preimmanent person of Jesus Christ, who should make a difference in our daily living. When we take a good look at the gospel truths that we must make applicable in counseling, we see foremost the God-man Christ and all that He is (Colossians 1:9-23). We see the provision of forgiveness and salvation in Him through faith. *Then* we see all that He has gained for us and made us (our position and identity, or the *indicatives*), as well as all that He deserves and has called us to (our practice, or the *imperatives*). As pictured on the next page, there is a great deal inherent in this gospel that we must help others appropriate.

There must be emphasis and balance in all aspects of the gospel when it comes to change or living the Christian life. Too little respective emphasis on Christ, our position, or our practice gives one a skewed view of the gospel itself and the Christian life also. This skewed view will perpetuate some kind of focus on self, and in this self-focused perspective, we will not perpetuate the full intent of the gospel—that we live to the glory of God, glorying in *Him*.

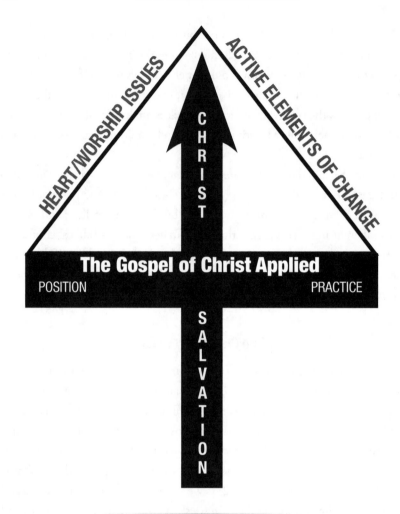

Don't Rock the Boat

If in our counsel we center mostly on our obligations (our practice) without our gaze upon the person of Christ and an appropriation of our position in Him, the focus will be on us with either *self*-righteousness or *self*-loathing. It follows then that while attention to our practice or our sanctification may be present, it is also problematic since we minimize the pleasures and the power and the imputed righteousness of Christ. This lack of emphasis on our position in Christ creates an overemphasis on *our* work and is work in our own strength (John 15:5; Philippians 2:13; Colossians 1:29). It is not work that glorifies God from the heart, and it will not result in lasting change. In this case, true heart worship and other important heart attitudes fall short and/or become nonexistent. The worship of idolatrous lusts and the turning to false refuges is inevitable (Jeremiah 2:13; Galatians 5:16; 1 John 2:15-17). Here's how we can picture our counseling if it is imbalanced in this way.

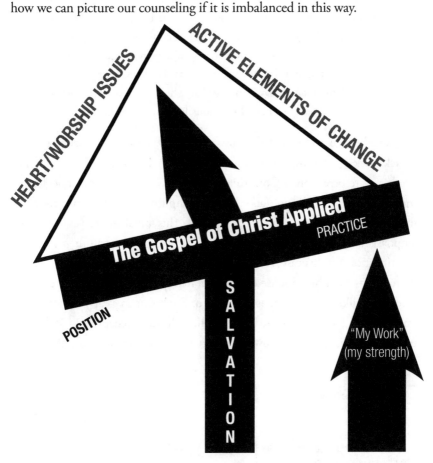

This is not the life that glorifies God and that Christ died to procure for those we seek to help. We certainly do not want to encourage anyone towards this Pharisaical and hopeless pursuit of change. From God's perspective, any effort on our part should always be a matter of depending on His power at work in us.[2] The kind of imbalance pictured above fosters pride, a performance-driven life, legalism, and moralism. With this kind of counseling imbalance, it is easy to carry on counseling without true salvation. We must continually spotlight all that Christ is and all our position in Him means. The importance of the indicatives in counseling is well stated by pastor, author, and Gospel Coalition council member Kevin DeYoung:

> We ought to positively glory in the indicatives of the gospel. The indicatives ought to fuel our following of the imperatives. Our obedience must be grounded in the gospel. Sanctification is empowered by faith in the promises of God. We need to be reminded of our justification often and throughout our Christian lives. Our pursuit of personal righteousness will not go anywhere without a conviction that we are already reckoned positionally righteous in Christ.[3]

Another way to think about this kind of imbalance in counseling is when we acknowledge the gospel in the *narrow* sense (our believing in Jesus—His life, death, and resurrection [1 Corinthians 15:1-8]), while assuming or neglecting the gospel in a *broad* sense (all Christ accomplished and what our salvation means for us today [e.g., Ephesians 1:3-14]). This imbalance leaves the greater emphasis of our counseling on practical life change and on our part of our sanctification. In this case, there is not enough connection of the gospel in a narrow sense or a broad sense to practical living. And, in reality, there is little true, Christlike growth. But as the book of Ephesians so clearly indicates, the imperatives (chapters 4–6) are based on the indicatives (chapters 1–3). In contrast to Ephesians, here is how we might mistakenly try to apply the gospel in counseling.

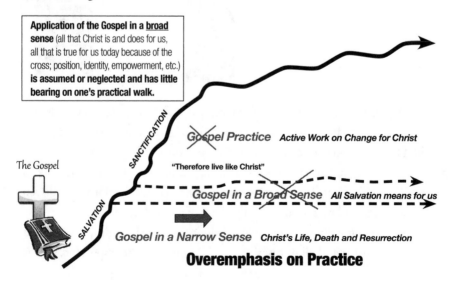

On the other hand, if we center primarily on our position in Christ and all that we have in Him and do not emphasize our practice as well, there is another kind of gospel distortion and hindrance to growth.[4] Again, the focus is primarily on self, so true worship is affected and emphasis on the active elements of change and one's practice are lacking. This second imbalance can be pictured like this:

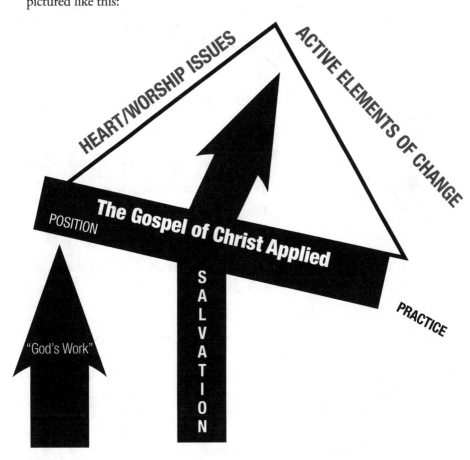

This particular gospel distortion in counseling addresses the gospel in a narrow sense, focuses primarily on the gospel in a broad sense, while matters of practice are seen as minimally important or assumed to flow naturally. While the gospel in a narrow sense and the gospel in a broad sense are well applied to practical living, there is still a gospel lack. This lack can lead to an almost Keswick ("let go and let God do it all") view of sanctification: In this case, "Let go and let 'the gospel.'"[5]

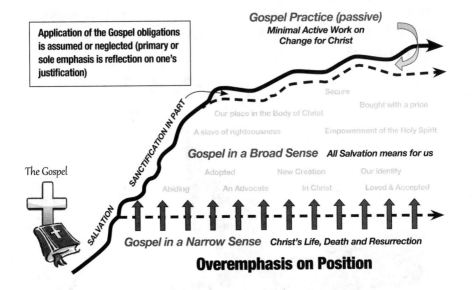

Overemphasis on Position

In addition to addressing the former imbalance, DeYoung stresses the importance of not just centering on justification with all its privileges and implications:

> The New Testament gives us commands, and these commands involve more than remembering, revisiting, and rediscovering the reality of our justification. We must also put on [Romans 13:14; Ephesians 4:24-32], put off [Romans 13:14; Colossians 3:12-14], put to death [Romans 8:13; Colossians 3:5], strive and make every effort [1 Timothy 4:7-10; 2 Peter 1:5]…Yes this effort is always connected to gospel grace. But we cannot reduce effort to simply believing in justification [verse references mine].[6]

In this imbalance, we might perpetuate that dealing with heart issues alone is all one needs for change. Or, we may see law (God's moral law) as the enemy of the cross or grace, rather than understand that living *under* the law or *for* the law or *through* the law (seeking justification by it) are the real enemies of the cross (Galatians 3:21-24). With this imbalance, we may become all about grace, but this shortsighted "grace" does not really dependently work to please Christ out of gratitude (Titus 2:11-14).[7]

While it is true that the gospel in a *broad* sense is indispensable to change, and even though it is our very motivation for gospel practice, those caught up in this particular imbalance will not believe in real effort through the power of Christ (1 Timothy 4:7-10, 2 Peter 1:5-7). Inevitably, it will lead to stunted growth or even license (fleshly living).

As we contemplate these important matters, it is helpful to realize that we are all prone to imbalance of all sorts. Thomas Schreiner of Southern Seminary offers the same caution as DeYoung, while encouraging us to avoid all types of reductionism:

> We must remember that Paul's theology is multifaceted...It is possible to diminish the centrality of justification, but it is also possible to exaggerate its importance so that other aspects of Pauline soteriology are shoved into the background...It is imperative to avoid reductionism, as if justification were the only part of Pauline theology.[8]

Keeping It Real

A balanced and properly emphasized gospel highlights all three of its aspects with the gospel in a *narrow* sense being unfolded and practically applied into the gospel in a *broad* sense, and the gospel in a *broad* sense being unfolded and applied into gospel *practice*. The gospel must be unfolded and exercised in this way for a new working worship, identity, mind-set, and service. If not, the gospel will not be operating with the right motivations or with the right end—to the glory of God (Ephesians 1:3-14). With all three aspects of God's gospel, we face the fiery darts of the evil one, the world, and our own flesh. While there is certainly some natural flow from one aspect of the gospel to another, there is not enough to impact the Christian walk rightly and renew ingrained habits in a timely manner without an alertness in one's walk, and a dependent "holy sweat" (work) to renew the mind, plan changes, and choose Christ. This more biblical perspective can be pictured like this:

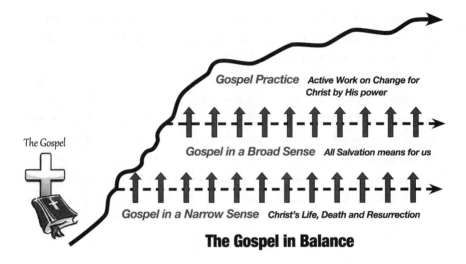

The Gospel in Balance

Again, Schreiner offers us a good word:

> ...the imperatives that dominate this text [Ephesians 4:22-24] should never be sundered from the indicatives. Romans 13:11-14 reminds us, however, that the indicatives do not rule out the need for the imperatives. Even though believers have already "put on Christ" (Gal. 3:27; Col. 3:10) and put off the old person (Col. 3:9), *they* must also put on Christ (Romans 13:14)...The tension between the indicative and the imperative is due to the already-but-not-yet paradox that characterizes Paul's theology.[9]

Putting It All Together

As we have a proper gospel balance, we are able to employ rightly the other crucial aspects of biblical counseling. As we have seen, this is true because the imperatives are so dependent on the indicatives and the gospel must permeate all we do.[10] As we deal with past suffering and sin in the lives of those we counsel, we will draw from the gospel who God is, what He is doing, what He can do, and for the believer, a new identity. As we discover and address the real-life agendas or worship of those we counsel, we will apply from the gospel why we were created, what God deserves, and what He has done for us. As we press those who are changing from within to actively apply biblical principles for change, we will point them back to the great love of Christ, who we are in Him, and dependence on all His resources—which are each found in the gospel.

All this being true, it is paramount that we really do specifically, thoroughly, and biblically deal with matters of the past and present with the gospel and practical worship, and with what God provides and asks of us in the change process. This brings us back to the biblical picture of the three counseling emphases with which we began.

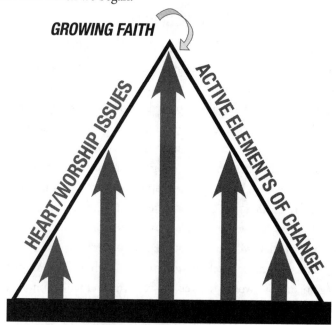

GROWING FAITH

HEART/WORSHIP ISSUES

ACTIVE ELEMENTS OF CHANGE

The Gospel Applied

There are all kinds of distortions that can arise when any key element of biblical counseling is misunderstood, minimized, or missing. Even more basic is the reality that The Gospel Applied, Undivided Heart Worship, and The Active Elements of Change all must be carried out by the vehicle and exercise of *faith* or trust in the Triune God (Romans 3:22; Galatians 2:20; Hebrews 11:6; James 2:26). The character and deeds of God must permeate each emphasis. And so, like the triangle that holds this paradigm together, faith becomes an integral part of the counselees' apprehension of the biblical help we offer.

In the book *Christian Spirituality*, Sinclair Ferguson writes:

> In Christ's incarnate, crucified, risen, and glorified humanity lies the sanctification I lack in myself. The question therefore becomes: How are his sanctification and my need for it brought together? According to the New Testament, it is by the ministry of God's Spirit and by the exercise of the believer's faith...Faith involves trusting in and resting on the resources of Christ as though they were our own.[11]

The Bottom Line

I am personally and deeply indebted to those individuals, authors, and institutions that have highlighted one or more of the key essentials of scriptural counseling or have spoken to the imbalances that have arisen through the years. Each concept has biblically impacted my own counseling in needed ways, but not without struggle. Now, I am often reminded that, as biblical counselors, we must all work hard to avoid tunnel vision, reductionism, and scriptural imbalances that stem either from ignorance or from a reaction to other imbalances or lacks we have experienced or observed. One imbalance cannot be corrected by another one. Furthermore, seeing only one crucial part of biblical counseling as "the whole enchilada" will result in isolated development of biblical concepts that will do our counselees a disservice.

So, to the biblical counseling movement as a whole, I humbly offer some encouragements. We would do well to avoid fragmentation among us that is perpetuated by a singular emphasis or biblical error. Instead, in humility, we must work hard to fill out or change any of our own weaknesses or imbalances according to the Scriptures. And, with each new or refreshed biblical conviction on how to help people, we must be pressed back to the Scriptures to see it in the context of *all* God says. We must purpose to bring God's whole picture of counseling into focus by considering the whole counsel of His Word. If these things are taken seriously, then even the triune representation of the biblical counseling paradigm that I have offered could undergo some changes or additions in the future.

What is the bottom line of this chapter? We dare not say (similar to some in the Corinthian church—1 Corinthians 1:10-13), "I am of applying the gospel in counseling," or "I am of addressing practical change in counseling," or "I am of addressing the heart and heart worship in counseling." Instead, we must be able to say, "I am seeking to be, more and more, a counselor of God's kind—emphasizing faith, emphasizing the application of all aspects of the gospel (of Christ) and what it means, emphasizing heart and worship issues, and emphasizing all the active elements of change by Christ's power and for His glory." And, we must say, "I am one who will continue to learn, grow, and faithfully adjust the emphases of my counsel to what God has revealed in His Word."

The Pursuit of Holiness

Lee Lewis and Michael Snetzer

Many people believe that once we receive salvation in Jesus Christ, we have reached our destination. While it is true that we have come to the end of one life, it is equally true that we have been raised to live another (Romans 6:4). It is not only an end, but a beginning. It is as though our King has taken on the role of a master gardener. He has staked His claim on our very hearts and has every intention of producing something beautiful and useful for His kingdom purposes. The soil of our former lives produced nothing but weeds. Even the apparent flowers of our former lives were really weeds planted as counterfeits and their very presence, if not uprooted, will continue to steal nutrients from the soil. In order for this field of weeds to become a garden, something that up to this point has been foreign must be planted in it that over time will bear fruit. The beauty and usefulness of the garden is dependent on the skill of the gardener, the receptivity of the soil for fruit-bearing seed, the ongoing nutrients on which the garden must feed, and to the soil's willingness to give up unfruitful weeds.

Understanding the Destination

The destination of God's people is a majestic garden, with the beauty of the garden bringing glory to the Master Gardener. Regardless of the droughts, storms, heat, or the stubbornness of the soil, He will accomplish His plans. This garden may at times look hopeless, but once He stakes His claim, He will accomplish His vision. Believing we have "arrived" at this wonderful destination when we are saved is a misunderstanding of how the Master works. When we are saved, we are set apart to be used for different purposes. We have a long road ahead of us before we arrive at the destination. Using an Old

Testament example, the Israelites were delivered miraculously from their slavery to Egypt, but were not brought directly into the Promised Land. Instead, they were led into the wilderness. Now it must have been exhilarating to have been brought out in such a miraculous way; however, they would soon find that the wilderness had its own set of difficulties. These difficulties have redemptive purposes in preparing God's people for their destination. This preparation, known biblically as sanctification, has an ultimate destination called glorification. Knowing God has good purposes in our lives as we face difficulties helps us to endure those difficulties. Having the Master Gardener's vision informs our current reality (Romans 8:28-30).

Examining Sanctification

Sanctification is the "gracious operation of the Holy Spirit, involving our responsible participation, by which he delivers us from the pollution of sin, renews our entire nature according to the image of God, and enables us to live lives pleasing to him."[1] It is the process of making us holy, a process that is not complete until our death. This process brings freedom in Christ (2 Corinthians 3:17-18), not from difficulties, but in the face of them.

Sanctification is nestled in Romans 8:28-30 as the idea of being "conformed to the image of his Son." This text outlines the process of salvation—namely, that God foreknew before time began and predestined who He would call, justify, sanctify, and glorify. God opens our hearts to receive the truth and respond in faith in our effectual calling. We are then justified by the grace of God, which flows from Christ's atoning work on the cross as we repent and believe in the gospel. We receive His righteousness and through His work are accepted by God. It is only on this basis (justification) that sanctification can occur.

Sanctification is the evidence of our justification and brings hope for the promise of glorification. Justification is "the acceptance of believers as righteous in the sight of God through the righteousness of Jesus Christ accounted to them"[2] (see Galatians). This happens as the seed of Christ is deposited in our hearts. In time, this seed will produce fruit. The fruit is Christlikeness, or sanctification—it is progress in actual holiness. If there is no fruit, over time we must begin to question whether the seed was planted. If we see the fruit of Christlikeness, then we would suspect the seed of Christ has been planted (Luke 6:43).

For those who have not responded to the gospel in faith, all efforts in participating in the fruits of sanctification are futile. Therefore, a biblical counselor's role to those who have not yet been justified is to expose the futility of self-efforts against the hope that the gospel offers. Attempting to be sanctified without first being justified amounts to dead religion.

When we step back from these particular verses to look at the whole of Romans 8, we see this redemptive process takes place amidst suffering. If we misunderstand the gospel as one of prosperity, we will surely think we are on the wrong road when suffering comes our way. Instead, we can take great comfort that regardless of our current difficulties, God will use it for His good purposes and that nothing that has been given to us in Christ can be taken from us. We also find that none of these difficulties can separate us from the love of God. In fact, it is in these seasons of difficulties that He teaches us of His sufficiency and sustains us by His grace. As important as it is to understand these truths, it is equally important that we not merely apply biblical platitudes to these difficulties, but instead enter into our counselees' plight and encourage them to cry out, "Abba Father."

The Plan: The Gospel of Jesus Christ

In light of this goal, it must be understood that apart from the gospel of Jesus Christ, true holiness is impossible. The world will offer a myriad of strategies that appear to be shortcuts toward our destination, but we must recognize them for the counterfeit substitutes that they are. Just as Satan tempted Jesus in the wilderness to take matters into His own hands to get what was already His by following him, so the enemy will attempt to mislead us by offering what appear to be shortcuts to a vibrant garden. There are manmade ways of enhancing our garden and accelerating growth through chemical fertilizers and pesticides which, on the surface, appear to be beneficial, but long-term disrupt the balance of our garden, sometimes destroying in the process that which is necessary for health. The result is often unnatural-looking fruit that has been enhanced artificially and looks plastic. What's more, these chemical agents often leave residue in the soil, contaminate the groundwater, and kill "good" insects and bacteria. The gospel alone offers both the seed and the environment necessary for healthy growth. There are no shortcuts or acceptable substitutes; there is only one way.

Empowered by the Holy Spirit

Paul raises a vital point through some questions he asks in Galatians 3:1-3:

> O foolish Galatians! Who has bewitched you? It was before your eyes that Jesus Christ was publicly portrayed as crucified. Let me ask you only this: Did you receive the Spirit by works of the law or by hearing with faith? Are you so foolish? Having begun by the Spirit, are you now being perfected by the flesh?

Not only is it through faith in the gospel that God justifies a person, it is also the gospel that enables a person to live a new life. Paul warns the church that they will not be perfected apart from the Spirit's work. They must continue in the same manner that they started.

Grace-Driven Effort

We also see from Hoekema's definition that sanctification is a "gracious work of the Holy Spirit" that requires our participation. We have been made holy in a passive sense (justification); however, practically speaking we are to be active in our pursuit of holiness (sanctification).

For some who have been justified, biblical counselors need to help strengthen them in what is already true of them in Christ. The truths of what the Son has accomplished in reconciling them to the Father as new creations in Christ should be savored. They must have solid footing in the gospel indicatives if they are to successfully contend for the gospel imperatives or commands of God that should flow out of their lives in response to this glorious gospel.

For others who have been justified, we will have to press them onward to the gospel imperatives. While they are already resting in the gospel indicatives, they have been negligent to press on toward holiness, claiming there is no need to do so in light of what they have already been given. This, too, is a misunderstanding of the gospel as they confuse sanctification with justification. There is a failure to take responsibility for personal holiness, which robs them from living out the Greatest Command and, in turn, the Great Commission. If they negate responsibility for the sin that proceeds from them by claiming imputed holiness, they cannot repent, and because repentance is a necessary part of ongoing spiritual growth, they will remain immature. Such negligence of their garden will inevitably detract from its beauty and usefulness. Sanctification requires their responsible and active participation.

There is nothing wrong with effort when it is a response of faith to the gospel message. We go wrong in trying to earn God's grace, which, by definition, can't be earned. The grace of God not only saves us, it enables us to live new lives. He is not only our future hope, but our present help. We have been brought from one kingdom into another and called into action. We are to be busy working in the garden, but if we are to understand the seriousness of the battle and what is at stake, we must understand that there is a war going on deep within the garden.

Understanding the Enemy and the War[3]

The enemy of God is a real personal evil set up to oppose the kingdom of God and steal His glory. Satan and demons work to influence the world and entice the flesh. Prior to our conversion, we were enemies of God, and now we have been redeemed and are being equipped for the service of our King. This means that we have been enlisted to eradicate evil as we are empowered by the Spirit. We are to put on our armor and take seriously our call. We are to strategically pray against the temptations of the world and the enticements of the flesh, and pray for deliverance from spiritual strongholds.

Through the gospel, sin, Satan, and death will be eradicated. The fruit of our garden will be our love for and ministry to those who are suffering in the advancement of the kingdom. If we understand the source of injustice contrasted to the power of God which has been made to dwell in us, we will not be so fearful to engage when faced with demonic opposition.

Mortification and Vivification

Sanctification has two parts: mortification and vivification. *Mortification* might be thought of as "putting to death things that rob our affections for Christ." *Vivification* might be thought of as "filling ourselves with the things that stir our affections for Christ." In sanctification, God has chosen us, set us apart, and is creating something wonderful to be displayed for His glory (Matthew 5:14-16) and useful for His kingdom (Matthew 5:13).

For a garden to be beautiful and productive, it must be tended to. What happens when you fail to tend to the garden? It becomes overgrown, and any produce present in the garden rots. Our hearts might be considered soil (Matthew 13:1-23), and for our garden to be beautiful requires both weeding and feeding. God requires our responsible participation in these activities. Mortification is like pulling weeds, ridding our hearts of those things that detract from the beauty of the garden and rob it of its nutrients. Vivification is like feeding our garden proper nutrients so in time it produces a harvest.

In order to truly uproot the weeds in our life we must not just examine and turn from our immoral behavior, we must also look beneath the surface to the roots that are producing the weeds. Through the Word of God, the Spirit illuminates what is going on beneath the surface. It is also the work of the Spirit that brings rain, which softens the ground so that the roots come out easily. He will reveal the various forms of idolatry and pride which drive our ungodly behaviors. Many weeds have thorns, and these may be seen as self-protective ways of trying to keep the Gardener from taking hold of the weed. It is only by faith (trusting the Gardener) that these weeds will be pulled. This means submitting to His will and asking Him to do what only He can do. This means repenting of our attempts to uproot the weeds in our garden through our own self-efforts.

You cannot divorce the mortification of sin from life by the Spirit. In other words, you cannot find freedom by merely stopping certain things without being filled by something else, something greater. This means that we must not only examine the root, repent of our sin, and ask for God to uproot it, but that we also must delight in the gospel and all that it promises.

Matthew 12:43-45 teaches that when an unclean spirit has gone out of a person, it seeks rest, but finds none. Then it says, "I will return to my house from which I came" (verse 44). When it comes, it finds the house empty, swept, and put in order. Then it brings with it seven other spirits more evil than itself, and they enter and dwell there. Then the last state of that person is worse than the first. This passage suggests it is not enough to merely quit doing wrong; you must replace that wrong with something right.

Thomas Chalmers, in his famous sermon "The Expulsive Power of a New Affection," states, "A moralist will be unsuccessful in trying to displace his love of the world by reviewing the ills of the world. Misplaced affections need to be replaced by the far greater power of the affection of the gospel."[4] In vivification we find life through the Spirit as we engage in activities that stir our affections for Christ. This fills us so that we have fruit to offer the world. It is when we are filled with the Spirit that the things of this world lose their luster.

Hebrews 12:1-3 calls us to lay aside certain things and look to Christ. We tend to look in the direction we intend to pursue. Pursuit reveals what we love. Show me your pursuits, and I'll tell you what you love. Not only do we pursue what we love, we resist what we hate. We are to lay aside weights and sins that hinder us from running the race with endurance and pursue that which should be the treasure of every believer—intimacy with Christ. *Christian hedonism*, a phrase and concept introduced by John Piper in his book *Desiring God*, gets to the heart of this idea. As believers, our pleasure is ultimately found in Him, and when that is the case, all other pleasures pale in comparison. As we get more of Him, the pleasures of this world become less enticing. In this way, the stirring of our affections displace our love of this world.

Temptations of Mortification

There are two temptations that arise when we decide to deal with the weeds in our lives. Both fail to address the roots. One results from laziness, the other from deceit. Imagine that you have a front yard full of weeds. If you mow over the weeds, they will look like grass for a day or two. It is easier and seemingly more efficient to just mow the weeds down rather than take the time to pull the weeds and plant grass seeds in their place. Spiritually, we often don't want to take the time or effort to examine our hearts and expose the ugly roots of pride and idolatry that drive sinful behaviors. We would rather just say that what we did was wrong and try harder, rather than confessing the roots and repenting of our ugly pride and idolatry. However, because we don't address the root, we find the same weed growing back again and again.

The second temptation is based in deceit and involves our tendency to want to bring in good-looking topsoil and cover up the ugliness of the weeds. We cover over our sins by putting on an outward display of good behavior. In doing so, we live in denial and deceive ourselves and others in the same way that false prophets told God's people there was peace when, in actuality, there was no peace (Jeremiah 6:14).

Now, there are some weeds that look like flowers. From a counseling perspective, these reflect the not-so-noticeable ways that counselees tend to cope with living in a sinful world rather than overcoming sin through faith in Christ. Outwardly they look okay, but in reality, they're not. This calls for discernment on the part of the counselor.

To truly get rid of the weeds, they must be uprooted. And the ground must be soft for this to happen. This requires rain, which comes from the heavens.

Temptations in Vivification

If all we do is we feed our garden but never harvest the fruit and use it in ministry and mission, it will rot. Spiritual obesity occurs when we are always learning but never applying or exercising what we have learned. We are not just to be hearers, but doers of the Word. I remind those whom I counsel that the application of the truths that we talk about in counseling is 100 percent their responsibility, and that it is 100 percent my responsibility to counsel them in accordance with the truth, motivated by love. We are to exercise our faith active in love.

Without proper nutrients, our garden will bear little fruit. If we fail to feed on those things that bring life by the Spirit, we will be miserable. To bear fruit, we must abide in Christ (John 15:1-7).

We must also take care to make sure the soil in the garden hasn't hardened such that any nourishment that is put down is unable to penetrate the soil. There are some people who are always around the truth, but if we were to ask them what God is teaching them, they would not be able to tell us. It doesn't matter how much Bible one reads or knows if its truths aren't penetrating our hearts and having an impact on how we live.

Discipline

God disciplines those He loves (Hebrews 12:5-11). This should be a comfort (Psalm 23:4) to the children of God, as it would not be love if a father allowed his children to do whatever they wanted or walk toward death without intervening. Hebrews 12 tells us that discipline is not pleasant, but has purpose. God's intervention in our lives is a sign that He loves us. We should also see the discipline that comes through His instrument, the church, as a sign that He loves us and wants to lead us to life. Using our illustration of the Christian life as a garden, discipline is analogous to pruning. Pruning keeps us from growing contrary to the Master Gardener's intended purposes and removes non-fruit-bearing branches from our lives.

Spiritual Disciplines[5]

In Jesus' response to a question about fasting in Mark 2, we see that the spiritual disciplines are not an end unto themselves but a means to an end. The Pharisees want to know why Jesus' disciples do not fast, not realizing that the One whose presence they should be seeking through fasting is standing right in front of them. The Pharisees represent the self-righteous—those who believe that it is their religious practices that make them righteous, as opposed to seeking after the One who is righteous.

Spiritual disciplines are those things that we practice in order to come into the presence of God, sit at His feet, and learn of His ways. They should be practiced with our eyes looking to Him, not at ourselves. The spiritual disciplines posture us under the waterfall of His grace, bringing our heart into alignment with His.

Redeeming Suffering

God's use of grief, suffering, and trials to bring about sanctification is a consistent theme in the Scriptures. Suffering comes because of our own rebellion (sin); it comes because of someone else's sin (abuse); or it comes because of the Fall (sickness, persecution, spiritual warfare).

This is where Romans 8:28 is such a tremendous hope and truth. God is absolutely sovereign over all things. No form of suffering can derail God's redemptive work in His people.

> In this you rejoice, though now for a little while, if necessary, you
> have been grieved by various trials, so that the tested genuineness of
> your faith—more precious than gold that perishes though it is tested

by fire—may be found to result in praise and glory and honor at the revelation of Jesus Christ (1 Peter 1:6-7).

This is an incredible picture of the purposes of God through suffering. The faith produced through the fire has no equal and cannot be destroyed.

In Deuteronomy 8:2-3, we see that God's purpose for "desert experiences" is to reveal our inability to find satisfaction for our thirst with anything other than Himself.

> You shall remember the whole way that the LORD your God has led you these forty years in the wilderness, that he might humble you, testing you to know what was in your heart…that he might make you know that man does not live by bread alone, but man lives by every word that comes from the mouth of the LORD.

God exposed the Israelites' deep need for Him by taking them through the wilderness. His provision and protection cared for them perfectly during their trial.

Biblical counseling relies on the sovereign purposes of God to bring about holiness in His people, believing that God works all things together for good (Romans 8:28-30). This truth provides tremendous hope for the believer. But, what are some of the specific matters revealed on a heart level through suffering?

Reflecting again on Deuteronomy 8, we see God exposing in His people a propensity to seek refuge and salvation from somewhere other than Himself. The Scriptures identify this as idolatry, which is a deeply rooted heart issue. Paul Tripp contends in his book *Instruments in the Redeemer's Hands* that people are created to worship. Therefore, everyone worships something. It is impossible for a person to be neutral when it comes to worship. After God brings about a regenerate heart, the nature of the flesh is such that our hearts will at times seek to worship created things above the Creator. Suffering always reveals idols of the heart.

Suffering is not just difficult because of what is directly endured. Temptation often becomes a major factor in the midst of suffering. James 1 talks about temptation amid trials that entices the flesh (verse 14). God does not and cannot tempt, but it is in these periods of great angst that temptation can be as strong as it ever has been. These are the moments during which sinful affections of the heart are exposed. During the trial, God presses His child to bring about a greater dependence on and worship of Him and simultaneously reveal the heart as temptation presents itself to the sufferer.

Consider being in a difficult season of suffering at a time when hope is waning. Fear begins to creep in that God will not bring deliverance or be a refuge. It is at this time that Satan might tempt with a false security or refuge. Thomas Watson calls this temptation a medicine for security.[5] The relief that temptation proposes, although temporary, becomes very appealing. It is in this moment that at least two things are being revealed: (1) the propensity of the heart to seek refuge outside of God, and (2) the opportunity to press into God in the midst of suffering and temptation. In Matthew 4, after Jesus is baptized and the Spirit descends on Him, the Spirit leads Him into the wilderness. Satan presents several temptations that take this form of false refuge. Jesus perfectly submits to the will of the Father and in doing so resists the devil's schemes. His obedience shows that no trial or suffering (regardless of the outcome) supersedes what God is doing.

The human propensity toward self-reliance is also exposed during times of trial and suffering. The prideful heart says it can do better than God. It screams, "I know better; I am sovereign!" When King David took another man's wife (Bathsheba) into his bed and he later discovered she was pregnant, he attempted to manipulate and control the outcome. His plans were foiled, and he ended up sending Uriah to his death in battle. David acted independently of God and at no point positioned himself under the Lord. The Bible has many other examples of men and women, who during moments of self-reliance, acted independently of God. Rarely will a person vocalize something as blatant as, "I'm sovereign and I know best," but even a hint of suffering can quickly expose a self-reliant heart. There is more trust in self and what self can control than in what God can offer or can do in and through suffering.

The Importance of Gospel-Centered Community Under the Authority of the Church

There is no substitute for the body of Christ. A healthy church provides an environment of redemptive relationships that provide the nutrients necessary to enrich spiritual growth. The church provides opportunities for gospel-saturated community to be experienced. Because all other communities lack some component of this, including the private practitioner's office, it should be the agenda of every biblical counselor to encourage involvement in this community.

The lives and testimonies of the redeemed provide a nutrient-rich environment that stimulates growth. Consider compost. This fertilizer is rich in nutrients and provides key organisms that ward off disease. Compost helps aerate the soil, allowing heaven (the air) to mix with earth (the soil). It is incredible that the refuse of our former lives can be redeemed to provide a nutrient-rich environment so that the gospel can take root and produce fruit in the lives of others. Our very lives testify to Christ's love, power, and truth as the Holy Spirit brings life from what was once dead. The church offers hope, help, and healing.

A church becomes fruitless when its testimony becomes one of self-righteousness and legalism. Then their focus is on their own goodness rather than the goodness of God amidst their refuse. From such pride comes all forms of spiritual disease.

A healthy community saturated with the gospel will walk humbly with one another (Matthew 18:4). The church will be a safe place for the weak, the wounded, and the lost. It is "a place where it is okay to not be okay" (see Matthew 18:5), "but not okay to stay there" (see Matthew 18:8-9). This environment is produced as the church responds in faith to the gospel message. Faith in Him becomes the very air we breathe, which sustains us. The church acts as a garden where heaven and earth come together to produce fruit. The Holy Spirit, like rain, washes us clean and softens the soil. Jesus Christ, the Son of God, like the sun, provides light and warmth in an otherwise dark and cold world.

The church is also to guard against those who plant false teachings that will produce bad fruit or plant weeds that detract from the usefulness and beauty of the garden. The best way to promote a beautiful lawn is plenty of grass—the healthy grass literally chokes out the weeds.

We must also be watchful for predators. There are those who come to the church as parasites whose agenda is to suck the resources of the church. And once they are gone, they are gone. There are also those who come in like foxes to prey on and steal from the garden.

Churches that are tolerant of false teaching and do not protect the garden will err on the side of license by allowing sin to reign, which creates a toxic environment for the garden and can choke it out.

A healthy church will make sure sin doesn't take root by practicing Christian accountability and church discipline. When a fellow believer is caught up in sin and thinks he is okay, it is not okay to let him remain that way. Where there is no discipline, there is a lack of love, for as we saw earlier, God disciplines those He loves.

On a related note, private practitioners should realize their limitations when it comes to dealing with sin in people's lives, for counselors do not operate as a church. They should be members in a church, involved in gospel-saturated community, and accountable to the church. All of us who are private practitioners outside the church are in a sense always trying to work ourselves out of a job. We want whatever biblical benefit the counselee is receiving in our private practice to ultimately be found in the body of Christ, which should offer a better context for the life-on-life relationships necessary for sanctification to occur.

This community context goes well beyond an hour-a-week counseling session. It is difficult to get a good sense of what is happening in a counselee's life through meeting once a week. The body of Christ is about doing life together, and by doing life together, sin is revealed. And where sin is revealed, there is an opportunity for relationships to be healed. So whenever it is possible to do so, a counselor should support and serve the church rather than attempt to replace it. In addition, God has given specific authority to the institution of the church to govern His people. For this reason, consents to disclose counseling information should be obtained so that church members are able to be held accountable to their local body.

The evidence of God's grace in the life of the church is unity and love. Two primary responses of faith to the gospel of grace are repentance when we sin and forgiveness when we are sinned against. These graces are granted through faith in the gospel. If we fail to respond to the gospel by faith, we will harbor unforgiveness and continue to walk in unrepentant sin. This will lead to division within the church, where neither love nor unity will testify to the Spirit's work. A healthy church will be a beautiful garden with healthy fruit.

In addition to providing the nutrients, the church also provides the trellis, or the structure and strategies necessary for shaping the growth of the garden. Since our sanctification will result in works that help advance the kingdom among the nations, a coordinated effort will insure that no tribe, tongue, or group is left unreached. The church universal is meant to cover the earth. Organic growth is good and should be encouraged, but it is often haphazard. It is important that the church provide strategic and organized mission and ministry opportunities that enable a continuity of effort and the possibility of the systematic eradication of the enemy. What spectacular display of God's glory will be seen as every tribe, tongue, and nation is gathered and represented within this great garden! Just imagine the sights, the smells, the sounds, the tastes, and the feelings of being a part of this majestic garden that worships God and testifies to His greatness (Revelation 7:9).

For counseling to be biblical, or even Christian for that matter, the gospel of Jesus Christ must be the only hope and answer given for the elimination of sin and suffering common to our humanity. One ambassador of Christ who bears a message of reconciliation and speaks the truth in love has more to offer than the aggregate efforts of all other forms of counseling.

The Weapons of Our Warfare

Bob Kellemen and Dwayne Bond

As we think biblically about spiritual growth, we would be naïve to ignore spiritual warfare. The apostle Paul didn't. Having filled his letter to the Ephesians with salvation truths ("gospel indicatives") and sanctification truths ("gospel imperatives"), he concludes by urging them (and us) to be strong in the Lord's might and to put on the whole armor of God. "For we do not wrestle against flesh and blood, but against the rulers, against the authorities, against the cosmic powers over this present darkness, against the spiritual forces of evil in the heavenly places" (Ephesians 6:12).

Paul chose a word—*wrestle*—which in his day empathically communicated a life-and-death battle. Wrestling matches in the Greco-Roman world were won when the victor was able to press and hold down his prostrate antagonist by the neck—pinning his opponent to the ground by strangling. At times, the loser had his eyes gouged out, resulting in blindness.[1]

So that we might avoid spiritual blindness, Paul exhorts us to understand and "stand against the schemes of the devil" (Ephesians 6:11). Many of us, when we think about spiritual warfare and overcoming the adversary, start thinking eerie thoughts of demons and exorcisms. Rather than such eerie thoughts, however, Paul and the rest of the biblical authors focus on:

- renewed minds that understand Satan's strategy
- renewed hearts that apply Christ's counterstrategy

As we relate spiritual warfare to spiritual growth, we'll follow this biblical pattern by exposing the evil one's crafty schemes and disclosing Christ's victorious plan for demolishing Satan's strongholds.

Tempted to Rebel[2]

The Bible exposes the two-pronged attack in Satan's basic bait-and-switch scheme:

- First Satan tempts us to rebel against God.

- Then Satan condemns us for rebelling against God.

Satan mounts his mutiny against God through a deceitful stronghold: God is untrustworthy. In subtle and not-so-subtle ways, he places God's heart on trial by whispering insidious lies: "God is holding back on you. He wants you to jump through hoops in order to earn His love. He's stingy. He doesn't have your best interests in mind. You're better off trusting in yourself. Your resources and functional saviors work better than waiting on and trusting in Him." To counteract Satan's challenge to God's good heart, we need to expose his seducing strategies.

Seducing Strategy #1: Enticing Us to Distrust God's Good Heart

Satan's kryptonite is separation through slander. He slanders God to us and us to God. His devious design lures us away from God and tempts us to rely on ourselves. The original lie reveals the nature of all his lies—Satan wants us to doubt God's generous goodness (see Genesis 3:1-6).

Moses warns his readers with these words: "Now the serpent was more *crafty* than any other beast of the field that the LORD God had made" (Genesis 3:1, emphasis added). "Crafty" suggests shrewd, brilliant malevolence—a being who is clever enough to package his venomous hatred in sugar coating. He simply wants some information, right? "Did God actually say?" He is only after a little conversation, right? "Hath God said?" He seeks simple clarification, right? "You must not eat from any tree in the garden?"

"Hath God said" seduces Eve to ask, "Why is God a 'must not God?'" The serpent is not simply saying, "Do I have it right?" He is implying, "God said what?!"

God, of course, had said, "You are *free* to eat from *any* tree in the garden; but you must not eat from the tree of the knowledge of good and evil, for when you eat from it you will surely die" (Genesis 2:16-17 NIV, emphasis added). The serpent sidesteps, alludes, and ultimately ignores God's generous benevolence and twists His one prohibition—a protective prohibition meant to teach God-dependence and intended to spare us from the consequences of self-sufficiency.

The serpent is not finished. He blatantly calls God a liar: "You will not surely die" (Genesis 3:4). Then he shoots the poisoned arrow. "For God knows that when you eat of it your eyes will be opened, and you will be like God, knowing good and evil" (verse 5). "God is withholding! God is terrified that He might have to share some of His glory. God hoards His gifts so He alone can enjoy them."

Satan wants us to see God as our enemy, thus disconnecting us from God. Thwarting the pursuit of supreme joy, delight, and provision is his aim. Rather than seeing God as our gracious Creator who creates beings in His image with a will empowered either to obey or rebel, Satan deludes us into seeing God as our cruel Taskmaster who suppresses our freedom and demands that we grovel. The marquee scrolling across our minds trying to reinterpret life reads: "God-Against-Us." This becomes the dominant lens through which our flesh interprets life. We no longer give our loving Father the benefit of the doubt. Instead, we view every event as conclusive proof that God is against us.

Sin is like a malicious virus that relentlessly seeks to erase our memory of our trusting relationship with our trustworthy God. What if Adam and Eve had reminded each other that every good and gracious gift comes down from the Father of lights? What if they had recalled that God gives us richly everything to enjoy? Because they did not, they became susceptible to Satan's second seducing strategy.

Seducing Strategy #2: Enticing Us to Trust Our Own Heart

Doubting God inevitably leads to trusting self. In Genesis 3:6, Adam and Eve eat the forbidden fruit, and their fall is complete. In Genesis 3:7, they realize their nakedness and *cover their shame on their own.* Imagine what might have happened had Adam and Eve cried out to God between Genesis 3:6 and 3:7:

> Then the eyes of both of them were opened and they realized that they were naked. Standing exposed as failed and flawed male and female, naked before Him with whom they have to deal.

Then the naked man and the naked woman heard the song of the LORD God as He was walking in the garden in the cool of the day, as He always had for fellowship. And they stayed.

Adam cried out to God, "I am unworthy to be called Your son, for I have sinned against You in my self-sufficiency. I have failed to be the courageous and responsible male You designed and called me to be. I have been a coward rather than a guardian. Make me like one of your animals, for I am soulless."

Eve cried out to God, "I am unworthy to be called Your daughter, for I have sinned against You in my self-sufficiency. I have failed to be the completing female You designed and called me to be. I have poisoned rather than nourished and cultivated. Make me like one of Your animals, for I am soulless."

Instead, the LORD God slew the innocent animals He had created. He shed blood. Carefully, tenderly, He made handcrafted robes of righteousness for His son and daughter.

Then He ran to them, threw His arms around them, kissed them repeatedly, and whispered gracious assurances of His love in their ears. The Father said to His angelic servants, "Quick, bring the best robes that I have handcrafted and put them on My son and daughter. Put rings on their fingers and sandals of peace on their feet. Bring the fatted calf and kill it. Let's have a feast and celebrate. For this son and daughter of Mine were dead and they are alive again." So they began to celebrate!

Grace means never having to cover our sin. But Adam and Eve, having doubted God's goodness, do not embrace His grace. Instead of depending upon God, they depend upon self. Being naked and afraid, they ashamedly hide. As terrified rebels, they turn their backs on and run from God. Seeking righteousness through their own efforts, they sew fig leaves together to make coverings for themselves. They attempt to make themselves attractive and acceptable by trying to beautify their ugliness.

In the flesh we use every strategy at our disposal, every scheme we can imagine, to not need God's grace. What fig leaves do we sew to cover our shame? What view of God does such shame and hiding suggest? Whenever we mistrust God's good heart, we end up trusting our own fallen hearts.

Condemned for Rebelling

Once we succumb to Satan's scheme, we might imagine that he would applaud us. "Atta' boy! Now you're getting it. You're on my team now." But nothing could be further from the truth. Instead, once we bite his bait, he lures us in, fries us, and eats us alive. "You fool! You sinner! How could you have disowned God? Now He hates you. You're ugly, unwanted, filthy, puny, and putrid. What a mess you're in. Run. Hide. Be ashamed. Be afraid."

Condemning Tactic #1: Accusing Us to God

First Satan tempts us to sin, and then he taunts us for having sinned. Puritan writer Thomas Brooks explains how Satan presents the pleasure and profit of sin, but hides the misery that follows:

> He paints sin with virtuous colors. After having tempted us to sin and to mind sin more than Christ, then he makes us believe that we are not good because we were beset by temptation and cannot enjoy God as we once did. The moment we give in to temptation, Satan immediately changes his strategy and becomes the accuser.[3]

Consider three passages picturing Satan's condemning narrative: Job 1–2, Zechariah 3:1-10, and Revelation 12:7-10. In Job, Satan accuses Job of being a fair-weather follower of God. In Zechariah, he slanders the filthily attired priest, Joshua. In Revelation 12:10, he is rightly labeled "the accuser of our brothers." Satan not only accuses God to us; he accuses us to God.

And how does God respond? He looks to the cross; He looks at His Son. "Who shall bring any charge against God's elect?" (Romans 8:33). The answer, of course, is Satan brings the charges. However, the answer is much more than that. God is saying, "No one can bring charges that stick, charges that condemn." "If God is for us, who can be against us? He who did not spare his own Son but gave him up for us all, how will he not also with him graciously give us all things?" (Romans 8:31-32).

Satan is always against, but never victorious. Since Christ died for us while we were His enemies, certainly now that we are His family, His grace covers our sin. His grace covers our disgrace. Therefore, nothing in all creation, including the powerfully evil creature Satan, can ever separate us from the love of God that is in Christ Jesus our Lord.

Condemning Tactic #2: Accusing Us to Ourselves

Satan fights a futile battle to persuade God to condemn us. Unfortunately, he's more successful with his attempts to convince *us* that we are contemptible. Martin Luther experienced and overcame these demonic character assassinations:

> The Deceiver can magnify a little sin for the purpose of causing one to worry, torture, and kill oneself with it. That is why a Christian should learn not to let anyone easily create an evil conscience in him. Rather let him say, "Let this error and this failing pass away with my other imperfections and sins, which I must include in the article of faith: I believe in the forgiveness of sins, and the Fifth Petition of the Lord's Prayer: Forgive us our trespasses."[4]

Satan seeks to fill our souls with shame that separates. "Give up on life. Throw in the towel." Paul labels it worldly sorrow that produces death (2 Corinthians 7:10). Satanic shame involves self-contempt and self-disgust that causes us to despair of all hope that God could love a sinner like us. Condemning shame convinces us that God has forever justly rejected us. Godly sorrow, on the other hand, is guilt that leads us to return to God. It is guilt that escorts us to grace. It reminds us of our absolute dependency upon Christ's grace and invites us to come home to our forgiving Father. Shame separates; sorrow connects.

Condemning Tactic #3: Accusing Us to and Through One Another

If we have faith like Luther, we can overcome Satan's second condemning methodology. However, before we celebrate prematurely, we should remember Satan's persistence and remind ourselves of his third condemning tactic. He not only accuses us to God and to ourselves, he also accuses us to and through others.

James is aghast that out of the same mouth we release words that praise our Creator and words that curse those made in His image (James 3:9-10). He calls this a "restless evil, full of deadly poison" (James 3:8). More than that, he identifies the source of our bitter envy, selfish ambition, and divisive speech— it "is earthly, unspiritual, demonic" (James 3:15).

Luther's practical eye, trained by a lifelong battle against Satan, helps us to see the connection between our devouring words and Satan's diabolical methodology:

> There is no person on earth so bad that he does not have something about him that is praiseworthy. Why is it, then, that we leave the good things out of sight and feast our eyes on the unclean things? It is as though we enjoyed only looking at—if you will pardon the expression—a man's behind. The devil gets his name from doing this. He is called Diabolos, that is, a slanderer and reviler, who takes pleasure in shaming us most miserably and embittering us among ourselves, causing nothing but murder and misery and tolerating no peace or concord between brothers, between neighbors, or between husband and wife.[5]

Diabolos loves division. He attempts to separate us from God through shame that tempts us to run, hide, and cover; he strives to separate us from ourselves through shame that produces self-contempt and the disintegration of our shalom; and he toils to separate us from one another through shame that divides and conquers.

In the midst of Satan's insidious seductions and shrewd tactics we could be tempted to give up, to raise the white flag of surrender. Yet God calls us "more than conquerors" (Romans 8:37). We are superconquerors, superheroes! How? What is Christ's victorious counterstrategy in our spiritual warfare against the prince of darkness?

Christ's Counterstrategy

God is the eternal community of selfless oneness who graciously created us to revel in and reveal His goodness (Genesis 1; John 1; John 17; Ephesians 1). Could any script be better written? Could any lead actor or actress ever receive a better role?

What's the problem then? A great liar, the great Liar, attempts to rewrite the script. Satan, the sinister Antagonist, sneaks in his revisions. Paul warns us about them. "See to it that no one takes you captive by philosophy and empty deceit, according to human tradition, according to the elemental spirits of the world, and not according to Christ" (Colossians 2:8). It is an alluring script with vicious hooks designed to captivate our soul's attention.

At the end of life, each of us must answer the question, Whose story captured my soul? Our role in the story is to counter Satan's subversion. "We destroy arguments and every lofty opinion raised against the knowledge of God, and take every thought captive to obey Christ" (2 Corinthians 10:5).

We live our lives amidst two competing interpretations of life. In this competition, this warfare, "we are not waging war according to the flesh. For the weapons of our warfare are not of the flesh but have divine power to destroy strongholds" (2 Corinthians 10:3-4). So how do we wage war? What is Christ's counterstrategy, and what is our role in it?

Victorious Strategy #1: The Battlefield Scouts— the Naked Eye Versus the Spiritual Eye

When suffering comes our way and besetting sins assault us, how do we interpret life? When life's expectations take a painful U-turn and leave us with a new reality, how do we perceive life? Paul informs us how *not* to interpret our life story: "You are judging by appearances" (2 Corinthians 10:7 NIV). "Appearances" literally means "according to facial expression," or what we might call "with eyeballs only." We see what only the flesh can see—mere external appearance, what is outward, only on the surface, skin deep.

God has given us all that we need to see life with spiritual eyes. When Paul and Barnabas heal a man lame from birth, the citizens of Lystra and Derbe shout, "The gods have come down to us in the likeness of men!" (Acts 14:11). Paul and Barnabas respond with outrage and embarrassment.

> We also are men, of like nature with you, and we bring you good news, that you should turn from these vain things to a living God, who made the heaven and the earth and the sea and all that is in them. In past generations he allowed all the nations to walk in their own ways. Yet he did not leave himself without witness, for he did good by giving you rains from heaven and fruitful seasons, satisfying your hearts with food and gladness (verses 15-17).

Our God has not left us without witness. No one can look at life's gifts and doubt the goodness of the Giver. No one, that is, with spiritual eyes. When we interpret life with eyeballs only, God holds us without excuse. And justly so.

> The wrath of God is revealed from heaven against all ungodliness and unrighteousness of men, who by their unrighteousness suppress the truth. For what can be known about God is plain to them, because God has shown it to them. For his invisible attributes, namely, his eternal power and divine nature, have been clearly perceived, ever since the creation of the world, in the things that have been made. So they are without excuse (Romans 1:18-20).

When we observe life with eyeballs only, we will not see God's goodness, especially when life is bad. Romans 1 teaches that *when life stinks, our God-perspective shrinks, and when our God perspective shrinks, our hearts stink.*

But Christ endures the stench and moves toward us with holy love (Romans 1:16-17). God has not abandoned us in our evil world. With spiritual eyes, with faith eyes, we see Him and His goodness everywhere (Acts 17:24-31). His fingerprints are visible and detectible. "He has fixed a day on which he will judge the world in righteousness by a man whom he has appointed: and of this he has given assurance to all by raising him from the dead" (verse 31).

Faith is the assurance of things we can't see with eyeballs only. Without faith it is impossible to please God, because anyone who comes to Him must believe that He exists and that He *graciously rewards* those who earnestly seek Him (cf. Hebrews 11:1-6).

The role of biblical counselors is to facilitate the discovery of a greater God awareness through spiritual eyes that look at life through scriptural lenses. Faith is the awareness that God's name is Rewarder. Faith perceives that God in Christ is graciously good, forgiving those who deserve judgment (2 Corinthians 5:21).

Victorious Strategy #2: The Battlefield Weapons— the Battle for Our Minds

Life, then, is a battle for our minds. How do we fight the battle? What's our strategy? When Paul explains that we do not "wage war" as the world does (2 Corinthians 10:3), he uses the Greek word *strateia*, meaning "strategy." In Paul's day, strategy was inseparably linked to generalmanship—the tactics and war plans of the highest-ranking military officer. Two generals hand us our marching orders. Which general's strategy will win our minds?

Satan's grand strategy is to blind us to God's true nature. Being the father of lies, the creator of the lying narrative, he attempts to cause us to see God as the Evil Emperor, Darth Vader, or Ming the Merciless. He wants us to view God as malevolent.

Biblical counselors scout his subterfuge. He tempts us to reinterpret our image of God—God is a bully, Christ is our prison warden, and the Holy Spirit is an impersonal force. Satan also deludes us into reinterpreting our relationship to God—God is our enemy.

Biblical counselors now know Christ's counterstrategy. He opens our eyes to the true nature of life. God is our pursuing Father, and we are His adult sons and daughters. Christ is our forgiving Groom, and we are His virgin brides. The Holy Spirit is our inspiring Mentor, and we are His best friends and disciples.

Two generals present us with two strategies—this is the battle for our minds. When Satan's lying salvos assault our position, what weapons do we use? Our weapons are our Father's weapons—far superior to human weapons, abilities, traditions, and philosophies (2 Corinthians 10:4).

The word "weapons" speaks of a siege implement, a battering ram. These are not defensive weapons. They are offensive. The very gates—the protective walls that guard a city on a hill—of hell shall never prevail against them. They will fall. What sort of weapons can demolish demonic reasoning? Truth. The Word. The truth about who Christ is and who we are in and to Christ.

In C.S. Lewis' novel series The Chronicles of Narnia, Aslan, the great lion, is the Christ-figure. The evil White Witch captures him, binds him, and kills him. The four children, Lucy, Edmund, Susan, and Peter, forfeit hope. Exhausted from battle and weeping, they sleep. Upon awaking they're horrified to see mice gnawing upon Aslan's dead body. But upon further, closer, inspection, they realize that the mice are actually eating away the ropes that bind the great lion king. Before their eyes they see him rise. With their own ears they hear him roar. They're ecstatic, yet confused. "How? Why? What?" they stammer.

Aslan hushes them. He explains the evil, finite, temporal magic of the White Witch. With a twinkle in his eyes, he tells them, "But she did not know of the deeper magic from before the dawn of time." The White Witch, Satan, and all who follow them perceive life with eyeballs only so they know only of the evil magic *in* time. We, with faith eyes, see the deeper magic from *before* the dawn of time. We perceive the eternal power and gracious goodness of God, who raises the dead.

The weapon of our warfare is the gospel story, the "magic" from before the dawn of time that raised Christ from the dead. This resurrection power, Paul tells us in Ephesians 1:18-23, is the same power that is at work now within us.

Victorious Strategy #3: The Battlefield Soldiers—Biblical Counselors as Spiritual Friends/Spiritual Soldiers

Our role as biblical counselors is to remind broken people of the gospel script. We're soldiers in a battle standing back-to-back as spiritual friends speaking God's truth in love. We provide grace relationships of compassion and present grace narratives with discernment, using the weapon of truth to take down enemy lies and take captive enemy plans.

Our General commands us to destroy strongholds, arguments, and every pretension that sets itself up against the knowledge of God (2 Corinthians 10:4-5). The word "destroy" means to take down by force by demolishing the foundation. It pictures knocking the props out from under someone, knocking him off his feet.

In high school wrestling, the best wrestlers are those with the best take-downs. As a wrestling coach, when I (Bob) teach young wrestlers to do take-downs, I teach them that their opponent's arms are like a moat or a gate that prevents them from reaching the castle. Their castle's foundations are its legs. To take someone down, they have to take control of their opponent's legs by knocking them out from under him.

We wrestle against principalities and powers. We must take down and dethrone their foundational strongholds, arguments, and pretensions. "Strongholds" is a military term referring to a fortress or fortified place. The word came to be used metaphorically for anything on which someone relies. In 2 Samuel 22:3, God claims the title of our Stronghold.

So what is Paul saying? We must rip the foundations out from under all bastions of human reasoning that say, "I don't need God!" We must demolish every non-God story of life. We must pulverize every God-is-not-good life narrative.

In their place, biblical counselors are to apply the victorious gospel narrative. "You were buried with Christ in baptism and raised with Him through the powerful working of God. You have been made alive together with Christ, your sins forgiven and your debt canceled—nailed to the cross. He disarmed the rulers and authorities and made a public spectacle of them, triumphing over them by the cross" (cf. Colossians 2:12-15).

Angela as a Case Study

Consider Angela, who struggles with despair, perfectionism, and self-sufficiency. Imagine that she has alertly and humbly traced her battle to deeper heart issues. She confesses that in the fortress of her heart, she's clinging to the lie that "I need to be perfect to be whole. I know that God doesn't want me to take life into my own hands, but I feel so safe when I'm in complete control of everything. Like I finally have it all together." Angela's relying on her perfectionistic self-sufficiency as her stronghold—her place to find life, her fortified safety zone.

Elyse Fitzpatrick helps us to see the connection between these strongholds and arguments or imaginations. "Our beliefs about the sources of joy (through finding a spouse or success, for instance) are frequently experienced as colorful imaginations that captivate our hearts."[6]

Angela does not imagine in black in white. She imagines in living color, technocolor, big screen, jumbotron. Her thoughts of a perfect life, a perfect family, perfect friends, and a perfect church are incredibly attractive. This is exactly what Paul pictured with the word "arguments" (2 Corinthians 10:5). It's the same word used in Hebrews 11:19 regarding Abraham's reasoning—his mental calculations. In her moments of despair, Angela is adding up reality. "Trusting God to fix the messes in my life does not measure up to the wonderful way I feel when I prevent any messes from ever occurring. I feel so alive. So fully safe!" In those instances, she shuts her thoughts off from God. Her deliberations are warped, out of joint. She fails to factor God into the equation of her life.

According to Paul, all such thoughts smack of arrogance. They're pretentious images that ascend like the Tower of Babel over the landscape of our minds shouting, "We have vaulted above God! We can make life work apart from Him!" Paul insists that we implode these top-most perches of audacious pride. For such pride rises above and against the knowledge of God, acting as if He is unworthy to be retained in our thoughts.

Angela began to experience lasting victory when she recognized the horrors of her sin. "I'm saying that God is smaller to me, less significant in my mind, than I am. When I surrender to my controlling, demanding perfectionism, I'm chucking God's holiness, His majesty, and His beauty right out the window." Further, she said, "When I reject His forgiveness and work to earn back His acceptance, I'm acting as if I can save myself. I'm like Eve putting on a fig leaf thinking I can make myself presentable to God!"

A biblical counselor interacting with Angela would want to help her to see with spiritual eyes who God is and who she is in Christ. This follows the passion of our Commander-in-Chief, who orders us to take captive enemy plans (2 Corinthians 10:5). Literally, we are to make them prisoners of war without any rights or power. What do we take prisoner? "Thoughts." Paul uses the word *voēma,* meaning "plans, plots, schemes." He chooses the identical word in 2 Corinthians 2:11 for Satan's schemes, designs, and plots. Satan's scheme is simple. His plot goes like this: "You don't need God. He's not so hot anyhow. You can make it on your own." At root, all sin follows this same plot line, this same story line. When we sin we say, "God? I don't need God. He doesn't come through for me anyway. Doesn't really care, not when it counts. I'll make life work quite well on my own, thank you."

As Angela's biblical counselor, we want to help her to pluck out her eyeballs-only thinking, and we want to do it in a creatively powerful and uniquely personal way. "Angela, here's the picture that I'm sensing. You've been handed two blueprints for your life. One instructs you to build your lovely, oh-so-perfect life upon your own skillful organizational abilities, your logical mind, and your perceptive competency to scout out pending doom. From a human perspective, you've done very well. The dollhouse that is your life is immaculate. The problem is, you haven't invited God into your home. Plus, others don't feel comfortable there because they fear messing with your Good Housekeeping life.

"The other blueprint terrifies you, yet attracts you. When the Architect hands it to you, He does so with a calmness that has the power to quiet your agitated soul. Looking at His blueprint, you notice splashes of color here, dashes of personality there, creativity in this corner, and possibilities in that one. You also detect, horror of horrors, some clutter, some unfinished rooms. A speck of dust. Lint on the carpet. You're tempted to race for the vacuum, but then you see all the guests thoroughly enjoying themselves. They feel comfortable, not only in your home, but also with you. They feel invited, wanted, necessary. Most importantly, the Architect lives in your imperfect home, shaping it daily more and more into His desired design."

Imagine Angela's response. "I don't like that first picture. Yet there's no denying that it's me to a tee. As for the second picture, you're right. I hate it and I love it. It does scare me to death. It makes me feel naked, like I'm giving up everything I've ever depended on. Yet, I love it, I want it, at times I've tasted it. To give up being always-busy-Martha and become restful-relational-Mary...wow. That's what I want. That's what my family wants. That's what God made me for."

14

The Hope of Eternity

Nicolas Ellen and Jeremy Lelek

What you hope for determines what you live for. What you hope for determines *who* you live for. Hope misplaced can devastate you. In the book of Proverbs, the author writes, "Hope deferred makes the heart sick, but a desire fulfilled is a tree of life" (Proverbs 13:12). Hope, therefore, is directly tied to desire. As such, hope is appropriately understood as a product of the inner workings of the soul. It springs forth from within while being intricately connected to a final end (a desire) that is perceived to be good, pleasurable, and fulfilling. If you long for hope, ask yourself, "What do I want that I believe will bring ultimate good, pleasure, and a sense of being fulfilled?" Conclusions drawn from this question will shape a distinct worldview that will serve to inform your perception of reality. This perception can often be the dividing line between "heart sickness" and thriving as a "tree of life." Perspective, therefore, is extremely important when considering the pathway to genuine hope.

Pray for Proper Perspective

If you have ever been interested in modern literature that illustrates the power of God in the midst of terrible suffering, you may have come across the classic book *The Hiding Place*, written by Corrie ten Boom with John and Elizabeth Sherrill. It is a firsthand account of a family during World War II who was placed in Nazi concentration camps because they had hidden Jews in their homes. Two of the sisters arrested, Corrie and Betsie, through a series of remarkable events, end up in the same camp, Ravensbruck.

While there, they were not only forced to come to grips with the fact that God had allowed them to experience such travesty, but they also had to contend with the fact that the barracks where they were assigned were heavily infested with lice and fleas. Could God not spare them from even this? Corrie struggled with this fact, and for a while, her perspective led her down the pathway of a sickened heart. Because she and her sister were facing such horrendous conditions, her hope started becoming fixed upon the slightest possibility of any relief or comfort. Everywhere she looked, both day and night, there was misery. Sleeping in a bed without bugs crawling all over her body didn't seem like much to ask from God.

When Corrie's longings were never realized, her animosity and confusion towards her Creator began to flourish. Her frustration became evident when her sister, Betsie, was encouraging Corrie to thank God for *all* things, including the tiny insects that were embedding themselves into her skin. After hearing her sister's counsel, Corrie rebutted, "Betsie, there's no way even God can make me grateful for a flea."[1] Without her realizing it, God was setting the stage to disrupt Corrie's faithless obstinacy, and it would be His eternal hand that would make all the difference.

Ravensbruck was a new setting for the ten Boom sisters. What they soon realized was that even though the conditions were far worse than anything they had thus far experienced, hassle from the prison guards was all but nonexistent. When the 1500 or more women prisoners packed into a room designed for just over 100 people, they were basically left to themselves. This was far different than the previous barracks where they were constantly barraged and assaulted by the Germans. This new "liberty" allowed Corrie and her sister to start Bible studies in the evening, which changed the very atmosphere of the living quarters, not to mention the lives of the women with whom they were imprisoned. Towards the end of her life, Betsie explained the reason for this phenomenon to Corrie:

> "You know we've never understood why we had so much freedom in the big room," she said. "Well—I've found out."
>
> That afternoon, she said, there'd been confusion in her knitting group about sock sizes and they'd asked the supervisor to come and settle it.
>
> "But she wouldn't. She wouldn't step through the door and neither would the guards. And you know why?"

Betsie could not keep the triumph from her voice: "Because of the fleas! That's what she said, 'That place is crawling with fleas!'"

My mind rushed back to our first hour in this place. I remembered Betsie's bowed head, remembered her thanks to God for creatures I could see no use for.[2]

Eternity had been realized in the present, and that which served as Corrie's source of despair suddenly blossomed into the very thing that brought her hope! Her perspective had changed *everything!*

As happened with Corrie, when our perspective changes, all else changes. This is especially true when we consider the idea of eternal hope. As with Corrie, when we seek to develop a proper perspective, it is imperative to consider the eternal as it influences the here-and-now moments of life. Clearly, in biblical counseling and in Christian living, a biblical perspective of eternity carries profound implications for our moment-by-moment experiences.

While this topic would take an entire book to adequately consider, there is a well-known prayer in the Bible that sheds much light on the issue. It is the prayer of Jesus, who uttered these words: "Our Father in heaven, hallowed be your name. Your kingdom come, your will be done, on earth as it is in heaven. Give us this day our daily bread, and forgive us our debts, as we also have forgiven our debtors. And lead us not into temptation, but deliver us from evil" (Matthew 6:9-13).

Although this entire prayer reveals for us the intersection between the present and the eternal, we'll focus our consideration on verses 9 and 10: "Our Father in heaven, hallowed be your name. Your kingdom come, your will be done, on earth as it is in heaven."

Our Father in Heaven, Hallowed Be Your Name

Jesus is teaching His disciples several things here. First, He is highlighting the literal interpersonal reality of prayer. Prayer is communion with that which is eternal. It is speaking to the One in whom there is found no beginning or end. When we pray, we are speaking to the One whose eternal purposes and designs are unfolding as our present realities. In order to find hope in them, we must seek *Him* and *His* perspective. This requires a keen understanding of the redemptive nature of our existence, which points us to the glorious gospel of Christ.

When we pray, we are not only communicating with God, we are reminded that humanity is in perpetual relationship with eternity. The very apex of this reality is recognized in an eternal Person. Prayer awakens our hearts to the vivid reality that the privilege of communion with God resides in the finished work of Jesus Christ.

Consider the writer of Hebrews, who encourages the believer with these words: "Let us then with confidence draw near to the throne of grace, that we may receive mercy and find grace to help in time of need" (Hebrews 4:16). Upon what basis was he making such a plea? It was none other than the "great high priest who has passed through the heavens, Jesus, the Son of God" (Hebrews 4:14).

Prayer is an activity that brings to bear on our futile minds the reality that petitions to God are not simply about our present moments of struggle and the need for Him to give us the answers we desire. Rather, it exposes the miniscule nature of our finite realities as they are overshadowed by the eternal magnificence of God. Prayer holds the potential of thrusting upon our awareness the awesome reality that we are taking part in something far more expansive than the simple here and now. Prayer connects us with the One who is eternal, prompts us to recall our purpose in reverencing His name, and reminds us through our circumstances of His eternal purposes as realized in the divine narrative of the gospel of Jesus Christ.

Your Kingdom Come, Your Will Be Done

Recognizing our true state as creatures called to revere the name of God while treasuring the gospel, it becomes apparent that this thing we call the time-space continuum is never truly unfolding outside the context of eternity. We could make the case that eternity is NOW. Jesus taught His disciples to pray, "Your kingdom come, your will be done, on earth as it is in heaven" (Matthew 6:10). Even as you read this sentence, there is activity unfolding in the heavens, the likes of which we are not currently entitled to completely know.

However, God, in His grace, has granted us a glimpse into what is on display in the heavenly places. Consider the words of John: "After this I heard what seemed to be the loud voice of a great multitude in heaven, crying out, 'Hallelujah! Salvation and glory and power belong to our God..." (Revelation 19:1). He later writes, "The twenty-four elders and the four living creatures fell down and worshiped God who was seated on the throne, saying, 'Amen. Hallelujah!' And from the throne came a voice saying, 'Praise our God all you servants, you who fear him, small and great'" (verses 4-5).

The scenes John described when he recorded his visions of heaven are captured in one word: worship! They convey the essence of Jesus' words when He was teaching those around Him to pray, "Your kingdom come, your will be done, on earth as it is in heaven." The great hope, the deepest existential purpose of humanity, rests in this: that by grace our hearts would be opened to God's merciful invitation to mirror on earth that which is perpetually transpiring in heaven—the grand celebration of all creation in bringing glory to the living God.

This reality is made possible only through the transforming regeneration of the heart. Such a conversion opens the heart to those things that are transcendent, and sets forth a process in which every here-and-now experience becomes profoundly interconnected with the eternal. It is an interconnection in which God is passionately making creatures on earth that properly cherish as their chief end the glory and enjoyment of Him alone. That is the stuff of eternity, and it should be reflected in our daily lives here on Earth.

The bottom line is this: Our deepest hope resides in God's glory. Going back to our original question, we may ask, Do we find it good, pleasurable, and fulfilling to seek God's glory as our final end? Is it this that brings us a sense of hope, regardless of our situation? If so, then the implications of eternity are having a marvelous influence on our perspective, and hope will likely be a steady companion.

However, because we're creatures with a propensity to sin, disappointment serves as a rich context to understanding what truly captures our hearts in a given moment. It is where the objects of our hope that poison the heart are exposed, and the eternal promises of the Savior to redeem His own burst forth in real time (Titus 2:11-14). So, when such poison is discovered, what must we do?

Purify the Poison in Our Hearts

There are many who believe they have biblical hope, but in reality it is worldly hope. How can we tell the difference? First, the Bible says "There is a way that seems right to a man, but its end is the way to death" (Proverbs 14:12). Worldly hope is based on human wisdom instead of godly wisdom. Worldly hope claims, "All my problems would be solved if I had a better job." "I would be happy if I was married to the right person." "If people would just listen to me, everything would be fine." These ideas reflect a mind that is set on self with strong resistance to the will of God.

Second, worldly hope is built on an improper interpretation of Scripture.

> Therefore, beloved, since you look for these things, be diligent to be found by Him in peace, spotless and blameless, and regard the patience of our Lord as salvation; just as also our beloved brother Paul, according to the wisdom given him, wrote to you, as also in all his letters, speaking in them of these things, in which are some things hard to understand, which the untaught and the unstable distort, as they do also the rest of the Scriptures, to their own destruction (2 Peter 3:14-16 NASB).

For example, distorted interpretation of the Bible may sound like the following: "Because God owns it all, I should never be without." "Because God is my Father, I should be healed of all diseases." "God will give me anything I want if I just ask for it." Such misinterpretation, while sounding hopeful, actually sets the stage for immense hopelessness when things don't work out accordingly.

Third, worldly hope is birthed by the passions of ungodly men:

> False prophets also arose among the people, just as there will also be false teachers among you, who will secretly introduce destructive heresies, even denying the Master who bought them, bringing swift destruction upon themselves. Many will follow their sensuality, and because of them the way of truth will be maligned; and in their greed they will exploit you with false words; their judgment from long ago is not idle, and their destruction is not asleep (2 Peter 2:1-3 NASB).

Conclusions drawn from this mind-set may reflect the following: "If I treat people right, I will not be mistreated by others." "If I can believe it, then I can achieve it." "There is a perfect mate for everyone." "Surely if I serve others, they will return the favor and serve me." All these perspectives have one thing in common: They are based on things that God never promised. There is no surety that these things will happen. One is left waiting for something with no guarantee at all that it will come to pass. Worldly hope is just that—worldly. Our minds are consumed with the cares and riches and pleasures of this life. We are not focused on the hope that is to come through Christ Jesus our Lord. Instead, we are consumed with the things that Jesus said would rust and that moths will destroy. Our treasure is on Earth instead of heaven. In light of this, we are to consider the following:

> Brethren, join in following my example, and observe those who walk according to the pattern you have in us. For many walk, of whom I often told you, and now tell you even weeping, that they are enemies of the cross of Christ, whose end is destruction, whose god is their appetite, and whose glory is in their shame, who set their minds on earthly things (Philippians 3:17-19 NASB).

> The eye is the lamp of the body; so then if your eye is clear, your whole body will be full of light. But if your eye is bad, your whole body will be full of darkness. If then the light that is in you is darkness, how great is the darkness! No one can serve two masters; for either he will hate the one and love the other, or he will be devoted to one and despise the other. You cannot serve God and wealth (Matthew 6:22-24 NASB).

When we shift from personal purity to personal happiness, we lose biblical hope because we are not focusing on God's agenda, we are focusing on our own. God's agenda is guaranteed and our agenda is not. Hope in our agenda leads us into a game of chance in which we have no idea of the outcome. This false hope is poison to our hearts.

If we want to escape this way of living, we must purify this poison from our hearts. In order to do this we must identify the things in life that we have wanted above loving God and loving others—things which have become the lust of our lives (James 4:1-3). Whenever we treasure things of this life more than the God of eternal life, we will find ourselves wanting things of this world too much. The result is that we will place our hopes in the temporal pleasures of this life rather than the pleasure evermore found in Jesus Christ.

We must confess this as sin to God and turn away from those things in this life that we have made more important than God (Proverbs 28:13). We must evaluate every person, place, product, perspective, position, or pleasure we have looked to in place of the promises of God, and turn away from those things accordingly.

God is a compassionate God. He has given us a conscience that convicts us, and the Holy Spirit, who empowers us to respond to our convictions in a God-honoring way. Purifying the poison of our hearts will happen as we focus on putting off the sin in our thoughts, words, and actions and focus on walking in what is right (Ephesians 4:21-24). Then we will find purity and peace for our hearts (Philippians 4:6-9). As we purify our hearts of this poison, we can begin to experience the love of God, which results in expecting what God has promised. This will lead us back to biblical hope (1 John 3:1-3).

Pursue the Proper Practice of Obedience

As we purify the poison in our hearts, we must pursue the proper practice of obedience. We are not called to just turn from sin. We are also called to replace sin with right living in the areas where we have sinned. There can be no genuine hope developed without pursuing the proper practice of obedience. Obedience that is sincere toward God will lead God to make Himself known to us in ways whereby we can experience the benefit of being in His presence (Psalm 16:11; John 14:21). This can develop genuine hope in what God has promised to come as we experience the benefits of being in His presence.

We must come to a place where we seek to understand our goals within the various situations of our lives. As we evaluate all our cares and concerns in life, we must distinguish between what we expect and what God has commanded and promised in correlation. As we do so, we can learn God's agenda as a means to interpret our life situations accordingly. Learning God's agenda should be used to help us distinguish between our roles, responsibilities, and concerns and God's sovereignty in relation to the various situations we encounter in life.

As a result, we should accept God's sovereignty in a matter while learning to assume responsibility according to our God-given role. This will bring peace to our hearts as we anticipate the blessed future to come.

Pursuing the proper practice of obedience should lead us to focus on what God has promised for the future and our present situations. It should lead us to develop stability in our faith in Jesus Christ our Lord. Pursuing the proper practice of obedience should lead us to expect God to perfect the things concerning us (Psalm 138:8), to anticipate our heavenly home (John 14:1-4), as well as to expect our glorified bodies (Philippians 3:20-21).

The more we pursue the proper practice of obedience and lean on God and what He has promised, the more we will forsake a life of sin while pursuing a life of holiness (1 John 3:1-3). As we embrace the reality that God is perfecting those things concerning us, we will rest in God's ordering of our steps (Psalm 37:23). We will be consumed with the cares, riches, and pleasures of God's kingdom. We will be focused on the treasure that is to come through Christ Jesus our Lord.

Praise the Perfect Priest

If we are going to live a life of genuine hope, there must be a praise of the perfect Priest: Jesus Christ. Christ makes intercession for us to God the Father. Consider that reality for a moment. Jesus is praying for you and for me. Since He is always pleasing to the Father, what prayer could He pray that would be denied by God the Father? This perfect Priest prays perfect prayers for us. Since He prays the Father's will for our lives, we can expect that to be realized in our lives.

When we consider some of the things Jesus prayed for while He was here on earth, it should make us realize what He valued for us versus what we value for ourselves. He prayed for our oneness, protection from the evil one, our sanctification, and our experience of genuine love from God the Father (John 17:1-26). Our Lord and Savior Jesus Christ is worthy of all praise. Our lives, therefore, should be centered daily on the praise of the perfect Priest. How different our lives would be if we focused less on our problems and more on our Lord and Savior Jesus Christ, who is greater than our problems!

We must praise the perfect Priest for being a dependable anchor for our lives (Hebrews 7:11-19). We must also praise Him for the reality that He will never leave us nor forsake us (Hebrews 13:5-6). In addition, we must praise the perfect Priest for the fact that He will be our help in time of need (Hebrews 4:14-16). Moreover, we must praise Him for the guarantee that He will help us make it through every trial and temptation we face (Hebrews 13:5-6). Finally, the perfect Priest is to be praised because we know that He will provide for all our needs (Philippians 4:19).

Prize the Precious Product of Heaven

So, what is your hope? Where do you seek to find solace for your spirit when this fallen world presses down upon you? Is your hope in a better marriage or a better-paying job? Does your hope reside in overcoming some issue of sin that has plagued you for years? Is it in no longer being depressed, anxious, or angry? Does your sense of hope reside in who is elected as the next president or the conservative agenda or the liberal agenda? Is it in a better school for your children? By what is your mind governed that shapes your perspective of hope? The potential list is endless. The reason for this rests in the fact that *our hearts are wired for worship, and our worship is directly tied to our sense of hope.*

Consider Paul, for example. He was a very astute theologian. Prior to being arrested by the all-consuming grace of Jesus Christ, his primary ambition was to exhibit excellence as a good, law-abiding Jew. As such, his entire hope rested on keeping the law of Moses. This was so until he was confronted with the glory of Jesus Christ. He wrote: "Look out for the dogs, look out for the evildoers, look out for those who mutilate the flesh. For we are the circumcision, who worship by the Spirit of God and glory in Christ Jesus and put no confidence in the flesh—though I myself have reason for confidence in the flesh also" (Philippians 3:2-4).

Paul made it very clear that of all people, he had great reason to put confidence in the flesh. After all, he was "circumcised on the eighth day," was "of the people of Israel," and "of the tribe of Benjamin." He described himself as "a Hebrew of Hebrews; as to the law, a Pharisee; as to zeal, a persecutor of the church; as to righteousness under the law, blameless" (Philippians 3:5-6). In other words, in every area of his life in which he could gain a sense of hope, he excelled.

Paul's life was centered on works. He orchestrated his entire existence around rules and laws that he believed were essential. While many Christians today might have a hard time relating to such a way of life, the reality is that *all* people operate by some form of self-imposed law. This is true even of the nonbeliever. Consider the following modern-day "laws" that dictate the lives of many in our own culture (maybe even us):

- You must be attractive.

- You must be successful.

- You must be healthy.

- You cannot endure stress or pain.

- You must be a moral person.

- You must have well-adjusted children.

- You must feel good about yourself.

- You must accept yourself.

- You must believe in yourself.

- You must find a spouse.

- You must find the *perfect* spouse.

- Your children must attend the best college.

- Husbands, you must be spiritual leaders.

- Wives, you must be respectful.

- Children, you must honor your parents.

- You must have daily devotions.

Our culture is enslaved by such futile, self-imposed laws. Take, for example, the United States. For some Americans, they, like Paul, can boast, "I was born in a great country. I was born to a successful family. I am an American of Americans. As to success, I am the ultimate entrepreneur. As to zeal, I have conquered the pinnacle of my career ladder. As to being a good person, I'm tolerant of everyone." Such people generate a lifestyle centered in their values and these values have served in shaping their objects of hope. The cultural pressures to fulfill such laws can prove daunting, and before long, the "prize" to which these individuals have committed their lives are exposed as the fraudulent counterfeits they truly are. When success or marital bliss or flawless health or good children begin to escape them, suddenly the hopeful, meaningful, exciting lives they thought they had disappear as a fleeting vapor. Hopelessness becomes their most consistent companion. The good news here is that the believer in Jesus Christ has been rescued from this tragedy.

Consider again the words of Paul:

> Indeed, I count everything as loss because of the surpassing worth of knowing Christ Jesus my Lord. For his sake I have suffered the loss of all things and count them as rubbish, in order that I may gain Christ and be found in him, not having a righteousness of my own that comes from the law, but that which comes through faith in Christ, the righteousness from God that depends on faith—that I may know him and the power of his resurrection, and may share his sufferings, becoming like him in his death, that by any means possible I may attain the resurrection from the dead (Philippians 3:8-11).

Paul's perspective had changed! Now that his eyes were opened to the value of Jesus Christ and the gospel, all other hopes and virtues were forced into their proper place. Paul's tone lends to the idea that not only had his previous objects of hope been devalued, but when compared to Jesus Christ, all of them were absolutely contemptible! His sense of the sacred underwent a complete transformation, and his heart was opened to the only source of hope accessible to the human race—Jesus Christ. As God's grace taught Paul to value the only thing of *genuine* value, all other means of hope were diminished to rubbish. This is the pathway to hope.

Biblical hope of this nature is a progressive reality for the believer. It is not a state of being that is achieved in a given moment remaining static throughout the rest of one's life. The hope of which Paul speaks is experienced in the ebb and flow of our broken experiences as they are infused by the sovereign grace and purposes of God. Paul never said, "I've arrived!" Instead, he candidly confessed,

> Not that I have already obtained this or am already perfect, but I press on to make it my own, because Christ Jesus has made me his own. Brothers, I do not consider that I have made it my own. But one thing I do: forgetting what lies behind and straining forward to what lies ahead. I press on toward the goal for the prize of the upward call of God in Christ Jesus (Philippians 3:12-14).

If you read closely, you will quickly see that Paul wasn't saying he was going to forget the great failures and sins of his past. No. Instead, he was saying, "All the things in which I once placed my hope, and in which I performed exceedingly well, I now abandon. And I don't just abandon them; I actually despise them in comparison to Jesus!" His object of hope was now centered on the eternal.

Notice also Paul's humility. He wasn't boasting as though he had attained the perfect understanding of the gospel as it applied to his daily life. He hadn't perfectly valued the gospel as he should, and he knew it. What did he do though? He pressed on. He pressed on to an eternal call that he now had in Christ Jesus—a call revealed in the words of his Master, who taught his disciples to pray, "Your kingdom come, your will be done, on earth as it is in heaven" (Matthew 6:10). Paul valued Jesus and His kingdom, and no matter what he faced, he knew the experience of divine hope.

The transcendent value of God's eternal gospel infused a hope in Paul that would not shift with the temporal realities of life. Whether in prison, shipwrecked, or being tortured, Paul's hope rested in God. He was now an ambassador of another kingdom, and the recognition of this eternal truth caused him to consider all other things in life as refuse.

Peace that Passes Understanding

This is biblical hope—that our hearts would be so radically changed by the grace of God that those things we treasure as invaluable would be cast into the cesspool of all things idolatrous in order that our affections would crave nothing but Christ crucified, and that all such longings entail for His chosen. If, as biblical counselors, we engender hope anywhere else for those we serve, we rob them of the peace of which Paul speaks, the peace that transcends the capacity of human intellect!

Worse still, we rob them of the pleasure of rejoicing in the mighty King of kings, the very purpose for which they were created. May we seek to engender hope in Him alone as we fulfill our current call in His eternal service.

Part 2

A Practical Methodology of Biblical Counseling

15

The Biblical Counseling Ministry of the Local Church

Rob Green and Steve Viars

We hope that by this point in the book you are rejoicing in the gospel of Jesus Christ. We trust that you are thinking deeply about your union with Christ and how that union frees you to love and serve your risen and returning Savior. We pray that you are marveling at the Spirit's work in your life—that by virtue of Spirit baptism, you have been made part of the body of Christ. We hope that you have even more confidence in the work of God in the lives of people and the sufficiency of the Scriptures that God gave us. We trust that these truths are resonating so deeply in your soul that you are compelled to do something with them—to see your church intimately involved in meeting people in the midst of their sin and suffering, and to seek opportunities to be an instrument in the hands of our wonderful Redeemer.

A Church *of* Biblical Counseling

In fact, to be even more specific, we pray that you want your church not only to *have* a counseling ministry, but to *be* a counseling ministry. You want your church to be a place where the sufficiency of Scripture and the doctrine of progressive sanctification permeate everything. You want your church to be a discipleship factory. In fact, you want to be so intentional about discipleship that you are not simply talking about the folks in your church who are doing great, but you are also concerned about the ones whose wheels have fallen off. If this describes your thoughts, then this chapter is for you.

Faith Church has been seeking to be a church that *is* a counseling ministry for a very long time. We not only want to be a place where hurting souls can find help and hope; we also want to be a church that teaches, counsels, and disciples so that issues can be prevented or solved before they reach the point of critical mass. Yet we will be the first to confess that we have learning and growing to do at every level. Our regular failures are constant reminders that we are always dependent on the Lord, always in need of His grace, and always prone to allow our own sinfulness to shine more brightly than the glorious work of God.

At the same time, however, since 1977 we have been doing *something*, and the Lord has blessed our feeble and sometimes foolish efforts. In the last thirty-five years, the attendance at Faith Church has grown from 300 to 1800. The number of counselors serving on a weekly basis has grown from four to twenty-five. By God's hand of favor, we are now one of the largest counseling centers in our community (with 140,000 residents, including those at Purdue University), offering well over 3000 hours of free counseling to both the community and our church family. Our training ministries (the annual Biblical Counseling Training Conference, our training that occurs each Monday in eleven-week blocks, and our regional conferences) have given us the privilege of being involved in training 2500 other vocational and ministry lay leaders in 2012 alone. The regional conferences have occurred through incredible partnerships with churches that have the same desire that we do—to *be* a ministry where counseling and discipleship truths are part of the fabric of the church.

In addition to the formal training done with those outside our church, there is training within our church. Hundreds of our own members have attended the conferences and lay counseling classes offered within our church. Most of our small group leaders, our Adult Bible Fellowship teachers, our deacons, and our ministry leaders have taken part in the training. Some have continued to improve their skills and joined our formal counseling team. Most have simply worked to be godly influences in their various places of ministry. Their "counseling" role has included praying, meeting over coffee, one-anothering, being accountability partners, having godly homes, and being godly influences in their workplaces and neighborhoods. In other words, we want biblical counseling, one-anothering, and discipleship to influence every ministry and every family within our church.

In our view, formal counseling is required when struggles of sin and suffering reach a point of crisis, but informal counseling occurs *all the time*. Both are necessary for the church to *be* a counseling ministry. We believe that being a church *of* biblical counseling is part and parcel of the mission God gave His church.

The Mission: Win the Lost, Disciple the Saved

God gave the church a mission. Some individuals and churches spend far too much time focused on things other than that mission. Committees are organized for all kinds of things, but oftentimes decisions are not made and commitments are not kept. Before long, people come to the church house wondering why the carpet is blue rather than wondering if any unsaved people have walked on that blue carpet recently. Too much time is invested in the wrong things. With that in mind, let's look at three Bible passages that help to define the church's focus.

Making Disciples—Matthew 28:19-20

In Matthew 28:19-20, we learn Christ's Great Commission: "Go therefore and make disciples of all nations, baptizing them in the name of the Father and of the Son and of the Holy Spirit, teaching them to observe all that I have commanded you. And behold, I am with you always, to the end of the age." There are two observations we would like to make about this text.

First, making disciples is the central command in verse 19. If you were to evaluate everything in your church through the grid of whether it was assisting in making disciples, then it is very possible you would determine there are some things your church should stop doing and other things your church should start doing. Certain committees, meetings, and possibly even services may not be accomplishing that mission. Maybe intentional discipleship through biblical counseling is a missing component.

Second, this text explains that we are to be baptizing and teaching. It is through baptism and through teaching that disciples are made. Again, the same question is relevant: Are your church's efforts contributing to these tasks? In other words, are there trained leaders in your church who can help others understand how Scripture encourages them with their marriage, their parenting, and how to develop a closer and deeper relationship with Jesus? These things need to happen. Pastor James MacDonald says it well: "If you have been in ministry for very long, you know that there are some knots that can only be untied in a more personal time of sharing God's Word one on one."[1] Preaching, yes; teaching, yes; but is there personal ministry of the Word?

Equipping God's People to Speak the Truth in Love— Ephesians 4:11-16

Paul develops the church's call to discipleship in Ephesians 4:11-16:

> He gave the apostles, the prophets, the evangelists, the shepherds and teachers, to equip the saints for the work of ministry, for building up the body of Christ, until we all attain to the unity of the faith and of the knowledge of the Son of God, to mature manhood, to the measure of the stature of the fullness of Christ, so that we may no longer be children, tossed to and fro by the waves and carried about by every wind of doctrine, by human cunning, by craftiness in deceitful schemes. Rather, speaking the truth in love, we are to grow up in every way into him who is the head, into Christ, from whom the whole body, joined and held together by every joint with which it is equipped, when each part is working properly, makes the body grow so that it builds itself up in love.

Note that God has given gifts, in the form of people (prophets, evangelists, pastors, and teachers), to the church for the express purpose of equipping. While the leadership is certainly involved in doing the ministry, the leadership was never designed to do it alone. God expects the leaders to equip and He expects the people to want equipping. That is how effective, God-honoring ministry works. Survey your congregation. Ask them questions like these:

- If your friend secretly told you that he has a pornography problem, what would you say and do next?

- If a couple in your church confessed that they were contemplating divorce, then what would you do?

- What would you say to your friend whose parents were recently killed in a car accident?

- What would you tell your friend with a wife and three children the day after he lost his job?

- What would you do if you learned that your best friends, the ones you thought had it all together, argue and scream at one another on a regular basis?

In our experience, the vast majority of church folks don't know what they would say or do. In fact, some might do absolutely nothing. These responses from our dear folks are not necessarily their fault. Maybe they have not been equipped to deal with problems like these.

In addition, notice the warning in Ephesians 4:14—this equipping is to help prevent believers from being vulnerable to "every wind of doctrine... human cunning...deceitful schemes." Many believers, at least for a time, are susceptible to unbiblical ideas. They are easily swayed by human opinions. For example, when they are told by others it's okay to live together before you get married. Or they are told they should seek a divorce because their marriage is just not working out. We are talking about the kind of advice that people in our church receive that has nothing to do with Jesus, the gospel, or the Word of God. All too often there are churchgoers who take action according to unbiblical advice they hear from others. Counseling and counseling training helps to overcome people's tendency to believe whatever they hear. It helps them to stand firm in the grace of Christ even in the midst of competing voices. It helps them to run to the rock that is higher than they are when they have people telling them different things.

Notice as well that Ephesians 4 explains that everyone in the church should be growing and maturing in order to properly contribute to the body. For those who still want to believe that the pulpit is sufficient for making this happen, it is time to wake up. We have preached thousands of sermons, so we are not enemies of the sermon; we believe in the strong proclamation of the Word. But we also recognize that many of the people who raise their hands in worship on Sunday morning raise their hands in anger Tuesday night. Many of those who close their eyes and sing great songs of the faith on Sunday morning close their eyes and sing music contrary to the gospel on Thursday afternoon. The same man who has heard dozens of times that he is supposed to love his wife like Christ loves the church spends his days loving himself and demanding his wife love him too. The parents who speak eloquently about legalism and hypocrisy on Sunday morning are legalistic and hypocritical themselves.

Somewhere, somehow there is a disconnect between what people say they believe and how they live. Maybe that is one of the reasons Paul's ministry was both public and in homes (Acts 20). Maybe the struggle from theology to practical living is a bit larger than many of us are willing to concede. We have to take into consideration that some of God's children will grow as they should through the ministries of the church and others will need more personal time and attention.

The Maturing of God's People—Colossians 1:28-29

Paul develops this equipping ministry concept further in Colossians 1:28-29: "Him we proclaim, warning everyone and teaching everyone with all wisdom, that we may present everyone mature in Christ. For this I toil, struggling with all his energy that he powerfully works within me."

Note first that there is urgency in this text. Observe the number of times that "everyone" is used. This urgency is also seen in the phrase "struggling with all his energy." Paul does not rely on his own strength, but on the power of Christ in him. It is with this energy that God supplies that Paul is able to carry on his ministry of proclamation, warning, and teaching. To say it another way, there are some things that just have to be done *now*. They cannot wait. They are too important to be put on the back burner. For Paul, there was a mission to accomplish that demanded a level of urgency.

We also notice that Paul was focused. He had a clear goal, and he would not veer to the right or to the left from it. We can't help but wonder how many emails Paul would have skipped over, or how current he would have been with the news of the day, or even how vigorously he would be rooting for his favorite sports teams or athletes. Our ability to have information quickly is both a blessing and a curse. Our ability to function in a fast-paced society sometimes encourages us to focus on nothing of lasting value, just running from one temporal thing to the next.

Just as we saw in Matthew and Ephesians, so it is also here—the mission involves the maturing of God's people. We should never forget that we are in the disciple-making business, and disciples are to grow up. They are to mature. They are to learn how to skillfully navigate through our broken world with a godliness that shines like a city on a hill. Maturity is a work of the Lord, and the Lord often uses us to accomplish this task. He allows us to meet, to talk about life and about the Word, and works in and through us.

Our point in considering all three of these passages is that the mission God has given us implies maturity, teaching, and completeness. Bob Kellemen, in his book *Equipping Counselors for Your Church*, wisely calls the first chapter "More than Counseling: Catching God's Vision for the Entire Church."[2] His point, and ours, is that biblical counseling is part of the way that maturity, teaching, and completeness occur within the body of Christ. We believe that throughout Scripture, this involved both a public and private ministry of the Word: a ministry of proclamation and a face-to-face ministry around the Word.[3]

God desires that we have a ministry that is effective both when things are going well and when sin and suffering have penetrated the camp. The methodological approach given in the Scripture is multifaceted, and so must be our ministry. When the wheels come off, there must be a counseling ministry available to help people return to a functional and vibrant part of the body of Christ (Galatians 6:1-5). When the wheels are shaking, there should be personal ministries to help folks tighten the lug nuts. When the wheels are solid, there should be ministry to others.

In addition, there is clearly an evangelistic call in Matthew. Churches may talk about evangelism, but counseling offers a tremendous opportunity for folks to do evangelism rather than talk about doing evangelism. When an unbeliever seeks biblical counseling, it's an opportunity to present Christ as the answer to their needs. Instead of us going to them and giving them a message they don't want, our non-Christian counselees come wanting an explanation for the challenges they are facing in their lives. They are coming on our turf and wanting our answers because no one else has been able to provide satisfactory answers to their deepest questions.

The mission of disciple-making, winning, baptizing, teaching, and maturing people is a huge task. It is a task that God has asked His children to work toward. While we always recognize our dependence on the Lord's work, we also get busy working at the mission. In our judgment, a church that counsels all the time and in every ministry is seeking to fulfill that God-given mission.

The Importance of Process in Fulfilling the Great Commission

Our goal is to demonstrate that our mission requires a private ministry as well as a public one. We hope that you agree that *being* a church that *is* a counseling ministry is part of the fulfillment of the Great Commission. We hope you understand that part of the evangelistic mission can be accomplished through counseling and that part of teaching, completing, and maturing followers of Jesus is being there to help minister the Word during difficult times.

But in fairness, you also know that understanding something and doing something are not the same. So the remainder of this chapter will describe how a church goes about the *process* of being a counseling ministry and using counseling as a tool to help fulfill the great commission.

Commitment to Biblical Counseling from Every Level of Leadership, Especially the Top

Regardless of your church's leadership structure, for a church to become a counseling ministry, there must be support from the top. The areas that the leadership values will be discussed from the pulpit, they will be funded by the church budget, they will be celebrated during church family gatherings, they will be discussed in small groups, and they will be reflected in how individual families talk about their church at work, school, and in their neighborhood.

So if a church wants to be known as a missions church, then missions will be discussed, funded, and celebrated. If a church wants to be known as having the coolest music on the planet, then music will be discussed, funded, and celebrated. You get the point—your church culture will be driven by the leadership, and more specifically, by the pulpit. If the leadership is interested in developing a counseling ministry, then training, support, and funding will be available. Teachers and leaders say a lot of things, but it is their heart that is adopted by those who follow them. People understand the passions of their leaders. If personal ministry is not a passion of the leadership, then being a counseling ministry is not going to occur.

So what about the situations in which the top leadership will not drive biblical counseling, but it is supportive of letting a segment of the church do biblical counseling? In cases such as this, one changes the expectations, influences graciously, and trusts in the sovereign Lord. Being a biblical counseling church is not likely in cases like this, but having a vibrant counseling ministry through which people are won to Christ and believers are growing by overcoming sin and trusting in the midst of suffering can still happen.

If you are in this situation, here are three things you can do: First, thank God for any counseling ministry that you do have. It is much better to have something than it is to have nothing. Second, share stories of the Lord's work in people's lives with the leadership team. It may be possible to invite counselees to speak to the church family, a Sunday school class, an adult Bible fellowship, or a small group, and share what God is doing in their lives. As you do so, you are giving God glory by allowing them to lift high the name of Jesus. Third, graciously encourage the leadership team to receive training themselves, to be actively involved in counseling, to give opportunities for further testimonies of God's amazing grace.

Recruit Individuals to Serve and Provide Training

Paul reminds us in 1 Corinthians 12 that every part of the body is important. Practically, this means that some people could serve as counselors, and others should be serving the body of Christ in other ways. In our situation, there are two ways that counselors join our formal counseling team. Sometimes we see individuals who possess a level of giftedness with the Word and with people, and we will pursue them directly. We ask them to consider serving in personal one-on-one ministry. In other cases, we provide some initial counseling training to a number of folks and see who "bubbles up" from that group. Who is attentive? Who seems to be developing a passion for counseling? Who seems to have the tools necessary to minister effectively on a personal basis? In other words, we are intentional about the individuals who should be equipped.

Once the potential counselors are identified and given initial training, then a second phase of counseling preparation begins. In our ministry, we use the

National Association of Nouthetic Counselors' (NANC) certification process as a training guide because they are one of the few groups that has a long-standing record of certifying biblical counselors. They require that trainees read quality counseling material so that they are familiar with solid biblical counseling literature.[4] The counseling and theology exams ensure that all our counselors are able to articulate basic evangelical doctrine and have an understanding of biblical counseling and the counseling process. And at the final stage of the process, which in our opinion is the most valuable, trainees are paired up to co-counsel with an experienced counselor for a period of time. We directly supervise their counseling and give them suggestions for improvement. Only after our potential counselor has completed NANC certification and has received approval from our pastors does a person join our formal counseling team.

So now what? You have a church leadership that supports the ministry at every level, encourages people to get involved, and recruits and trains those God has gifted to serve in personal ministry of the Word.

A System in Place that Makes Counseling Available to the Church Family Without an Unhealthy Stigma

Dealing with terminology is one of the challenges to being a counseling ministry. After all, some people are intimidated by the word *counseling*. They think counseling is only for those individuals who are facing a major crisis or who are mentally disturbed. In reality, counseling, as we have defined it in this book, is for everyone. So, how do you lose the stigma of counseling?

First, talk about counseling, sounding out the stereotypes and associations to the word. Clarify what you mean and don't mean. Often a word takes on a different meaning for someone after you talk it through. Let me (Rob) give you an example:

The first time I saw John Piper's book *Desiring God*, I was turned off by the subtitle: *Meditations of a Christian Hedonist*. I did not know John or his ministry. Nor did I look through the book. What I "knew" was that hedonism was bad. It is kind of like nasty medicine. At this point I have to say that Mary Poppins is a liar—there *is* some medicine that goes down hard no matter how much sugar you put with it. The term *Christian Hedonism* sounded like an oxymoron. It sounded like a medicine that could not be made tolerable. But later, when I took the time to read the book, I learned that John was trying to redeem the notion of hedonism. He was redefining it from a biblical perspective. Once I understood that, I appreciated his work and all that *Desiring God* was teaching and trying to accomplish.

Some people might perceive the word *counseling* the same way I originally perceived the term *Christian Hedonism*. Perhaps they think it involves lying on a couch, looking at ink splotches, or even the Bob Newhart "Stop it!" approach. But counseling is actually a theologically rich and deeply personal ministry founded on the Word of God and dependent on the work of the Lord. As you talk about counseling in this manner, the idea of counseling will begin to lose its stigma.

Second, be transparent about your own faults. While you want to avoid talking about your faults too much, there are incredible ministry opportunities for ministry that open up when people know you have struggles in your life as well. Space limitations prohibit going into more detail on this, but the book of Hebrews explains that both the ministry of the Old Testament high priests and the high priestly ministry of Jesus are based on a "weakness" argument. In other words, they were in the perfect position to minister to others because they understood the weaknesses of the people they were serving. When people know that you struggle, they will be less afraid to share their own struggles. They will sense you'll be slow to judge and quick to be compassionate.

Third, encourage those who have received counseling to refer others to the counseling ministry. When one person in your church receives help and tells one of their friends, that helps to diminish the stigma.

In these ways, your church culture can move from a "counseling is only for really messed up people, and I am not one of those" to a "everyone needs counseling of some kind, and praise God there are people who can offer that counsel on the basis of Scripture."

A System in Place that Makes Counseling Available to Your Community

A church that is interested in *being* a biblical counseling church will, at some point, develop a counseling ministry that is available to the community. In our case, we decided to offer counseling to our community free of charge on Monday afternoons and evenings. Our primary source of counselees is through word-of-mouth recommendations, but we also attempt to advertise our counseling services enough so that people in our town know we are here. As long as a person in our town is willing to allow us to talk to them from the Bible, then we are happy to meet with them.

The system we use is quite simple. First, people who want to receive counsel call our office, and we explain the type of counseling we offer, the times we do the counseling, and then ask if we can send them some basic information for them to read, fill out, and return to us.

Second, we fit them into an available time slot, recognizing that some counselees will need to be counseled either by a person with experience in a certain area or by one of our more mature counselors. In other words, we attempt to match counselees with counselors in a way that encourages the counseling will go well.

Third, we have the counselees begin their appointments, and the process goes on from there. Again, it's a rather simple setup, and counselees know up front we will offer counsel from Scripture.

Here are some of the benefits of having a community-based counseling center:

One, it can serve as a means of evangelism into the community. Some of our counselees are now in our church because the Lord drew them to us at one of their lowest moments and we were the ones who were there to help them. The waters of our church's baptismal tank have been sloshed around repeatedly by former counselees who have given their lives to Christ.

Two, it can serve as a tool for church growth. Some believers live as though church is not very important. Their Christianity is weak. And when trials or difficulties come along, because they haven't grown in spiritual maturity, they aren't sure how to respond. Many of our counselees fit in this category. Some of these folks may have even stopped going to church for several years, then returned because someone ministered to them during some dark moments in their life.

Three, it provides us with the opportunity to be a friend to other churches. Not long ago a couple asked us to counsel them. We soon discovered that they were members at a sister church. We contacted their pastors, and their pastors asked that we stop counseling until they had time to talk to the couple first. In the end, the elders at that church asked if we could be involved in the counseling. In other words, we had the opportunity to encourage and help a couple with the blessings of their church. Instead of creating a rift, the counseling ministry was able to come alongside a sister church and offer assistance.

Four, it helps the entire church to cultivate an outreach mentality. As a church family sees the effectiveness of offering biblical counseling to our community, it will respond more readily and eagerly to other community outreach events sponsored by the church.

To Him Be Glory in the Church and in Christ Jesus

It is a joy and privilege to carry out the mission that Christ gave, in part, by *being* a counseling ministry and not simply having one. It is a mission worthy of careful thought, and worthy of our wholehearted involvement, time, energy, and financial resources. It is taking the message of Jesus and putting it on a hill for all to see. As we carry on this vital work, we cling to the promise found in Matthew 16:18—"I will build my church, and the gates of hell shall not prevail against it"—as well as the promise in Ephesians 3:20-21: "Now to him who is able to do far more abundantly than all that we ask or think, according to the power at work within us, to him be *glory in the church and in Christ Jesus* throughout all generations, forever and ever. Amen" (emphasis added).

The Health of the Church and Biblical Counseling

Deepak Reju and Mark Dever

Rob was overwhelmed, and for a few minutes, he just stared at the thousands of people who surrounded him. He was in the middle of a refugee camp, and the needs were well beyond his worst nightmares. The State Department officials, humanitarian relief organizations, and medical staff were all competent and extremely hard workers, but the needs were still overwhelming. There was far too much for them to handle on their own.

To some degree, as a counselor, you can relate to this, right? You are in a daily battle to care for people's needs, distress, and suffering. Yet the sheer volume of folks who struggle, and the extreme nature of their difficulties, at times can be overwhelming for you. You have a sea of people sitting just outside your door who need help. They call, email, and text. Their requests and demands are constant and unyielding.

That's the problem. The million-dollar question is, What's the solution?

Here is our answer: *Let the church fight this battle with you.* Don't take this on by yourself. Imagine a church in which the members work *together* to meet these overwhelming needs. The person assigned the role of counselor is not the only one caring for all these struggling people; the church *as a whole* is working to build one another up in love and unity.

Is this really possible? Could you teach the people in your church to care for one another? It is possible if your church is *healthy.* We want to help you think about what a local church's counseling ministry might look like when the church as a whole is healthy.

Picture a symphony. Counseling in a healthy church is like being a conductor in an orchestra. You conduct healthy Christians to make beautiful music together. The "musicians" listen to the conductor and to one another. They coordinate their playing to produce harmonious, inspiring music—a musical masterpiece!

Most counselors never get to the point of conducting, but instead get bogged down in the trenches. They do their best to handle all the problems that come at them every day. But the weight and burden of caring for *all* these people is at times just too much. What if we said it doesn't have to be that way? What if members of your church could partner with you to care for struggling Christians? What if they were committed to doing spiritual good for each other? What if they were willing to step into the messy parts of the Christian life and to try their best to help out? What if they were serious about loving one another and building one another up? As a counselor, do you believe that this is even possible—that church members and leaders would really desire to share this burden with you?

You don't have to fight counseling battles alone. If your church is healthy, it is definitely possible for the people in the congregation to counsel one another with the Word. Church leaders and church members can come alongside of you to help you care for struggling Christians. Counselors who go at it alone forsake one of God's greatest means of change: a loving, unified, self-sacrificial church.

If we've sufficiently gotten your attention, then read on. But before we can get the people in a church to care for one another, we have to first understand what a healthy church is.

What Is a Healthy Church?

A healthy church is one in which each member lovingly submits to the good of the whole. Under the ministry of God's Word, they strive for unity. In the strength of the Spirit, they pursue spiritual growth together. With a growing awareness of their sins, they are willing to gently confront and live transparently with one another. They learn and grow, forgive quickly, walk patiently with one another, pray for humility, and wait expectantly for the Savior to return.

Paul writes in Ephesians 4:11-16:

He gave the apostles, the prophets, the evangelists, the shepherds and teachers, to equip the saints for the work of ministry, for building up the body of Christ, until we all attain to the unity of the faith and of the knowledge of the Son of God, to mature manhood, to the measure of the stature of the fullness of Christ, so that we may no longer be children, tossed to and fro by the waves and carried about by every wind of doctrine, by human cunning, by craftiness in deceitful schemes. Rather, speaking the truth in love, we are to grow up in every way into him who is the head, into Christ, from whom the whole body, joined and held together by every joint with which it is equipped, when each part is working properly, makes the body grow so that it builds itself up in love.

Pastor-shepherds pray, preach God's Word, exhibit Christlikeness in personal relationships, and pour themselves into people. As they do this, they equip believers "for the work of ministry"—church members use their gifts to build one another up for the sake of the common good (1 Corinthian 12:7; 1 Peter 4:10). Paul uses a body metaphor to describe the building up of the church. Just as a body grows and develops, so also should the church. The end goal is "mature manhood" (Ephesians 4:13). Maturity is marked by believers growing up into "the stature of the fullness of Christ" (verse 13). As pastor-shepherds preach and teach the truth about Christ (Ephesians 4:21), the church grows as it strives to be like Christ.

Christ is the head of the church, so He will lead, guide, and direct the body. He will supply what is needed for His people's spiritual growth. In Colossians 2:19, Paul describes Christ as the head, "from whom the whole body, nourished and knit together through its joints and ligaments, grows with a growth that is from God."

Each member has an interdependent role to play, so if one selfishly overperforms or lazily underperforms, the body will not function properly. Church life is not a selfish striving for what I want; it is about a local body of believers growing in Christ *together*, with each member lovingly submitting to the good of the whole. As the church follows Christ, it grows and builds itself up in love as each part does its work.

If you were to survey a group of Christians and ask about the characteristics of a healthy church, they would probably come up with a list of traits that no one would dispute. A church should be loving, unified, missions-minded, prayerful, giving, self-sacrificial, and worshipful. But is that all that is needed to create a healthy church? The Bible describes for us a number of practices that contribute to church health, which we'll now examine. A good analogy to keep in mind is this: If we're trying to maintain a healthy *physical* body, we would pursue a balanced diet, exercise, getting enough sleep, and so on. So what should we pursue to cultivate a healthy *church* body?

Here are nine practices that help to build a healthy church:

1. *Church health centers on God's Word.* Since the very beginning, when God spoke the world into existence, men and women have been called to live according to God's Word. More than just a book, God's Word was made flesh as the Son of God came to earth to dwell among us. Man does not live by bread alone, but by every word that comes from the mouth of God. Thus, the expositional teaching of Scripture is of primary importance. As we explain what the Bible says and vigorously apply it to people's lives, God's Word convicts, converts, builds up, and sanctifies God's people (John 17:17; 1 Thessalonians 2:13; Hebrews 4:12; 1 Peter 1:23). Ultimately, success in a church is measured by faithfulness to God's Word.

2. *A healthy church is grounded in biblical theology.* Biblical theology is theology that is thoroughly Bible-based. It reflects right thoughts about God from His Word, and not just our own opinions.

3. *A healthy church is gospel-centered.* The gospel is the power of God for the salvation of everyone who believes, and it is the only way for sinful people to be reconciled to a holy God. Everything in a church's life flows from the gospel.

4. *A healthy church thinks biblically about evangelism.* Christians tell non-Christians the good news about what Christ has done to save sinners. A healthy church fosters an eagerness to tell the gospel to the lost.

5. *A healthy church thinks biblically about conversion.* As God uses His people to communicate His Word to lost souls, lives are changed. God gives life to the spiritually dead (Ephesians 2:5) and sight to the spiritually blind (2 Corinthian 4:3-6). In conversion, people repent of sin (Mark 1:15) and trust in Christ (Romans 3:21-26).

6. *A healthy church thinks biblically about spiritual growth.* When placed in the fertile soil of God's Word, the new believer will grow (Philippians 1:6). Spiritual growth is a normative expectation for Christians in healthy churches.

7. *Healthy churches are filled with committed Christians.* Christians should commit to attending, loving, serving, giving, and submitting to a local church. Church membership is a conscious commitment to a local body of believers that ties a person to others. Much more than just a casual association, the New Testament refers to some people being on the inside and others on the outside of a church (2 Corinthians 2:5-7).

8. *Healthy churches are willing to remove unrepentant sinners in order to preserve their gospel witness to the world.* Sadly, there are times when a person refuses to repent of sin and the church can no longer affirm his profession of faith. The healthy church will remove him from membership and participation in the Lord's Supper (Matthew 18:15-20; 1 Corinthians 5:1-13).

9. *Healthy churches are committed to raising up godly men to preach, teach, guide, and shepherd.* Churches should not be led by a power-hungry, CEO-style pastor, but by a plurality of godly, qualified men called elders. God gives these pastor-elder-teachers as gifts to the church to lead and guide her.

How does that sound to you? When a church is healthy, the instruments harmonize and the music is resplendent. Word-centered, gospel-saturated, spiritually growing and committed Christians tell unbelievers about the truth and hold one another accountable for sin. They pour themselves into each other,

244 CHRIST-CENTERED BIBLICAL COUNSELING

and are quick to forgive and eager to reconcile. Believers and leaders are Word-directed and Spirit-filled. Those are the marks of a healthy church.

But is all of this just a fairy tale? Is a healthy church too good to be true? No. The Bible says it is possible.

Why is a healthy church so hard to imagine? Probably because we are so accustomed to seeing *unhealthy* churches. In Ephesians 4:14, Paul describes unhealthy churches as populated by immature and gullible children who often fall into trouble and are very unstable. He compares them to a ship being tossed to and fro by waves and carried by the wind. Unhealthy churches are full of immature Christians with erratic spiritual lives, who are led astray by bad doctrine, poor teaching, human ideas, and deceitful methods.

Churches become unhealthy when the people are exposed to watered-down, moralistic, and Christless teaching that exalts self-help and human wisdom over God's Word. Leaders spend more time studying business practices, marketing strategies, and church-growth fads than they do studying God's Word. Members are more interested in lauding their gifts and socializing than serving one another. Unity is difficult to achieve because everybody is a consumer, except perhaps the pastor, who is expected to do all the work of ministry. Faithfulness to God's Word is irrelevant; if the church is growing numerically, then it considers itself successful.

If this sounds familiar to you, it may be because you spent some time in a church like this. The cacophony of sounds, the discord among the members, a lack of self-sacrificial, loving servants, the disharmony of the congregation, the worldliness of the leadership, and the shallow teaching contributed to a church that looks and sounds more like the world and less like what is described in God's Word (James 4:4). Surely there is a better way to do church.

What Difference Does Church Health Make for Counseling?

A healthy church is not some utopian paradise, something that is only possible in heaven. A healthy church is both biblical and possible this side of glory, and having such a church can make a tremendous difference in your counseling ministry.

Word-Centered People Are Better Prepared to Face Real Life and to Counsel Others

When I (Deepak) worked in private practice, I saw counseling clients from several local churches, some of whom had been taught well and firmly grounded in the Word, and others who had not. The Word-centered folks had an anchor that helped them remain stable in a fallen world; the rest were tossed to and fro by bad doctrine, poor teaching, and human fads, with no anchor to help secure them.

If a pastor and his leadership team are committed to teaching and applying God's Word, and making it central to everything in the life of the church, then God's Word will become foundational in the life of the believers (Matthew 7:24-27). Word-centered churches produce Word-centered people who are eager to share the Word with those around them who are struggling.

A continual diet of the Word satisfies, and it builds an appetite for more. The psalmist writes, "I will delight in your statutes; I will not forget your word" (Psalm 119:16), and "How sweet are your words to my taste, sweeter than honey to my mouth!" (verse 103). Popcorn and candy might taste good, but feed them to children at every meal and they'll get sick. They will not grow up to be healthy and strong. Similarly, shallow sermons entertain, but they don't produce spiritual vigor. Adults will never grow out of their spiritual immaturity. A healthy church that consistently feeds the Word to its people builds a bigger appetite for the Word. Members come to counseling eager to grow in Christ and to learn how the Word applies to their difficult circumstances.

Those who live on this kind of diet will grow in their discernment and understanding of life. "Everyone who lives on milk is unskilled in the word of righteousness, since he is a child. But solid food is for the mature, for those who have their powers of discernment trained by constant practice to distinguish good from evil" (Hebrews 5:13-14; cf. Psalm 119:130). Christians who constantly train themselves with the Word in the context of a healthy church will enter counseling more capable of discerning the good and evil in a situation.

Word-centered people have a better sense of what to avoid and where to go. Unlike the proverbial fool, who consistently gets into trouble, the wise person grounded in God's Word is protected against sin, folly, and evil. "How can a young man keep his way pure? By guarding it according to your word" (Psalm

119:9; cf. verse 11). The Word steers this young man away from evil, and illumines the right path. "Your word is a lamp to my feet and a light to my path" (verse 105). Word-centered people who enter counseling will be more eager to fight sin and follow the guidance set out in Scripture. Because they know more of the depth of their sin, they are more willing to allow other church members to help them stay on that right path.

Word-centered people have more hope. The psalmist, writing under difficult circumstances, finds hope in God's Word: "You are my hiding place and my shield; I hope in your word" (Psalm 119:114). "I rise before dawn and cry for help; I hope in your words" (verse 147). Word-centered people enter counseling with a greater sense of hope because they trust in God's Word, and they are more likely to share the hope of God's Word with others who are struggling.

Word-centered people are more capable of correcting and training one another. Paul writes to Timothy, "All Scripture is breathed out by God and profitable for teaching, for reproof, for correction, and for training in righteousness, that the man of God may be complete, equipped for every good work" (2 Timothy 3:16-17). Scripture is God's Word, literally His words "breathed." These words help us to teach, correct, exhort, build up, and direct one another. The Word-centered person is more likely to receive this correction with humility and a genuine desire to change.

Word-centered people in a healthy church are hungry, hopeful, better able to avoid evil, more discerning, and better equipped to grow in godliness. What if someone like this showed up in your office for help? What if, rather than being recalcitrant, they sought counsel, adhered to wisdom, desired to love wisely, and were eager for truth?

Don't get us wrong—even a healthy church has its share of messed-up folks. After all, what is a church? It's not a place for the self-righteous, but a hospital for sick, weary, discouraged sinners. Yet the percentage of people who live Word-centered lives is much greater in healthier churches. Your counseling ministry can be much more of a delight (and less of a burden) as you counsel in a healthy church. As a counselor, you need to ask: How grounded is my church in the Word? Do I see the teaching ministry of the church transforming the lives of our members? How can I help my church (and not just my counseling ministry) become more Word-centered?

Committed Church Members Will Be Involved

When Betty shares with Debbie that she is struggling, what does Debbie do? Does she offer to pray for her yet do nothing more? Does she get overwhelmed and send her friend to the doctor? Does she call the pastor and pass off the problem to him?

Unfortunately, Debbie is not unlike many of the members in your church. Too many Christians today have an expectation that only pastors and professional counselors are qualified to care for struggling members. They assume that all of the difficult issues in Christian discipleship (such as eating disorders, marital conflict, depression, suicide, family conflict, and addictions) are issues that "average" Christians can't help with. They believe that such difficulties should be handed over to the pastor or counselor with specialized training.

Yet the Bible describes Christians being involved in one another's lives even when things are difficult:

- "A new commandment I give to you, that you love one another: just as I have loved you, you also are to love one another. By this all people will know that you are my disciples, if you have love for one another" (John 13:34-35).

- "Love one another with brotherly affection. Outdo one another in showing honor" (Romans 12:10).

- "Owe no one anything, except to love each other, for the one who loves another has fulfilled the law" (Romans 13:8).

- "Accept one another, then, just as Christ accepted you, in order to bring praise to God" (Romans 15:7 NIV).

- "I myself am satisfied about you, my brothers, that you yourselves are full of goodness, filled with all knowledge and able to instruct one another" (Romans 15:14).

- "...with all humility and gentleness, with patience, bearing with one another in love..." (Ephesians 4:2).

- "Be kind to one another, tenderhearted, forgiving one another, as God in Christ forgave you" (Ephesians 4:32).

- "Encourage one another and build one another up, just as you are doing" (1 Thessalonians 5:11).

These passages are speaking to Christians, and the general direction of all of these texts is to oblige Christians to love one another—to be devoted to each other; to honor and accept each other; to be patient, kind, compassionate, and forgiving; and even to instruct one another.

In a healthy church, the members have an expectation that it is *normal* for believers to care for and counsel one another with the Word. It is *normal* to be invested in each other's lives. No one has to give them permission to initiate love for one another and be invested in each other's lives. There is no counseling program to sign up for, no formal training that must be done, and no list of formally approved steps that must be followed in order to help someone who is struggling.

Granted, most Christians would look at the list of problems in a church and run the other direction! Fear, or the possibility of being overwhelmed, or a desire to not get involved in the messy things all keep average Christians from trying to help. But there is no excuse. A Christian who is armed with the Word and the Spirit can always do something to help.

As a counselor, you need to ask: Do the members in my church expect that all the difficult problems will be handled by the pastor or professional counselors? Are they too quick to refer prospective counselees to someone who is more professionally trained? Even if the situation requires the help of a pastor or counselor, are the members of your church still willing to stay involved? Or are they too scared to get involved in the messy parts of Christian discipleship?

Leaders Will Shepherd

Several pastors helped to counsel a young lady who visited our church, and she said, "The leaders in my home church did a lot, but they weren't involved in my life." That's not unusual. Many pastors would rather preach God's Word and keep their distance than invest in a personal, one-on-one counseling ministry. Most pastors counsel because they have to, not because they want to, and if they could, they would rather pass that responsibility off to someone else. But should that be the mind-set of a pastor? Peter writes:

I exhort the elders among you, as a fellow elder and a witness of the sufferings of Christ, as well as a partaker in the glory that is going to be revealed: shepherd the flock of God that is among you, exercising oversight, not under compulsion, but willingly, as God would have you; not for shameful gain, but eagerly; not domineering over those in your charge, but being examples to the flock. And when the chief Shepherd appears, you will receive the unfading crown of glory (1 Peter 5:1-4).

Pastors are to be shepherds—those who daily care for and tend to the needs of the sheep in their flock. They are to look to Christ, who is the Chief Shepherd, and model wise shepherding to others. Christ doesn't superficially teach His sheep from a distance; He knows His sheep and His sheep know Him (John 10:14-15). Christ doesn't just deal casually with His sheep; He paid the ultimate price by willingly laying down His life for them (John 10:11). Unlike those who don't care for the sheep and run away when trouble comes, the Good Shepherd endures through good times and bad (John 10:12-13).

Pastors in healthy churches recognize that active, deliberate, loving shepherding is a fundamental part of their job description. Their willingness to counsel the sheep and to be personally involved can make a tremendous difference in the lives of those who are hurting. Anyone (whether paid or lay) who serves as a pastor should recognize their biblical responsibility to care for, instruct, and shepherd the sheep. Pastors shouldn't do this because they must, but because they are more than willing, as God wants them to be (1 Peter 5:2). They are eager to let their lives serve as godly examples (Hebrews 13:7) and set godly expectations for the flock under their care (2 Peter 5:3).

In healthy churches, the pastor's life, not just his words, sets the tone for the church. He is an example for others of what careful, wise, loving counsel and care might look like, both in times of crisis and in daily self-sacrificial living. If the pastor doesn't want to counsel and care for the members, how could we ever expect church members to want to do this? If pastors are unwilling to be self-sacrificial with their time and lives, how will members ever learn to care for one another? A healthy church culture of counseling and care is built on the backs of humble, godly men who set the example for their congregation. Their lives will model what Christian living should look like.

Counselor, ask yourself: Do your church leaders care about counseling? How invested are they in the lives of the members? How well do they know their sheep, and how well do the sheep know them? What can you do to help them become better counselors? If they don't care about shepherding and counseling, how can you help them grow in their desire to care for the sheep?

How Do I Get Health?

As a counselor, lay person, or pastor, you might be thinking, *My church is not healthy. What do I do? How can I bring change? How can we become a healthy church?*

Think Corporately

One of the biggest problems in counseling today is what we call the silo effect. For decades, the model for counseling has been built around the one-on-one engagement of counselor and counselee. A sinner cares for a sinner, helping to solve problems, provide direction, and give some sense of hope, but counselors often don't have the time or energy to think of care outside of the bounds of the counseling session. Most counselors think *individually.* They run their own show, or even if they are part of a counseling center, they spend most of their time in one-on-one settings.

Could counseling be more than just one-on-one? What would it look like to go beyond the counseling office and to have an effect on the entire congregation?

In healthy churches, counselors don't think only about the individual in front of them, but strategize about the church *as a whole.* How do we change the culture of the church? How do we make it normal for all Christians to assume a responsibility to counsel the Word? How do we help the leadership grow toward an eagerness to counsel and shepherd?

When I (Mark) first hired Deepak, I told him that 80 percent of his work should be devoted to individual counseling and 20 percent should involve training of the congregation. But I also said that, in time, those numbers should reverse. Eventually, 20 percent of his efforts should be preoccupied with individual counseling, and 80 percent with equipping the congregation. As the Lord uses Deepak to raise up others who are competent to counsel, Deepak should be spending less time doing actual counseling and more time equipping members of the congregation to do the care themselves. If you are a pastor or counselor, could you do something like this in your church? What would it take to transform the entire culture of your church?

Build a Church Culture

The first step is to think about the church's culture of discipling and counseling. *Discipling* is a broader term that applies to the one-on-one Christ-centered mentoring that older Christians do with younger believers (cf. Titus 2). *Counseling* is a subset of discipleship and deals with the more problematic and difficult aspects of life to handle, like marital conflict, depression, eating disorders, addictions, self-harm, and suicidal thinking.

Every believer is expected to disciple someone and to be discipled, and is capable of doing so without any formal training. All they need is a willing spirit and a Bible. On the other hand, members may not know how to care for Christians who are struggling with more severe problems. Even if they are willing to help, they may not know what to do, what to say, or where to go in the Bible for help. While everyone has the ability to disciple or be discipled, counseling might require more guidance from pastors and counselors.

A Culture of Discipling

When a church has a culture of discipling, the whole personality of the church is one of making and caring for disciples. Discipling is in the DNA of the church. This is the way Christians expect to live and care for one another. Do the members of your church see it as normal to care for one another? If not, how can you help them live more proactively as disciplers?

Here are ways you can build a culture of discipling:

- *Emphasize a commitment to church membership.* Are the people in your church committed to the congregation? A commitment to the church, and not just a consumer mind-set, sets the foundation for disciple-making. A commitment to the church *as a whole* makes a difference in people being willing to sacrifice time and energy to invest in one another.

- *Teach an expectation of disciple-making and reinforce it.* For anything to change in your church, members must first be taught from God's Word. When Christians see the expectation coming from the pages of Scripture, their motivation will come from God's Word, and not just the pastor's exhortations. So teaching a biblical expectation for every member to be discipling is key to building a culture of disciple-making.

- *Create reproducible fruit.* Andy poured himself into Ryan when the latter was a young believer. While Andy discipled and cared for him, Ryan came to understand what Christian discipling should look like. Then Ryan was able to disciple Bob. In this way the disciple-making mind-set is not just taught, it is caught. Once it is taught and caught, it can be passed on to others.

- *Model discipleship in front of others.* As we mentioned earlier, church leaders need to set an example for discipling. They need to be willing to model one-on-one discipling, even if doing so comes at great cost.

- *Structure your services so they encourage discipleship.* Our Sunday evening services are not a miniature version of our Sunday morning services. Rather, we make it a time during which the church members share, encourage, exhort, teach, and most importantly pray for one another. I (Mark) will often share prayer requests like, "Let's have someone pray tonight that our members live with transparent relationships in which we are not scared to ask hard questions and be vulnerable," or "Let's pray that our members see it as normal to build their lives around a church."

We could tell you many other ways to build a culture of discipling in your church, but our goal here is not to give you a cookie-cutter recipe for success. No, the point is to encourage you to think about what would work best for you corporately. How can you build a culture in your church that nurtures the expectation that everyone is to be a disciple-maker?

A Culture of Biblical Counseling

The culture of counseling is built on the backbone of our commitment to membership and discipling. The logic goes this way:

- If Christians are committed to the church *as a whole*, then they will be more invested in discipling.

- If the members are faithful in discipling other Christians through Bible study, prayer, and mentoring, then they are more likely to deepen that involvement when things get messy in the lives of the people they're discipling.

If a culture of discipling is already in place in your church, the next obstacles you will often face are fear and lack of confidence when disciplers face the unpleasant and complicated parts of their friend's lives. Even if your members are regularly involved in the lives of others, they often have a knee-jerk reaction when they run across the difficult problems in the Christian life. They call the pastor. They give the person the name of a good counselor. They offer to pray. But honestly, they are just too scared and insecure to do any more.

That's where deliberate investment and training of members of the congregation can be a big help in dispelling the fears and building the confidence of the members.[1] A combination of public teaching and private small-group instruction can help instill the basic concepts of biblical counseling, like a theology of sanctification and a theology of care. You might think, *I barely have time to counsel; how am I supposed to write and teach others?* Fortunately, a combination of both self-published curriculums (John Henderson's *Equipped to Counsel: A Training Course in Biblical Counseling*) and more formal curriculums (CCEF's core curriculum series, including *How People Change* and *Instruments in the Redeemer's Hands*) have become available over the last few years. Most of these resources are user-friendly and very easy to understand. If you have a few mature Christians in your congregation, take them through a biblical counseling curriculum with the express goal of equipping them to teach it to others. Don't delay. Pick one of these resources and start investing in your church!

Be Proactive, Not Defensive

Most counseling ministries are characterized by a defensive posture—that is, you are putting out fires as they come to you. A husband is leaving his wife. A young man is struggling with a porn addiction. A young lady doesn't want to live anymore. And the list goes on and on.

The fires are real, and legitimately need your attention. However, if all you are doing is spending time with the struggling members of your church and you are not building proactively into your church's culture, then you are being shortsighted and limiting the effectiveness of your ministry.

How much time out of your schedule are the weak sheep consuming? Are you actively setting aside time to invest in the congregation as a whole? While it may seem costly at first (especially if your compassionate heart makes it hard for you to say no), over the long haul, taking the time to raise up a culture of discipleship and counseling can bear a lot of fruit.

Working at changing an entire church's culture, and not just a few individuals, is a long-term project. It takes patience and persistence. It's like building a symphony orchestra—it requires careful attention to all the parts so that in the end, the music is balanced and harmonious. It takes vision for you to go beyond the day-to-day to think about what might be possible in the future. It takes a growing hope that the church *as a whole*, and not just a few competent individuals, can make a difference. It takes a belief that God has not abandoned His bride, the church, but daily is building her up for the sake of His name.

Healthy Church, Better Counseling, Greater Impact

Healthy churches matter. They matter because healthy churches produce growing Christians. They matter because healthy churches produce more unity. They matter because suffering Christians are counseled and shepherded by leaders, counselors, and members alike. They matter because counseling doesn't just help a few, but the entire church. How does that sound to you? Sounds beautiful, doesn't it?

What would it mean for you to build a culture of discipling and counseling in your church? If you are a counselor, get out of your silo. Don't sell yourself short; build up the church as a whole. Don't be satisfied with just helping *a few* when you can start changing *the entire culture* of your church. Take out your conductor's baton and start conducting some beautiful music as the members of the church love one another and bear one another's burdens in Jesus' name.

The Personal, Private, and Public Ministry of the Word

Kevin Carson

Change. Amazing word, meritorious goal. Change is the goal, the objective, the target, the purpose of counseling. Often when people seek counseling, they desire some kind of change—in circumstances, in others, or in themselves. Thankfully, God provides a way for change. Jesus prayed that God would change people with the truth: "Sanctify them in the truth; your word is truth" (John 17:17). And not just any truth, but God's truth. Jesus used the word "sanctify," which has to do with God setting aside something as holy, to consecrate, dedicate, sanctify it.[1] In a world where not just people in the universe are broken but the universe itself is broken, sanctification means that the individual person changes in relationship to responsible personal choices in honoring God as well as in his response to the inevitable challenges associated with suffering.

God's goal is for every believer to become like Christ (Romans 8:29). Becoming like Christ involves the whole person—all one's character and conduct. This means when the believer makes a personal choice (where responsibility is evident) or personally responds to difficult circumstances (being sinned against, personal illness, financial difficulties, among various other pressures), the believer consciously chooses to respond as one who is set apart unto God.

Jesus, of course, is the perfect example of this in every way; He is the one believers emulate. This is possible only as the believer is under the influence of the Spirit and the Word, as Jesus asked the Father to sanctify or help people change through the truth, which is God's Word. Therefore, if life change is the context of counseling and the Bible presents the necessity for it, then pastors, counselors, friends, church members, and family members must by necessity learn how to minister the Word.

The anticipated benefits and practical outcomes of the ministry of God's Word in the believer's life are important to daily ministry, especially to biblical counselors as they serve other believers. God's Word, empowered by the Spirit in the life of the believer, is the beginning point of change. It just starts the process; change takes time and is not an event. Learning the Word and becoming efficient in meditating on it places the believer in the right location to enjoy its intended results. However, the results come only with practice and careful attention to one's personal relationships, where love abounds as one grows intimately with God in Christ through the gospel and consistent application of discernment. So the ministry of the Word is essential for each aspect of growth to take place as God intends.

Poor Attempts at Ministry of the Word

Clearly, ministry of the Word is important. That being the case, biblical counselors strive to minister God's Word with excellence. In the past, however, biblical counselors have received criticism regarding their practice. An honest look reveals that some of what claims to be biblical counseling is woefully lacking and does not meet the challenge of excellence at ministering the Word. The failures to minister the Word with excellence fall into three categories: those who counsel inaccurately, those who counsel incorrectly, and those who counsel inconsistently.

Some Minister the Word Inaccurately

Inaccurate counsel relates to the counselor's use of the Scriptures. Although most congregations expect the pastor or preacher to understand the text and explain it accurately, some counselors use the Bible with too little regard to accuracy. This may occur in one of several ways in the counseling process: taking verses out of context; proof-texting (where one finds a few words that sound good and fit what he wants to say but make for inaccurate use of the text); overgeneralization or overemphasis of a particular word, verse, point or theology; misinterpretation of the text; misapplication; and the list goes on. Although the counselor is using the Bible itself, it is in some way used inaccurately.[2]

Some Minister the Word Incorrectly

Incorrect ministry of the Word relates to those who incorrectly view the Scriptures and resultant change as something different than what they actually are. They use the Bible incorrectly because they see it for what it is not. There are three primary ways they misperceive the Bible: First, they fail to see and understand the sufficiency of Scripture (as discussed in chapter 6 by Steve Viars and Rob Green). Second, they use the Bible almost as if it were a magic wand, and use it with the expectation that upon hearing, memorizing, or quoting certain verses over and over, the counselee will instantly or automatically change. The counseling essentially comes down to this: "Take two verses and call me in the morning." However, ministry of the Word is more than just the quantity of verses, as if more is better; the counselor must understand the benefits of time, patience, and discernment in learning individual passages. The third way counselors use Scripture incorrectly is by viewing the Bible as a set of loosely held together verses (similar to an encyclopedia). They listen to the counselee share the problem, then turn to a concordance and plug in the right verse for the situation. It's almost like a counseling version of "Name That Tune."

Each of these incorrect views of Scripture misses two aspects of ministry of the Word. First, they miss the wisdom component of counseling on the part of the counselor. The counselor must take time to listen, reflect, and interpret what is said from the counselee in light of biblical wisdom. And second, the goal in counseling is to *minister* the Word, not merely *dispense* it. The counselor must take the time to clearly explain, illustrate, and apply the text for the counselee. When done accurately, this means the counselor will use a limited number of passages used in any given counseling session. It may be easy to think, *If one passage is good, two or three will be better.* However, one passage is all that is necessary if the counselor takes time to minister it effectively.

Some Minister the Word Inconsistently

Inconsistent counsel of the Word relates to the counselor's tendency to use a particular style or section of the Bible in the counseling process without balance of the whole. The Scriptures were written with built-in tension between texts and its resultant theology. For instance, some make the commands of Scripture the primary mode of counseling. Counseling has a "Just do it!" sound, where the counselees are challenged to go live obediently in their own power. Take the book of Ephesians, for an example. The counselor may counsel primarily from the ethical instructions in Ephesians (chapters 4–6), which includes many direct commands, and rarely, if ever, counsel from the thanksgiving/body section (chapters 1–3), which deals primarily with necessary foundational material related to one's position or union in Christ.

On the contrary side of this issue, however, some counselors may spend so much time in the narrative or wisdom literature portions of Scripture, or in the body of the epistles, that the counselees never understand explicitly what God wants them to do in a particular situation. The counselee has all the right commitments, appropriate motivation, and solid foundation, but still struggles in a particular instance of knowing how to change or what to do. This counseling can be fuzzy or unclear, even though it is true to the text. The challenge is to counsel with the whole counsel of God so that the counselee receives a good and appropriate balance of the biblical text.

Ministry of the Word Begins with How the Counselor Handles the Word

The desire of every biblical counselor should be to do ministry of the Word with excellence. And excellence begins with the way the counselor handles the text. If the Word of God is essential for change by the Spirit, and the counselor is the one responsible for choosing the passage, explaining it, and helping apply it, then the counselor must develop the skills that are necessary for understanding and applying the Bible with excellence. Paul wrote, "Do your best to present yourself to God as one approved, a worker who has no need to be ashamed, rightly handling the word of truth" (2 Timothy 2:15). It is contradictory to say that we are *biblical* counselors and that the Spirit of God uses the Scriptures to change people if we consistently get the Bible text wrong. Therefore, the counselor must understand and appreciate the basic differences between the meaning of a text and its significance.

Understanding Meaning

To minister the Word, we must begin in the text. The goal is to accurately know and communicate what the Bible text means. This process is referred to as *exegesis*—the process of discovering the author's intended meaning as communicated in and through the text.[3] The question to answer in any particular text is, What did the author intend to communicate to his original readers? He consciously wrote to communicate a specific message to the reader; that message is fixed in the text, does not change, and is discoverable with contextual clues.[4] This message is the meaning of the text.

There are no doubt a number of inherent difficulties to discovering the meaning of any text, such as genre (different categories of writing), culture, history, and language, among others. Even though exegesis is difficult, the hard work it requires is a necessary process so that we properly understand the meaning of the texts we are sharing in our ministry of the Word. Essentially, we want to know (1) what was said, (2) where it was said, (3) to whom it was said, and (4) why it was said.

Understanding Significance

Whereas there is only one meaning in any specific text, a meaning that is fixed and unchanging, there are any number of significances. Basically, significance captures the relationship between the specific passage as it is related to something else, such as a person, concept, or situation. It builds a connection between the truth as given to the intended audience and the truth as expressed in relationship to a contemporary reader or listener—in this case, our counselee. Often this is the area we call application, implication, or wisdom.[5]

The questions we can typically ask as we contemplate the significance of a passage are: (1) What is the relationship of the meaning to the counselee's situation? (2) What do these verses reveal about God—who He is or what He does? (3) What do these verses reveal about people—me, my counselee, people in general? (4) What should be done in response to this passage—what is explicit in the text? What is implicit? What looks wise as a result of the passage's meaning? (5) How does this passage help me in loving God or loving my neighbor? Now, there will be times when Bible passages have answers for some of the questions and not others.

Walter Kaiser provides a specific warning with regard to working on the significance of a passage: "It is important...to make certain that the consequent or implicit meaning that we attribute to a text is one that accurately reflects the fundamental truth or principle in the text, not a separate or different one."[6] His point is to be carefully observed. It is inappropriate for someone to draw an application or significance from a text where the fundamental truth being applied is inconsistent with the fundamental truth being taught to the original intended audience. The fundamental truth (the timeless truth, eternal truth, or central truth) of the passage is that truth which crosses all generations as intended by the original author.

Suppose we have a counselee who is experiencing marital difficulties. We consider with her Philippians 4:13: "I can do all things through him [Christ] who strengthens me." The fundamental truth is that by the power of Paul's union in Christ, he can be content in every situation regardless of the inherent difficulties. Paul's contentment is not based upon his sheer willpower; but instead, it is based upon the power of Christ in him. This can be applied in a variety of ways. Given the questions above: (1) Paul was in a tough circumstance in which it would have been easy to not be content, just as the counselee is also in a tough circumstance where contentment is not easy. (2) Christ provides her with strength in this incredibly difficult circumstance. (3) Her contentment is not based upon her own willpower; her contentment is by the power of Christ, who strengthens her. (4) She can be thankful for the strength Christ provides and go to Christ in prayer, demonstrating her dependency. (5) Her love and trust for God can grow because God has provided her strength to endure this difficulty. She also can focus on demonstrating Christ's love to her spouse through the strength Christ provides to her.

What would be inconsistent in terms of significance and meaning? If we were to tell her, "If you try hard enough, you can change your husband, because you can do all things in Christ." Or, if we were to suggest that she take a step of faith financially and go on a lengthy cruise with her husband to work on their marital difficulties if—after all, she can do all things through Christ.

Neither answer, however, is consistent with the fundamental truth in the text. These answers would be no more accurate than telling Christian athletes they can make a touchdown or score a free throw or win the game because they can do all things through Christ. The meaning (fundamental truth) and significance (relationship to the contemporary circumstance) must be congruent with each other to evade any of the errors discussed above in prooftexting or misapplication.

There are two general warnings to heed with regard to meaning and significance. First, we want to be very clear with the counselee about the point at which we transition from discussing meaning to discussing application/wisdom/significance. Mixing the two categories without distinction leads to confusion for the counselee. We do not want to lead a counselee to believe the significance of a particular passage is in fact its meaning. For instance, the Bible says for a husband to love his wife (Ephesians 5:25)—that is the meaning. Our suggestion for him to find ways to express his love for her—that is significance.

We also want to be careful not to mix our wisdom regarding a text with God's commands in a text. This will also lead the counselee to confusion. If the Bible commands it, the counselor has the authority to share it as a command. If it is the counselor's wisdom based off of a command, then the counselor needs to clearly identify it as a wisdom-suggestion. Using the same example as before, the Bible says for a husband to love his wife—that is the command. If needed, we may suggest for him to put the dirty clothes in the hamper (and not on the floor) as a demonstration of love—that is wisdom, and not a command.

Ministry of the Word in Day-to-Day Ministry

With a solid commitment to the importance of the ministry of the Word and a sincere desire to handle the biblical text with excellence, that brings us to what this looks like in day-to-day living. How do we take this essential component of biblical counseling and wed it with moment-by-moment ministry? In what ways can we expect to do our ministry in the life and practice of the local church?

Paul's labors at Ephesus demonstrates well what ministry of the Word looks like in day-to-day ministry. As Paul talks to the Ephesian elders for the final time of his life, he reminds them of his ministry to the church in their city (Acts 20:18-22). Here, Paul refers to three forms of ministry of the Word. First, he explains how he carefully evaluated his own heart for an appropriate motivation and response to tough circumstances in ministry (20:18-20). This infers the *personal ministry of the Word*—where Paul judges his own ministry against the characteristics of a Christlike follower. He determines that even in the midst of significant, life-threatening trials, he continued his labor as a servant of Christ with tears and in humility.[7]

The second and third forms of ministry are explicit: *public and private ministry of the Word.* Initially, Paul reminds the Ephesian elders that he gave them the truth; he ministered the Word. "I did not shrink from declaring to you anything that was profitable...from declaring to you the whole counsel of God" (20:20,27). So, Paul provided that which was helpful, the very Word of God. He also describes how he provided it—through preaching and teaching. And he further explains where he did it—in public and from house to house. He publicly ministered the Word in the synagogue and in the lecture hall of Tyrannus (Acts 19:8-9). He privately ministered the Word from house to house.

In Acts 20:31, we can see how seriously Paul took his task of ministering the Word: "for three years I did not cease night or day to admonish everyone with tears." The Word of God is crucial if we intend to benefit those to whom we minister. No matter what the *look* of our ministry (personal, private, or public), the Word of God cannot be divorced from our practice. The content (God's Word) is the vital link that creates continuity between the personal, private, and public ministry of the counsel of God. The form of ministry is the means to the necessary end—that is, the ministry of the Word. Yes, "Preach the Word" (2 Timothy 4:2). But also "Counsel the Word," and "Self-counsel/ live the Word."

The Personal Ministry of the Word

"Self-counsel/live the Word" relates to the personal ministry of the Word. It is often said among biblical counselors that in order to be a good biblical counselor, you must first be a good counselee. This statement reminds us that what we bring to the counseling moment in terms of our character and relationship with God is vitally important. More than in any other model of counseling, the biblical counselor's personal character serves as a litmus test to the authenticity of the counsel given. Paul realized this, and he encouraged others to not only examine his lifestyle, but also to imitate him (Philippians 3:17; 4:8-9).

Self-counsel means the daily perpetual invitation to heart searching, heart repentance, and heart renewal through God's Word. In other words, it is the examination of our own heart (i.e., thoughts, motives, desires) and behavior by taking the penetrating light of God's Word and letting it carefully examine every part of our life (Colossians 3:16).[8] Jesus cautions His followers to start with their own eye/heart before ministering to others (Matthew 7:1-5). In addition, the writer of Hebrews warns that any believer can be deceived by sin—and thus needs to "take care" that it doesn't happen (Hebrews 3:12-13). Therefore, the personal ministry of the Word must not be overlooked or the value of it underestimated.

Paul gives timeless advice to Timothy when he writes, "If you put these things before the brothers, you will be a good servant of Christ Jesus…train yourself for godliness" (1 Timothy 4:6-7). Paul wants Timothy and others to focus their efforts on the consistent, diligent practice of righteousness. He further writes, "Practice these things, immerse yourself in them, so that all may see your progress. Keep a close watch on yourself and on the teaching. Persist in this, for by so doing you will save both yourself and your hearers" (4:15-16). Paul makes the priority clear—start in your own heart and life before you begin focusing on others. Before you work on your theological system and before you move toward others in ministry, make a conscientious effort to walk in the power of the Spirit through the Word. Motivated by the love of Christ and concern for others, you carefully watch your own heart continually with the hope of faithful perseverance and meaningful ministry to others.

There are two types of absolutely critical questions we need to ask ourselves throughout the self-counsel process. First, "What does God want me to change in my life?" In other words, where is God working? What does God have His finger on and desire to see changed? What and where are the areas of struggle? What or who do I want to serve and obey? These questions are questions of insight. Basically, as we read the Word of God and discover its meaning, these questions can help us think through its significance in our life at this time.[9]

However, we must not stop with just these answers. We also need to ask, "What am I doing about it?" Given the area that God wants to change, how are we working on it? It is easy to be insightful (get answers to the questions above) and think that we have changed. However, we do not want to confuse insight with change. Simply said, "Change has not taken place until change has taken place!"[10] We want to make a concerted effort to determine what we can do to help facilitate change in our own life and seek accountability from others as we enjoy the personal ministry of the Word.[11]

The Private Ministry of the Word

"Counsel the Word" relates to the private ministry of the Word—the one-on-one, face-to-face counseling component most characteristically discussed as biblical counseling. There are two issues pertinent to the private ministry of the Word. First, the counselor must never forget the importance of handling the text accurately. Often, little attention is paid in education to the exegesis process, even seminary education in biblical counseling. Just as it would be irresponsible to preach without knowing the text, it is also irresponsible to counsel without knowing the text. We counsel the Word. In Christ, the Spirit of God uses the Word of God to change counselees into Christ's image. Therefore, the meaning of the text must be central to our ministry of the Word.

Excellent biblical counseling always regards truth as paramount, yet it is hard sometimes to discern between truth and error. Paul writes to Timothy, "Have nothing to do with irreverent, silly myths." He continues, "Devote yourself to the public reading of Scripture, to exhortation, to teaching" (1 Timothy 4:7,13). Paul expects Timothy to know the difference between truth (God's Word) and error (myths). Probably most counselors would laugh if you insinuated that they could share information in counseling from daytime television talk shows, where the message and advice often includes spirituality without a clear or accurate God-orientation. However, without taking the time and effort to learn the biblical text, what would keep any one of us from misinterpreting or misapplying the Bible? Without careful thought and diligence, any one of us could be no further from error than a persuasive book or article by a well-meaning Christian. Therefore, the desire to minister the Word with excellence must drive our efforts in preparing for counseling.

In consideration of helping our counselees with clear application or wisdom (significance) from a Bible passage, there are several additional questions we can ask: (1) What applies to the counselee's thinking? (2) What applies to the counselee's conduct? (3) What applies to the counselee's attitude? (4) What applies to the counselee's affections/wants/loves? When considering these questions, look for specific principles in the text to determine what the relationship is between the text and the counselee's situation, and at the same time, check to see if it is consistent with the fundamental truth of the passage.

So, what passage do we minister then? There are four principles to consider as we determine what passages best fit a counselee in a particular situation. First, consider our counselee's attitude and openness to the Scriptures. Is this counselee primarily interacting with us as a sinner (someone responsible for known sin), as a sufferer (someone who is under pressure or facing trials), or as a saint (someone who is responding from a clear sense of the gospel but just needs encouragement)? Paul seems to use the following categories (see 1 Thessalonians 5:14): Does this counselee know what to do but is refusing to do it? Is this counselee learning what to do but is scared to do it or does not know how? Or, is this counselee so weak that any hope of doing what is right is seemingly impossible? The answer to these questions will help you determine what Scripture passages may best minister to this counselee.

Second, we want to consider what this counselee's heart is gripped by at this moment.[12] It's possible that the primary issue on our counselee's mind/heart—through which we can begin ministry—is not necessarily the presenting problem or the ultimate problem we will deal with. However, it provides us an opportunity to begin to provide hope, care, mercy, and the love of Christ to this person.

Third, listen and determine whether the counselee has a functional understanding of grace and the gospel. How does union in Christ, position in Christ, and the power of Christ fit into this counselee's functional theology? Is this counselee responding in a manner consistent with what Christ has already done for and in this believer? Is the counselee aware of what Christ provides now and into the future?

Finally, we can ask, "What passage of the Bible, if heard and obeyed, will help this counselee here and now?"[13] Are there issues of wisdom and folly that need to be addressed? Is there a particular issue of sin that needs immediate attention? It's possible the counselee is living a life void of wisdom and needs help with discernment. Ministry of the Word here may look more like encouragement and be filled with practical wisdom.

Regardless of where we start, private ministry of the Word must always rest solidly upon a passion to use the Word of God accurately and a passion to minister to one of God's children with Christ's love.

The Public Ministry of the Word

"Preach the Word" relates to the public ministry of the Word, (i.e., preaching, teaching, or writing). Public ministry provides many opportunities to minister the Word with wisdom and excellence. By definition it is different. Private ministry is face-to-face; public ministry is many faces. Private ministry is meaning, significance, specific circumstance; public ministry is meaning, significance, many different circumstances. The challenge of preaching for life change is to take the meaning of a passage and communicate its contemporary relevance to an entire congregation.

Basic Elements

There are three basic elements to keep in mind as we prepare for public ministry of the Word. Paul said to Timothy, "Until I come, devote yourself to the public reading of Scripture, to exhortation, to teaching" (1 Timothy 4:13). The opportunity to minister can be divided nicely into the three parts: read your passage, explain your passage, and apply/communicate the significance of your passage. Using the principles discussed earlier in the chapter, (1) study the text, (2) determine the fundamental truth, and (3) consider the audience. In the preparation process, allow enough time after understanding the meaning to consider carefully the significance. Considering the audience takes time and thought; this can only be accomplished after we know the meaning and fundamental truth. We ask, "How does this passage connect to real people with real problems?"

Three Steps to More Effective Public Ministry

First, we need to recognize our natural tendencies in preparation. Typically, we will either enjoy soaring high in the clouds of meaning, or we will find it hard to get the meaning plane off the ground. If we enjoy the study process, the text engages us. The technical concepts stimulate our thinking. The connections are fascinating, the facts riveting. We will tend to soar high above the audience in meaning—and will love every minute of it. On the other hand, some will find it fun and natural to hardly get the text plane off the ground. We understand our culture at street level well. We know movies, music, menus, inner-city, style, and marketplace concepts. However, we may not grasp exactly how the text actually connects meaningfully and consistently at the street level. Neither tendency is wrong; the reality is we must be a student of both. How does Jerusalem or Philippi meet our city? How does the church at Ephesus connect with our church? How does God's wisdom expose, engage, and evangelize the world's wisdom?

Second, as counselors, we do one-on-one private ministry of the Word on a regular basis. Our private ministry connects our public ministry with life lived. Our public ministry engages the same kinds of people we see and hear privately in counseling—people with lost jobs, financial concerns, relational difficulties, health concerns, family problems, personal problems, and the list goes on. They are sitting in front of us; and there are many of them all at the same time. This brings up a bit of a different challenge. In private ministry, we have the privilege of reading an intake form; we contemplate the real issue as we ask many questions of the counselee. With both time and opportunity, we are able to look for themes and patterns in the person's life and respond to them directly. However, in public ministry, we do not enjoy those benefits. Instead, we bring all of those private ministry experiences with us into our study. We pray with them in mind. We study with not just a passion to know; we study with a passion to know *and* share meaningfully at the life-lived level. Our public ministry can profit as we participate in private ministry, small groups, and service projects. We will find it easier to bring our meaning plane close to the ground because we know the geographical contour of our audience well.

Third, we can't be afraid to keep it simple. What makes for a fun and necessary discussion in seminary does not always connect with the people in the audience. Please understand that there is never an excuse to be sloppy, inaccurate, imprecise, or not clearly comprehend the text. In fact, we must know it so clearly and accurately that we can speak it in simple terms. The goal is not to sound deep; the goal is to be clear and helpful. We do public ministry with hurting people who need truth accurately explained in simple terms and concepts. We can ask: (1) Are there key terms that are hard to understand? (2) If I described this passage in counseling as I have it prepared for public ministry, would my counselee get it? (3) What illustrations can I use that are consistent with the meaning of the text and help build comprehension?

The Privilege of the Ministry of the Word

Recognizing the importance of the Bible to the change process, biblical counselors strive to minister the Word with excellence in personal, private, and public ministry. Jesus prayed, "Sanctify them in the truth; your word is truth" (John 17:17). The next time you pick up your Bible to consider your own heart, sit down to help another person in counseling, or prepare to present a passage publicly, contemplate how privileged you are to participate in the process of ministry to God's people in Christ.

In the book of Job, God rebuked Job's counselors because they spoke inaccurately of God (Job 42:7). James writes, "You know that we who teach will be judged with greater strictness" (James 3:1). Paul challenges us to rightly handle the word of truth (2 Timothy 2:15). He also calls us ambassadors who have the word of reconciliation (2 Corinthians 5:18-21). Jesus simply says to Peter, "Feed my sheep" (John 21:17). How sobering. What a privilege!

18

The Transformational Tie Between Small Group Ministry and Biblical Counseling

Brad Bigney and Ken Long

Small groups are the ministry that churches initially love but after they head down that path for a while, they sometimes come away disappointed. Churches and their leaders will become all excited about starting a small group ministry because of all the hype they've read in the latest book or heard at the latest conference. They come away believing that all their problems will be solved if they can just get their people connected in a vibrant small group ministry. So they spend a lot of ministry capital establishing a small group ministry, only to find out that it's not the magic elixir they'd hoped for. What's more, they end up with a whole new set of problems and concerns they feel unprepared to address. For this reason, many small group ministries are constantly in flux, with the church leadership trying to make, and then remake, the ministry over and over again.

So how does a ministry that appears to offer so much promise leave so many pastors jaded and tossing the idea of small group ministry back onto the "we've tried that before" pile? It's the high percentage of failures, along with the incessant number of small group ministry "makeovers," that compels us to write this chapter.

One of the main reasons for failed small group ministries can be symptomatically understood from the following incident that actually took place in a church (not ours, thankfully!). At the close of their weekly small group meeting, a young couple that had been attending the group hung around until everyone else had left so that they could speak with the leader couple alone. After a few minutes of nervous chit-chat, the young couple began to open up and pour out their hearts about a significant problem they were having in their marriage. The leader couple gave their full attention, listening intently and compassionately, and then they spoke a word of counsel. They said, "With issues like that, you should consider joining another group."

Right there is the Achilles' heel of the entire small group ministry movement. We're convinced a key reason for the high percentage of failed small group ministries and constant makeovers is that churches have not intentionally developed their small groups to be a place of *grace and growth* for all of the walking wounded who come through our front doors.

Most churches today have not structured their ministries to get down into the nitty-gritty of people's lives. When personal problems begin to surface, they are overwhelmed and ill-equipped to respond in a loving, biblical way. Too many churches don't know how to give hope or help to real people who have opened up about the struggles they're facing, nor do they have a plan for equipping their small group leaders to do so. And so the small group ministry either limps along in a superficial way or falls apart as leaders become overwhelmed by issues they were not equipped to deal with effectively.

In this chapter, we want to paint a new picture of a small group ministry that can give hope and help to those who participate in such groups. Even struggling small group ministries can be revitalized *by refocusing the purpose of the small group on spiritual formation and by tying the small group ministry to the church's biblical counseling ministry.* These two ministries should work hand in hand together—small groups and biblical counseling.

In fact, we would go so far as to say *don't start a small group ministry without an equally vital biblical counseling ministry.* Don't even think about it—not if your goal is spiritual growth and transformation. If you're happy with superficial yak 'n' snack groups, then don't worry about a biblical counseling ministry, and don't bother with reading the rest of this chapter. Just make sure your leaders make it absolutely clear to everyone in their group that we're not here to dig into the real stuff we're all wrestling with. Keep it safe; keep it superficial.

The Purpose of Small Group Ministry

So where should you start? The best place is to make sure everyone has a clear understanding of the purpose of the small group ministry. If that's unstated or unclear, then you can count on lots of confusion and a high turnover rate among your small group leaders.

So what should be the purpose of the small group ministry? Well, there are a lot of reasons why small groups exist in a church—none of them bad, but a lot of them unclear and peripheral to what's going on in the heart and soul of a church. Often the name attached to the ministry gives the reason for its existence—for example, Care Groups, Men's Bible Study, Ladies' Groups, or Growth Groups. Many churches looking for a way to meet the personal and physical needs of their people in a loving, decentralized manner will establish Care Groups. Others want their men to dig into the Bible, so they start a Men's Bible Study. Still others want to emphasize growth for the kingdom so they have Growth Groups modeled after the principles contained in Carl George's book *Prepare Your Church for the Future* (Tarrytown, NY: Fleming H. Revell, 1991).

But careful and prayerful thought should be given to the purpose of the small group ministry of any church. Don't just put some chairs in a circle and start one. A small group ministry should deliberately and directly enhance the primary ministry of the church. So before you can determine the purpose of your small group ministry, you must first answer the question, What is the primary ministry of the church? Do you know? It can be seen clearly in Ephesians 4:

> Now these are the gifts Christ gave to the church: the apostles, the prophets, the evangelists, and the pastors and teachers. Their responsibility is to equip God's people to do his work and build up the church, the body of Christ. This will continue until we all come to such unity in our faith and knowledge of God's Son that we will be mature in the Lord, measuring up to the full and complete standard of Christ. Then we will no longer be immature like children. We won't be tossed and blown about by every wind of new teaching. We will not be influenced when people try to trick us with lies so clever they sound like the truth. Instead, we will speak the truth in love, growing in every way more and more like Christ, who is the head of his body, the church (Ephesians 4:11-15 NLT).

Ephesians 4:11-15 drives home the fact that God has given Spirit-gifted people "pastors and teachers...to equip God's people...[to] build up the church, the body of Christ" (verses 11-12). So the goal of building up His church is to have all of God's people to "be mature in the Lord, measuring up to the full and complete standard of Christ" (verse 13). Or stated another way, "growing in every way more and more like Christ, who is the head of his body, the church" (verse 15). In other words, a primary purpose of the church, depending on one's theology, is for the whole church to participate with the Spirit (see 2 Corinthians 3:18) in the transformation of God's people to be more like Christ.

So if spiritual formation is the purpose of the church, then personal transformation should intentionally be the purpose of the small group ministry. Bible study is great. Fellowship is wonderful. Evangelism is essential. But changing and growing to be more like Christ should be the purpose of the small group ministry. And believe it or not, it's possible to focus on Bible study and still not arrive at personal transformation unless the leaders are trained and reminded to be pointed in that direction.

The way to encourage such transformation is for the group to spend their time intently studying the Word of God or a theological book based on the Scriptures, with an emphasis on applying the truth to their lives. You say, "But aren't most churches and small groups focused on this already?" We don't think so. Most Bible studies are focused on knowledge with possibly some private application considered. Usually what happens is the group leader gives a mini-lecture, while the participants dutifully "spank the blanks" in their study guide or workbook. Occasionally the leader will ask some inductive questions about the text, but even then the questions are often focused on facts rather than life application.

And don't hear what we're *not* saying. We're not saying that Bible knowledge is irrelevant; we're saying it's not enough. And we're saying that small groups are the place to push past Bible knowledge and on to life application so that we can see people's lives transform more and more into the image of Christ. *A transformational small group focuses on everyone giving and receiving hope and help from God's Word to spiritually mature in Christ.*

So a small group intent on encouraging personal transformation is focused on asking questions with spiritual formation in mind. Take, for instance, a small group discussion of James 1. Because the text deals with trials, the leader would press each member of the group to think about a personal trial in their own life and to humbly share about it with the others. To spark a spiritual discussion that moves below the surface of "Hey, how ya' doin'?" the leader might ask: "Looking at verse two, what difficulty or trial are you personally facing right now in your own life?" After hearing from everyone who is willing to answer the question, a follow-up question might be: "On a scale of one to ten, with ten being the highest, what is your joy quotient right now as you persevere through this God-given trial?"

Notice how a small group leader, with the help of a series of questions, can provide fertile ground for each person to really examine his or her attitude of submission to God's Lordship in their life, which is indicated by the level of joy he or she is experiencing in the midst of the trial. Obviously, such a discussion would lead naturally into a meaningful time of prayer for each other that would rise above the prayer requests typically shared at church prayer meetings, which are usually focused on minor surgeries and the problems of other people outside of the group whom we've never met.

In the scenario just described, the small group leader's transformational target is to help each member of the group to move toward greater submission to God during a trial. God has commanded us to be joyful in our trials (James 1:2). So how are we doing? Of course we're not asking that someone be joyful if he or she has cancer. But a person can be joyful that in this horrendous trial, their Father's steadfast love, which endures forever (Psalm 100:5), will use even this circumstance for His glory and their good. For God's good work to be made complete in a believer, he has to "count it all joy" when he "meet trials of various kinds" (James 1:2). In other words, the passage is teaching us to not waste our trials, but to be good stewards of them. Our small group members need more than just help in understanding this. They need help doing it and living it. And that's where the small group ministry should focus.

A small group's time spent in the Word should be interactive, with everyone sharing where they are in their own lives and encouraging others in their walk. And so often, it's others around us who can see where God wants to grow us even before we see it ourselves. In a small group setting, others can see areas where we need wisdom and prayer (James 1:5). So the small group becomes a greenhouse or incubator for spiritual growth, with everyone spurring one another on to love and good deeds (Hebrews 10:24-25), giving hope and help that enables everyone to keep moving forward, by God's grace. This, of course, is all hinged upon allowing others to speak into our lives.

The Place of a Small Group Ministry in the Overall Church Structure

The leadership at our church, Grace Fellowship Church (GFC), believes that the transformational process of becoming "more and more like Christ" is the primary purpose for why God has called us together as a church. So the small group ministry focuses primarily on personal transformation for everyone who calls GFC home. For more than sixteen years now the leadership at GFC has trumpeted that "small groups are the heart of the church." And in saying that we make two things clear: first, the importance of transformation, and, second, the decision to make small groups the place or the context in which God accomplishes this. GFC's Ministry Relationships (see below) shows how transformation and small groups fit into the overall picture of GFC.

GFC's Ministry Relationships

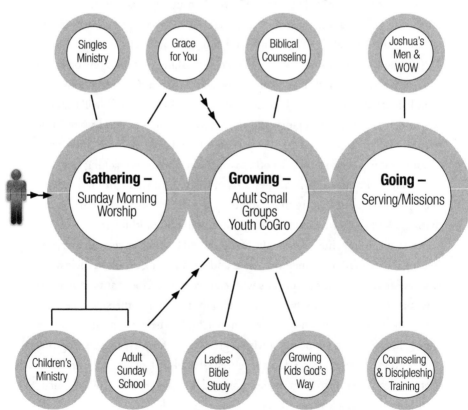

First, notice that the three large circles represent the three primary ministry areas of GFC for adults: Gathering, Growing, and Going. As indicated by the person on the far left of the diagram, most people are first exposed to GFC through the "Gathering" aspect, or corporate worship services on Sunday. From that first exposure to GFC, newcomers are intentionally directed into a small group where they can form personal and transformational relationships with other believers at close range. Plugging into a small group is represented by the large center circle, "Growing." Once a person is plugged into a small group, they're encouraged to look for ways to serve and give their life away in ministry to others, both inside and outside of our church family. This part of our church life together is represented by the third circle, titled "Going—Serving/Missions."

We want our people breathing in and breathing out the grace of God in all three areas of ministry—Gathering, Growing, and Going. Focusing on these three areas of Gathering, Growing, and Going is our version of the simple church presented in Thom Rainer and Eric Geiger's book titled *Simple Church* (Nashville: B&H Books, 2006). And it's freed us up from trying to run dozens of ministries that offer dozens of programs to our people. Instead, we're focused on the promotion and resourcing of three circles that we believe are helping keep our church moving in the right direction and focused on the right things because it all produces the right result—disciples of Christ who look more like Jesus and less like themselves as time goes on.

God has called us to more than buildings, bodies, and bucks. He's called us to make disciples, to see people changing and growing and living out the great truths of the gospel and resurrection hope! Every church should have a yardstick that helps them to measure their effectiveness against what God has purposed for them to be. Andy Stanley, along with others, refers to this yardstick as "a win" in *Seven Practices of Effective Ministry* (Sisters, OR: Multnomah, 2004). The leadership of any church should ask themselves what has to happen for their ministry to be "a win." We're delighted when we hear someone say, "Oh, I love the preaching and worship" or "I have so many friends here." But "a win" for us is when someone says, "Since being a part of this church, I have grown spiritually more than ever before in my life." For us, that's "a win," and by God's grace, we have the joy of hearing this often.

I (Brad) received an email from someone new in our church family that said, "I know you probably hear this a lot, but maybe not often enough. You, Ken, the other pastors, and the Grace family are amazing! My wife and I never felt so discipled anywhere else. The Grace family really walks in a God-honoring way. For the first time I can truly say I feel like an actual 'disciple' of the Lord instead of just 'one of the people in the crowd hearing a message'...if that makes sense. Thank you and the church for living it out and creating disciples!"

Training for Small Group Leaders

Maybe you're getting excited as you read this, but you're thinking, *Where am I going to get the people who will lead small groups that are more than yak 'n' snack and are focused on transformation? Won't it be a hard sell to do small groups this way?* Maybe at first, but not if the church leadership makes this one of their top priorities—and they should. For a small group ministry to be focused on personal transformation, you have to make the selection and training of your small group leaders a top priority. Your church leadership should be praying, looking, and funneling potential small group leaders into an intentional training process—you should be identifying and raising up new leaders and apprentices on a constant basis. Why? Because not just anyone can do this. We're looking for more than just an outgoing personality and a spiritual pulse!

The small group leader needs to be equipped to carry out the vision of pushing beyond Bible information and on to personal life transformation. Certainly, the small group leader must have "a growing relationship with God and a heart for the people of God in the group."[1] In addition, the guidelines you establish for those who serve as small group leaders should make it clear you expect them to demonstrate good theological understanding, personal spiritual maturity, and the fact they are being used by God regularly as an instrument for transformation in other people's lives. Clearly defined expectations for the leader will promote a unified and effective ministry for both the participants of every small group and the small group leaders themselves. Though rigorous, such guidelines will help toward fulfilling the goal that your small group leaders have a fruitful, long-term ministry.

Typically at GFC the leader of a small group is either a single male or a married couple. In the groups led by a couple, both husband and wife are involved in the spiritual growth and care of their people, but the husband will lead the group's time in the Word.

The GFC guidelines for becoming a small group leader are as follows:

1. A member of Grace Fellowship Church (1 Peter 5:2-7)

2. Has served as an apprentice for a GFC small group and has been recommended by their small group leader, who completes a Ministry Referral Form (2 Timothy 2:2)

3. Has completed Fundamentals of Biblical Counseling training (Romans 15:14; 2 Timothy 2:15)

4. Has participated in Joshua's Men (JM) or Women of the Word (WOW) leadership training in our church (1 Timothy 4:16)

5. Demonstrates being "spiritual" and being used by God to "restore others in a spirit of gentleness" in the transformational process (Galatians 6:1-2)

6. Has completed the Small Group Written Interview and it has been accepted by the director of small groups and/or elders

7. Has been interviewed and endorsed by the director of small groups

Everyone who becomes a small group leader first serves for a time in an already-established small group as an apprentice (see guideline #2). This allows for a small group leader to disciple a potential leader for his (and her) growth both spiritually and in the ways of shepherding brothers and sisters in the small group. As time goes on, the leader will give the apprentice increasing opportunities to oversee responsibilities relating to the transformation of the other participants.

Another component of the training for apprentices is completing the Fundamentals of Biblical Counseling training. This is the initial 30 hours of biblical counseling training based on the National Association of Nouthetic Counselors (NANC) model. Having this biblical counseling background has been invaluable for our small group leaders. When a soul-care issue comes up in a small group, our leaders can know with confidence that the Scriptures have answers. By the Spirit's power, the leader will be able to give hope and even some initial help from God's Word.

In the cases where a couple leads a small group, both husband and wife are required to complete our leadership training program. We expect our men to go through the Joshua's Men (JM) program, and we ask their wives to go through Women of the Word (WOW). JM and WOW are for training leaders in biblical theology and its practical everyday applications to one's life. For two years, JM and WOW participants meet once a month for three hours to discuss a reading assignment by sharing their written answers to questions we've provided for them.

For JM, one year is devoted to working through the majority of *Systematic Theology* by Wayne Grudem (Grand Rapids: Zondervan, 1994). The second year is devoted to reading nine theological books: *Knowing God* by J.I. Packer (Downers Grove, IL: InterVarsity Press, 1973), *Trusting God* by Jerry Bridges (Colorado Springs: NavPress, 1988), *The Discipline of Grace* by Jerry Bridges (Colorado Springs: NavPress, 1994), *Seven Reasons Why You Can Trust the Bible* by Erwin Lutzer (Chicago: Moody, 1998), *Why Small Groups* by C.J. Mahaney (Gaithersburg, MD: Sovereign Grace Ministries, 1996), *The Heart of Anger* by Lou Priolo (Amityville, NY: Calvary Press, 1997), *Disciplines of a Godly Man* by R. Kent Hughes (Wheaton, IL: Crossway, 1991), *The Complete Husband* by Lou Priolo (Amityville, NY: Calvary Press, 2007), and *Spiritual Leadership* by J. Oswald Sanders (Chicago: Moody, 1980). Also, during this intense time of training the men and women memorize over fifty Bible verses related to their readings. These two years are an incredible time of equipping and growing! It's such a joy to see the men and women becoming "like great oaks that the LORD has planted for his own glory" (Isaiah 61:3 NLT).

Continual Training for a Small Group Leader

Once the trainees become small group leaders, they are asked to participate in an advanced-level counseling and discipleship training class each year. We want to make sure the small group leaders continue to get a fresh vision for what helping people become more like Christ really looks like. We also want to keep before them the fact that, with the Bible in hand, they are more than able to jump into this kind of ministry, even though many churches are reluctant to have the laity do such ministry. Many believe that only ordained ministers and those with college degrees in biblical studies are qualified to really help people change and grow. Yet Paul assured the Christians in Rome that he was "confident...that you also are full of goodness, filled with all knowledge, able also to admonish one another" (Romans 15:14 NKJV).

The Necessity for a Counseling Ministry

As you can imagine, significant personal issues will arise during the discussions that take place in transformational small groups. While GFC small group leaders are able to handle most of the soul-care issues that arise in their groups, there are exceptions. Because they are already busy providing "personal discipleship" for the eight to fifteen people in their group, people who need "personal long-term intensive discipleship"—or what is commonly referred to as biblical counseling—may need to be cared for by others. For many small group leaders, there simply isn't enough time to also do long-term biblical counseling.

Fortunately, there is a way to handle the more difficult issues that will arise in transformational small groups. The people who need more intensive personal discipleship are referred to the church's counseling center. Among the issues referred to the counseling center are life-dominating sins such as adultery, alcohol or drug abuse, pornography addiction, persistent unbelief, sexual abuse, crippling fear, etc.

Steve Viars, the senior pastor of Faith Church, Lafayette, Indiana, illustrates this by telling the story of a person floating down a river in a boat. But then the boat gets trapped in an eddy and keeps bumping into the shore, no longer making any progress down the river. General and personal discipleship are represented by the person making progress down the river or toward growth in Christlikeness. The eddy represents a life-dominating sin that impedes any spiritual growth. Not until the boat is freed from the eddy will it continue its journey down the river. Likewise, not until a person is freed from life-dominating sin will he or she resume growing spiritually.

Sometimes outside help is required in such a situation. Someone else needs to help move the boat out of the eddy, or to come alongside the sinning believer and offer help in the form of biblical counseling, whereby the sinning believer is helped by loving confrontation and instruction from the Scriptures. The goal is for repentance to take place so the believer will get back on the paths of general and personal discipleship.

As can be seen, to have a successful transformational small group ministry requires the availability of a biblical counseling ministry that can help care for the people who require long-term personal discipleship. If long-term biblical counseling is not available, a well-intended transformational small group ministry will eventually shift its focus. Those who are still ensnared in their sin will get frustrated whenever the group talks about change and growth. They'll desire change, but without the help of a spiritually mature person who can come alongside them (Galatians 6:1-2), they will lose hope.

Eventually, a group that started out with the purpose of transforming lives will shift into more of a Bible study or a care group that focuses mainly on acquiring more Bible information or on changing people's circumstances. The leaders of a church need to ask themselves, "Is this the risk we want to take by not providing the support of a biblical counseling ministry? Would God be pleased with such a shift in emphasis in the small group ministry?"

We have seen churches start a transformational small group ministry, but for one reason or another, neglect the development of a biblical counseling ministry. Eventually they end up having difficulties. Either the pastoral staff becomes swamped with counseling requests because no one else is able to do the work of biblical counseling, or the small group ministry becomes less focused on spiritual formation and growth. Neither situation is satisfactory.

Conversely, a church that has a counseling center but no small group ministry faces problems as well. Churches that do not have small groups to help out with more ordinary kinds of personal discipleship may end up with an inordinate number of biblical counseling cases. This is especially likely in a church where there is transformational preaching and teaching. The people will become hungry to change in the direction that they have been challenged, and because they're not able to get ongoing personal discipleship via a small group, they turn to the biblical counseling ministry for help. Many of these people could be effectively cared for in a transformational small group ministry. What's more, once people have been helped with intensive discipleship through biblical counseling, where do they turn for ongoing personal discipleship if transformational small groups do not exist?

What we're advocating is that a church that desires to be transformational should consider having an interdependent biblical counseling ministry *and* a small group ministry. Our observations have been that this model is suitable for both small and large churches. In 1996, as a church plant, Grace Fellowship adopted this model when there were only 80 people attending the service each Sunday morning. Today, the average Sunday attendance is around 1800, and the emphasis on growing in Christlikeness has remained unchanged. We're thankful that about 75 to 80 percent of the adults who call GFC their home church are participating in a transformational small group. For sixteen years, the purpose of GFC has remained unchanged as we've recognized the need to have both a biblical counseling ministry and a small group ministry functioning in an interdependent relationship.

In fact, these ministries and their interconnectedness are needed now more than ever before for Grace Fellowship to continue being a transformational church. As a church grows larger, one of its main concerns is making sure it can provide spiritual care for all the people whom God brings through the doors on a Sunday morning. Pastors are to equip the saints for the work of ministry, but they're not called to do all the work of discipleship. Works of ministry for lay people should involve more than just volunteering in the church nursery; it should include caring for the souls of others (Romans 15:14; Galatians 6:1-2). The integrating together of a small group ministry and biblical counseling ministry fosters Ephesians 4:11-12 involvement by all the people in a church. Each small group leader will typically care for eight to fifteen people.

With this model, our pastors don't spend the bulk of their time caring for the people one-on-one. Rather, they are able to spend a greater percentage of their time assisting and caring for the small group leaders as they shepherd the people in our church family. We do have one pastor who leads the counseling ministry, and the work of that ministry is carried out largely by trained lay counselors. This fulfills the God-given mandate for pastor-teachers to help all their people be involved in ministry to their level of giftedness (Romans 12:4-8; 1 Corinthians 12:7).

Currently we have about sixty transformational small groups, and the counseling ministry is usually caring for thirty to forty individuals or couples involved in long-term counseling, or what we would call intensive discipleship.

A team of about thirty counselors do the counseling, and fourteen of these are NANC-certified counselors. We're thrilled that the majority of the counseling cases, about 60 percent, are handled by lay counselors.

God has been actively at work among us, and we've just been trying to humbly keep up with what He has entrusted to us. When we first started out we didn't have all the details of ministry figured out, but we did start with the idea of not just doing church but of deeply desiring to cooperate with God in His work of transforming the people in His church (see 2 Corinthians 3:18). In response to our meager efforts, we've seen God do exceedingly, abundantly beyond all that we could ask or think (Ephesians 3:20).

19

The Goal and Focus of Spiritual Formation

Robert Cheong and Heath Lambert

Mike looks happy. He is married to his high school sweetheart, and they have a beautiful daughter in college. Mike loves his wife, she loves him, and their daughter thinks they are both wonderful parents. While there have been occasional arguments, their family is genuinely happy and has always been that way. Mike has a great job at a Fortune 500 company, where he has worked for twenty-five years. He has a nice home in a desirable part of town, a time-share, a boat, a 401K, and all three members of his family drive new cars. Mike is also active in church as an assistant community group leader. He is always helpful, usually in a good disposition, and has many friends.

Though Mike looks happy, he isn't.

Mike is locked up with anxiety. As he talks, he describes a life dominated by worry. The fact is most of the things in Mike's life have a price tag attached. With Mike's upscale life comes mortgages, second mortgages, membership and service fees, tithes, taxes, college tuition, and car payments. In addition to being stretched financially, Mike feels overextended with his time. An increasingly competitive work environment and a constricted economy have led to ever-increasing demands at work. That, in turn, has led to increased pressures at home.

Mike's wife is becoming concerned about the distance developing in their relationship. With their daughter at college, she assumed they would spend more time together. Instead, they spend less. If all of that weren't enough, Mike feels guilt in connection with a recent sermon in which the pastor challenged everyone to redouble their efforts in serving the church.

Mike doesn't know what to do. He wants to retire, but knows his family can't sustain their lifestyle without his quarterly bonuses which will vanish when he receives the company watch. He wants to spend more time at home and church, but doesn't know how to do that with his boss breathing down his neck. As a result, Mike is worried about his job, his marriage, and his life-style and standard of living. He is worried that his friends and leaders at church will think he is not as involved as he should be. He has come to counseling looking for help to relieve the pressure.

So how would you help Mike? What does he need? The answers to these questions are long, because counseling with Mike will require many conversations about a lot of things. He needs to learn priorities, simplicity, self-control, and contentment. He needs to learn what it means to turn from a heart that is selfishly ambitious to a heart that rests in grace and is thankful for all of God's goods gifts. He needs to learn how truly to serve, and how to turn from doing his good works to be seen by others. Mike needs all of this, and more.

Yet more than anything else, what Mike needs is to be formed into the image of Jesus. He needs to learn to abide in Christ so that the life of the Savior flows through and empowers everything he thinks, says, and does. Mike needs all kinds of things, but fundamentally he needs to learn what it means to walk in a life-giving relationship with Jesus.

When Christians talk about spiritual formation, they are talking about what are often called the spiritual disciplines—journaling, fasting, solitude, prayer, Bible reading, and other similar activities quickly spring to mind. A conversation about such disciplines is important. Such a discussion, however, can sometimes lose sight of the fact that those disciplines are not goals in and of themselves. Instead, they are a means to something much greater—namely, Jesus Christ. The goal of the disciplines—of spiritual formation—is Christ Himself.

When understood in this way, it is not hard to see why, as biblical counselors, we should be interested in spiritual formation. We are interested in this topic because we are interested in Jesus. We are not merely interested in dispensing life tips, nor are we narrowly concerned about changing behavior. As important as these things are, we as biblical counselors are satisfied with nothing less than counselees becoming conformed to the likeness of Christ.

Biblical counselors want Mike, you, and those you counsel to look more like Jesus Christ when the counseling is complete. Any counseling that does not pursue spiritual formation through an intimate relationship with Jesus by faith as one of its chief goals is not worthy to be called *biblical* counseling.

Spiritual Formation and Abiding in Jesus

The Bible uses several different terms to talk about the Christian goal of becoming more like Jesus. It is referred to as training (1 Timothy 2:7-8), disciplining (1 Corinthians 9:27), walking (Galatians 5:16,22-24), maturing (Colossians 1:28), and transforming (2 Corinthians 3:18), just to name a few. In John 15:1-11, Jesus refers to this goal as abiding. All the varied terms the Bible uses to refer to the goal of being formed into the likeness of Christ have different nuances and emphasize distinct benefits. For example, the meaning behind "abide" emphasizes the need Christians have to rest in Jesus and receive from Him His life, which conforms us into His image. It is this theme of abiding—as it appears in John 15:1-11—that we wish to unpack in this chapter on biblical counseling and spiritual formation.

Jesus says, "I am the true vine, and my Father is the vinedresser...Abide in me, and I in you. As the branch cannot bear fruit by itself, unless it abides in the vine, neither can you, unless you abide in me" (John 15:1,4). The Gospel of John is well known for the usage of the "I AM" sayings. In these sayings, John quotes Jesus making a metaphorical statement about His identity which states a specific benefit from the incarnate "I AM" to His people. Jesus is the gate through whom His people can enter and find pasture (John 10:9). He is the bread of life on whom His people can feed, and be eternally rid of their hunger (John 6:39). He is the way, the truth, and the life who affords access to the Father (John 14:6). He is the resurrection, in whom Christians live even though they die (John 11:25). He is the light, who keeps His followers from walking in darkness (John 8:12). He is the good shepherd who lays down His life for the sheep (John 10:11).

John 15 records the last of these "I AM" statements, in which Jesus declares Himself to be the true vine. The statement is ripe with biblical significance. The imagery of the vine is one God frequently uses to speak of His people Israel in the Old Testament. One very interesting aspect to note about the use of this metaphor, however, is that every time God uses it to talk about His Old Covenant people, it is always in connection with the failure of the vine (for example, Ezekiel 15). In the midst of repeated illustrations about the failure of the vine of Israel, Jesus comes along and declares that He is the *true* vine.

As the true vine, Jesus is the fulfillment of everything His Old Covenant people were supposed to be but could not be apart from Him. Jesus declares Himself to be the vine that His people need for sustenance and life. Just as a branch cannot bear fruit unless it is connected to the vine, neither can people have life if they are not connected to Christ. This passage is about spiritual formation that comes through a vital, life-giving union with the Son of God. It calls people to spiritual formation—not with the language of discipline, but with a vibrant invitation to live and abide in Christ Himself. This passage gives hope to all of us because we all fail at being "spiritually disciplined enough" to please God. But what does it mean to abide? If abiding in Jesus is critical to being formed into His likeness, then how can we make that happen?

Abiding and the Spiritual Disciplines

John's language of abiding rings with themes of life rather than discipline, but that does not mean that it does not have anything to do with what are often called spiritual disciplines. In fact, Jesus links abiding to three practical and tangible realities—Bible reading, prayer, and obedience.

In John 15, Jesus calls us to abide in Him by dwelling in His Word. He says, "If you abide in me, and my words abide in you…" (John 15:7). A few chapters earlier in John, Peter rightly said to Jesus: "You have the words of eternal life." Jesus' words are words of life. So if we want to have His very life flowing through us, we must regularly take in His life-giving words. Of course, this happens by reading the Bible because it is there that we have an inspired and trustworthy living word written so that we would believe in Him and have life in His name (John 20:31). When we draw near to Christ through His Word, the Spirit transforms us, exposes us, and comforts our hearts (Romans 12:2; Hebrews 4:12; 2 Corinthians 1:3-5).

In this same passage, Jesus also calls us to abide in Him by seeking Him through prayer. He says, "If you abide in me, and my words abide in you, ask whatever you wish…" (John 15:7). First, Jesus talks of our need to abide by listening to God's Word as He speaks to us. Now, Jesus talks of our need to abide by speaking our words to God. This is a beautiful picture of relationship. Abiding is not a divine monologue, but a high and holy interaction between the Father and His children. Jesus wants us to come to the Father asking requests that have been shaped by the words we take in from Scripture. One of the most important means of abiding, and of spiritual formation, is approaching the throne of grace and talking with the Father through prayer so that we might receive mercy during our time of need (2 Corinthians 3:18; Hebrews 4:16).

Finally, Jesus calls us to abide in Him by obeying His commands. He says, "If you keep my commandments, you will abide in my love, just as I have kept my Father's commandments and abide in His love" (John 15:10). This is important. Abiding is not limited to those things that are obviously spiritual, like prayer and reading Scripture. It has also to do with living all of life in ways that honor God (Romans 12:1). Abiding by living life as Jesus commands is not about legalistic drudgery, but is fundamentally a matter of experiencing Jesus' love. The text is clear: We abide in love when we keep Jesus' commandments. If we desire to be spiritually formed into the image of Jesus, we must deny ourselves, take up our cross, and follow our Redeemer in obedience (Matthew 16:24).

Jesus' threefold approach to abiding is also seen in Philippians 4:4-9:

> Rejoice in the Lord always; again I will say, Rejoice. Let your reasonableness be known to everyone. The Lord is at hand; do not be anxious about anything, but in everything by prayer and supplication with thanksgiving let your requests be made known to God. And the peace of God, which surpasses all understanding, will guard your hearts and your minds in Christ Jesus. Finally brothers, whatever is true, whatever is honorable, whatever is just, whatever is pure, whatever is lovely, whatever is commendable, if there is any excellence, if there is anything worthy of practice, think about these things. What you have learned and received and heard and seen in me—practice these things, and the God of peace will be with you.

There is an emphasis on *word* here as Paul encourages Christians to think on what is true. There is an emphasis on *prayer* as Paul encourages Christians to make their requests known to God by prayers and supplications. There is also an emphasis on *obedience* as Paul encourages Christians to practice the things they have learned, and received, and heard.

Abiding with Christ in prayer, Bible reading, and obedience are the primary means that Jesus gives His people to grow close in relationship to Him. It is important to make clear, however, that it is not through the practice of these disciplines that we come to know Christ in the first place. Abiding is a sweet grace, but it is a grace that flows *from* our salvation, and not a grace that *leads* to our salvation. In John 15:3 Jesus says, "Already you are clean because of the word that I have spoken to you." Notice that Jesus' exhortation for His people to abide comes after His declaration that they are already clean.

Why is this sequence important? One the one hand, we do not have to despair because our righteousness in Christ is not based on our works of abiding. On the other hand, we should not become passive in our walk in Christ because abiding with Christ in these practical ways reflects our righteous standing in Him. Such practical realities are good news. Abiding is about life, but it is not mystical and nebulous. Jesus calls us to abide with Him in ways that are practical and tangible. We do not have to be "super spiritual" in order to abide. We are already spiritual because of Jesus' cleansing Word and because He has brought us into union with Himself. The goal of spiritual formation is to grow in this spirituality by abiding in Jesus in prayer, Bible reading, and obedience to Jesus' loving commands.

Abiding and Unbelief

Perhaps you are wondering why Jesus commands people to abide when they are already His by virtue of the powerful cleansing word He has spoken. Jesus knew that His followers would struggle as a result of their indwelling sinfulness, the temptations of the world, and the lies whispered by the enemy. In a world filled with distractions and distortions, He knew His disciples would still be blinded and hardened by sin and would grow weary as they lived in a fallen world. They had a mission to complete and He knew that if they didn't abide in Him, they would fail to produce the fruit that comes with faithfulness.

Despite being saved by grace, we live in a world where we not only war against the enemies of darkness, but also our own unbelief. The root of our spiritual struggles as Christians is whether or not we will believe in all that Jesus is and has done for us through His finished work on the cross. This is why Jesus commands us to abide. We have already seen how Jesus' commands to abide are linked with drawing near to Him through His word, prayer, and obedience. As important as these activities are with regard to abiding in Christ, Jesus' call to abide involves more than *doing*. It also involves *believing*. In John 15, when Jesus summons us to an abiding relationship, He is asking us to believe in Him as the foundation of that relationship.

Jesus woos us to believe that His grace has spoken a powerful word that unites us to Him (John 15:3). He beckons us to believe that true life is found in Him, the true vine (John 15:4). He encourages us to believe that our lives are worthless without Him (John 15:5-6). He invites us to believe that God will be glorified in answering our prayers (John 15:8). He bids us to believe the love He has for us (John 10:9-10). In these ways, the call to abide is a call to believe. Whenever we fail to abide, we demonstrate unbelief in our hearts.

You might think, *I don't struggle with unbelief. I am a Christian. I believe.* Whether you realize it or not, your ongoing battle with unbelief drives all your sinful thoughts, emotions, desires, and actions. Even as Christians we still battle against God in our unbelief as we struggle to believe in Him and His promises, as we fail to place our hope in Him alone, and as we refuse to love Him and others. That is why God calls us as brothers and sisters in Christ to encourage one another daily, for our often-deceived and unbelieving hearts can cause us to turn away from the living God (Hebrews 3:12-14). Martin Luther, the great Protestant reformer, stated that unbelief is the essence and driving power of all sin:

> No external sinful work is done except a person rushes into it with his whole body and soul. Scripture takes particular notice of the heart and of the root and main source of all sins, which is unbelief in the inmost heart. Accordingly, even as faith alone justifies and obtains the Spirit and willingness for good external works, so unbelief alone sins and rouses the flesh and the desire for evil external works, as happened to Adam and Eve in paradise...Hence, before good or evil works are done (which are good or evil fruits), there must first be in the heart faith or unbelief, the latter being the root, sap, and main strength of every sin.[1]

As we examine Jesus' words about abiding, we must avoid a moralistic effort merely to pray harder, read the Bible more, or try to be more holy. Our efforts at being spiritually formed by our practice of the disciplines must be fueled by belief in the promises that underline and empower Jesus' commands.

Abiding and Glory

In John 15:8 Jesus says, "By this my Father is glorified, that you bear much fruit and so prove to be my disciples." Here, Christ teaches that the kind of spiritual formation we are discussing in this chapter ultimately leads to God's glory. Specifically, what leads to God's glory is the fruit that comes from abiding in Jesus. To understand exactly what it means for God to be glorified in our fruit-bearing, it is important to understand the nature of the fruit mentioned in this passage.

Jesus has spoken about fruit several times leading up to His words in John 15:7-8. In general terms, the fruit He discusses flows from our vital union with Jesus. Then in John 15:7-8, He explains the type of the fruit which glorifies the Father: "If you abide in me, and my words abide in you, ask whatever you wish, and it will be done for you. By *this* my father is glorified" (emphasis added). As we noted earlier, the phrase "If you abide in me, and my words abide in you" refers to Jesus' invitation to draw near to Him through reading and reflecting on His Word, and that "asking whatever you wish" is a reference to prayer. Thus, the fruit mentioned in this passage refers to God's answers to our prayers, which are shaped by the words of Jesus abiding in us. Fruit, in John 15, refers to God answering our Word-initiated prayers.

Fruit is what happens when God's people dwell in God's Word and ask God for the things they find in that Word, and God responds to those Word-informed prayers. Such fruit glorifies God for two reasons. First, the reason we, as God's people, are able to abide at all is because of His unilateral act of divine grace, in which He pronounces us clean in Christ. *We are not clean because we abide. We abide because we are clean.* The second reason this fruit glorifies God is because God is the One who produces the fruit by answering the prayers. The fruit does not come from our labor, but from God, who answers our prayers. This kind of fruit glorifies God because it stands as a testimony to His grace as He answers our prayers. This fruit is all of grace and, therefore, all for the glory of God.

Abiding and Joy

As Jesus concludes His words on abiding, He says, "These things I have spoken to you, that my joy may be in you, and that your joy may be full" (John 15:11). These words are fascinating. As we said earlier, when Christians talk about spiritual formation, they usually talk about the spiritual disciplines. That is not wrong. As we already explained, the Bible uses the language of discipline to refer to being spiritually formed into the image of Jesus. Our point here is to highlight the fact John 15:11 does not use the language of formation and discipline, but of abiding and joy. It is passages like this one that teach that pursuing a relationship with Jesus is not about drudgery, but joy.

Jesus tells us two things about this joy. First, the joy He wants us to know in abiding is *His* joy. He says that He has spoken these things "that *my* joy may be in you." Jesus knows the joy He is commending to us; He has experienced it. What is it? John 15:9-10 make this clear: "As the Father has loved me, so have I love you. Abide in my love. If you keep my commandments, you will abide in my love, just as I have kept my Father's commandments and abide in his love." These words teach that Jesus experiences the Father's love ("the Father has loved me"), and that Jesus abides in the Father ("I have kept my Father's commandments and abide in his love"). Jesus wants us to pursue the same living relationship with the Father that He pursues. When we do, the same God-oriented and God-honoring joy that motivates Him will enliven us.

Second, the joy Jesus wants us to know in abiding is *full* joy. Jesus wants to teach us how to have a life full of joy. He could have commended all sorts of wonderful things: marriage, church involvement, acts of service, hard work, vocational ministry, eating, or rest and relaxation. He doesn't commend any of those good things to experience fullness of joy. Rather, He commends abiding. He urges relationship.

If we are honest with ourselves, we have to admit we often talk about spiritual formation in terms of losing something. We set the alarm clock to get up earlier and lose sleep; we fast to make room in our hearts and schedule and lose food; we determine to pray and study the Bible before we accomplish any other task and lose time for work. But Jesus does not talk about spiritual formation in terms of *loss*, but *gain*. When we do what is necessary to pursue an abiding relationship with God, there is addition, not subtraction. God gains glory, and we gain a fullness of Jesus' own joy.

Abiding and Mike

Now let's get back to Mike and take a look at his struggle with worry and how it relates to abiding in Christ and spiritual formation. Mike finds himself overwhelmed and in a constant state of worry about his marriage, work, and involvement at church. Given his genuine relationship with Jesus, how might an unbelieving and deceived heart be the root, sap, and chief power of his worry?

In the Sermon on the Mount, Jesus commanded us not to worry about our lives—what we eat and drink, or about our bodies and clothing (Matthew 6:25). Mike is sinning against God because he is not being obedient to Jesus' command to avoid worry. But notice how Jesus connects His commandment to unbelief. A few verses later He says, "If God so clothes the grass of the field, which today is alive and tomorrow is thrown into the oven, will he not much more clothe you, O you of little faith?" (verse 30). Why does Jesus indict those who worry as those who possess "little faith"? When we worry about our needs and finances, we question God's ability to provide and care for us. Ultimately when we worry, we are telling God, "You are neither trustworthy nor in control, so I need to worry and scheme as I take matters into my own hands." In this way unbelief drives worry, for it is impossible to worry when we are trusting in the provision of our sovereign God.

Mike's failure to abide in Christ not only results in incessant worry, but also leads to his failure to obey Jesus' command to love others (John 15:12). He fails to love his wife because he does not believe that God's call to love his wife as Christ loves the church is more important than making ends meet. He avoids friends at church because he does not believe that God's call for him to live out his faith with other men in community takes precedence over his fears of what others might think about him. And he judges others in response to how he thinks others are judging him because he does not believe the gospel truth that there is no condemnation for those who are in Christ.

In Mike's world of worry, we do not see much evidence of him abiding in Christ or the fruit that comes from an intimate relationship with Jesus. Instead, we see him wracked by a prevailing unbelief that has undermined his faith and hope in Christ and his love for God and others. Mike needs a deep, abiding, believing union with Jesus. No amount of budgeting, simplifying his life, accountability, reconciliation, or time management tips—as important as these can be—will ever provide the abundant life that Jesus wants for Mike. Such a life comes only through an abiding relationship with Jesus—a relationship in which Mike draws near to Jesus through His living Word, by bringing his prayer requests to Him, and by seeking a life of obedience, all through faith in Christ.

Change will not come until Mike repents of his anxious unbelief, turns to Christ, and rests in the Lord's promises to give him true life. As Mike encounters the promises God has given in the Bible, and as he turns those promises into prayers, he will find new power to obey and live a life full of God-glorifying joy. And he will experience a real and lasting peace—one that surpasses all understanding and guards his heart and mind as he abides in Christ Jesus.

With Christ to Be Like Christ

Just like Mike, we tend to seek life in our ability to juggle the myriad of responsibilities and demands on our hectic schedules. We can also try to find life in our family, corporate positions, retirement accounts, quarterly bonuses, and track record. Where is God in all this? Where is the life that He alone can bring? Nowhere. Such false pursuits are not life-giving. They will always disappoint. They make promises they can never keep because they do not contain the life that is possessed in Jesus, our true vine. When we search for life and joy in anything other than God and His promises, we set ourselves up for hopeless worry and lifeless anxiety.

In this chapter, we looked at Mike and his anxious heart. We saw that he searched for satisfaction in "the good things of life," and that his worries were rooted in unbelief regarding God's provision. We could, however, just as easily talk about those who try to find satisfaction in sexual immorality because they do not believe that the love of Christ is enough. We could discuss those who struggle with rage because they do not believe God is in control as they live in His world and under His rule. The logic would be the same for those who lie incessantly because they do not believe anyone could ever love them after finding out about their failures and their flaws. We, too, will struggle with these problems and more when we fail to believe the tender promises of Christ and fight to be spiritually formed in Him by the spiritual disciplines we have discussed.

By God's sovereign wisdom and grace, abiding in Christ is the supremely powerful and foolproof means of conquering the wicked and poisonous sap of unbelief. Jesus commands us to abide in Him because He knows that we are prone to drift from Him and cease believing His Word. To those who seek spiritual formation in Christ, Jesus reminds us, "Abide in Me, because I am the true vine."

20

The Importance of Multiculturalism in Biblical Counseling

Rod Mays and Charles Ware

W hy does a book on biblical counseling include a chapter on multiculturalism? Does not the simple proclamation of the sufficiency of Scripture fill our churches with a diversity of saints that mirror our heavenly community?

The fact is that most of us function in a homogeneous environment, especially in our churches. While the United States is becoming the most culturally diverse nation in the world, less than 5.5 percent of Christian congregations are multiethnic.[1]

This lack of positive multicultural relationships, especially in the church, may have negative consequences. Counselees may lack any sense of responsibility, understanding of personal bias, and confidence in the sufficiency of Scripture to free one from sin regardless of his or her culture.

So what is culture? Hosea Baxter, the urban leadership professor at Crossroads Bible College, defines culture as "the sum of a society's way of thinking and doing. Culture will also include a society's institutions and the products of human work and thoughts." Professor Baxter further provides his view of culture from a biblical perspective as "beliefs and social behaviors that are informed or defined by divine revelation and therefore set the theological/social parameters within a society. Some of these beliefs and behaviors will be temporal and others will be eternal depending on the intentions and dictates of God."[2]

Does culture necessitate divisions within the body of Christ? Why is the evangelical church in the United States so segregated? Could it not be the practical, sociological will of God that churches be ethnically segregated? If so, would not the kingdom be better served by enhancing the homogeneous concept of church planting and discipleship that seems to have served the evangelical community well as far as church growth is concerned? Why not have black, white, Latino, Asian, etc. biblical counseling movements?

James Cone, a liberal theologian, expresses what is perceived to be the practical reality for the white evangelical church, the need for a black theology due to his distrust of white theologians:

> On the American scene today, as yesterday, one problem stands out: the enslavement of black Americans. But as we examine what contemporary theologians are saying, we find that they are silent about the enslaved condition of black people. Evidently they see no relationship between black slavery and the Christian gospel. Consequently, there has been no sharp confrontation of the gospel with white racism. There is, then, a desperate need for a *black theology,* a theology whose sole purpose is to apply the freeing power of the gospel to black people under white oppression.[3]

Is there any truth to Cone's assertion that there is a need for a black theology, even within an evangelical context? As biblical counselors, we must adhere to a biblical theology that addresses a variety of cultural realities. Concerning pastoral counseling of multiracial families, I (Charles) stated the following in the book *Just Don't Marry One*:

> A pastor has an awesome responsibility to speak the mind of God to the people of God as revealed in the Word of God. We do not simply study the crowd, find out what they want, and give it to them. While the Bible must be applied to the times, it is not to be subservient to the times. Thus unity across economic, cultural, and ethnic lines should be proclaimed not because it is the latest fad but rather because it is the clear teaching of the eternal Word of God.[4]

While we must be sensitive to various cultures, at the same time, we have a divine commandment to make disciples of all nations—all people groups (Matthew 28:19). The foundation of the gospel is a Jewish Savior. The gospel was given to and spread by, at the inception, Jewish disciples from Jerusalem to the end of the earth (Acts 1:8). Although there were cultural challenges, there was one body in Christ (Acts 6; 10; 11; 15; Ephesians 2–3). The biblical counselor must always remember that *the root problem is deeper than skin; it is sin.* The ultimate cure is not culture, but Christ.

While Christ is the universal cure for the human family, the Word of God warns us of possible cultural biases that may reside in the counselor. The biblical counselor needs to honestly and continually examine his or her motives and perceptions; otherwise, cultural bias may hinder one's counsel.

Multiculturalism and Biblical Counseling Self-Confrontation

Self-confrontation is a foundational value of biblical counselors. It would seem wise for those of us in a multicultural environment to examine ourselves to identify any cultural bias that might cloud our message. Culturally biased counselors, such as Jonah, for example, can still offer effective counseling (Jonah 4). But we desire a changed heart, like Peter's, that would grant us the humility warranted to address one from another culture with the transcendent Word of God (Acts 10–11).

Like the Pharisees of old, it is easy for us to add cultural layers upon the Word of God (Mark 7:3-13) that blind us to the naked truth needed to transform counselees into the image of Christ. The vision biblical leaders have of God's desire for others has been distorted by various bias-related attitudes:

- Jonah: ethnic and national (Jonah 4:1-11)
- The disciples: ethnic and gender (John 4:4-38)
- Peter: ethnic and religious (Acts 10–11)
- The early church: ethnic and cultural (Acts 15)
- The early church: economic (James 2:1-13)

Counselors need to be sensitive to possible national, ethnic, economic, educational, political, denominational, gender-related, generational, etc. biases that may distort our perception of the counselee's real problem. People, especially in the United States, represent very diverse cultural groups within many of our communities. In many cases, to encounter a different culture, we no longer need to cross the sea; we can do so by merely crossing the street.

Due in part to the ever-increasing cultural diversity in the United States, many have come to embrace secular tolerance, which seeks to affirm all and offend none by considering all truth claims of equal value. The biblical counselor dare not allow the absolute truth of God's Word to be washed away by the tidal waves of secular tolerance. While we affirm the existence of cultural differences, we hold that Scripture alone possesses the absolute transcendent truths that address the deepest needs of all humans.

As biblical counselors we must listen carefully to the text of Scripture to wisely discern transcendent truths from temporary cultural traditions. A profitable exercise is to exegete Scriptures that address absolute truths and issues of biblical cultural diversity. There are several passages we can examine for enlightenment concerning absolute truths not bound by culture: Proverbs 29:18; John 14:6; Acts 17:11; Galatians 1:8-9; Colossians 2:9; 1 Timothy 1:3-11,19-20; 6:20-21; 2 Timothy 2:14-19; 3:16-17; Titus 1:10-17; 3:10-11; 1 Peter 4:10-11; 2 John 1:7-11.

Since biblical counselors are convinced of the sufficiency of Scripture, it is imperative that passages granting cultural liberty on certain issues be examined. Here are some that are worthy of further investigation by all of us: Acts 15:1; Romans 14–15; 1 Corinthians 8-11; Colossians 3:10-15. After a proper interpretation of texts that demand culturally transcendent truths and cultural differences that do not seek to negate those truths be tolerated, we need to make careful application to those various cultures that might be represented in our counseling sessions.

When Cultural Perceptions Clouds the Message

We, as mature believers, are to learn continually. As we do cross-cultural counseling, we should be aware of historical and cultural events that may cloud the message due to a perception of the messenger—us! While this might not always occur, we should be aware of historical and cultural objections to Christ, especially when they relate to perceived and/or actual injustices perpetrated upon a group or culture by Christians. Possessing a general knowledge of diverse cultures enhances our ability to discern how we can best help counselees.

First Corinthians 9:19-23 indicates we have a biblical responsibility to understand the culture of a counselee and appropriately present the message for maximum clarity. Although this passage deals with evangelism, in context, it reveals several critical principles for those who counsel cross-culturally. First, Paul was willing to engage another culture. Second, he understood several cultures—for example, Jews, those under the law, those without the law, and the weak. Third, he was willing to make the adjustments necessary to clearly communicate the message. Fourth, he wisely expected that a clearly communicated message would save some, not all.

Engaging Other Cultures: No Contact, No Impact

Our confidence in effective counseling cross-culturally is rooted in the presence and power of God exhibited through the sufficient Word of God. We are an instrument of, not the source of, God's grace. Along with the command to make disciples of all people groups is the promise of God's presence (Matthew 20:19-20).

With this confidence, biblical counselors should seek to discover key characteristics of the culture of some likely counselees. Like the apostle Paul, we should willingly and confidently engage those of other cultures, believing that God will "save some" (1 Corinthians 9:22). Remember that the root cause of humanity's problem is sin, not the color of one's skin.

Cultural Competency: Understanding Several Cultures

We, as biblical counselors, should learn some of the history, heroes, values, smells, foods, family relationships, crime, suffering, views of shame, marital traditions, blended families, etc. of the various cultures that we may be counseling. In their book *Divided by Faith: Evangelical Religion and the Problem of Race in America* (New York: Oxford University Press, 2001), Michael O. Emerson and Christian Smith chronicle a history of segregation between black and white believers. For many who see Christianity as a tool of oppression and injustice to their people, the present is blurred by the past. The biblical counselor must not underestimate the barrier that past history constructs. Scripture says that "a brother offended is more unyielding than a strong city" (Proverbs 18:19). Biblical counselors need to acknowledge historical facts with humility while proclaiming truth with compassion (Acts 10). In fact, the challenge of broken relationships calls for wisdom from above (James 3:17).

Biblical counselors can silently project a multicultural message by using diverse resources. For example, the power of human heroes cannot be overestimated. Biblical counselors would be well served by gathering diverse positive role models of biblical truth. This is not to suggest using black heroes for black counselees, Latino for Latinos, and so on. No, it is better if we, as biblical counselors, have relationships and illustrations that model the God of the nations we proclaim. Beyond heroes, we should gather diverse, positive examples of cultural traditions different from our own.

Cultures place different values on things such as space, time, tone of voice, eye contact, volume, shame, etc. Ignorance of these differences may cause a counselor to misinterpret or unknowingly offend a counselee.

We must also be mindful that cultures change and individuals do not always fit within cultural stereotypes. These are among the reasons a counselor must learn to listen carefully.

Contextualization for Clear Communication

Many counselors are often reluctant to counsel cross-culturally due to their fear of a lack of cultural identification. We learn in 2 Corinthians 1:4-6 that God uses our personal trials to prepare us to minister to others who experience similar trails. Is it reasonable to conclude from this text that unless we experience the kinds of trials associated with a cultural group or we have some association with such a group, our counsel is useless?

As biblical counselors, we can speak to issues and cultures based upon the sufficiency of Scripture rather than personal experience. However, we would be well served to make adjustments when necessary to ensure the clear communication of our message in various cultural contexts. Paul affirmed that he made certain adjustments to identify with different groups. This meant that he studied cultures and humbly communicated in a manner that was culturally relevant. Paul, the mature believer, was willing to make cultural adjustments to clearly communicate his message (1 Corinthians 9:22). Likewise, we as mature biblical counselors need to take our knowledge of the history, heroes, and values of our counselees' culture and make adjustments for contextualized communication without comprising truth.

Save Some, Not All

Paul wisely expected that his cultural adjustments for a clear communication of the gospel would save some, not all. It is easy within our society to conclude that any counseling failure that involves giving cross-cultural counsel is due to cultural differences. The fact is that our counsel is not always effective even with those from our own culture!

God is no respecter of persons. All who respond to the truth will experience His freedom. We need to communicate clearly—with humility and compassion—God's eternal truth with the confidence that it speaks to the deepest needs of all humanity.

Biblical love for God and neighbor is the ultimate motivator for us to "become all things to all people, that by all means [we] might save some" (1 Corinthians 9:22). Christ's love drove Him from the glories of heaven to identify with fallen humanity. He became one of us so that He might die for us and save us. His sacrificial love was shown to us first, and that should be the basis of our love for others. As Christians, one of our identifying traits is love.

May the love of Christ compel us to live cautiously, freeing our hearts from cultural biases and prompting us to learn continually so that we might educate ourselves about cultural differences, listen carefully, and make cultural adjustments necessary for clearly communicating the biblical message. Then we can counsel courageously with the confidence that God will free some, not all, through His all-sufficient Word.

Critical Principles for Biblical Counseling in a Multicultural Environment

For many of us (especially in an older generation), it is a stretch to imagine ourselves living in other cultures with different values and assumptions about people and situations. The emphasis of multicultural awareness over the past couple of decades has been on the assimilation of varying languages and viewpoints into the prevailing culture, as well as the accommodation of dissimilar ideas and practices, rather than on the traditional American sociological view of the melting pot, which saw various cultures coming together under one ideal and goal (religious and economic freedom). There are three main presuppositions about humanity and culture that will provide for us a platform that assists our understanding of how to make biblical counseling accessible to those from every tribe and tongue and nation: the individual, the demographical background of the counselee, and contextualization.

The Individual

First, we must consider the individual. All men and women are created in God's image (Genesis 1:26). There is unity among all human beings as members of the human race, with further unity and connection among those who are members of the body of Christ, the church. As believers throughout the world, we share many common characteristics (Ephesians 4:4-6). However, there is great diversity among individuals with respect to gifts, abilities, personalities, spiritual maturity, community structure, cultural courtesy and connectedness, needs, dysfunctions, and problems.

This truth has several implications. We know that God will work through His Word, since faith comes by hearing, and hearing by the Word of God (Romans 3:17). What we call the perspicuity of Scripture reminds us that any person influenced and inculcated by any culture can understand the story of the Bible and the message of Scripture:

> All things in Scripture are not alike plain in themselves, nor alike clear unto all: yet those things which are necessary to be known, believed and observed for salvation, are so clearly propounded and opened in some place of Scripture or other, that not only the learned, but the unlearned, in a due use of the ordinary means, may attain unto a sufficient understanding of them.[5]

The theology of the Bible is the foundation for all biblical counseling. However, with respect to counseling methods and models, we must be flexible, taking into account the individual characteristics of both the counselor and the counselee. Counselors are called to meet people where they are and as they are, and not force others to agree or to change behavior, emotions, thinking, or beliefs by means of a standardized or fixed method. It is extremely important to consider a counselee's cultural norms, background, communication abilities, and comfort level in conversation with the counselor. Our methods must be tailored to the individual needs, culture, and personality of the counselee.

Demographic Background

Second, it is imperative to understand the demographical background of those whom we counsel. Our ability to minister is affected by demographic factors, including the socio-economic background of the person, his or her family dynamics, age and stage of life (young, single, married, with or without children, young or grown children, elderly), education level, language (multilingual), and other differences that form natural divisions in the population of the counselee.

These factors affect how much we are humanly able to accomplish (because of language barriers or educational and theological barriers) and how much we can expect to see people change in a given context. These demographical differences will also affect the style of counseling we use and the methods employed.

Contextualization

Third, because of the global nature of our times, contextualization is a necessary component of our counseling. The Bible demands that we move toward people and lift them up (Romans 12), not withdraw and oppress or put them down. According to Timothy Keller,

> "Contextualization" is adapting gospel ministry—the truth of the entire Word of God which describes God's creation, man's fall, God's process of redemption through the work of Jesus, and the hope of the glory to come—to the culture into which we are speaking by: 1) Examining our message to be certain that we do not communicate our own cultural norms and standards of thinking, emotion and behavior rather than the truth of God's Word, and 2) being careful to maintain the truths of the Bible that are unchanging and essential to faith in God through Jesus. The process of contextualization "incarnates" the Christian faith in order to invade a particular culture. It is the process by which we present the gospel, by and through our flesh, to people of a particular worldview in forms that the "receptor-hearers" can understand.[6]

Counseling can become a very moralistic practice of ministry if we refuse to contextualize the message of the Bible so it speaks specifically into the life of the counselee in the way he or she views the self, views God, and is able to understand how practical application of biblical truth should look in his or her everyday life. Distinguishing between cultural norms and biblical absolutes is crucial to counseling that is effective to change not only behavior, emotional responses, and the thought processes of the counselee, but also points the heart to God's mercy and the grace believers have received through the sacrifice of Jesus.

In 1 Corinthians 9:19-23, the apostle Paul specifically asks the Corinthians why they judge his life and his work. He asks open-ended questions as to what behaviors are allowed by the law and what thinking and behavior may put up barriers to the gospel of Christ. Paul encourages the Corinthians to be flexible in their thinking about what constitutes acceptable behavior and to look at Scripture to determine whether an idea or expectation is a biblical mandate or a function of the social pressures exerted by a particular culture. Likewise, we are called, as counselors, to be willing to flex our methodology so that the gospel and hope do not seem to be alien concepts to our counselees because of our limited ability to express the truth of the gospel in a way that connects with the world they know and understand.

Our Rescuer

Our world is changing. Global communication and our more mobile societies mean that the truth of living with and ministering in multiculturalism cannot be ignored if we are to be effective in counseling as we offer hope to a broken world. Consider the story of the Tower of Babel in Genesis 11. After the flood, all people on the earth spoke the same language. In the midst of this uniformity, they decided to build a tower or staircase to heaven so that they could be like (equal to) God. The people thought if they accomplished that, they would be able to live without God's authority and power ruling over them. But God showed them the foolishness of their efforts by suddenly causing them to speak in different languages so that they were unable to communicate. Men and women were scattered all over the world as they sought others with whom they could communicate and share life.

From that one moment in history we have the beginnings of the multiple cultures that exist today. And Revelation 5:9 tells us we'll see the world's multiculturalism represented among God's people: "They sang a new song, saying,

'Worthy are you to take the scroll and to open its seals, for you were slain, and by your blood you ransomed people for God from every tribe and language and people and nation.'" People from every color, tribe, and nation will be in heaven, singing in unison as they lift up music and praise to God. We cannot enjoy that right now because of people's attempt to raise themselves up to God's level through their own ingenuity and willpower. The citizens of Babel did not understand the kind of rescue and rescuer they needed.

The true Rescuer, the Redeemer, is the One we are to make known to the broken, the hurt, the confused—to those who would be free from the struggles of this fallen world. Our message to all cultures, by means of the ministry of biblical counseling, is that fallen people can never escape from a fallen world and raise themselves up to be in the presence of God by their own intelligence, will, and power. Instead, heaven must come down in the person of Jesus.

The Nature of the Biblical Counseling Relationship

Jeremy Pierre and Mark Shaw

In 1 Thessalonians 2:8 the apostle Paul pens some pretty friendly words to the believers in Thessalonica—words that may seem too friendly for a counseling relationship: "Being affectionately desirous of you, we were ready to share with you not only the gospel of God but also our own selves, because you had become very dear to us." From our cultural vantage point, we tend to think of counselors as therapists who apply various theories of health to their clients during a session, after which a pleasant secretary acts as boundary between counselor and counselee until the next appointment. We might imagine the client and therapist being a bit embarrassed when they run into one another at the grocery store or a school play. The relationship is largely contractual, not easily mixed with the events of everyday life. It is not exactly a friendship—at least, not the type of redemptive friendship displayed in Paul's words in 1 Thessalonians 2:8.

But when it comes to biblical counseling, friendship is central to the counseling relationship because it is a key aspect of the gospel. Paul's words display it; Jesus' actions prove it. In Jesus Christ, friendship has its ultimate—that is, its paradigmatic—display. He sacrificially gave Himself for the good of those He befriended—people who were the awkward and troubled types, people who did not offer Him anything particularly desirable in return. Yet to this group of dirty-footed friends He spoke in intimate terms: "This is my commandment, that you love one another as I have loved you. Greater love has no one than this, that someone lay down his life for his friends" (John 15:12-13).

Jesus compelled His followers to follow Him in befriending others sacrificially. But who could presume to love in the same manner Jesus did? The phrase "as I have loved you" cannot be domesticated. Jesus' love is not warm sentiment, but sober self-emptying. Such love is powerfully redemptive, piercingly truthful, intensely set on glorifying God. How can we dare claim to be such friends to others, particularly in the counseling relationship?

The answer comes in the preceding verses of this passage. Jesus' followers will display such love only as they abide in Christ and in His Word (verses 1-11). And as they do so, they prove to be His disciples in their befriending love for others (verse 12). And all this is to display the glory of God. Jesus said so Himself: "By this is my Father glorified, that you bear much fruit and so prove to be my disciples" (verse 8).

And so our vision of the counseling relationship begins to form around this task: to make disciples to the glory of God. And God uses the love of a Christian for his or her friend to accomplish this—a Word-dependent, Christ-trusting, God-glorifying love. Any other kind of love falls short of the calling of the biblical counseling relationship.

Having established a theological vision of the counseling relationship, we now consider how this relationship is structured around the main tasks of counseling in the forming of disciples. We explore how a biblical counselor's early efforts must be centered upon establishing what makes for a high-quality friendship based upon sacrificial love.

A Uniquely Structured Friendship

The counseling relationship is unique in that it is, at least for an apportioned time, more structured than a casual friendship. It is organized around a certain set of tasks—an *agenda*, to use a word we often shy away from with regard to a friendship. But this is an agenda in the positive sense—*an intentional structure for the eternal help of another*. In one sense, all Christian friendships should have this agenda; the biblical counseling relationship only puts a unique *structure* to this agenda.

First we establish a connection with counselees by understanding them and helping them understand themselves biblically. Then we show them the love of Christ as displayed in His person and work. Finally, we encourage them with the hope of seeing a way through their trouble. These tasks give helpful structure to the relationship as we seek to follow the biblical call of friendship.

Establishing Connection: Biblical Counselors Seek to Understand Counselees and to Help Them to Understand Themselves Biblically

People know intuitively whether a relationship is one of true investment or not. We can all tell the difference between the low investment of a casual acquaintance and the high investment of a dear friend. Biblical counselors establish a sense of investment in the people they serve by being an understanding, insightful friend.

An Understanding Friend

The counseling relationship requires the hard work of listening well. Not many interactions make a person feel more isolated than when they feel misunderstood. A person is more likely to feel misunderstood if he is handed answers that have not adequately considered the matter at hand. Offering an answer before one has heard a matter is folly and shame, according to Proverbs 18:13. A productive counseling relationship requires that the counselor understand as best he can how his friend experiences life, particularly in regard to the issues at hand. Friendship cannot flourish without such connection, and a counselor should be committed to listening well as a good friend.

An Insightful Friend

Having connected in this way, counselors can then help their friends understand their own experiences better. Have you ever noticed how a good friend will often help you understand yourself better by making casual observations or by asking just the right question as you relate something to them? A good friend can act as a mirror that helps you to see yourself more clearly. A good friend is often the best access you have to an outside take on your life. He sees things you don't, and by doing so, keeps you better grounded in reality. We all know people who live in isolation, their idiosyncratic thought processes rolling over and over in their minds, unchallenged by the perspectives of others. Soon their thinking solidifies into an unassailable bastion from reality. Good friends interrupt our constant gravitation toward self-reference.

Biblical counselors do this for others, only in a more structured way. They help people look carefully at how they think, what they desire, how they feel about certain things, what they are loyal to. They offer new, biblical interpretations of their experience. They help them understand both their inner and outer lives *from the perspective of Scripture.*

In keeping with the pastoral hearts of the New Testament writers, counselors are generous in their estimation of those they minister to, believing the best about them and going out on a limb to speak of their hope for them (2 Corinthians 7:16; Hebrews 6:9). At the same time, they help guard against the self-deception of sin's pervasive power (Hebrews 3:12-13) by challenging counselees to consider its quiet influence deep within (Romans 7:7-25). The counseling relationship is marked by both types of connection: confident hope and realistic vigilance.

Showing Love: Biblical Counselors Help People to Know Christ Better

The connection of friendship takes place in service to a more meaningful connection still. Through your friendship, Christ beckons people into relationship with Himself. And this is not any generic friendship, but the sharing of His righteousness so that people are made fit for the eternal blessings for which they were made (2 Corinthians 5:19-20). This relational invitation is not just for people who don't yet know Christ. Even those who have been Christians for a long time can lose sight of the love of Jesus Christ for them and all that God is calling them to be. There is no greater service you can give to a friend than to keep the love of Christ central to your relationship. Biblical counselors do this by being a friend who is wise in the Word and a friend who reminds people of Jesus.

A Friend Wise in the Word

Introducing counselees to Christ means introducing them to His Word. How else would we know about the cosmic demonstration of His love for people who did not love Him (Romans 5:8)? Where else do we see the sheer expanse of the love that surpasses knowledge (Ephesians 3:14-19)? Jesus equates abiding in His love with abiding in His Word (John 15:4-11). Receiving Christ means receiving His Word. Therefore, to be the best friend you can be to your counselee, you should have infectious love for the Word, unshakeable confidence in the Word, and familiarity with the Word.

Infectious Love for the Word: Psalm 19:10; 119:16

You can't teach a person to love something. But you can get him to feel the heat of your love for something. Counselors should display in their relationships a love for God's Word that compels others to love the Word.

Unshakeable Confidence in the Word: Isaiah 55:10-11; 2 Timothy 3:16-17

Counselors should be unembarrassed by their wholehearted reliance upon the Word of God. This is relationally compelling for spurring others toward greater confidence in the Word.

Thorough Familiarity with the Word: Psalm 119:10-11

We are familiar with what is important to us. Some people know the names of every Star Wars character and every class of starship in the movie series. We should be no less familiar with the Word of God. Our familiarity with the Word is a statement of its practical importance for daily living.

A Friend Who Reminds People of Jesus

We have an incarnational ministry. The most eloquent teaching, the most piercing insights, or the most effective methods mean nothing without love (1 Corinthians 13:1-3). This hard relational fact keeps us honest as counselors. Or better said, it keeps us dependent. Because we will not love those who are difficult to love had Christ not beat us to the task (1 John 4:19). Any love we show a counselee is merely a representative love. Counselors represent Christ's love in sympathy, in righteousness, and in service.

In Sympathy

Though sinless, Christ is nevertheless sympathetic with weakness and temptation (Hebrews 4:15), and we should be the same with confused, sinning, and suffering people. We are, in other words, representatives of the sympathetic High Priest who represents people before God in prayer. Good counselors grieve with the hurting and rejoice with the victorious (Romans 12:15) because that is what Jesus does.

In Righteousness

Friends mimic one another, both positively and negatively (Proverbs 13:20). In fact, imitation is one of the most powerful forms of teaching, and counselors ought not to underestimate it (1 Corinthians 4:16; 11:1; Philippians 3:17). A living, breathing example often brings to life what can seem abstract. This is especially true with concepts like *righteousness*. An important aspect of the counseling friendship is to display the righteousness of the One who shared His with us. Obedience necessarily springs from faith (Romans 1:5,16-17), particularly in regard to manifesting Jesus' love by caring for suffering people (James 2:14-17). Being a good friend is casting a living vision of how righteousness operates in real life.

In Service

Jesus was the ultimate friend; He proved His title in laying down His life for His friends (John 15:13). The heart of Christ is one that served undeserving people, and we need this in our counseling ministries. Without a servant's heart, we will relate to counselees primarily for what *they* can do for *us*—like give us the satisfaction of success or the affirmation of their gratefulness.

Instilling Hope: Biblical Counselors Help People Understand a Way Through

In times of great darkness, sometimes even a flicker of hope can change the course of a person's life. The amazing thing about Christian hope is that it is not mere wishful thinking, but the certainty of the Almighty's promise that His purposes for a person will not be lost in that darkness. A connected, loving friend serving as a biblical counselor has a unique opportunity to instill this hope in a counselee by being a hopeful friend, a friend who sees a way through, and a friend who motivates.

A Friend Who Is Hopeful

Sometimes the greatest encouragement comes when a friend displays hope in a situation you had long thought hopeless. A counselor acts this way for those she helps because of whom she trusts—God Himself. Sometimes your expectation of positive results will inspire a counselee's hope for positive change (Psalm 146:5). This expectation does not come from your skill as a counselor, any degree or certification, or any training. Instead, it comes from knowing Christ and having faith in Him that He will work for the good of the counselee according to His purposes for His own glory (Romans 8:28).

Biblical counselors have the responsibility of pointing counselees to Christ Himself, the object and source of hope. As one who points to the coming dawn when the night is at its darkest, the counselor points counselees to the glory of Jesus, which provides light for navigating life's dark circumstances.

A Friend Who Sees a Way Through

Many of us know the rising hope that comes when we talk with a friend who has been through the same kind of trouble we're experiencing and has given insight for getting through it. Advice like that is golden. A biblical counselor provides such hope to people struggling with particular troubles, giving preemptive warnings on potential hazards and positive strategies for making progress. The counselor knows enough about his friend to see the strengths and weaknesses of how he typically relates to life, offering him warning and encouragement as appropriate. This process can serve as part of what the apostle Peter calls "preparing your minds for action" (1 Peter 1:13). The language of planning and preparation in this verse is coupled with "set your hope fully on the grace that will be brought to you at the revelation of Jesus Christ." *Planning* and *hope* go together. A wise friend knows this, and helps a friend see what *specific actions steps of hopefulness* look like in the troubles he is facing.

A Friend Who Motivates

Few things are more motivating for exercise at 6:00 Saturday morning than a knock on the door from the friend you are training with. In fact, sometimes that knock is the only thing that can overpower the soft magnetism of the pillow. A biblical counselor is called to be that kind of friend. This motivation looks different depending on the state of the one being helped, of course. Following the counsel of 1 Thessalonians 5:14, "We urge you, brothers, admonish the idle, encourage the fainthearted, help the weak, and be patient with them all," a loving biblical counselor will learn to recognize where counselees fall in the complex spectrum of being idle, fainthearted, or weak. His attempts to motivate them will match the state of their heart. He would not admonish the fainthearted or simply encourage the idle. It would be wrong to do so and fail to bring real hope, which would demotivate the heart of the counselee. Just like the energetic friend at your door at 6:00 in the morning, the counselor helps motivate action that otherwise would be less likely to happen—for the health and success of the counselee.

Practical Guidelines for the Counseling Relationship

Thus far, we have considered a broad view of the counseling relationship. Now we move to some specific tips for managing this structured friendship well. We offer these as precisely that—*tips*, not immortal law. Different situations may demand quite different actions.

Set Proper Expectations

You as the biblical counselor are not the solution to anyone's problems. A counselee must not become dependent upon you, but rather upon the Lord. A biblical counselor trusts that Christ Himself will intervene in the life of the counselee. One of the best ways to foster a dependence upon Christ alone is to have clear guidelines in place, starting with prayer.

Prayer

The counselee should be aware that you are not God. Better yet, she should be aware that *you are aware* that you are not God. If God does not move, counselees are without hope. Dependence must be on the divine relationship, not on any human one. As a counselor, you must demonstrate this explicitly by *your* dependence upon the Lord. Every session should involve prayer, sometimes extensive prayer. Do not treat prayer as merely an introductory transition from talking about football to talking about serious things. In a sense, prayer is the main work you do in the session, and you should acknowledge it as such to the counselee. After all, if Christ was prayerfully dependent upon the Father, how much more should His followers be (Matthew 6:5-13)? Let the people you counsel hear frequently of your dependence upon the Lord for wisdom and your confidence that He alone grants it out of His abundant generosity (James 1:5-8).

Availability

Fostering a counselee's reliance upon God does not mean that the biblical counselor make himself inaccessible outside of the counseling session. As we said, the heart of the counselor should look like Paul's, who was ready to share not only the gospel but his very self with others (1 Thessalonians 2:8). Yet this heart should be displayed with propriety and discretion. Because of the intimate nature of counseling, you should create clear expectations for your availability through written documents such as consent forms that are signed at the outset of counseling. Whether contact will take place via phone calls, texts, emails, social media, and the like must be individually determined by each counselor and communicated clearly to the counselee. Here are some suggestions for maintaining propriety while showing availability.

Phone

Calls should be limited to certain hours of the day, except in emergencies. Sometimes you will need to help counselees discern what constitutes an emergency. The danger of phone contact is that the counselee will become too dependent upon the counselor, insensitive to the private life or busy schedule of the counselor, and seek quick solutions without allowing time for the counselor to ask the tough questions that give the whole picture of the problem at hand. Some counselors have counselees call an administrative assistant rather than provide a personal number.

Any phone calls that do take place should serve a specific purpose, and you can help set this expectation in the beginning by saying something like, "What particular question can I answer for you?" As you hear the answer, try to discern how much a phone conversation can accomplish and how much should be left to in-person counsel. Then direct the conversation accordingly. Also, try to end every phone call with prayer. It serves as a natural close to a conversation, and makes it clear to the counselee that God is with all who call on Him at any time.

Texts

Texts are immediate and brief in nature, making them particularly dangerous for a counselee to use as an avenue for sending impulsive thoughts. Do not counsel over texts. As a form of communication, it is inadequate for dispensing careful, patient advice. In most cases, counselees should be encouraged to use email if they'd like to communicate their thoughts in text format. Email is less intrusive and has less expectation of an immediate reply.

Email

Email can be an effective way of allowing counselees to organize their thinking. But it is best not to do too much counseling through email, particularly when a back-and-forth conversation begins to emerge. Email is best used to summarize themes and outline homework. Make it clear to the counselee that you may not have the chance to answer every email, but you will certainly read them and consider them as you work with him in person.

Social Media

Facebook, Twitter, and other forms of online contact can be helpful ways of knowing the interests and habits of your counselees. But given the public nature of wall posts, status updates, and tweets, these should be used with great caution. (Direct messages function basically as email and can be thought of according to the guidelines above.) You protect your counselee by keeping to a minimum any public inquiries about how they're doing or offhand comments about seeing them soon. The temptation of public social media is to make them feel special in front of others or to make yourself look like an attentive friend, but neither are worth the potential liabilities.

It is not always clear how to decipher between the use of email, phone, and in-person contact. If a counselor is not careful, this age of instant access will work against long-term productivity. You should think through both the advantages and disadvantages of using modern communication technology. Email, social media, and even phone calls do not adequately convey voice tone, nonverbal gestures, and the warmth of direct presence, all of which are significant aspects of effective communication. Basically, it is always best to meet face-to-face whenever possible and to use other means of communication as supplements. Whatever limits the counselor decides upon and sets at the beginning of the counseling relationship should be adhered to on a consistent basis because those limits will often be tested by the counselee.

Time and Duration

Setting up expectations regarding the time and duration of meetings is another challenge simply because some sessions will "break open" late or require long and involved explanation of complex details. But generally, you should keep to the schedule, particularly in the early sessions, when expectations are being formed. It is courteous to give counselees at least 24 hours' notice if you need to cancel, and they should offer the same courtesy to you.

Regarding demands for more time, for counselees who are putting forth a great amount of effort as evidenced by their commitment to working their plan, doing homework assignments, and seeking to obey Christ, counselors may want to offer more time in counseling sessions. For counselees who are failing to put forth adequate effort, counselors may want to shorten a session to allow the counselee more time to spend in prayer and working on biblical homework assignments. Doing this will help encourage a counselee to develop more reliance upon Christ than upon the counselor. When a counselee does not do the assigned homework prior to each session, that may indicate he has a poor understanding of the necessity of spending time with God first and foremost. In this case, a biblical counselor may have a counselee who must be admonished due to idleness (1 Thessalonians 5:14). On several occasions when I have counseled someone struggling with an addiction, I (Mark) have shortened the length of the counseling session and asked the counselee to spend the remainder of the time working on the assignment while I work simultaneously in the same room. This may seem brusque, but my purpose is exactly opposite: to encourage an obedient relationship with Christ not just in word but in action (James 1:22).

Limit of Counsel

Limiting your counsel to the person or couple in front of you is always wise. Many times, counselees will want you to counsel other people in their situation, such as outside family members. Requests for you to meet with additional people may be an attempt, on their part, to divert your attention from their own responsibility in the situation to someone else's. While this is not always the case, we recommend that counselors address the counselee's heart and culpability prior to considering any request to counsel other people. Once a counselor is satisfied with the progress of the primary counselee, then it may be appropriate to invite others into the counseling process. It is, however, helpful to remind a counselee with such a request that life in a fallen world means that relational discord will not be perfectly solved this side of heaven, and the counseling process cannot encompass every relationship connected with the counselee.

Initiating and Following Up

If you counsel under the authority of a local church, there will be no shortage of counselees from within the body of believers as well as from the community at large. Word of mouth, along with whatever forms of advertising the ministry publishes, will likely lead people to come to you. This is especially true in churches that set a vision for member care that emphasizes the value of the interpersonal ministry of counseling within its discipleship strategy. In these cases, it is helpful to appoint, on the church staff, an administrative assistant who can handle the scheduling of counseling appointments.

Initiate

At other times, you will be made aware of folks who need counseling but are unwilling to initiate it. In these cases, with the approval of the pastors or church leadership, a direct appeal in person is best. There is something powerful about personal presence in appealing to someone. The second best option is a phone call. Do not attempt to initiate contact via an email and certainly not a text. If the person remains unresponsive to the call for counsel, the church leaders should discuss the pastoral implications of guarding the person from the deceitfulness of sin (Hebrews 3:12-13). The goal is not to force a person into counseling, but to help him overcome any fears that stem from a lack of wanting to expose himself. Proverbs 28:13 reminds us, "Whoever conceals his transgressions will not prosper, but he who confesses and forsakes them will obtain mercy." Biblical counseling is meant to be a blessing and not a curse to the counselee.

Follow-up

Follow-up after formal counseling has ended is usually a good idea, and in some cases is necessary. Crisis situations usually require follow-up to monitor the health and safety of those who came through it. Even noncrisis situations, though, often benefit from a simple check-in, whether in the form of a phone call or a meeting. When formal counseling has ended, a counselor can schedule or simply recommend that counselees come back in six months for a check-in. Counselees still feel connected when this follow-up session is offered, and will understand that they are now expected to continue applying what they have learned in the counseling process, only now without direct supervision.

The goal of this follow-up meeting is merely to see if the counselee is maintaining the biblical perspective you have tried to instill, to see if he is discouraged or encouraged, and to offer prayer support. Usually counselees are quite grateful for a follow-up appointment.

Coordinate Your Ministries

The counseling relationship is merely one among many in a counselee's life. And a wise counselor will utilize those other relationships, particularly those within the church community. In our church, I (Jeremy) frequently conduct what I call ministry coordination meetings, in which we gather the counselees' supporting community to instruct them how best to minister to the counselee. These meetings include the counselees' fellow small group members and any pastors or friends who are closely involved in the person's life. I use our Sunday school time slot to hold these meetings because it is a convenient gathering time for many, and childcare is available as well. These meetings are infrequent enough for the individuals involved that they do not hamper people's regular involvement in the teaching ministry of the church, and the meetings are a highly effective tool for equipping our people to address the difficulties of life.

Mobilize Your Small Groups[1]

When a well-known political figure declared it takes a village to raise a child, she had the right concept but the wrong means. Her "village" was the federal government, but we know that the more ideal village is the church of Jesus Christ. Biblical counseling is no different: it takes a body of believers in a faith family. Churches with relationally intentional small groups can be a vital resource to a counselee who desires to pursue transformation by the power of Christ.

No one was created to live in isolation. We need each other, and Proverbs 18:1 reveals the heart motivation of those who prefer to live in isolation: "Whoever isolates himself seeks his own desire; he breaks out against all sound judgment." Counselees should be encouraged to live transparent, open lives with those whom they are closest. Perfect intimacy was a reality before the Fall (Genesis 2:25), and counselees who learn to be open and honest with fellow believers in the church will benefit greatly in terms of sanctification. It is ideal for a member of the small group to accompany a counselee in the counseling process, if possible. This serves two functions: It benefits the counselee in terms of additional prayer, accountability, encouragement, and support. And it benefits the small group member with further training in how to apply the truths of God's Word to people's hearts.

Involve Your Pastors

First Peter 5:2 makes it clear that God's overseers are willing shepherds, eager to care for their people. A pastor who can be involved in loving oversight of the flock has the opportunity to provide tangible blessings to any counselee in a number of ways. Counselees who are given pastoral care experience love and connection to the body of believers; they are provided discipline (Hebrews 12:7-12), and they learn to recognize the authority of God in their lives (Romans 13:1). Even if an individual pastor, elder, or other church leader is not involved in the counseling process itself, he can be an additional source of guidance and hope. Counselees truly benefit—and are often powerfully changed—when pastoral leaders extend loving oversight to them.

Empower Family and Friends

Relationships that are already established prior to the initiation of a counseling relationship can have a remarkable impact on a counselee's success. As described above, a wise counselor will involve godly people in a counselee's life in the counseling process. You can encourage the counselee to invite a spiritually mature family member or a close friend into a session or two in order to outline the themes of the counseling relationship and recruit their help for specific goals in the counselee's life. Again, this emphasizes the transparency and humility required for transformational growth within the body of Christ and de-emphasizes an expert model of counseling.

Redemptive Friendships

The counseling relationship is simply a structured version of Christian friendship. Structuring the relationship around the right goals and keeping a wise level of propriety will help keep it productive and enjoyable. But the foundation of a successful relationship is not the structure we have outlined. Rather, it is Jesus' sacred command to love one another *as He has loved us*. This standard is impossible apart from His redemptive love changing us first. From start to finish, the counseling relationship is dependent upon Christ's friendship to sinners. And we should not want it any other way.

The Central Elements of the Biblical Counseling Process

Randy Patten and Mark Dutton

The goal of this book is to equip biblical counselors to minister God's Word to hurting people with confidence, competence, and compassion. Building upon the robust and relational biblical counseling theology and methodology presented in this volume, we believe that the counseling process can be summarized by the following six practices:

- gathering pertinent information

- sorting out the problems

- involvement

- hope

- instruction: the path forward

- homework

The mere understanding of these aspects of the private ministry of the Word will not make you an excellent biblical counselor. But your comprehension of these principles and how they interact with one another in the counseling process will set you on the path toward being able to extend compassionate care. The degree to which you develop relational competency in each of these areas will significantly influence your effectiveness in counseling, whether it is done formally in a church office or informally at a coffee shop.

If it so happens that you are not as effective as you would like to be, it is likely in part because you are weak in one or more of these basic relational practices. As you read along, seek to identify the ways in which you can sharpen your skills in these six areas.

Gathering Pertinent Information

Jesus Christ, the Perfect Counselor, knows all things. We don't. Therefore, gathering significant data is an important part of a biblical counselor's work. Our ability to minister God's Word to hurting people with confidence, competence, and compassion is greatly influenced by how well we understand counselees and their circumstances, goals, and motives. Three Scripture passages provide helpful direction in accomplishing this goal.

Proverbs 18:13 says, "He who gives an answer before he hears, it is folly and shame to him" (NASB). We are foolish when we interact with our counselees about how they need to renew their thinking or change their behavior without first taking time to hear with compassion and understanding their life stories, current circumstances, concerns, and struggles. Solomon admonishes us to listen before we advise.

Proverbs 18:15 adds, "The mind of the prudent acquires knowledge, and the ear of the wise seeks knowledge" (NASB). The more clearly you understand how individuals view and make decisions about themselves, God, key relationships, and present challenges, the better prepared you are to minster God's Word meaningfully with them. That kind of information does not just fall into your lap; you will have to actively seek it.

Proverbs 18:17 alerts us that "the first to plead his case seems right, until another comes and examines him" (NASB). There are always two sides to every story, and sometimes more. Listening to only one party in a conflict will lead to imbalanced, partial, and skewed understanding. Wise counselors seek to obtain pertinent information from all the key parties in a conflict. They seek to have all the parties together at the same time. This allows everyone to hear the same thing at the same time and gives the counselor an opportunity to observe people's responses and interactions with one another.

Someone skillfully summarized the application of these three verses from Proverbs 18 by saying that biblical counselors are to listen for facts, listen actively for facts, and listen actively for *all* the facts. Here are four helpful strategies for gathering the pertinent information:

Go Back

Ask your counselees to give you a seven-to-ten minute life history, starting with when and where they were born. Ask them to tell you about their parents, what early home life was like, the relationship they had with their parents, and special interests as a child, adolescent, and teenager. Ask them to describe what school days were like, what they did after high school. Ask them to tell you about the individuals or events that had a significant impact on their lives.

You might say, "I'm not looking for someone to blame things on, but I do want to know about the various zigs and zags your life has taken and contributed to you becoming the person you are today." This is usually a rich data-gathering and relationship-building time.

Go Wide

Typically one major concern will prompt individuals or couples to seek help, but nobody has just one problem in life. Problems tend to overlap and build on one another. So make sure you seek to understand the big picture of your counselee's life.

That will involve asking questions about the counselee's health, spiritual life, family, work/school, social life, finances, and other current concerns. This is sometimes called "extensive data gathering."

Go, Go, Go, and Go Deep

The information most helpful to a counselor is frequently not obtained in response to questions number 1, 2, and 3 in a given area, but to questions 4, 5, and 6. It is when further probing is done that significant data comes to light.

"A plan in the heart of a man is like deep water, but a man of understanding draws it out" (Proverbs 20:5 NASB). Wise counselors will seek understanding that goes beyond the superficial and the obvious.

Go Open-Ended

Questions that elicit a yes or no answer can be helpful, and sometimes are the most appropriate. However, open-ended questions frequently provide more helpful information to a counselor. For example, a husband's response to the question, "Do you love your wife?" is usually predictable and not very enlightening. His answer to "In what ways do you demonstrate love to your wife?" is much more informative, especially if his wife is present and you can observe her reaction to his answers.

Sorting Out the Problems

The counselor who does a thorough job learning about his counselee's life, circumstances, and thinking patterns figuratively ends up with a large mound of problems on his desk. At this point, you are ready to break down this mound into smaller piles or categories.

Presenting Problem

The presenting problem is the particular event or circumstances that motivated the individual or couple to seek help. Frequently it comes with lots of emotion surrounding it. For example, you may receive a phone message from an obviously distraught mother who pleads, "Please call me right away…I don't care how late it is…our teenager is driving us nuts."

The presenting problem will have to be addressed in some way even though you may determine there are other important long-term problems to deal with. If you do not address what compels people to see you, they frequently will not come back.

Behavior

Who did what to whom? What happened, and when? Like a good detective, a careful biblical counselor will separate the facts from the emotions. Clearly understanding the facts is critical to developing a wise plan for helping the counselee.

One anxious woman phoned and, in between sobs, exclaimed, "My husband is leaving me…my marriage is over…I can't raise the kids by myself…I don't know what to do!" Further investigation revealed that the husband had left the house after a lengthy argument in which both the husband and wife made hurtful statements about the other and talked of life after divorce. After talking with the husband, the counselor learned that he had not filed for divorce or even consulted with an attorney. He did admit, however, that he had manifested sinful anger in both words and actions. Though he was very frustrated, he still desired to work things out with his wife. The facts of the situation were a lot different than what was reported initially.

Thinking

The way individuals think about the issues of life and living significantly affect their conduct. Proverbs 23:7 says of a person, "As he thinks within himself, he is" (NASB). Proverbs 4:23 adds, "Watch over your heart with all diligence, for from it flow the springs of life" (NASB). Repeated thoughts become deeprooted perspectives. They become the lens through which we view all of life.

Therefore, skilled biblical counselors will seek to understand how their counselees think about themselves, handling problems, God, culpability for current difficulties, etc. Look for thinking patterns that have been prevalent for a long time and are now affecting the person's current circumstances. This includes the counselee's habitual responses to difficulties.

Motivations

Why do your counselees do what they do and say what they say? What drives them? Who are they seeking to please? What do they want so badly that they are willing to sin to get it or to keep it? Who do they want to please more than God? The Scriptures call this an idol of the heart (Ezekiel 14:1-8 NASB) or lust (Ephesians 4:22 NASB).

The apostle Paul asked, "Am I now seeking the favor of men, or of God? Or am I striving to please men? If I were still trying to please men, I would not be a bond-servant of Christ" (Galatians 1:10 NASB). These are good questions for both the counselor and counselee to answer. Lasting change that pleases God begins with understanding and purifying one's motives.

Involvement

Another important part of the counseling process is gaining involvement with the counselee. While the definition of this term may differ in the different fields of counseling, involvement is a central element in the counseling process. A preliminary definition of involvement is "building a relationship with the counselee where you put yourself in a position to help."

We can have great spiritual impact on others as we work at establishing a relationship with them. Jesus, the Wonderful Counselor, established relationships with the people to whom He ministered—even to the point of calling His disciples "My friends" (John 15:14 NASB). Because we are ambassadors for Christ, we need to build a relationship with our counselees. We should put ourselves in a position to help them by building a relationship with them and fulfilling what Jesus expects from us as "the salt of the earth" and "the light of the world" (Matthew 5:13-14), and as we live as examples of a growing believer in Christ.

The amount of emphasis placed on involvement is determined by our view of our role as a counselor. God's Word places a great deal of emphasis on building relationships:

- Acts 20:31: "Be on the alert, remembering that night and day for a period of three years I did not cease to admonish each one with tears" (NASB).

- 1 Thessalonians 2:7-8: "We proved to be gentle among you, as a nursing mother tenderly cares for her own children. Having so fond an affection for you, we were well-pleased to impart to you not only the gospel of God but also our own lives, because you had become very dear to us" (NASB).

A detailed definition for biblical involvement is as follows: "Accepting the counselees as persons important to God, and coming alongside in concern and love to see their problems in order to help them find biblical solutions and change for God's glory and the counselee's benefit." Sometimes it's hard to build relationships, especially with those who have sinned in the ways many counselees have sinned. However, those problems can be overcome. The question at this point is this: How does a counselor establish or gain involvement with the counselee?

Be Available

We are to be available not just during the counseling session, but in between sessions, if necessary, for emergency situations. This shows you care about them and want to help.

Be Sensitive

We are to be sensitive to our counselees' needs. They may be hurting or suffering with certain circumstances or struggling with specific sins. As counselors, we need to deal with problems in the context of (1) "How can this problem make you more like Christ?" and (2) "How can this problem draw you closer to Christ?"

Be Your Own Person

You need to be your own person, so don't mask your value system. We always find Paul building deep relationships with people through ministering the truth in a loving manner.

Be Willing to Take the Counselee Seriously and Address the Problem with Biblical Answers

When a counselee says, "I'm a terrible person," don't reply with, "Oh, you're not so bad." Instead, ask, "What have you done or what are you doing that makes you see yourself as such a terrible person?" When you approach the counseling process in this manner, people will gain hope because they know you're taking their problems seriously—especially when you show them the appropriate biblical answers God has for the very situations they are facing.

Don't Be Manipulated by Counselees

They may have manipulated others with their anger attacks, facial expressions, or even crying. But as biblical counselors, we need to let them know that anything they might do will not cause us to get off track when it comes to providing biblical answers to their problems.

Be a Model of the Very Truth You Are Presenting

Paul said in Philippians 4:9, "The things you have learned and received and heard and seen in me, practice these things" (NASB). As counselors, we need to "be an example of those who believe" (1 Timothy 4:12). Among the outstanding characteristics of the Wonderful Counselor are that Jesus was loving, humble, and here to serve, not to be served. Throughout His ministry, He modeled how to build involvement with people. We can do the same with His help!

Hope

When counselees leave a counseling session, you want them to have far more hope than when they came into the session. If that happens, they will return for more counsel. A working definition of hope is this: "conveying an assurance that God is working good in our lives for His glory and our growth in Christ." We have to help our counselees understand that God is up to something good in their lives! There is a purpose for what is occurring—a purpose that can help them get to a better place in their walk with God and help them to experience "the peace…which surpasses all understanding" (Philippians 4:7).

It is amazing how much God's Word deals with this issue of hope:

- Psalm 42:5: "Why are you in despair, O my soul? And why have you become disturbed within me? Hope in God, for I shall again praise Him for the help of His presence" (NASB).

- Romans 15:4: "Whatever was written in earlier times was written for our instruction, so that through perseverance and the encouragement of the Scriptures we might have hope" (NASB).

- Philippians 1:6: "I am confident of this very thing, that He who began a good work in you will perfect it until the day of Christ Jesus" (NASB).

This brings us to five steps a counselor can take to help accomplish the goal of instilling hope in the counseling process.

Step 1: Cast a Vision of What God Can Do Through His Word and His Spirit in a Person's Life

Some people have not had the opportunity to see change take place in another person up close, or they can't point to any significant changes in their own lives. A counselor needs to help the counselee see that nothing is impossible with God (see Luke 1:37). This does not necessarily mean their immediate circumstances will change, but the way they respond to their situation can be dramatically different.

Step 2: Communicate the Promises of God and His Character During Times of Temptation

A key verse for hope is 1 Corinthians 10:13: "No temptation has overtaken you but such as is common to man; and God is faithful, who will not allow you to be tempted beyond what you are able, but with the temptation will provide the way of escape also, so that you will be able to endure it" (NASB).

Step 3: Illustrate How Victory Is Possible in the Midst of Human Frailty and Difficult Circumstances

Hebrews chapter 11, often referred to as the "Hall of Faith," mentions several examples of Old Testament figures whom God helped change and grow. Your own life could serve as a modern-day illustration for your counselees! Telling them about the changes that have taken place in your past could give them hope. You can also connect a counselee with another person or a couple who used to struggle with something that the counselee is struggling with now.

This is one of the key benefits of offering counseling services in the context of the local church—it allows you to connect counselees with others who have faced similar circumstances and learned how to make wise choices that glorify God. You might consider putting together videos or written testimonies from such people so you can use their life stories in the counseling process.

Step 4: Use Biblical Terminology to Describe Problems

When you counsel someone, describe their problem the same way the Bible does. For example, instead of using the term *an affair*, use the word *adultery*. Using biblical terms allows you to go to the Scriptures and give biblical solutions to the problems the counselees are facing. Those who attempt to soften their counsel by calling sin a mistake or a disorder of some sort end up removing accountability from the counselee and therefore rob him of any hope for change in his life. When you use biblical terminology, you give hope because God's Word provides answers for how conditions can be solved.

Step 5: Start with the Most Accountable and/or Responsible Person Before God

In marriage or parenting counseling, start with the husband. If one person is a Christian and the other is not, start with the believer—the result could be that the other counselee could come to know Jesus because of the change in that believer's life. With God being who He is given His character and attributes, there is always hope for every situation and for every person who will put their trust in God!

Instruction: The Path Forward

Biblical counselors are not afraid to be "directive." On the basis of God's Word, we interact with people about their thinking, motives, and behaviors. This happens because the Bible instructs us about how to please God with regard to our perspectives, behaviors, and heart longings. Hurting individuals will appreciate counselors who are willing to cut through the fog of complicated problems and provide biblical insight toward lasting solutions.

In 2 Timothy 3:16, Paul states, "All Scripture is inspired by God and profitable for teaching, for reproof, for correction, for training in righteousness" (NASB). Counselees will frequently need biblical wisdom in one or more of these four categories.

Teaching

Teaching refers to the proper desires, thoughts, and actions related to the issues of life and living. Because ignorance of God's Word and His ways is so prevalent, many counselees will need to be taught these truths. Even many professing Christians are uninformed of God's expectations regarding motives, marital roles, communication, anger, fear, worry, handling temptation, response to trials, sex outside of marriage, finances, work ethic, priorities, raising children, etc.

Reproof

Reproof refers to becoming aware of the ways in which we are not pleasing to God and admitting it. As 1 Peter 5:5 says, "God is opposed to the proud, but gives grace to the humble" (NASB). Some counselees are quick to admit their failings; others are self-righteous and defensive. When counselees recognize and acknowledge their sin, help them confess their sin to God and seek His forgiveness. You might also urge them to seek the forgiveness of other people if it's appropriate to do so.

Correction

Correction refers to standing up against that which has been knocked down. The Bible is profitable for teaching us how to clean up the messes our sin creates. This involves repentance, which is a change of mind that leads to a change of behavior. Wise counselors will not only teach a biblical perspective on the issues being addressed, but will also provide guidance on how to move forward and apply God's Word to a given situation.

Training in Righteousness

Training in righteousness addresses how to discipline thoughts, actions, and motivations so the future of one's life will be different from the past. It is not enough for a person to stop doing what is wrong; that person must start doing what is right and do it for the right reasons. Counselees will benefit from clear, precise, practical biblical teaching on renewing the mind (Romans 12:2), taking thoughts captive to the obedience of Christ (2 Corinthians 10:5), learning to put off the old man and put on the new (Ephesians 4:22-24), and disciplining oneself for godliness (1 Timothy 4:7-8).

Instruction in these four key areas may be provided in multiple ways. Some teaching can occur in the counseling sessions and be reinforced with assigned reading or listening. We are blessed in our culture with numerous resources that provide theologically sound explanations of God's Word and include clear, practical suggestions on how to apply scriptural principles to life. Such resources can help facilitate learning between the counseling sessions.

As counselors teach, they should seek to minister the Word rather than merely dispense it. Dispensing the Word is usually marked by turning to many verses in sequence and giving a short explanation and application for each one. This seems to grow out of the philosophy that if one verse is good, then ten verses are ten times better. The net result is instruction that tends to be a mile wide and an inch deep. Counselees benefit minimally.

To minister the Word means to select a key verse or passage which, when understood and applied by the counselees, will help them grow toward change in multiple areas of their lives. Once a passage is selected, it is read and explained carefully by the counselor. Then it is the counselees' turn to explain the passage. The counselor can further strengthen the counselees' understanding of the passage by demonstrating how obeying it will impact their lives. The counselor seeks to push the understanding and application to various life circumstances familiar to the counselees. This passage would then be assigned as homework for study, meditation, and possibly memorization. The counselees would also be given practical steps on how to implement the passage. This key passage would then be talked about in subsequent sessions, with each mention of it providing an opportunity for the counselor to stress the passage's meaning and application to the counselees' lives. Counselees benefit most from this type of instruction.

Homework

Homework is simply the application of God's truth to one's life. Throughout the New Testament there is an expectation that truth be put into practice on a regular basis. With regard to biblical counseling, homework helps counselees to obey the teaching found in God's Word so they will grow spiritually in the areas you are dealing with in the counseling process.

The Wonderful Counselor gave "homework assignments" to help others grow spiritually. For example, when Jesus was in the upper room with His disciples just prior to His crucifixion, He washed their dirty feet. He then gave them a homework assignment (a practical application of the teaching that He was the Teacher and Lord) and said, "If I then, the Lord and the Teacher, washed your feet, you also ought to wash one another's feet" (John 13:14-15 NASB). Jesus even went on to say, "If you know these things, you are blessed if you do them" (verse 17 NASB). It's easy for a person to want the benefits of Christianity, but not the responsibilities of the Christian life. Jesus made it obvious when He said, "If you love Me, you will keep My commandments" (John 14:15 NASB). Of course, one of the most direct statements about putting truth into practice appears in James 1:22: "Prove yourselves doers of the word, and not merely hearers who delude themselves" (NASB).

You might be asking, "What is the reason for giving homework to my counselees?" Good homework assignments are vital to the counseling process because they help counselees to grow and change in the ways they think and act. Simply talking about problems will not effectively help counselees. We have to help them *do* something about their problems. Good homework assignments help counselees to put truth into practice on a daily basis. In fact, counselees can walk out of the counseling session with a plan to put into practice the very things discussed in that counseling session! In this way, you affirm change is possible.

What does a good homework assignment look like? One of the first answers is to be specific, not fuzzy. For example, don't simply ask counselees to read the Bible. Instead, ask them to read specific relevant passages each day or two times daily, and list the ways these passages give them hope that they can change. You might ask counselees to read a specific verse three times daily, memorize it by day four, and be ready to quote it at the next session.

There also needs to be a balance between knowing and doing. You might expect your counselees to read a certain passage in God's Word or to read a chapter in a book that addresses the issues in their life. But then you need to ask the question, "Now what?" What do you want the counselee to *do* in response to the knowledge gained by reading that passage or book? A homework assignment could be for a husband to read 1 Corinthians 13 three times daily (knowing the truth), and to give one example per day of what he did to show love to his wife (doing the truth).

Homework assignments should be appropriate to problem(s) discussed in the session. If you address communication problems within a marriage, the homework assignments should address that very issue. When your counselees return for the next session, review their homework first. This communicates accountability, and little or no accountability tends to breed mediocrity. Then make sure you give a new homework assignment at the end of the counseling session.

Keep Growing

You can do it! You can be one who ministers God's Word to hurting people with confidence, competence, and compassion. The central elements of the biblical counseling process have been briefly described above. These are the signposts on the path to becoming an excellent biblical counselor. Here are some suggestions to help you on that journey:

1. Evaluate some of your recent counseling efforts in light of each central element. In which elements are you strong, and in which do you see room for improvement?

2. Plan your next counseling session around the central elements. How much time do you intend to give to each? How will you accomplish each? Evaluate the effectiveness of your plan and what actually happened afterwards.

3. Read regularly and repeatedly from foundational books about biblical counseling, like the ones listed in this endnote.[1] These books address the central elements in different ways. Working your way through such books on an ongoing basis will help you come up with ideas and strategies for aiding your growth in these basic practices of good private ministry of the Word.

The Diagnoses and Treatment of Idols of the Heart

Howard Eyrich and Elyse Fitzpatrick

Little children, keep yourselves from idols" (1 John 5:21). Idolatry—that's an interesting topic for a chapter written by twenty-first-century Christians, isn't it? Concerns about idolatry seem so out of place in our modern Western society. After all, not many of us burn incense before little bronze statues in our living rooms. Idolatry might have been a problem in the past or in some other culture, but it's not really that much of an issue for us now. Or is it?

How many accounts of Old Testament idolatry have you read about in the past six months? That question was recently asked of ten senior high school students and ten junior high students, and we're sure you've already guessed their answer: "None." We suspect that if we asked the same question of any twenty adults we would get the same answer—unless, of course, the individual happened to be working through a one-year Bible reading plan. Furthermore, it is highly unlikely that any one of these adults would have ever read all the Old Testament passages about idolatry in one sitting or progressed through a systematic study of these passages. Whether you're a Christian who reads much of the Old Testament or not, we're sure that the topic of idolatry is not commonplace fare when you get together with others for a cup of coffee.

Although there isn't typically much discussion about idolatry within Christian circles, within biblical counseling you will frequently hear phrases like *idols of the heart*, *heart issues*, or *curing the heart*.[1] These phrases are used, in one way or another, to identify some of the motivational issues with which Christians struggle and that biblical counselors seek to address. Because the consideration of idolatry is so routine within biblical counseling, we want to do two things for you in this chapter: First, using biblical accounts of idolatry, we will help you to understand the nature and function of idols as seen both in Scripture and in contemporary life. We will learn some basic principles on how to diagnose idolatry and the motivation behind it. And second, we want to provide some practical approaches to assisting Christians in their struggles with idolatry and the motives that lead to it. Of course, in a chapter of this length, it will not be possible to look at every biblical reference to idols and idolatry, so we'll be selective and representative. We hope this chapter will serve to whet your appetite for a deeper study of this topic.

Wanting Something Too Much

Most of us think about idolatry in terms of little stone statues outside of ourselves. But idolatry in its many forms actually begins within our own hearts. For instance, one form of idolatry happens when we lust after or want something so desperately that we are willing to sacrifice our principles of right and wrong to possess it. The Bible frequently uses the word *lust* to talk about a desire that is very strong. It does not refer solely to a sexual longing, which is how our culture typically uses the word. To lust after something—whatever it might be—usually means to want something more than we should, to the point we're willing to sin so we can obtain it. (In this chapter, we'll use the words *lust*, *desire*, and *idolatry* interchangeably to indicate a love or desire that has gotten too strong.)

Rebecca and Jacob as a Case Study in Heart Idolatry

For instance, in the book of Genesis we read the story of Rebecca and her son, Jacob, who both desired something too much. In this case, they were idolizing a good thing (God's blessing) and were willing to do something they knew they shouldn't in an attempt to get it. They lusted after something God had already promised them they would have, but they were unwilling to wait upon God's timing. Their desire for first place in the family motivated them to deceive Isaac to achieve their end. The promised blessing of a birthright had become their idol. Consequently, Rebecca sacrificed her marital relationship with Isaac and Jacob his relationships with his father (Isaac) and brother

(Esau). The birthright was what they were idolizing, and the power and position that it ensured in the family was what motivated them to sin.

Christians frequently fall into this kind of idolatry. Perhaps they want something good, like a godly spouse. They imagine how wonderful life would be if God would just hurry up and bring along Mr. or Miss Right. It often happens that the good desire for a godly spouse can become an idol that leads a person to compromise on morals or to date someone who isn't a believer. In this case, the desire for a spouse is an idol, and the security and love that a spouse seems to promise would serve as the motivation for pursuing that idol.

The Children of Israel as a Case Study in Heart Idolatry

Have you ever wondered what it was like to be one of the children of Israel in bondage under Pharaoh? Consider this for a few moments. At your mother's knee you would have learned about the man Joseph, who rose to great power in Egypt. After Joseph's death there came a Pharaoh who didn't know Joseph and began to make slaves of your ancestors. For nearly 400 years your forefathers were slaves, until God finally sent a deliverer for His people, Moses. Even so, for a while things got worse. Pharaoh ordered the slave masters to take away the supply of straw and still demand that the Israelites maintain the same production rate of bricks. But eventually God delivered His people after a series of incredible plagues, and He helped the nation to cross the Red Sea on dry ground. You would think that after all that, the Israelites would have trusted in God and believed that He loved them and cared for them—but they didn't.

While the people were on their way to the Promised Land, God called Moses to come up Mount Sinai and leave his associate, Aaron, in charge. After a while, when Moses didn't return, some of the people began to think he was dead. They became impatient and afraid. Soon their thinking spread like wildfire across the camp and the people cried out for Aaron to make a god for them who would lead them. The mob mentality took over and Aaron acquiesced. He called for all the gold the people had brought with them out of Egypt, and he used it to fashion a golden calf (Exodus 32:1-9). God informed Moses of the happenings in the camp and Moses returned to confront the people.

Do you think you would have joined that mob? Well, we won't speak for you, but our experience with our own hearts tells us that, yes, we would most likely have been part of the mob. At minimum, we would have been standing on the sidelines failing to oppose them. This mob was willing to sacrifice their relationship with Moses and God in exchange for an idol they could see and worship. They were impatient and lusted after a god that was more tangible, more like the gods of the Egyptians. They didn't want to wait in faith, so they took matters into their own hands. The golden calf was their idol, and the security offered by a god you can see, feel, and manipulate was their motivation.

This wasn't the only time that the nation of Israel gave in to idolatry. In fact, Israel's history is described in this way on several occasions: "Nevertheless... the people continued to sacrifice and make offerings on the high places..." (2 Kings 12:3; see also 15:4,35; 2 Chronicles 15:17). In other words, even when they seemed to be outwardly worshipping God, they were inwardly worshipping idols (Isaiah 29:13).

Now before we throw stones at the Israelites, perhaps we should consider what God has already done for us and how we've responded. The Father sent His Son, Jesus, as the Passover Lamb who came to take away the sins of the world (John 1:29). Through His sinless life, substitutionary death, and bodily resurrection, He brought us out of slavery to sin and the law, delivering us through the Red Sea by overthrowing our enemy behind us in great victory. Jesus has freed us from sin's dominion and God's just wrath—He has forgiven us, granted us right standing before God, and has promised to lead, feed, and guide us all the way through this journey into heaven.

These are glorious truths that all Christians affirm, and yet that doesn't stop us from falling into idolatry ourselves, as we'll soon see. None of us loves God with our whole heart, soul, mind, and strength (Matthew 22:38-40). We all have other loves or desires that take precedence over that one great desire, and our hearts are infected with the same virus that afflicted the ancient Israelites. In fact, one writer said that our hearts—yes, even the hearts of Christians— simply manufacture idols.[2] What follows is an example of this kind of idolatry.

Sara as a Case Study in Heart Idolatry

Sara (not her real name) is a college junior and the daughter of a couple in ministry. Her family was well known in the community and highly regarded as an exemplary Christian family. Her mother had a strong personality, whereas her father tended to be more laid back at home. Sara came and sought counseling with a self-diagnosis: She had an eating disorder. Data gathering revealed that she had a tendency to put on weight easily and her mother tended to "be on her case" about her eating habits. Her mother and father were high performers, high-profile people in the workplace. Sara valued both her parents' and her peers' acceptance.

The strong desire, lust, or idol that drove Sara's behavior, and particularly her "eating disorder," was her longing to have others approve of her. How she looked became her idol, her source of joy. She coveted a physical appearance that would give her acceptance and arrogantly determined that she should be able to control others' opinions of her through her outward appearance. In the process, she lost sight of her calling to glorify God in her life and became like the withering branch about which Jesus observed, "Just as the branch cannot bear any fruit unless it shares the life of the vine, so you can produce nothing unless you go on growing in me" (John 15:1-6, authors' paraphrase). In her preoccupation with her lust (James 4:1-5) and her desire to gain what she thought she needed, she ended up losing the joy and peace that come with abiding in Christ (John 15:10-11).

Worshipping Our Version of Happiness

Idolatry happens when we invest something—anything—with the power to bring us peace and joy, to give us what we should seek only from God. For instance, Sara foolishly thought she would experience happiness if everyone approved of how she looked and her mother stopped pestering her about her weight. The worship and trust of an idol had replaced her worship and trust of God. Like Sara, we all too easily end up pursuing something that we think will delight and satisfy us—something that becomes more important to us than God. We end up becoming like the craftsman Isaiah speaks of, who fashions an idol out of wood and then bestows upon it the power to satisfy him... all to no avail:

> All who fashion idols are nothing, and the things they delight in do
> not profit. Their witnesses neither see nor know, that they may be put
> to shame...No one considers, nor is there knowledge or discernment

to say, "Half of it I burned in the fire; I also baked bread on its coals; I roasted meat and have eaten. And shall I make the rest of it an abomination? Shall I fall down before a block of wood?" He feeds on ashes; a deluded heart has led him astray, and he cannot deliver himself or say, "Is there not a lie in my right hand?" (Isaiah 44:9,19-20).

At its core, all idolatry is deception, delusion. It is belief in the lie that something other than God's perfect plan for our lives will satisfy us. It is the delusion that we can invest a created thing (whether tangible or imagined) with enough power to bring us true life. Of course, the tragic reality is that we tend to be slow learners. We think, *Well, maybe it didn't work this time, but next time, I'll just try harder, or sacrifice more.* The most terrifying example of the absurdity of idolatry is seen in the way the people of Israel sacrificed their own children to the god Molech (Leviticus 18:21; 1 Kings 11:7). Can you imagine giving up one of your children to be burned in the hopes that such a sacrifice would ultimately make you happy? That's the deception and danger that's inherent in idolatry.

We All Want to Be Happy

The most sought-after commodity in human life seems to be happiness or joy (pleasure, satisfaction, fulfillment, or meaning). Seventeenth-century French philosopher and mathematician Blaise Pascal recognized this:

> All men seek happiness. This is without exception. Whatever different means they employ, they all tend to this end. The cause of some going to war, and of others avoiding it, is the same desire in both, attended with different views. The will never takes the least step but to this object. This is the motive of every action of every man, even of those who hang themselves.[3]

All people seek their own joy, pleasure, and happiness. And because we're all seeking after happiness or fulfillment somewhere, we have words that speak about the lack of joy, words that include sadness, disillusionment, depression, and despair. Everyone knows what it is to feel sad or disillusioned. We've all felt depressed at one time or another. At times (but not always) the reason we feel down is because we desire something that we are unable to attain. When

Sara couldn't look at herself in the mirror and feel satisfied, she was despairing and more determined than ever to buckle down and control her eating. When the Israelites feared a bad crop or were sad about the future, they sacrificed their children to Molech.

Proverbs speaks of this pursuit of happiness and the resulting sadness when it is delayed: "Hope deferred makes the heart sick, but a desire fulfilled is a tree of life" (Proverbs 13:12). When something we desire is postponed, we feel heartsick. On the other hand, when our desires are satisfied, we feel happy (at least temporarily). Again, this isn't something we need to stop doing, as if we could. No, we simply need to learn where our desires or longings will be truly satisfied.

One of the main personal benefits of abiding in Christ is Jesus' promise of joy: "These things I have spoken to you so that My joy may be in you, and that your joy may be full" (John 15:11 NASB). When we look to Jesus in faith, worship, and grateful obedience, we have access to the very thing that human beings seek everywhere else and fail to find. Sooner or later, all Christians have to learn that happiness doesn't come to us through the obtaining of some desired created object, but rather through relationship with Jesus Christ, the Creator and Lover of our Soul. It is only in His presence that we find true satisfaction, as Psalm 16 reminds us: "You make known to me the path of life; in your presence there is fullness of joy; at your right hand are pleasures forevermore" (Psalm 16:11). Real life, fullness of joy and pleasures are to be found only at the right hand of God, where the incarnate Christ prays for us. Everything else is vanity.

The Happiest Place on Earth?

However, all too often Christians follow the example of society around them and seek joy in all the venues offered by the world. Many of these venues are not sinful in and of themselves but can easily become so. For example, I (Howard) spent a week in Orlando with my daughter's family. We four adults were accompanied by five children who were ages six to twenty and were part of a crowd of 70,000 other people at a theme park. We were there to enjoy a break from intense works schedules and to build relational memories. I am sure many others who were there had the same motive. But I am also sure many of those people were seeking meaning and fulfillment from a day of fun at the park. For them, the theme park had become an idol. There was a sense in which they were worshipping. They were seeking from entertainment what they should have been seeking from God. No matter how the advertising reads, nothing on earth, either in Orlando or Anaheim, will bring us true happiness.

Counselors know that early January often brings a crop of depressed counselees. Many of these folks have banked on the Christmas season to bring them happiness, joy, or some kind of fulfillment. However, the season only served to empty their bank accounts and deflate their hearts. After sacrificing a chunk of their living budget for the next year upon the idol of the season, they discover that they are as empty as they were in October. They went into the Christmas season hoping to worship God, yes, but also with the goal of having their desire fulfilled. And because they weren't looking to God alone to satisfy them, they came away feeling empty, disillusioned, and heartsick. Hence, the counselor's phone rings—as it did with Charlie and Rita.

Biblical Counseling with Charlie and Rita

Charlie and Rita were a middle-aged couple who loved each other. However, it was also very evident that they were at their wits' end with each other. One of their primary problems was that they tended to fight over sex. Charlie had been exposed to pornography as a young teen and become addicted to it. In his late twenties, he broke this addiction. Rita was very much aware of his struggles and supported his fight with encouragement and prayer. However, the porn habit had filled Charlie with a set of passions at war within him (James 4:1). Before coming to counseling, the most recent fight with Rita had been over his being online ordering Christmas presents from a lingerie site. Out of this fight, Charlie came to realize that for him this site, although socially acceptable, was nevertheless pornography. God had convicted him and opened his eyes; he was a broken man.

God had granted Charlie the grace to confess to Rita that he was still worshipping the idol of sexual pleasure as a means to ultimate fulfillment and happiness. He admitted,

> In the final analysis, I have believed that sex is all about me. It is experiencing a fantasy that has not allowed you, Rita, to enjoy what

God gave us, and ultimately has not allowed me to enjoy what God designed. I have arrogantly sought the fulfillment of my fancy at the expense of God's good gift. Please forgive me!

From an early age, Charlie had believed the lie that the road to happiness for him led through the exploitation of women. Although at first he would probably have argued with this notion—Charlie didn't love women; he hated them. He thought nothing of the souls of the women he leered at. He did not love his sisters; he hated them as he used them in his fantasies even though he knew that he had been commanded to love his neighbor as himself. In looking at pornography he was pursuing what he thought would make him happy. It took the work of the Holy Spirit to free him from that devastating lie and to help him come to understand that true joy, especially in his sexual relationship with his wife, was available only as he trusted, worshipped, and sought to obey the Savior.

As Charlie grew in his understanding of God's love for him in Christ and of the Lord Jesus' sacrifice to provide everything Charlie needed to live a joy-filled, satisfied life, he was able to release his hold on the sin that had entangled him. He discovered that the compulsion to sneak a peek online would not satisfy him but rather, would in fact lead to destruction, guilt, and more sin.

Biblical Counseling with Sam and Julie

Sam and Julie had grown up in Christian families but in different cultures. In Sam's culture, the man was always the unquestioned leader in the home. Although humble male leadership in the home is biblical, that's not the kind of leadership Sam was exposed to. Sam's desire to be respected and unchallenged functioned as an idol in his life. This idolatry bore the ugly fruit of demandingness and anger in his marriage. In order to achieve his desire of being respected, he would use his strength, power, and anger to force Julie to conform to his wishes. After five difficult years of marriage, he had finally agreed to receive counseling. Then, after four or five sessions of biblical counseling, he commented, "I was reluctant to come for counseling, but these sessions have enlightened me. I am learning God's desire for me as a husband. As a result, we are experiencing His joy."

When Sam began to understand the humble leadership of his Savior, Jesus Christ, and what He was calling him to, he began to give up his twisted view of leadership and learned what it meant to wash his wife's feet in service and lay down his life for her in love (Ephesians 5:25). This Spirit-wrought transformation was a source of real joy to both him and Julie.

Some Questions to Consider

About now you might be getting glimpses of idols or lusts in your own heart, or in the hearts of those you counsel. Perhaps you've wondered for a long time why you struggled with anger or self-indulgence or self-pity, and now you're beginning to see how these outward sins can serve as a sign of something deeper going on in your heart—an idolatry, a powerful desire that motivates your outward actions. Remember, Christians continue to struggle with sin their entire lives, and frequently these sins have their origin in lusts that seductively draw them into the same failures over and over again. It's not enough to simply stop participating in some outward sin; instead, the Bible tells us that we've got to change the focus of our worship, our desires, our loves.

Some questions you might ask yourself or your counselee could include:

- *What is the lustful passion that is motivating the worship of this idol?* Sara's desire for approval, Charlie's lust for selfish pleasure, and Sam's need for respect all drove them to carry out sinful actions. Sara starved herself, Charlie viewed pornography, and Sam had angry outbursts.

- *How is the glory of God being exchanged for the glory of man?* (see Romans 1:23). Whenever something created becomes an ultimate desire in the heart, the glory that is due to God as Ultimate is being exchanged for something lesser.

- *What sinful tools are being utilized?* (see Galatians 5:19-21). In other words, what sin behaviors—such as anger, self-indulgence, self-pity, and worry—are being used in the attempt to achieve idolatrous goals?

- *What thinking patterns and behaviors (which normally characterize the unconverted) must be put off?* (see Ephesians 4:22).

- *What thinking patterns and attitudes must be renewed?* (see Ephesians 4:23; Romans 12:2).

- *What new thinking patterns and behaviors must be put on?* (see Ephesians 4:24).

Only a Stronger Love Can Kill Our Idolatries

As we seek to help ourselves and others overcome idolatries of the heart, one of the first things we need to work on is our belief systems. We need to begin seeing ourselves for who we are and recalling what God has already done for us, and how all-encompassing and immeasurable it is.

We Are Justified

One of the primary truths that we as Christians must believe as we pursue change in our lives is that the new person we want to become is already here. We have *already* been recreated "after the likeness of God in true righteousness and holiness" (Ephesians 4:24). At the very least, this means that in the sight of God, we *already have* true righteousness and holiness—that is how God sees us now, even in our ongoing struggles. He has declared that we have been justified, which means not only have we been completely forgiven of our sin (that is, just-as-if-I-had-never-sinned), but also that God sees us as if we had always obeyed just as Jesus did (Romans 3:24,26,28,30; 4:5; 5:1-9; 8:30-33; 1 Corinthians 6:11). For those who are in Christ Jesus, God boldly declares, "There is therefore now no condemnation" (Romans 8:1). That means that if Sara, Charlie, and Sam are truly one with Christ through faith alone, that even when they fail in their struggle against sin, God will not condemn them because He has already punished His Son in their place. This is the astonishingly good news that will work to transform our hearts and help us believe that the love God has given us in Christ truly is all we need!

When we soak our souls in the truths of the gospel, when we see how God has loved us by sending His own dear Son as an incarnate man, how Jesus lived in humble submission to His Father, gratefully obeying even to the point of enduring our death, how the Father poured out all the wrath that was due us on the Son He loved, how He then raised His Son from the dead by the Spirit, and how the ascended Son is even now interceding for His beloved ones, *how is it possible that we might be enticed by vanity or pride?* When we stop and think about the gospel, all the allurements of the world fade into ridiculous insignificance and we learn what it means to "love because he first loved us" (1 John 4:19).

We Are Reconciled

Ultimately, what we need is not simply for someone to tell us that we shouldn't starve ourselves, look at porn, or yell at our spouses, although that's not wrong to do. At the end of the day, what we need—and what will transform our hearts—is to dwell on the love of God: the free, everlasting, overflowing love He's demonstrated for us in Christ. It is in the light of this mind-boggling love that we, by the power of the indwelling Holy Spirit, are enabled to annihilate the delusions of idolatry. And that's the reason the apostle John, who talked about love incessantly, ended his first letter with the words, "Little children, keep yourselves from idols" (1 John 5:21). He had just spent hours reminding them of God's love for them in the incarnate Son, so he knew that they needed only one little reminder: *Now that you see how He's loved you, keep yourselves from loving anything more than you love Him.* Or as he put it in 1 John 3:1-3: "See what kind of love the Father has given to us, that we should be called children of God; and so we are...Beloved, we are God's children now...And everyone who thus hopes in him purifies himself as he is pure."

Longing for Christ Alone

Idolatry—yes, surprisingly, it's here in all of our hearts. And yet the Lord Jesus Christ has forever conquered our slavery to it and declared that we are His freely loved children. So, yes, let's help people discover their idolatries and their motives, but then let's also take them to the only One who can transform the heart and fill it with zealous, idol-conquering love.

24

The Power of Confession and Repentance

James MacDonald and Garrett Higbee

Bill and Lisa were deeply troubled, hurt, and looking for understanding. They had both contributed to a marriage that lost its vitality years before. Not until after they were empty nesters did it become apparent they were more like roommates than "one flesh." Each had a story, each had legitimate pain, each had sinned against the other. But how do you say you are sorry for going through the motions for a decade? Where do you start? For the person counseling Bill or Lisa, there has to be a healthy tension between compassionate listening and firm exhortation that prompts them to take responsibility for their part in the slow death of intimacy in their marriage.

Frequently when we ask counselees what kind of help they want, we may get an answer like "Help me cope with my circumstances," or "Get me out of this painful situation." In a marriage like Bill and Lisa's, the response is often, "Just fix my spouse, and we will be fine." It may take time and patience for such counselees to realize that the counselor's role is to help them each realize they need to let God change *themselves*! Neither they nor we can change their past or other people. Godly counsel always encourages people to invite and embrace God in the change process, no matter how painful that may be. The power of confession, repentance, and forgiveness is most clearly seen in the way those experiences change individuals and set them free.

The Power of Confession

Biblical counseling formalizes the kinds of interaction that should be happening on a regular basis among God's people yet is often overlooked or ignored. James 5:16 says, "Confess your sins to one another and pray for one another, that you may be healed. The prayer of a righteous person has great power as it is working." There is a lot of ancient wisdom in the process of confession that has made it one of the corporate spiritual disciplines recognized by the church through the centuries. Unfortunately, the power of confession has been severely undercut by making it a system or a prescribed form of spirituality that seems to acknowledge God but actually denies the power of God in the process (2 Timothy 3:5). Anonymous, stylized, and routine confession transforms a life-changing gift from God into a dull, uncertain, and powerless spiritual pretense. True biblical confession represents an encounter with God that leaves the confessor changed.

Confession in the classic sense is broader than admission of wrongdoing. Confession is telling the truth. It is transparency. The basic Greek term *homologeō* means "to agree with" or literally, "to speak the same thing." In John 1:20, for example, John the Baptist "confessed," "I am not the Christ." In Matthew 10:32 (see also Luke 12:8), Jesus uses this term, which the ESV translates "acknowledges," when He declares, "So everyone who acknowledges me before men, I also will acknowledge before my Father who is in heaven." When we tell others Jesus is our Lord, we are confessing Him. This is emphasized in the original Greek text of the New Testament by the expanded term *exomologeō*, which is the strong form found in James 5:16 quoted above as well as in the powerful prophecy in Philippians 2:9-11: "God has highly exalted him and bestowed on him the name that is above *every* name, so that at the name of Jesus *every* knee should bow, in heaven and on earth and under the earth, and *every* tongue *confess that Jesus Christ is LORD, to the glory of God the Father*" (emphasis added).

We must come back to the idea that confession definitely includes telling the truth about hard things. Even when suffering, we need to take a look at our own sins. "If we confess our sins, he is faithful and just to forgive us our sins and to cleanse us from all unrighteousness" (1 John 1:9). In the context of this chapter, confession is the verbal part of repentance. It's putting into words for God and someone else our acknowledgement of sin. Repentance is internal; confession is the external evidence of repentance. Both are required. According to Romans 10:9-10, this process occurs in salvation: "If you confess with your mouth that Jesus is Lord and believe in your heart that God raised him from the dead, you will be saved. For with the heart one believes and is justified, and with the mouth one confesses and is saved." The internal and external acknowledgement of Jesus as Lord must be preceded by the internal and external acknowledgment that as sinners we need what only Jesus as Lord can give us—forgiveness, eternal life, and salvation. David is a case study on repentance. His confessions in Psalm 32 and 51 are powerful examples of a broken and contrite heart and God's amazing forgiveness.

While there is general agreement that "confession is good for the soul," biblical counseling adds immeasurable depth to that truism. People may concur with the idea that telling the truth rather than lying is a good thing, but the Bible spells out the process and makes it much more than getting something off your chest or some kind of cathartic psychological housekeeping. In Proverbs 28:13, we see a clear two-step process: confess and forsake. In 1 John 1:9 the Word says "if we confess," making it clear that forgiveness is part of our ongoing relationship with God and is contingent on confession. Without agreement with God in our heart and without repentance, there is no true outward confession.

We often instinctively know that we want forgiveness from God and others, but when we are unwilling to acknowledge *why* we need forgiveness (because we are sinful, broken people), God's forgiveness remains beyond our reach. We want to experience it without the crisis of admitting that we can't have it unless it is given to us by mercy and grace. So, we keep hunting for a reason in ourselves that will make us worthy of God's forgiveness rather than openly confessing that we are not worthy and can only receive what God offers to a humble spirit that has nothing to offer in exchange.

In the context of a biblical counseling relationship, confession can take on many forms. The first choice the counselee must make involves how much of the truth he or she will disclose to those in the counseling process. As happened with Adam and Eve in the Garden of Eden, where sin began to ravish mankind, we have a tendency to want to cover up our shame, make excuses for our sin, and hide from God and others. For the Spirit-led counselor, prayer takes on several significant roles in the process of drawing out or hearing confession. First, we pray for wisdom to discern what may be partly hidden. We will never see others as clearly as Jesus "saw" the woman at the well and her needs, but a prayerful reliance on God will often surprise us with insights that may help us as well as the counselee understand their situation.

Second, prayer will often encourage the counselee toward greater disclosure as we demonstrate dependence on God and deliberately place them and their needs in God's hands. Consider, for example, the context of James 5:16 with its emphasis on confession and prayer. When we respond to a counselee's truthful confession by confessing Christ and His power in prayer, we are accomplishing James' instructions.

An experienced counselor knows that the power of pain, shameful secrets, and sins is chiefly in their insistence on remaining hidden and unconfessed. As we create a safe place for the counselee to confess sin, the power of repentance becomes the starting place for hope and a deeper abiding in Christ. There is really no way to bear up under someone's burden or restore someone gently if sin that is present is not confronted and confessed. The saying, "You're only as sick as your secrets" has been borne out in experience and by biblical examples. Sin can declare its presence in a myriad of destructive ways while staying under cover, but exposure to light and truth thwarts Satan's plan and sin's power. This doesn't mean that confession is painless. Rather, it often causes great pain. The big lie is hidden in the mistaken belief that withholding confession will create less pain, when in fact it prolongs and deepens pain.

Imagine a splinter that is deeply embedded and painful. You pull out the part that is visible. Only a fool would not acknowledge or remove the part everyone can see. The problem comes when you leave the embedded portion of a splinter hidden under your skin. You know it has not been fully extracted, but you talk yourself into thinking it is all out. Days later you are dealing with a throbbing and pain you never thought possible. If you continue to ignore the splinter eventually the area around it will go numb, but it will also become infected. Likewise, we carry needless pain and tangle ourselves in relational knots as we neglect the prompting of the Spirit to make things right with God and others. True repentance seeks to remove every last fragment of the splinter.

The true power of confession comes from the One receiving that confession with a heart willing "to forgive us our sins and to cleanse us from all unrighteousness." Biblical counseling at its best disarms the counselee's fears that confession will only lead to greater feelings of guilt and more judgment from God. And it helps the counselee see that the Righteous Judge is also filled with loving-kindness and is ready to forgive. In fact, the real loss in hidden or unconfessed sin is the lack of intimacy the counselee experiences with God Himself.

The Power of Repentance

The personal impact and powerful effects of the external confession depend on the depth and breadth of the internal repentance. We as counselors can witness the external aspects, but only God has full view of what is going on inside. Nothing is hidden from Him: "The LORD said to Samuel, 'Do not look on his appearance or on the height of his stature, because I have rejected him. For the LORD sees not as man sees: man looks on the outward appearance, but the LORD looks on the heart'" (1 Samuel 16:7). In the context of biblical counseling, we recognize God's presence and providential impact in every relationship, and we admit that we are not always privy to the details of that work. It's for our good and His glory (Romans 8:28-29) that God is always up to more than we can see. That's why the Spirit-led biblical counselor recognizes the Holy Spirit is the change agent in the process. And it's why the process of confession is first vertical (to God), then leads toward horizontal reconciliation (with others).

Who doesn't love hearing testimonies about what God has done in people's lives? We could listen to such all day. That is, unless these people boasting of God's grace have hurt us, or worse, hurt the ones we love. What do we do when justice seems neglected and silent? Instead of listening and rejoicing over God's grace, that's when we bring down the judge's gavel. *Grace is too good for them.*

Such was the mind-set of Jonah, which sent him on his infamous Mediterranean cruise in the complete opposite direction from God's itinerary. More than just disobedient, Jonah thought in some silly, small way that he could keep God's kindness from reaching his enemies. Jonah had pronounced himself their judge, and no one could object—Nineveh most certainly didn't deserve God's mercy. But somewhere in the bowels of a fish, Jonah realized that he didn't either. There in that protected, surreal, secret place, God finally got Jonah's attention. He could have let Jonah drown. He could have let him endure some second-rate life in Tarshish. But in His kindness, God went for a full reversal. He put Jonah in a place where he could finally grieve over his sin and recognize that he was to blame for his own wrong choices (See Jonah 1–3 and Romans 2:2-4).

This "fish gut" setting is often paralleled in the counseling relationship. We meet people when they've been tossed overboard and swallowed by a fish of unmanageable circumstances or consequences. They've been engulfed. They are gasping for air and groping in the dark, and they can't see any way out. Listening to their story, we may not be able to see any way out either.

Biblical counseling isn't just a set of pat answers the world can't give. Ultimately, it's about what God can do. He can make a way where there seems to be no way. The greatest gift we can give a hurting person is the encouragement to wait on God, invite God in, or acknowledge God's presence in the situation—choices he may well have resisted because he was playing God's role or fell into unbelief doubting God's trustworthy care. In horizontal conflict our focus will almost always be on the situation or the other person. It is not until we are at peace with God that we can become ambassadors for Christ, and that, in turn, makes horizontal reconciliation possible.

Isaiah 50:9-11 states how God wants us to learn the art of waiting upon Him with trust—an art Jonah needed to learn. Now Jonah didn't think he was ever coming out of that fish. Read his prayer in Jonah 2, and you hear a man wrapping up the last seconds of his life. He thought to himself, *I'm going to be standing before God in just a moment, so I'd better make things right with Him now.* Jonah had no idea what God was prepared to do the moment he repented. Most people in a counseling situation don't have a clue about God's redemptive plans for them either. Their immediate encounter with God through confession and repentance may leave them feeling like they've been thrown up on the shore, just as Jonah was.

In Jonah's case, once his heart returned to God, it didn't take long for the spit-up, bleached-out, poster-boy-of-the-second-chance to get on the road to Nineveh. As he had promised, Jonah *confessed* God's great salvation to the people he loathed, and he ended up watching God rain a downpour of mercy on the wicked. Jonah's call to "repent, or else" coursed like a mighty river through the streets of the vast city. And as Jonah preached doom, the people understood the righteous anger of a holy God, turned from their horrific ways, and repented in sackcloth and ashes. From the greatest to the least, the people of Nineveh threw themselves on God's mercy. And God heard their cry.

With the same outrageous grace that spared Jonah, God now spared Nineveh. His kindness drew them to repentance, and His mercy overruled revenge. As hearts were revived, they recognized their sin for what it was and humbled themselves under God's mighty hand. And to no one's surprise, God stepped toward the people of Nineveh with open arms. God does that with all of us and wants us to emulate His patience with one another (see Romans 2:4). The absolute essential thought in all of this is *repentance*.

Repentance is the funnel through which all personal revival flows. Repentance is the natural next step on our journey when we have seen God's holiness exalted before our eyes, when we have been brought to a place of personal brokenness about our own sin through the tsunami of consequences that devastate our experience as the aftershock of personal sin. Repentance is the first step in the personal cleanup of the wreckage that sin brings. Refusing repentance always takes us down and never takes us up. Repentance alone opens the way to a fresh outpouring of God's favor in our lives. And the repentance that clears the way for us to experience God's grace and forgiveness in salvation echoes throughout the rest of life as we learn our lesson over and over (much as Jonah still had a lot to learn about personal repentance even after God used his words to spark a mighty revival in Nineveh). This side of eternity, the necessity of repentance must never be removed from the agenda of our dealings with God and others.

Repentance doesn't mean we no longer recognize others may have had a hand in our pain. But it's necessary if we're going to experience a right relationship with God and others. We are not able to get out of the whirlpool of bitterness and set ourselves on the solid ground of forgiveness without repentance.

Repentance Is a Good Thing

Trust us on this one: We all want more repentance in our lives. Though it's not an easy or pleasant thing, it is a good thing. If you want to get to a better place with God, get repentance. In the counseling setting, repentance is ground zero of a renewed relationship with God. It's about forgetting for the moment what others have done or not done and coming to terms with what God requires *of us*! Jesus never hesitates to call even extremely religious and self-righteous people to repent.

The church at Corinth was the most problematic church in the New Testament. The people in this worldly church were filled with themselves; they were carnal and divisive. Compared to the spiritual chaos around them, they were barely getting by. Compared with God's expectations, they were definitely falling short! In 2 Corinthians Paul refers to an earlier corrective letter he had written to them: "Even if I made you grieve with my letter, I do not regret it" (7:8). Apparently the earlier letter was to the point, as in "Hey, repent, or else! I mean it—knock it off and repent or you're gonna get it, big time!"

Sometimes a counselee will have to receive a hard word that he'd rather not hear in order to get to the place he wants to be. Paul felt that tension after he had written his strong, rebuking letter. Yet he said, "I do not regret it— though I did regret it, for I see that that letter grieved you" (7:8). Apparently the Christians in Corinth were wounded and offended by the truth, but only temporarily so. Eventually they repented! Paul knew that only after the believers in Corinth were wounded by the reality of their sinfulness could they begin to experience the renewing power of God's Spirit at work in their lives. Paul rejoiced "not because [they] were grieved, but because [they] were grieved into repenting" (7:9).

Speaking the truth in love is the heart of biblical counseling. It is the hard work of talking about personal sin and the depravity of self that can lead each of us to a changed life through repentance. It's this life-change that makes hearing the hard truth not only worthwhile, but cause for rejoicing. Repentance is the moment that everything changes. We drop the feeble excuses, plausible lies, and the failed self-righteousness. We step out from behind our shield of blaming others and face what God has for us. As difficult as it is for us to repent, it usually comes as a renewing shock to discover that God is not reluctant or unwilling to unleash His overwhelming benefits upon our lives. Even now, heaven is bursting with the grace and mercy of God, which will shower upon our parched hearts at the moment of genuine repentance. Picture it now by faith: all of God's favor, all of God's grace, all of God's blessing, billowing like rain-laden clouds ready to deliver a mighty downpour of revival into our lives. This comes only through repentance.

Understanding Repentance

No wonder repentance was the method in the mouth of every biblical messenger. "Repent!" was the one-word sermon from every Old Testament prophet. Isaiah, Jeremiah, Ezekiel, Hosea—all of them preached this one-word message: repent. It was plagiarism to the max. They would show up before a group of people and say, "Good morning...repent! Let's pray." This blunt method and message moved God's people.

Now in case you're thinking this was just an Old Testament thing, consider the prominence of repentance in the New Testament. Jesus, John the Baptist, and the apostles all emphasize repentance as preliminary to salvation (see Matthew 3:2, Mark 1:15; 6:12; Acts 2:37-38). In fact, in Luke 15:7, Jesus makes an amazing assertion: There's more joy in heaven over one sinner who repents than over ninety-nine other people who say, "I'm kind of tired of reading about repentance. I think I'll lie down now and take a little nap."

What was true in Old and New Testament times has an uncanny way of being true today. Repentance should always be on our list of considerations. Our daily times with God should never exclude the question, "Lord, where in my life do I need to repent today?" Repentance is never just about "back then" as in history, or even "back then" as when we surrendered ourselves to Christ. Rather, it is always among the possibilities for now, for today. This is why we have said that repentance is the funnel through which all personal revival flows.

Repentance Is Change Inside Me

Repentance is change in every way and at every level. Repentance is change in me—not a change of spouse, not a change of job, not a change of where I live or who I hang out with. Repentance is change in the place where it's needed most—inside me.

If you study all the Hebrew and Greek terms used for repentance, you get this three-part definition: *Repentance is a recognition of sin for what it is, followed by a heartfelt sorrow, culminating in a change of behavior.* Repentance is change at every level of your being: in your mind (*I see it for what it is*—recognition of sin), in your emotions (*I grieve over my sin*—heartfelt sorrow), and in your will (*I determine to change my behavior*—producing a specific plan of action for change).

Repentance Is a Work of God

Repentance is a powerful gift that God gives to a person who wholeheartedly seeks Him. In fact, only God can give someone a repentant heart. Note that 2 Timothy 2:25 says, "God *may perhaps grant* them repentance…" This is a crucial distinction in biblical counseling. We know where repentance originates, and that there is another "Counselor"—the Holy Spirit—in the room.

A typical therapeutic relationship involves two people working on one person's problems; biblical counseling, by contrast, is based on the premise that two people *and God* are working together on one person's problems.

As you've been reading along you may have thought to yourself, *But I don't feel grief over my sin.* God will help you with that if you ask Him. Maybe you even believe your actions or attitudes are not wrong even though God's Word says they are. Again, what you desperately need is to seek God and ask Him to change your mind *and* heart about sin.

All in all, repentance is not easy. If it was, everyone would do it. Only God can grant us repentance about all that we have done and failed to do. There are no quick fixes to arriving at that point. When repentance does come, so does its fruit.

The Fruit of Repentance

In 2 Corinthians 7:9-11, Paul mentions five results of repentance. We've grouped them here in the order we believe a repentant person experiences them:

Grief over Sin

Paul begins, "You felt a godly grief...godly grief produces a repentance that leads to salvation" (verses 9-10). In the original Greek text of the New Testament, the word for "grief" is *lupeo.* This word is used twenty-six times in the New Testament. One-fourth of these uses occur in this passage, making this the most concentrated statement in all of Scripture about the feelings that accompany repentance.

If you're really repentant, you're going to feel grief over sin. Genuine conviction over sin and repentance from it will result in pain and shame about the wrong choice you made. Don't shut it out; don't let it morph into a toxic shame. Mourn, wail, and weep (see James 4:8-10).

When you see your sin for what it is in contrast to the exalted holiness of God, you should lose your grip on the attitude, "I have it totally together." The people in Scripture who made real contact with God ended up feeling low, like a worm (see Genesis 18:27; Job 42:6; Isaiah 6:5; Luke 5:8). When you connect with God, you understand that *God is everything and you're not that much.* Real contact with God produces a sense of immense unworthiness. It results in deep humility. It puts *everything* else in life—even the hard things—in perspective. In biblical counseling, you'll see the truth of James 4:10 affirmed over and over again: "Humble yourselves before the Lord, and He will exalt you." And 1 Peter 5:6-7 offers the encouragement that as you humble yourself you can get better, for God's care is right behind you.

Soul anguish is not a bad thing. True repentance begins with heartfelt sadness about what you've done to God. At the heart of every choice to sin is a rejection of God. When you choose to do wrong, you're saying, "You're not enough, God. I need this too. You have not met my needs, so I'm going out on my own this time." But then repentance comes and says, "How could I have acted this way toward God? How could I treat His love so poorly when He's given me so much?"

Real repentance recognizes that a choice to sin is a choice against God. As you grieve over your sin and see it the way God sees it, a second mark of true repentance follows quickly.

Repulsion over Sin

Grief over sin leads very soon to feelings of repulsion toward that sin. In 2 Corinthians 7:11 Paul says, "See what earnestness this godly grief has produced in you." The word "earnestness" implies diligence. When you're really repentant, you pour serious energy into putting your sin behind you. Repentance brings with it a new urgency about your relationship with God and strong negative feelings toward anything that would injure it. You say to yourself, *What used to be so attractive to me now repulses me. I'm indignant about it; I'm strongly opposed to it; and I'm resolutely determined that it will always be repulsive in my eyes.*

When you repent, the sin that once gave you private satisfaction now makes you want to vomit because you see it for what it really is.

Restitution Toward Others

When repentance occurs, you will feel an urgent desire to go to the people whom your sin has wounded and fix the fallout. You desire not only to be right with God, but also to be reconciled to the people injured by your sin—that's what restitution is all about. Some Bible translations render this part of 2 Corinthians 7:11 as the "avenging of wrongs" (NASB) and a "readiness to see justice done" (NIV). For an example of restitution after repentance, see Zacchaeus' story in Luke 19:1-10.

Restitution is a mark of genuine repentance. That's why Paul said the Christians in Corinth possessed "eagerness to clear [themselves]" (2 Corinthians 7:11). Restitution involves going to a person and saying, "What I did or said to you was wrong, I'm truly sorry I did that. I don't have any excuses. Will you forgive me? I want to make this right if I can."

Repentance doesn't demand anything, but it does request reconciliation. Repentance means we admit being the reason for the conflict and any separation that may have occurred. Repentance is not concerned with the other person's contribution to the problem—there's already been enough blame shifting. Rather, it confesses that *I* haven't been what *I'm* supposed to be, so *I'll* make it right as much as *I* can and leave the rest with God. Repentance is doing what *I* need to and what *I* can do.

Revival Toward God

After repentance from sin comes revival toward God. Paul characterizes a repentant person's renewed relationship with God in the words "what fear, what longing, what zeal" (2 Corinthians 7:11). Previously, the Christians in Corinth were involved in all kinds of sexual sin and they didn't care what God thought. But their repentance increased in them their fear of the Lord. Fear of God is a good thing—"the fear of the LORD is the beginning of wisdom" (Proverbs 9:10). The fear Paul observed in the repentant Corinthians was an increased awe and respect for God. They were feeling a kind of holy terror over having offended God.

The repentance expressed by the Corinthian believers resulted in an increased passion for the things of the Lord. Paul marveled, "What longing!" (verse 11). A revived heart will show a greater zeal for the things of God.

This is the place not many people know to go. Spiritually speaking, this is the road less traveled. But you can make that journey, and if you do, others will begin to observe in you "what longing" after God! True repentance draws us closer to God than we were when we started, bringing with it a fresh awe and fear of God.

Readiness to Move Forward

So many people spend their lives lamenting what they see in the rearview mirror. But genuine repentance eliminates that persistent regret. As Paul says, "Godly sorrow produces a repentance...without regret" (verse 10). When repentance is genuine, the human heart experiences cleansing. And by God's grace, it moves beyond the kind of self-punishment that's stuck in the past and can't or won't move into the future. You know repentance is truly happening in a person's heart when he gets locked in on what's ahead and he experiences freedom from what's behind.

On the Road Toward Forgiveness

Speaking of looking ahead, repentance opens the road to forgiveness. Though costly, forgiveness is another powerful step in drawing closer to God, living in peace, and completing the reconciliation process. God's forgiveness is uncompromisingly complete. Not so with many people. You don't repent demanding forgiveness from the injured party, but reconciliation is a sweet fruit and is always to be sought, if possible.

So what does biblical forgiveness look like? We are glad you asked. In the next chapter we will focus on forgiveness. We will try to clear up some of the most common misconceptions regarding forgiveness as we explore the necessity for it, both asked for and granted in the life of every believer.

25

The Power of Forgiveness

James MacDonald and Garrett Higbee

If our counseling is truly Christ-centered, then the topic of forgiveness will inevitably come up in the journey toward growth and change. Right up front, we want to make the point that there are *no* lasting relationships without forgiveness. Relationships don't develop strength and longevity because two people always agree or get along well. Rather, they survive because forgiveness is the glue that overcomes the unavoidable offenses that occur in a fallen world. While few of us will ever have to forgive the magnitude of sin some victims of heinous abuse or cruelty have had to endure, who hasn't been hurt by someone? Who has never held a grudge or felt betrayed? Sometimes the hurts go deep. Biblical counseling does not put a Band-Aid on a gaping wound, but neither does the fullness of the gospel allow us to settle into a role of victim. So what does real forgiveness look like? Why is it so hard? What compels us as Christians to forgive terrible atrocities and personal offenses?

Throughout chapter 24, as we talked about repentance, we touched on the matter of forgiveness, which is the hoped-for result that awaits us beyond repentance and confession. God's forgiveness leads to the fear of the Lord and motivates our forgiving others, which is one of the most Christlike actions we can display toward those around us. It all starts with the reality that every single person needs God's forgiveness, the answer to the universal judgment in the proclamation that "all have sinned and fall short of the glory of God" (Romans 3:23). And once we are aware of our depravity, we can then confess our sin and know God's forgiveness. If those we counsel do not understand their desperate need for the atoning work of Christ at the cross, and they are not humbled by the finished work of Christ, then mustering up forgiveness for another's sin will be frustrating, superficial, and often a mere performance with no enduring fruit.

Think for a moment about who it is you need to forgive. Do you have a mental list now? Most of us already have a list, but the title of it is usually "People I *Can't* Forgive," or "Hurtful, Hateful, and Despicable Humans I Will *Never* Forgive." Now that's a problem. And we need to see it as a problem. As Christians, we have been forgiven a towering list of offenses done against a holy God. We say, sometimes quite casually, that God has forgiven us, as if such action is easy for God…because everything is easy for God, right? Well, not exactly. We don't use terms like *hard* or *easy* when it comes to God. He simply *does*. And in the way that He has freely forgiven us, we are to forgive others.

C.S. Lewis, talking about the very center of practical Christianity, said, "Everyone says forgiveness is a lovely idea, until they have something to forgive."[1] Speaking in the aftermath of World War II, Lewis followed up that statement with several postwar examples illustrating how easy it is to speak glowingly about the ideal of forgiveness while at the same time reserving for ourselves the right to withhold forgiveness based on how much we've been offended or hurt.

Now, we're aware that God understands our struggle. When He took on humanity, He experienced the full range of human life, including a packed portfolio of offenses done against Him: attacks, lies, threats, manipulation, betrayal, and more. Among His final words was a prayer that we often apply to Jesus' immediate circumstances, but the prayer actually encapsulated His entire life: "Father, forgive them, for they know not what they do" (Luke 23:34).

The Forgiveness *Crisis*

Much of what we hear in counseling sessions about the matter of forgiveness is profoundly negative: "I can't forgive him." "She won't forgive me." "If there really is a God, how could He forgive me?" And tragically, what sometimes passes for biblical counseling is actually the dispensing of cheap forgiveness, which, much like cheap grace, has little effect on those receiving the prescription.

A conversation between Peter and Jesus clearly illustrates what's at stake when we talk about forgiveness and why it isn't a simple matter: "Then Peter came up and said to him, 'Lord, how often will my brother sin against me, and I forgive him? As many as seven times?' Jesus said to him, 'I do not say to you seven times, but seventy times seven'" (Matthew 18:21-22). Earlier in this passage we are told that if a brother sins against us, we are to go to him. Go *to* him. If someone sins against us, we don't go tell other people about it. Rather, we go directly to the person who committed the offense against us and work it out with him.

Now, Peter is fine with that and knows the law. He knows that forgiving others three times is godly and is in line with the teaching of the Pharisees. He was probably thinking, *Well, the Pharisees say to forgive three times. But I want to impress Jesus. I'm shooting for the A-slot in disciple world. So I'll be generous and forgive four...um, five...um, six...um, seven times. Seven will blow Him away!* So Peter speaks up and says, "Lord, how often will my brother sin against me, and I forgive him? As many as seven times?" (verse 21). Notice that he has more than doubled the number set by the Pharisees. Peter was probably thinking, *Aren't I awesome?*

But Peter doesn't have long to gloat over his generosity. Jesus responds, "I do not say to you seven times, but seventy times seven" (Matthew 18:22). What?! Jesus' point here is not that you can say, "I forgive you" 490 times and then—ding!—you don't have to forgive anymore. He is saying, "Forgive always, forgive every time, and forgive before you come to Me in worship." He sets a standard that requires supernatural power and comes only from one who realizes he is forgiven!

Crucial in all this is an understanding of what forgiveness means. Forgiveness is *the decision to release a person from the obligation that resulted when he or she injured you.* In a counseling setting, a clear understanding of forgiveness brings both the weight and the necessity of the decision into focus. When you injure a person, whether knowingly or unknowingly, you create an obligation. You take something from that person—such as his time, money, pride, or dignity. And if you take something from your brother, then you owe him. For the hurt and injured party, the legitimacy of his claim should be acknowledged before the necessity of forgiveness is discussed.

It's easy to think that forgiveness means that nobody pays—that the debt is simply erased. But the truth is that if you take something from someone and he forgives you, he is making the costly decision to release you. In his forgiveness, he is covering the debt you owe. That decision (to release you from the obligation by taking it on himself) creates a crisis of the will and ultimately a moment of truth spiritually.

When a person releases someone else through forgiveness, the one who forgives is paying the debt. He is absorbing it, covering it, forgoing what is due him. He releases the offender from what he owes. It's not unlike what happens in our relationship with God. When He forgives, He pays. That's the story of the gospel, isn't it?

This necessity of paying another person's debt is an underlying factor that makes forgiving a crisis for us. Because the debt was unfair in the first place, we instinctively hesitate to pay it ourselves. But our "reasons" for *not* forgiving all turn out to be rationalizations. And if we insist on holding out for an apology, we are missing the point that even a sincere apology doesn't cancel the debt any more than sending a note to my bank that says I'm sorry I'm six months behind on my mortgage will cancel the debt (or the added interest!). When a person comes to us and says, "I was wrong. Will you forgive me?"—now that's a crisis moment! Whether someone asks sincerely or not, we can become so self-protective or embittered that we justify our unforgiveness with what we think are plausible rationalizations.

Consider five common rationalizations for holding someone hostage through a refusal to forgive:

1. I can't forgive this because it's too big. All the more reason *not* to refuse to offer forgiveness. The bigger the issue, the harder the forgiveness? The *more* reason there is to forgive! The bigger the issue at hand, the more you *shouldn't* want to carry it.

2. Time will heal the wound. We say, "I'm going to flip some pages on the calendar. I'm going to ignore what my father did, what my mother did, what my sister did, what my boss did, what my college professor did, whatever it is someone did to me."

But time heals nothing. The wound is still there. It's just as sensitive and sore as it used to be. You can avoid it. You can push it away. But someday you'll be at the mall, you'll be walking somewhere, you'll go into church, you'll be at a concert somewhere, you will be out on the street, and you will bump into that person and you will find out your wound is just as sore and sick as it ever was. It hasn't healed.

3. I'll forgive when the other person says he is sorry. "I'll get rid of this burden when the other person apologizes. But until then, I'm going to carry this grudge with me everywhere I go."

Newsflash: That person isn't going to apologize.

And if by God's grace a miracle were to happen and the person realized he was wrong and came to you asking for forgiveness, if you're nursing your grudge, you're not going to accept his apology. You won't be ready for restoration.

4. I can't forgive if I can't forget. That is completely backward. In reality, you can't forget until you are willing to forgive. A refusal to forgive is the decision to regularly review the offense. It is the decision to keep looking at it, keep feeling it, keep bearing with the discomfort. The fact is, as long as you are unforgiving, you are never going to forget what happened. Only when you are willing to forgive will you get it out, release it, and begin the healing.

5. But if I forgive, the person will just do it again. So you might have to carry two or more of these offenses? The very real possibility of another offense should be a huge motivation for getting rid of the first one by forgiving it. Otherwise, you'll only become more burdened by the accumulated weight of another person's offenses against you. It's crucial to realize that forgiving someone doesn't mean you are welcoming multiple offenses. More on this in a moment.

When you refuse to forgive, you may feel like you're the one in power. You may think you are in control in some small way. But in reality you're held captive to what happened because you're not letting it go. As explained earlier, forgiveness releases the situation and lets the healing begin. Yes, a refusal to forgive may make you feel powerful, but it's a false power.

Forgiveness, however, surrenders the power to demand retribution. Forgiveness gives up the right to "send any more bills to that person." It releases the other person—and you as well! When you forgive, you're no longer trapped in a self-destructive unwillingness to forgive.

Withholding forgiveness is an ineffective way to punish someone else and is destructive to the person who has been hurt. *It's like drinking the poison of bitterness and expecting the other person to die.* Though we might think forgiving others isn't what's *fair* for us, it's what's right and healthy for us!

Once we deal with the forgiveness crisis, as intense as it might be, we are then able to move on to the forgiveness process. Let's look now at this process as it relates to counseling. This is where biblical counseling can be tremendously helpful. People sometimes wonder why they still feel waves of hurt and even moments of bitterness after they've forgiven someone who hurt them. We can help them understand that the decision to forgive is not only an immediate release of the other person, but is also the beginning of the road to spiritual and emotional health.

The Forgiveness *Process*

The forgiveness *crisis* takes care of a person's relationship with someone else regarding an offense. Then the forgiveness *process* works through the healing and change that is required within a person to correct all the residual effects of the original offense and the damage caused by unforgiveness. Note the wisdom from God's Word in relation to this process:

> Do not grieve the Holy Spirit of God, by whom you were sealed for the day of redemption. Let all bitterness and wrath and anger and clamor and slander be put away from you, along with all malice. Be kind to one another, tenderhearted, forgiving one another, as God in Christ forgave you (Ephesians 4:30-32).

The process of forgiveness is very important. We don't want anyone to think that just because he or she says, "I forgive," those words are going to be the end of it. After that crisis moment of forgiveness comes the process of forgiveness, at which point the forgiver needs to train the mind to think differently, to be renewed. And that involves three crucial commitments: The person who was hurt will no longer bring up the offense (1) to the offender, (2) to others, or (3) to himself.

I (James) was driving with my wife Kathy one evening after preaching on this subject and I said to her, "Did you think of something you needed to forgive?"

She said, "I did."

I said, "What was it?"

She said, "I won't bring it up to other people anymore."

I thought, *Wow, isn't that great?* She wasn't going to bring it up to me. Or to others. And most difficult of all, she wasn't going to bring it up to herself. She wasn't going to obsess over it anymore.

And yet there are times when, after we've forgiven someone, we will find ourselves spinning back toward unforgiveness. That's why forgiveness is a serious process. We have to pray and confess our unwillingness to forgive as sin to God. Back when we forgave another person, we shifted the interaction about the offense from between the two of us to between God and us. That's part of the "payment" we discussed earlier. And each time we revisit unforgiveness, we end up going back to the forgiveness crisis. That's when we need to say, "Forgive me, God. I said I was going to leave that behind. You saw how I was thinking just now. That's not what I promised."

When we forgive someone, we have made ourselves accountable to God. Now it's just Him and us working on changing our heart and mind. If we honor the process of forgiveness, God will, by His Word, renew our mind.

What Forgiveness Is *Not*

It is very helpful to remind the counselee of the promises of forgiveness, but it is also helpful to teach him what biblical forgiveness does *not* demand of him. This can melt away any resistance as he realizes he is not being asked to enable sin or prevent someone from receiving justice. And forgiveness does not negate the wrongness of the offender's words or actions.

James 2:13 declares, "Judgment is without mercy to the one who has shown no mercy." And Jesus promised, "Blessed are the merciful…" (Matthew 5:7). Mercy is *not* giving someone what they deserve. Now, just because you've forgiven your offender doesn't mean you're interfering with God's judgment or His refining work in the person who hurt you. God will still do what He intends to do, and that's between Him and the offender. Our heart should be toward mercy. If someone is indebted, the debt has to be paid. That's what the cross is all about. The debt created by sin has to be paid.

And in the same way the debt had to be paid by the Son to satisfy the Father, so the debt has to be paid by someone. It can't just be left unpaid. When someone has sinned against you, you pay it by extending forgiveness. You absorb it. You cover it. You get beyond it. You pull it up yourself and deal with it and get past it. Remember, forgiveness is a decision to release a person from the obligation that resulted when he injured you. But forgiveness does not ignore the future nor fail to consider what changes might have to be made in the relationship.

Here are four things forgiveness does *not* do:

1. Forgiveness is not enabling. "My mother has an overspending problem. She's often used money in a way that is destructive to her and others. I can forgive her for what she did without giving her a credit card."

To forgive doesn't mean you have to let the person carry out destructive behavior again. Forgiving is not enabling.

2. Forgiving is not rescuing. "My fourteen-year-old son shows immense unkindness and disrespect to our family. He took our car out for a ride and he drove it into a tree and he destroyed it. We're still making monthly payments on the car, and yet we no longer have the car."

You can forgive your son yet still require him to get a job to help pay for a replacement car. Forgiveness does not require that you rescue the person who did wrong. The person can still be held accountable for the consequences of his or her bad choices. And furthermore, you don't have to risk repeat offenses. For example, imagine that your father is an angry, violent man who hurts you when he is drunk. You can forgive him for his actions, and at the same time, decline his invitation to a New Year's Eve party. You don't have to risk injury again in order to forgive.

3. Forgiveness is not negating the sin or denying the pain. You may have to mourn loss, weep over consequences, and bear the weight of what may have been set in motion for years to come. God comforts the grieving; He gives grace to the humble. He will set things right either here on earth or for sure in heaven. So mourn, and suffer in the fellowship of Christ, but do not let bitterness take hold in your heart. Entrust the matter to the One who judges justly (see 1 Peter 2:23).

4. Forgiveness is not always a repair of the relationship. While you should be willing to pray for those who persecute you and keep peace as far as it depends on you (see Romans 12:14-18), doing so does not always lead to reconciliation. Reconciliation cannot happen unless the offender comes to you with godly sorrow, acknowledges the sin done against you, and confesses his part in it. So when you forgive, know that reconciliation might not take place. You can pray that it does, and you can hope for it, but you can't force it. Forgiveness does not require that you walk back into the hands of a perpetrator, nor does it mean trust has been reestablished with the one who sinned against you.

The Profile of an Apology

We have talked a lot about counseling the offended party, but what about the offender? There are moments in counseling when things seem to shift from a selfish perspective to a Godward orientation. Conviction sets in, and things go vertical. One such moment is when someone asks, "If I really wanted to be forgiven by someone, how do I approach him? How do I seek forgiveness from someone whom I've hurt?" Jesus pictured a moment like this in His parable of the prodigal son:

> When he [the prodigal] came to himself, he said, "How many of my father's hired servants have more than enough bread, but I perish here with hunger! I will arise and go to my father, and I will say to him, 'Father, I have sinned against heaven and before you. I am no longer worthy to be called your son. Treat me as one of your hired servants'" (Luke 15:17-19).

For the offender, the scary thing about apologizing (and the reason people are hesitant to say they're sorry) is the possibility that the person who was hurt might say, "No, I won't forgive you!" If that happens, then the offender could end up feeling hurt as well. If we don't appreciate that risk, we won't take an apology seriously. Consequently, an offender is inclined to try to minimize the risk of exposing himself to such rejection—and that, in turn, ends up weakening or nullifying the apology.

Here are several ways offenders will minimize the chances of rejection and thereby nullify their apology:

First, the offender will consider the statement "I'm sorry" to be sufficient as an apology. However, unless you are talking about a minor infraction like spilt milk or sneezing on someone, saying, "I'm sorry" is not adequate when an offense is personal. It is merely a report of how the offender feels that doesn't take into account what the other person feels, or the offender's need to have the other person release him from the debt he incurred when he hurt the other person. In fact, saying, "I'm sorry" doesn't even invite a response from the person who was hurt. Therefore, saying, "I'm sorry" is not sufficient to serve as a request for forgiveness.

Second, an offender will undercut a confession by slipping in an excuse. He will say something like, "I know I hurt you, but I was having a really bad day." "I realize I betrayed you, but I was tricked." It's easy to come up with such excuses. And the person who was hurt could just as easily respond, "I want to forgive you, but it doesn't sound to me like you really want forgiveness."

Third, the offender will try to spin the apology by making it a conditional statement. That is, he will say, "*If* I hurt you, I'm sorry." "*If* I offended you, I apologize." In this way, the offense becomes the problem of the person who was hurt, rather than the responsibility of the offender himself. For an offender to take this approach is demoralizing to the person who was hurt, for it refuses to acknowledge responsibility and instead, shifts the blame to the person who was wronged.

Here's a rule we should all follow: An apology is a "no *buts* or *ifs* zone." An authentic confession has three parts: an admission of wrongdoing, a request for forgiveness, and room for a response. This is what such a confession would look like: "I was wrong when I _____; will you forgive me? [Silence.]" Acknowledge the debt; ask to be released; then wait for a response. In the case of the prodigal son in Luke 15, the son correctly declared his admission of wrongdoing, but his father interrupted his confession because he was so eager to forgive—in fact, he had already forgiven his son. He was just waiting for his son to return.

For many of us, "I was wrong" is the hardest phrase to speak. Yet they are the words that verbalize our need for forgiveness. If we can't admit we were wrong, then we can't ask for forgiveness. But if our apology is genuine, and it is accompanied by an arrangement for restitution, we will often find hurt people willing to release us from the debt we incurred when we hurt them.

Our Motive for Forgiveness

In Ephesians 4:29-30, Paul writes, "Let no corrupting talk come out of your mouths, but only such as is good for building up, as fits the occasion, that it may give grace to those who hear. And do not grieve the Holy Spirit of God, by whom you were sealed for the day of redemption." Do you know what Paul is talking about here? He's spelling out a compelling reason we ought to be ready to forgive others every day of our lives.

If you are a Christian—if you have acknowledged and repented of your sin and received the gospel by faith in Jesus Christ—then something amazing has happened to you and in you. The Bible promises that if you are born again, you have the Holy Spirit living within you. Do you believe that? You are sealed with the Holy Spirit (see Ephesians 1:13-14). Part of God's gift to you is Himself! The Holy Spirit is God's down payment on everything you're going to get in heaven. When you gave your life to Christ, He gave the Holy Spirit to you. You were reconciled to God, and this should drive your reconciliation to others.

What's more, God said He will never leave you or forsake you (Hebrews 13:5). This refers to the ministering presence of the Holy Spirit in your life. And when Scripture says, "Do not grieve the Holy Spirit of God" (Ephesians 4:30), we can understand that as evidence that the Holy Spirit won't go anywhere. He won't leave you. Everywhere you go, He goes. Everything you say, He hears. Everything you feel, He bears with. And when you're unforgiving, you grieve the Holy Spirit.

The word translated "grieve" is the Greek term *lupeo*; it means "to wound" or "to injure." We grieve the Spirit of God when we refuse to forgive and we cultivate bitterness in our hearts. Because the Spirit lives within us, He has to live alongside the damaging, destructive, and sinful choices we make. He is present when we hang on to our injury and disappointment with people instead of releasing it through forgiveness.

That's why Scripture warns us to not grieve the Spirit. Our desire to preserve our fellowship with God's Spirit should motivate us to be willing to forgive others. His presence is a continual reminder that Christ has forgiven us, and therefore, we ought to forgive each other. In this context, Paul then concludes Ephesians 4 with an amazing challenge: "Be kind to one another, tenderhearted, forgiving one another, as God in Christ forgave you" (verse 32).

The Forgiven Forgive

Here is a truth to remember: The forgiven forgive. They forgive others just as Christ forgave them.

As much as we might try to help counselees as they struggle through the forgiveness crisis and the forgiveness process, we have to get them to realize that the crucial "other rail" the train of life runs on is the matter of being willing to forgive. People who are unforgiving need to be reminded of the forgiveness they received from their loving heavenly Father at the time of salvation.

Those who do not recognize or appreciate the forgiveness God has given to them in Christ are unlikely to offer forgiveness to others. Those who won't forgive demonstrate that they don't really understand God's forgiveness, or that they haven't accepted it.

A refusal to forgive is a cancer of the soul. It punishes everyone in its path; it cuts a swath of destruction across one's life. And the fallout is huge. Remember the story in Matthew 18:23-35 about the king who forgave a servant whose debt was so immense that it couldn't be paid? Look at the fallout that occurred when the forgiven servant refused to forgive someone else who owed a much smaller debt. The servant forgiven by the king was incredibly fortunate considering the extent of his debt. Yet he very quickly made his situation a lot worse. By his willingness to accept the forgiveness of the king (God) and his refusal to extend forgiveness to others (his fellow servant), he proved that he had never really experienced the forgiveness of the king. And he ended up with neither the freedom of forgiveness nor the joy of forgiving. If a person wants God to bless, heal, and restore his life, marriage, and family, he must be willing to forgive.

We cannot counsel biblically for long before we end up dealing with sinners in need of inward repentance and outward confession. The beauty of urging counselees to take these steps is that doing so will lead them toward something infinitely more powerful and life-changing: forgiveness from God. According to 2 Corinthians 5:20, we have been given the ministry of reconciliation. The reconciliation process is always vertical first (with God) then horizontal (toward others) so that peace can be accomplished. Don't let the lives entrusted to you wallow in the shame of sin or in the bitterness of an unforgiving heart. Don't settle for worldly sorrow. Pray for and admonish those you counsel to walk in repentance and to forgive just as they have been forgiven in Christ.

26

The Ministry of Soul Care
for People Who Suffer

Bob Kellemen and Greg Cook

Blindsided. In football, the word pictures a quarterback who is about to throw a pass toward one side of the field, but is viciously tackled from the other side—his blind side. He never sees it coming. Being blindsided accurately depicts the disorienting nature of suffering.

Job was blindsided. Like the man born blind and his parents (John 9), Job did nothing to "deserve" what he received. He was blameless and upright, one who feared God and shunned evil (Job 1:1). Wealth taken, health gone, family killed, Job was tempted to question the rules and the Referee of life. Job wished for an official to rule on the hit he took, but he found no arbiter (Job 9:33). Not knowing the backdrop to the story as we do (Job 1–2), Job cried out with the laments that all sufferers can relate to: "Why? How long? What did I do to deserve this?"

We All Suffer and Need Comfort

Sufferers routinely approach counselors with an implicit or explicit demand for an *explanation* for their suffering. Suffering creates confusion, and human explanations offered for suffering only end up increasing the frustration. Looking at suffering from a human, temporal perspective merely magnifies the agony of suffering (Psalm 73:2-16).

Offering the Counselee a Biblical Viewpoint and Support

As biblical counselors, we rely on more than our experience (personal or observed) or the explanations to suffering that come from human reason. We offer an alternative way of looking at suffering by viewing it through the lens of Scripture. More than that, we offer to journey with our suffering friends.

Biblical counselors understand that many of the issues people struggle with are not the result of their direct personal sin, but rather the result of living in a fallen world. What is a biblical approach to helping hurting people find God's healing hope? How does a biblical counselor share God's sustaining and healing comfort? How do we walk with others through the valley of the shadow of death?

Viewing the Counselee as Sufferer, Sinner, and Saint

As a biblical counselor, how do you view your counselees? A well-rounded approach is to consider each believer a sinner, sufferer, and saint.[1] We do not need to choose *between* sinner, sufferer, or saint, but rather, we can readily embrace the biblical reality that we *all* sin, we *all* suffer, and those who have been regenerated are *all* saints with a new identity in Christ.

When we deal with a person's presenting problem, our tendency is to gravitate to one of these perspectives at the expense of the others. For example, if we view the counselee as facing an identity problem, then we could err in the direction of seeing the person as a saint to the exclusion of the implications of the flesh and its deceptive presence. Or, we may tend to emphasize the need for compassion and see a counselee as a sufferer, and fail to address the counselee's new identity in Christ (2 Corinthians 5:17; 2 Peter 1:3-8; 2). Or we may neglect to address the counselee's ongoing battle with the flesh and sin.

Comprehensive and compassionate biblical counseling seeks to address every counselee as sinner, sufferer, and saint, rather than to focus on just one or two of those areas. One counselor captures this balance well: "Pastoral care is defective unless it can deal *thoroughly* with these evils we have suffered as well as with the sins we have committed."[2]

We All Need a Shepherd to Follow

The Bible offers many examples and instructions for dealing with suffering well. A perfect example is what we read about our Savior in 1 Peter 2:19-25. In this passage, Peter explains that Christ's response to unjust suffering provides us with an example so that we "might follow in his steps" (1 Peter 2:21).

In Christ-centered biblical counseling, it is imperative that the biblical counselor continuously points sufferers to Christ's example and provision.

Christ-Centered Suffering: Mindful of the Father

Christ's focus on the Father was uninterrupted even when He suffered on the cross. In the most intense suffering ever experienced, Christ's focus remained steadfast upon the Father. His final words on the cross were Father-focused, even though His pursuit of the Father met with silence (Psalm 22:2; Matthew 27:46).

Jesus gives us the perfect example to follow in not giving in or giving up. Mindful of His Father and His Father's character, He endured (1 Peter 2:19-20). Many types of suffering demand justice as a condition of relief from suffering. Jesus, however, entrusted Himself to the God who judges justly (1 Peter 2:23) because He knew justice would eventually be accomplished.

A common temptation in the midst of suffering is to focus our attention on our suffering (our circumstance, our pain, and our seemingly hopeless future) and *away from* our Father. We become impatient with waiting through the silence of unanswered prayers in the midst of suffering. We cease trusting that God exists and that He rewards those who wait on Him (Hebrews 11:6). To combat these temptations, Peter calls us to a Christlike perspective: "If when you do what is right and suffer for it you patiently endure it, this finds favor with God" (1 Peter 2:20 NASB; see also Romans 5:2-4; James 5:10).

Christ-Centered Suffering: Rejoicing in the Father

Because Jesus' source of constant rejoicing was His Father, He was able to face even suffering with joy. Thus Peter witnessed what the writer of Hebrews records—that "for the joy that was set before him [Jesus] endured the cross, despising the shame" (Hebrews 12:2). He did not commit sin, nor was there any deceit, reviling, or threatening (1 Peter 2:22-23). In the same way that Christ looked to the Father and rejoiced, we are to look to Christ and rejoice (see Matthew 5:10; Hebrews 12:2: 1 Peter 1:6-8; 4:13).

Peter offers a perspective sometimes overlooked in the process of giving meaning and understanding to suffering:

> Beloved, do not be surprised at the fiery trial when it comes upon
> you to test you, as though something strange were happening to you.
> But *rejoice* insofar as you share Christ's sufferings, that you may also
> *rejoice* and be *glad* when *his glory is revealed*...if anyone suffers as a
> Christian, let him not be ashamed, but *let him glorify God* in that
> name (1 Peter 4:12-13,16, emphasis added).

Paul also encourages us to "consider that the sufferings of this present time
are not worth comparing with the *glory that is to be revealed to us*" (Romans
8:18, emphasis added). Psalm 22:8 demonstrates the same emphasis: "He trusts
in the Lord; let him deliver him; let him deliver him for he delights in him!"

Praise in the midst of suffering seems more focused, more real, and more
beautiful than the praise offered in the midst of material blessing. Habakkuk
waited quietly for the day of trouble, but was noisy with praise as he responded
with rejoicing to his adversity (Habakkuk 3:16-19). While we should identify
with suffering counselees by showing compassion, we also need to help them
to face trials with praise to the Lord and confidence in His plan (Psalm 22:22-
24; 1 Peter 3:13-16; 5:1,10-11).

Christ-Centered Suffering: Interceding to the Father

If we're honest, we can admit that we are tempted to threaten those who
cause us suffering. If we think we can overpower them, we may even go so far
as to offer a physical threat. If not, we can at least threaten to cut off the relationship.

What about our Savior? He interceded. "Father, forgive them, for they
know not what they do" (Luke 23:34). He actually prayed for those who were
causing His suffering (see Isaiah 53:12; Matthew 5:44; Luke 22:32; Romans
12:12,21). Not prayers of imprecation, but rather, prayers of forgiveness. Jesus
knew what we are prone to forget: that those who sin need forgiveness more
than cursing. Their sin has already cursed them because sin by its nature is
enslaving and separates us from each other and from God.

In prayer, we take our sufferings to the only place help can be found—
our Father. Biblical counselors serve others well by leading them to the throne
room. This is where the faithful have always gone with needs for deliverance,
perseverance, and hope. Biblical counselors listen carefully for the attitude of

prayer in those we serve because it reveals important information about their heart (i.e., there is a profound difference between voicing anger *at* God and bringing our frustrations *to* God).

We must also graciously warn that though healing (in terms of a change of circumstances) should be sought from the Father (James 5:13-15), it should not be presumed. Jesus' example for asking that the cup be passed (Mark 14:36) should be instructive and encouraging lest we develop a bitterness toward God for His supposed failure to answer. Our will and His will are too often moving in opposite directions (see 2 Corinthians 12:8-10; James 4:3).

We Are All Called to Be Biblical Soul Care-Givers

What the Counseling Process Can Look Like

As vital as it is to build a foundation of Christlike and Christ-centered responses to suffering, biblical counseling is much more than preaching a passage or teaching an outline to a suffering friend. What does it look like in real life to come alongside others with caring biblical comfort?

It never looks quite like the linear approach that you'll see on the following pages. Giving biblical counsel to a sufferer is a complex, back-and-forth, relational, soulful process (see 2 Corinthians 1:3-11; 1 Thessalonians 2:8). Picture it like "spaghetti relationships" (messy, intertwined) or like a spider web interwoven with countless links and interconnections. It is real and raw, loving and engaging.

Parakaletic Comfort: Called Along Side to Help[3]

Comfort is a powerful word both in the English and the original Greek text of the New Testament. In English, it highlights *cofortitude*—the idea that we are fortified when we stand together, that we are strengthened when others weep with us and grieve with us (Romans 12:15).

In the Greek text, "comfort" derives from a compound word—*para kaletic*, or *para klesis*. It means "one called alongside to help." In John 14, John uses this Greek term when he describes the Holy Spirit as our Comforter/Counselor. He is our encouragement Counselor, called alongside and even inside to help us after Jesus' ascent to heaven. In 2 Corinthians 1:3-7, Paul uses the same root word nine times in five verses to describe the calling of the members of the body of Christ to come alongside, empathize with, and encourage one another during times of affliction. God calls each of us to be *parakaletic* biblical counselors—biblical soul care-givers.

What is the focus of biblical soul care? We sometimes miss the profound biblical truth that when we minister to the suffering our goal is not only to care, but also to help them to grow. We need to link our ministry to the suffering with the ministry of sanctification—growth in grace. Satan wants people to think that when life is bad, God is bad. We help people to understand that even when life is bad, God is good. We help suffering people to *find God even when they can't find relief.*

Soul Care by Sustaining: "It's Normal to Hurt"

Biblically and historically, soul care begins with sustaining. In sustaining, we communicate to suffering people that *it's normal to hurt*. We give them permission to grieve. We join them in acknowledging with candor that life is bad. We listen to their earthly story. We enter deeply and personally into the reality that the world is fallen and it often falls on us. To illustrate these biblical truths, we will follow "the ancient paths" (Jeremiah 6:16) and learn from the "great cloud of witnesses" (Hebrews 12:1) who have gone before us.

Listen to Your Spiritual Friend's Earthly Story: 2 Corinthians 1:3-8

As soul care-givers, before we do anything else, we must listen to our spiritual friend's earthly story. This is so basic, but so often we miss it. We rush in quoting Romans 8:28, saying that God works all things together for good to those who love Him. *But while we are talking about God, we forget to listen to our friend talking about life.* How can we possibly relate truth to life if we've not listened to our friend's life narrative?

We learn much about listening to our friend's earthly story from Octavia Albert. Albert was an ex-enslaved, college-educated African American pastor's wife from Louisiana. In the 1870s, she ministered to many other ex-enslaved men and women by listening to their stories of suffering.

One of those individuals was Charlotte Brooks. Of Brooks, Albert writes, "It was in the fall of 1879 that I met Charlotte Brooks. I have spent hours with her listening to her telling of her sad life of bondage in the cane-fields of Louisiana."[4]

If we would simply do what Octavia Albert did, then we would be miles ahead in our spiritual friendships: *spend hours listening to sad stories*. Rather than rescuing and compulsively fixing, we need to listen to stories of suffering.

It's not easy, but it is biblical. In 2 Corinthians 1:3-8, in the context of comforting one another, Paul tells the Corinthians that he did not want them to be ignorant of what happened *to* him and what was happening *in* him. He had suffered greatly in Asia Minor—*external* suffering. And now he was suffering greatly in his heart—*internal* suffering. He felt the sentence of death; he despaired even of life (2 Corinthians 1:8-9). As happened with Paul and the Corinthians, we must listen as our friends share about his internal and external suffering.

Empathize with Your Spiritual Friends' Earthly Stories: Romans 12:15

As important as it is to listen, if we stop there, then we run the risk of simply being data collectors. Sustaining is not so much about gathering information as it is about entering souls. As we listen to our spiritual friends' earthly stories we need to empathize with them in their stories. Empathy is not a secular Trojan horse. It is a biblical word and a scriptural concept. Think of the term *em-pathos*: to enter the pathos or the passion of another, to allow another person's agony to become your agony, to weep with those who weep (see Romans 12:15).

Notice how Octavia Albert allowed Charlotte Brooks's agony to become her own. "Poor Charlotte Brooks! I can never forget how her eyes were filled with tears when she would speak of all her children: 'Gone, and no one to care for me!'"[5]

Albert pictures for us the essence of sustaining: We need to *climb in the casket*. This rather macabre imagery is totally appropriate. When we engage people like the apostle Paul, who feels the sentence of death, who despairs even of life, we enter their agony by climbing into their casket, so to speak.

Not only must we feel what another person feels, we need to express and communicate that we get it, we feel it, we hurt too. Consider how Octavia Albert does so with Aunt Charlotte. "Aunt Charlotte, my heart throbs with sympathy, and my eyes are filled with tears, whenever I hear you tell of the trials of yourself and others."[6]

What Octavia modeled in 1879 the church has long called "compassionate commiseration." *Co-passion:* to share the passionate feelings of another. *Co-misery:* to partner in the misery of your spiritual friend.

Comfort Your Spiritual Friends in Their Earthly Stories: Hebrews 4:15

You may be thinking, *Sustaining is hard work; it had better be worth it!* You're right—it is hard work. And yes, it is worth it. Because sustaining empathy brings comfort—that cofortitude that we mentioned above. Another African American illustrates this for us.

Olaudah Equiano was born free in 1745 in Benin. At age ten, he was kidnapped along with his older sister. Sold and separated from one another several times, he described their reunion. "The only comfort we had was in being in one another's arms all that night, and bathing each other with our tears."[7]

Ponder that: being in one another's arms bathed in comforting tears. People often need our silence more than they need our speeches. They need our presence, not platitudes and simplistic solutions.

Years later Equiano wrote a letter of confrontation to the slavers who continually separated him and his sister. "Are the dearest friends and relations still to be parted from each other, and thus prevented from cheering the gloom of slavery with the small comfort of being together, and mingling their sufferings and sorrows?"[8]

Equiano beautifully portrays the truth that *shared sorrow is endurable sorrow.* God never intends for us to suffer alone. As we mingle our sufferings and sorrows, two become stronger than one, and the one is empowered to endure. Imagine what might have happened had Job's wife shared his sorrow rather than urging him to give up on God. We need to follow the model of the ultimate Spiritual Friend, who sympathizes with our weaknesses and thus empowers us in our weakness (Hebrews 4:15-16).

Enter Your Spiritual Friends' Earthly Stories: John 1:14; Romans 9:2-3

Our calling from God as soul care-givers becomes more and more intense. We are also to *enter* our spiritual friends' earthly stories. Again, Equiano illustrates this truth for us. "Happy should I have ever esteemed myself to encounter every misery for you, and to procure your freedom by the sacrifice of my own!"[9]

Do we understand what he is implying? It is similar to what Paul said in Romans 9:2-3. He was willing to trade places with his unsaved Jewish friends and suffer being accursed—that is, suffer hell if it meant their salvation.

We can speak of this as *incarnational suffering*—suffering that enters into the world of another person. Suffering that cares so much that, if possible, it would endure substitutionary suffering. It is what Jesus did. Seeing and empathizing with our earthly story, Christ left heaven, left the Father, came to earth, was born in our likeness, and then suffered *on our behalf.* That's incarnational suffering.

Point Your Spiritual Friends to Jesus in Their Earthly Stories: 1 Peter 5:1-4

And that's why, ultimately, we don't want to point people to ourselves. We want to point our spiritual friends to Jesus—the ultimate Spiritual Friend. When we view ourselves as under-shepherds, as Peter did in 1 Peter 5:1-4, then people will see Jesus in us.

That's exactly what occurred with Octavia Albert and Aunt Charlotte, as Charlotte describes her response to Albert's care. "La, me, child! I never thought any body would care enough for me to tell of my trials and sorrows in this world! None but Jesus knows what I have passed through."[10]

Octavia Albert was *Jesus with skin on.* Her care gave Aunt Charlotte a human taste of Jesus' care—a taste Charlotte thought she would never receive this side of heaven.

Engage in Sustaining Trialogues with Your Spiritual Friends: Matthew 18:20

We are not passive as we listen to our spiritual friends' earthly stories. Instead, we interact back-and-forth not only in a dialogue (the two of us), but in a trialogue—the human counselor, the human counselee, and the Divine Counselor—forming a three-way communication through the Word of God.[11]

In the *pulpit ministry of the Word*, we don't experience the same level of give-and-take as we can have in the *personal ministry of the Word*. In personal ministry, we can target our spiritual conversations and our scriptural explorations to match and fit our spiritual friends' circumstances. Consider a few sample sustaining trialogues that are representative of interactions you might have with friends who are enduring suffering.

- "I'm so sorry for all that you're going through with your daughter's illness. I ache for you."

- "If it were me, I think I might be feeling _____. How does that relate to how you're feeling?"

- "Who has been a source of comfort for you? Who has wept with you?"

- "What do you think the Bible teaches about feeling and expressing pain, anger, and even doubt in a situation like yours?"

- "The apostle Paul admitted that he despaired. How do his feelings compare to yours?"

- "What would it sound like or look like if you were to voice your grief the way Job did or in the form of a lament psalm?"

- "How does it impact you that Jesus is your High Priest who sympathizes with your suffering?"

Soul Care by Healing: "It's Possible to Hope"

Sustaining is vital. Climbing in the casket is necessary. However, biblical soul care also must journey toward healing hope. Sustaining says, *"It's normal to hurt."* Healing says, *"It's possible to hope."* Sustaining provides empathetic permission to grieve. Healing offers encouragement to grow. Sustaining faces the fact that life is bad. Healing reminds people that God is good. Sustaining listens to the earthly story. Healing listens together to God's eternal, heavenly story.

As biblical counselors we should picture ourselves pivoting back and forth between the earthly story and the eternal story—one foot at all times in both worlds. We should listen with both ears: one to our friends' temporal stories of hurt, and the other to our Father's heavenly stories of hope. Biblical counseling resides in both worlds.

Stretch Your Spiritual Friends to the Larger Story: 2 Corinthians 1:9-11

We start the healing process by stretching our spiritual friends to the *larger* story. Remember how, in 2 Corinthians 1, we left Paul in the casket of despair? When we read the rest of the passage, we see Paul's acknowledgment that his external and internal suffering happened so that he might not rely on himself but on God, who raises the dead (2 Corinthians 1:9).

That's what healing does. It encourages people to read the rest of the story, to see the larger picture, to trust in the God who raises dead people.

That's necessary because *when life stinks, our perspective shrinks*. When hard times come, we tend to have a small, narrow, negative, earthbound perspective.

That's not just a natural phenomenon. That's initiated by Satan. He attempts to *crop Christ out of the picture*. When it comes to digital photography, we can crop people and things out of pictures with ease. That's what Satan seeks to do. He joins our natural inclination toward a shrunken perspective and he tries to crop Christ out of the picture. Our role as spiritual friends in healing is to *crop Christ back into the picture*.

How do we do that? There are many principles, but sometimes we make it much harder than we have to. In sustaining we naturally ask, "How do you *feel* about that?" In healing it should become just as natural for us to ask, "What do you think *God is up to in this*?" Just as we ask *feeling questions* in sustaining, we can ask *God questions*, spiritual questions, larger-story questions in healing.

That's exactly what Paul did in 2 Corinthians 1:9. He brought God back into the picture. He saw God's spiritual plan with spiritual eyes. *But these things happened so that you would not rely on yourself, but on God, who raises the dead.* God allowed Paul's suffering so that Paul would learn to *celebrate the empty tomb*—to rely on God, who raises the dead, and not on himself.

Stretch Your Spiritual Friends to God's Story:
Ephesians 3:14-21

Stretching our friends to *God's* story involves helping them to know God better and to live their lives on the basis of a *biblical image of God*. Perpetua, the first female martyr of the church, illustrates this truth. Barely over twenty, a mother of an infant child, and a recent convert, she is jailed and told that unless she recants her confession of faith made at her baptism, she will be killed.

Refusing to recant, she's imprisoned. While in prison she pens the story of her life. On the first page she shares her purpose by explaining that her book was "written expressly for God's honor and people's encouragement."[12] Even on her way to martyrdom, Perpetua is focused on healing encouragement that glorifies God.

As Perpetua and her fellow converts were being marched to their death, they were witnessing to the crowd. We're told that "they were exhorting the people, warning them to remember the judgment of God."[13]

If anyone ever had an excuse to focus on *life is bad*, it was Perpetua. If anyone could be tempted to crop Christ out of the picture, at this moment it would have been Perpetua. Instead, she remembers the future and focuses on the *eternal character of God*—our God of holy love who guarantees that while in this life things can go horribly wrong and be terribly unjust, from His perspective, all will be well. Like Perpetua and her band of brothers and sisters, we need to cling to our image of God's holy love—that He is simultaneously and continuously in control and caring, all-powerful and infinitely loving, above us and near us.

Toward the end of her life, others took over the writing of Perpetua's life story. They describe her final moments. "Perpetua followed with a quick step as a true spouse of Christ, the darling of God, her brightly flashing eyes quelling the gaze of the crowd."[14]

On her way to death, with her eyes Perpetua shuts the mouths of the boisterous pagan crowd. How? By clinging to the image of *who she was in Christ*. To them she was entertainment. To Christ she was the darling of God.

When we are hurting, when our spiritual friends are struggling, when Satan tries to crop Christ out of the picture, we must remind one another whose we are: We belong to the God of holy love. And we must remind one another who we are: In Christ, we are the beloved of God. As Paul prays in Ephesians 3, together with all the saints we need to grasp that we are *infinitely loved by our infinitely loving God.*

Stretch Your Spiritual Friends to the Eternal Story: Romans 8:17-39

Perpetua and her friends stretched one another to the *eternal* story. Perpetua's friend and fellow martyr, Felicitas, was pregnant. According to Roman law, she could not be executed until after her baby was born. Her fellow Christian martyrs hated that she would have to be martyred alone. Of them it was written, "Her friends were equally sad at the thought of abandoning such a good friend to travel alone on the same road to hope."[15] Felicitas joined them in praying that she would give birth early so that she could be executed with them. And that's exactly what occurred.

Amazing! Most of us would plead for every extra hour and day possible. Most of us would not perceive the road to death by the sword to be the *road to hope.* But these martyrs did. And, they perceived that in the body of Christ we are to travel this road *together*, not alone.

Perpetua, Felicitas, and their friends shared Paul's Romans 8 perspective that our suffering today is not worthy of being compared to the glory that will be revealed in heaven. *Eternal hope provides an eternal perspective.*

Witnesses watching the martyrs' final hours shared this testimony: "The day of their victory dawned, and with joyful countenances they marched from the prison arena as though on their way to heaven. If there was any trembling, it was from joy, not fear."[16]

The day of their *victory?* Only if one has an eternal perspective. They were able to weave into their circumstances the eternal truth that we are more than conquerors through Him who loves us so. Nothing shall ever separate us from the love of God in Christ—not even death.

Stretch Your Spiritual Friends to the Spiritual Story: 2 Kings 6:15-17

Once again, Perpetua is our model. "But that noble woman stubbornly resisted even to the end. Perpetua was singing victory Psalms as if already crushing the head of the Egyptian."[17]

We need more *as if* living. As if living looks at life with spiritual eyes, with faith eyes. It does what Perpetua was able to do. It does what Elisha did. He and his servant were surrounded, vastly outnumbered by the enemies of God. Elisha, with spiritual eyes, saw that those who were with him were more than those who were with the enemy. His servant surely thought that Elisha had finally lost it. And then Elisha prayed, "O LORD, please open his eyes that he may see" (2 Kings 6:17). We need to pray that prayer for our spiritual friends.

Stretch Your Spiritual Friends to the Scriptural Story: Engage in Healing Trialogues

With one foot pivoting in our friends' earthly stories, our other foot is pivoting in God's heavenly stories. We merge the two realities by stretching our friends to the *scriptural* story as we engage in healing trialogues—the bridge between two worlds. Consider a few sample healing trialogues that are representative of interactions you might have with your suffering friends:

- "God's timing and ours are often light years apart. What are you experiencing as you wait on God?"

- "Satan wants to use your suffering to suck the life out of you. How can you connect to Christ's resurrection power to find new zeal for God?"

- "How can you relate Paul's perspective on his suffering in Romans 8:17-39 to your life? How could taking on his eternal perspective alter yours?"

- "God is holy and loving. What impact does God's changeless character have on you as you face this?"

- "How have you been able to worship God in the midst of this?"

Notice in these healing scriptural trialogues how we can use God's Word to light our spiritual friends' path. We tend to use the Scriptures like a floodlight that we shine directly *in* someone's eyes immediately after they've been wandering in the dark. What happens? They're shocked and become further blinded. That's not how we can best use God's Word. Instead, we are to treat it as a flashlight that we hold *together* to shine *on* their path so they can see God's comfort, encouragement, and direction along their healing journey (see Psalm 119:105).

We Are All Michael Oher

The movie *The Blind Side* portrays the true story of offensive lineman Michael Oher. Both on the playing field and with his adoptive family, Michael learns to protect people's blind side. He learns to "have their backs."

We are all called by God to be Michael Ohers. With suffering, the blind side is not so much about unexpected suffering, since Jesus promises that in this world we *will* have trouble (John 16:33). Suffering's blind side focuses on combating Satan's attempt to use suffering to blind us to God's good heart, His holy love, His affectionate sovereignty. To counter Satan's scheme, soul caregivers protect each other's blind side by engaging in compassionate relationships focused on truth and love.

The Biblical Understanding and Treatment of Emotions

Jeff Forrey

One of the more puzzling aspects of people trying to understand themselves can be their experience of emotions. Love, hate, fear, happiness, sadness, awe, anger, etc., are all a part of our human experience. However, understanding *why* people experience certain emotions and understanding *how* to respond to troubling emotional experiences can be a challenge. In recent years, the study of emotions has drawn quite a bit of attention from psychological researchers and philosophers.[1] They have raised questions among themselves about the "nature" of emotions (or even if it is appropriate to use *emotion* as a descriptor for such widely different experiences like joy, fear, hate, and love). They have tried to determine how people can "regulate" their emotional experiences rather than having those experiences "highjack" their lives.[2]

Secular psychologists and philosophers interested in understanding emotions are at a disadvantage; their efforts will be skewed because they ignore God our Creator. They might come up with useful observations, but we should expect that their conclusions will be tainted in some way by their "suppression of the truth" (cf. Romans 1:18).[3]

For Christians, understanding emotional experiences begins with considering what the Bible says about human nature as created by God, as distorted by the Fall, and as restored through redemption in Christ. In this chapter, I will sketch the basic contours of this model and then offer an example of how to use this information in a case study.

What the Bible Says About People as Emotional Beings Created in God's Image

For emotions to be understood biblically, we need to understand how they reflect God's design for humanity. There are three intersecting dimensions offered by the writers of Scripture regarding our Creator's design:

1. A *theological* dimension on our role in God's creation, centering on being made "in the image of God."

2. A *psychosomatic* (body/soul or body/heart) dimension, highlighting initiation of lifestyle choices by the "heart" that are expressed by means of the "body."

3. A *social* dimension, recognizing the profound influence that other people have on our daily choices.

The Theological Dimension: Imaging God in Creation

Perhaps there is nothing more fundamental—or profound—about the Bible's description of humanity than what we read in Genesis 1:26-27:

> God said, "Let us make man in our image, after our likeness. And let them have dominion over the fish of the sea and over the birds of the heavens and over the livestock and over all the earth and over every creeping thing that creeps on the earth." So God created man in his own image, in the image of God he created him; male and female he created them.

Human beings—as male and female—are made in the image/likeness of God. That characteristic of human beings sets them apart from the other living creatures that were made during the creation week. The other creatures were made "according to their kinds"—according to some template God had in mind. For humans, however, *God Himself* was the template. What does it mean to be "God's image"? At the very least, based on Genesis 1:27-28, it means to *represent God* on earth: "And God blessed them. And God said to them, 'Be fruitful and multiply and fill the earth and subdue it' " (Genesis 1:28). Exercising dominion over the other creatures on earth mirrors God's universal dominion.

Being God's image, however, must also imply a *relationship with God,* because our dominion was granted to us, and we are meant to rule over the earth *in submission to God.* This was the point behind the test mentioned in Genesis 2:16-17. If Adam and Eve failed to submit to God's will (crystallized in the prohibition about eating the fruit of the tree of the knowledge of good and evil), then they would forfeit the very life He had given them. Thus, given the information in Genesis 1–2, being made in God's image means *human beings are made by God for God's purposes.* By God's design, then, emotions are involved in relating to Him and serving His purposes.

The Psychosomatic Dimension: The Interaction of Heart and Body in Daily Experience

Although this dimension is given considerable attention elsewhere in this book, it is important to be reminded that all of one's lifestyle choices come out of the heart (Proverbs 4:23). Sometimes biblical writers use images that communicate whatever *fills* the heart (that is, the immaterial control center of the person—i.e., the standards, values, ruling desires of a person) eventually *flows out* in the person's behavior, speech, attitudes, and emotions (for example, Luke 6:45). Sometimes biblical writers use images that communicate the *condition* of the heart *controls* the person's lifestyle choices (for example, Ezekiel 36:26; Ephesians 4:18). Both ways of describing the heart's role presuppose some kind of relationship with God, whether it is intimate or distant. The theological and psychosomatic dimensions of emotionality intersect.

When Jesus refers to the treasures of the heart in Matthew 6:19-21, He communicates that the heart stands for the values or standards that are important to a person. The treasures of the heart direct the way a person lives his or her life, and they will be a reflection of the person's attitude toward God. That lifestyle has three components:

1. Thinking patterns: interpretations and assessments of situations made in the light of the person's values

2. Behavior patterns: activities in situations that are dictated by the person's values

3. Feeling patterns: internal physical responses that energize the person's responses in situations

Though the heart initiates lifestyle choices, those choices are expressed *through* the body. Thus, behavior choices require working skeletal muscles. Thinking patterns require activity in the brain's frontal lobes. Feeling patterns reflect the integrated working of the nervous and endocrine (hormonal) systems. Furthermore, since all three components—behavior, thought, and feeling—arise from the heart, they all will reveal some of the treasure of the heart, and they all can influence one another.

Emotions are best understood as psychosomatic (whole-person) phenomena. They typically represent a certain assessment of a situation relative to the person's values, which, in turn, prompts a feeling state that motivates or prepares the person for a stereotypical behavioral response—again, relative to the person's values. Therefore, emotions have two components: an *internal experience* (arousal) and an *external expression* (behavior, body language, facial expressions).

The internal experience of an emotion is what goes on in the heart and what is felt in the body. For example, fear involves the assessment that a situation is dangerous, which is accompanied by physiological signs such as tense muscles, sweating, and labored breathing. These physiological signs are the "feelings" of fear.[4] Happiness involves the assessment that a situation is favorable to a person (consistent with the treasure of the heart), accompanied by the feeling of increased energy (see Proverbs 17:22).

The external expression of an emotion is what can be seen in stereotypical facial expressions or behaviors if the person chooses to show it.[5] For example, fear mobilizes the body for a defensive reaction, such as running away. Happiness is often demonstrated by smiling, laughing, or more energetic displays such as dancing (see Proverbs 15:13; Psalm 150). The observation that emotions are associated with stereotypical behaviors or facial expressions points to their function in the social dimension described below.[6]

Emotions can be either *reactive* or *proactive*. They are reactive when they occur after a person encounters a situation that was not planned for or anticipated. They are proactive when they motivate the person to anticipate and plan for a future situation. Either way, they will reveal in some measure the condition or contents of the person's heart.

The Social Dimension: Relationships with Other People as Part of God's Design

After the breathtaking narration of God's work of creation, and after the narration of His amazing accommodations for Adam in the Garden of Eden, we should be shocked by the stunning comment in Genesis 2:18: "Then the Lord God said, 'It is *not* good ...'"[17] What was missing was a partner for Adam, a fact that God impresses upon Adam through the exercise of naming the creatures in the Garden. "The man gave names to all livestock and to the birds of the heavens and to every beast of the field. But for Adam there was not found a helper fit for him" (Genesis 2:20). God created Eve and presented her to him. Adam's exuberant reaction to seeing Eve (Genesis 2:23) reminds us, once again, what God had made was very good!

By God's own assessment, we know that the creation of Eve was necessary to His purposes for humanity. Humans are not supposed to be solitary. Human beings are designed for relationship with God *and* for relationship with other human beings. Consequently, if emotions factor into our relationship with God, then logically they factor into our relationships with others too. The social dimension to emotionality intersects with the theological dimension.

The social dimension extends beyond marriage or other types of one-to-one relationships. People band together and organize themselves into *societies*—networks of people who agree to live together under certain rules for the common good. Societies also produce their own *cultures*—the complex of ideas, behaviors, attitudes, values, traditions, and material artifacts shared by the group that shape its members' way of life and is intentionally passed on to the next generation. Consequently, emotional experience (the internal, subjective component) is shaped by one's societal norms and cultural heritage. For example, the law of Moses prohibited the eating of certain types of animals (Leviticus 11:1-47). As that cultural value was practiced and then passed on from generation to generation in Jewish society, violations of it would evoke a specific emotional reaction within devout Jews: *disgust*. Peter exhibited this reaction when he saw the vision of animals lowered in a sheet and was told "kill and eat." "Peter said, 'By no means, Lord; for I have never eaten anything that is common or unclean'" (Acts 10:13-14).

Emotional expressions (the external, behavioral manifestations) also are shaped by societal/cultural expectations. One illustration of this is the elaborate mourning rituals associated with ancient Near Eastern deaths (for example, see Joshua 7:6; 2 Samuel 3:31,35-36; Ezra 10:6; Job 1:20; 2:11-13; Lamentations 2:10). Another illustration is given by the young woman in the Song of Solomon, who wished that her lover was a blood brother so that she could kiss him without the stigma their culture placed on public displays of affection by unrelated people (8:1).

What the Bible Says About People as Fallen Emotional Beings

Following the thrill of Adam's receipt of God's gift, Eve, we read about the tragedy of their disobedience to God in Genesis 3. Genesis 3:6 summarizes the essence of human sinfulness with straightforward brevity: "So when the woman saw that the tree was good for food, and that it was a delight to the eyes, and that the tree was to be desired to make one wise, she took of its fruit and ate, and she also gave some to her husband who was with her, and he ate." Eve—and Adam—disregarded the clear command of God, and their disobedience was motivated by the lure that eating of the tree would "make one wise." This phrase needs to be understood in the light of the serpent's temptation recorded in verses 4-5: "The serpent said to the woman, 'You will not surely die. For God knows that when you eat of it your eyes will be opened, and you will be like God, knowing good and evil.'" The serpent's temptation had a hard core: blatant denial of God's word—"you will not surely die." Yet it also had the softer covering: the enticing prospect of being "like God"!

For the reader of Genesis, this is quite a twist in the story line. Whereas in Genesis 1 being "like God" is the Creator's intention for humanity, in Genesis 3, it is a *perversion* of the Creator's intention. What accounts for the difference? In Genesis 1, being "like God" means following God's purposes; in Genesis 3, being "like God" means replacing God's purposes with one's own purposes. "Knowing good and evil" in Genesis 3:6 seems to imply *determining or experiencing what is good or evil personally rather than understanding it based on God's instruction.*[8]

Immediately upon eating the forbidden fruit, Adam and Eve experience the fallout of disobedience: embarrassment, shame, vulnerability, fear, even a form of irritation ("The woman whom *you gave* to be with me, *she gave me* …"). Here we see that direct connection between one's relationship with God and one's relationship with others. God's design remains, but it is experienced in a twisted and painful way, which is conveyed by the new emotional experiences Adam and Eve had after their sin.

Before the Fall, emotions would have functioned in ways that supported God-honoring living. Since the Fall, they have functioned in ways that reflect sinners' desire to be independent of God. This means that (1) although not all emotional experiences will be obviously destructive or wrong, (2) they will ultimately serve the creature and not the Creator. Consider Jesus' teaching about loving others in His Sermon on the Mount:

> You have heard that it was said, "You shall love your neighbor and hate your enemy." But I say to you, Love your enemies and pray for those who persecute you, so that you may be sons of your Father who is in heaven. For he makes his sun rise on the evil and on the good, and sends rain on the just and on the unjust. For if you love those who love you, what reward do you have? Do not even the tax collectors do the same? (Matthew 5:43-46).

Jesus refers to a type of "love" found among the unsaved. Evidently, it looks similar to Christian love in some respects, but ultimately it is inadequate because it is not motivated by a desire to honor God. It only serves the nonbeliever's personal agenda. In contrast, Jesus expects God's children to live above and beyond what might be seen in the nonbeliever's life. "You therefore must be perfect, as your heavenly Father is perfect" (Matthew 5:48). As always, the condition or contents of the heart are central to understanding human experience.

When Paul had to address grief among the Thessalonians, who thought their deceased loved ones would miss the second coming of Christ, he wrote, "We do not want you to be uninformed, brothers, about those who are asleep, that you may not grieve as others do who have no hope. For since we believe that Jesus died and rose again, even so, through Jesus, God will bring with him those who have fallen asleep" (1 Thessalonians 4:13-14). Grieving with "no hope" means experiencing loss without the anchor of God's love and promises. Grieving without hope is grieving as if God does not exist. Paul wanted the Thessalonians to grieve properly—to grieve like their losses mattered to God and His promises applied to them.

In general terms, if the treasure of one's heart is valuable only to the person and not to God, then it is unrighteous, and it will prompt speech, thoughts, behaviors, and feelings that are like "a polluted garment" to him (see Isaiah 64:6). Sinful (self-serving) emotions will prompt sinful actions; not having a proper relationship with God will result in sinful reactions to life circumstances. Anger can progress to murder (as in Matthew 5:21-22). Fear can lead to suicide (as in 1 Samuel 31:1-6). Living as if God does not care can result in anxiety (as in Matthew 6:25-33). Living contrary to God's kingdom agenda can result in bitterness (as in Jonah 4).

What the Bible Says About Christians as Redeemed Emotional Beings

Just as the Fall affected all aspects of our lives, so does redemption. The effects of redemption are described in terms of *reversing* the effects of the Fall and *restoring* the capacity for people to fulfill God's original intentions. There is always a challenge, however. Though Christians might be freed from the penalty and enslaving power of sin, they are still surrounded by its presence.

Restoring the Image of God

When Paul describes the Christian life in Ephesians 4, he first reminds his readers not to succumb to the temptation of living like their unbelieving neighbors:

> Now this I say and testify in the Lord, that you must no longer walk as the Gentiles do, in the futility of their minds. They are darkened in their understanding, *alienated from the life of God* because of the ignorance that is in them, *due to their hardness of heart* (verses 17-18, emphasis added).

Then Paul encourages a new lifestyle that specifically recalls God's original intention for humanity in Genesis 1. They were "to put off your old self, which belongs to your former manner of life and is corrupt through deceitful desires, and to be renewed in the spirit of your minds, and to put on the new self, *created after the likeness of God in true righteousness and holiness*" (verses 22-24, emphasis added).

No differently than in other aspects of our lives, emotional experiences and expressions can reflect either alienation from the life of God with a "hard heart" or a likeness to God with a "renewed mind."[9] We already have seen from Genesis 1–2 that imaging God means representing God and relating to Him. Paul's description of redemption adds another element: reflecting God's character. Godly character generates godly (God-honoring) emotions.

Categorizing Emotions as Righteous or Unrighteous

Christians should be intentional about nurturing righteous emotions as part of their spiritual formation. For the typical American, this conclusion might sound odd. It is not uncommon to read comments such as, "Feelings are neither good nor bad; everyone has them, and feelings by themselves don't cause problems. Each of us—adult and child—is entitled to whatever feelings we have. However, what you *do* with your feelings may be hurtful or inappropriate."[10] This reasoning is also heard within the church: "As Christians, it is important to understand that negative emotions are not sinful. Feelings, both negative and positive are not right or wrong; they simply are. You are human and therefore you feel."[11] It is true that everyone does have "feelings" (here it is clear "emotions" are meant by the authors); they are part of God's design for human nature.

However, the connection of emotions with the values/treasure/standards of the heart or mind does mean that emotions can be "right" or "wrong"— and perhaps more profoundly, it allows for emotions to be *commanded as virtues* or *prohibited as vices*. Here are some examples:

1. "Count it all joy, my brothers, when you meet trials of various kinds" (James 1:2) is an emotion-laden imperative connected to the presumed value of "perfection/completeness" in the Christian life: "For you know that the testing of your faith produces steadfastness. And let steadfastness have its full effect, that you may be perfect and complete, lacking in nothing" (verses 3-4). Perfection here means something like fully committed, prepared, or fit for God's purposes. James assumes that the prospect of being "perfect and complete, lacking

in nothing" will be incredibly exciting—and motivating—to his readers. Thus, joy can be nurtured by a focus on that which believers should desire.

Contrarily, disdaining the values of the world underlies an alternative emotion-laden imperative in James: "Submit yourselves, then, to God. Resist the devil, and he will flee from you. Come near to God and he will come near to you. Wash your hands, you sinners, and purify your hearts, you double-minded. Grieve, mourn and wail. Change your laughter to mourning and your joy to gloom" (James 4:7-9 NIV). Grieving, mourning and wailing are entirely appropriate expectations for believers once they realize their sin.

2. "By this we know love, that he [Christ] laid down his life for us, and we ought to lay down our lives for the brothers. But if anyone has the world's goods and sees his brother in need, yet closes his heart against him, how does God's love abide in him?" (1 John 3:16-17). "Closes his heart" paraphrases the more literal translation "shuts up his bowels," a way of describing a compelling compassion that moves an observer to alleviate another's suffering. Contrary to the thought of some, love *cannot* be reduced to an "act of the will" any more than it can be reduced to "just a feeling." It arises out of a heart energized by the power of the Holy Spirit and imprinted with the character of God (Galatians 5:22; 1 John 4:7-17). Therefore, such compassion is not optional for those who claim to be children of God. The love of God and the sacrifice of Christ should be so valued by believers that a similar compassion motivates their disciples' acts of mercy.

3. Just before and during the conquest of the Promised Land, God tells His people they should not fear the people in the land whom they had to displace (Deuteronomy 31:1-8; Joshua 10:7-8). The Israelites were to be so focused on the promise of their almighty God—He was giving them the land they had to take—that they could face the people they were supposed to displace rather than be intimidated by them.[12] A proper focus of the heart would enable the Israelites to fulfill the Lord's expectation.

Assessing One's Experience and Expression of Emotions

Nurturing righteous emotions begins with first assessing one's current emotional experiences (centering on the standards and values of the heart; what arouses the emotion) and expressions (the behaviors energized by the internal state). Both arousal and expression can be evaluated as either "righteous" or "unrighteous," providing this grid for assessment:

EMOTION ASSESSMENT GRID		
COMPONENTS OF [EMOTION]	CHARACTERISTICS OF UNRIGHTEOUS [EMOTION]	CHARACTERISTICS OF RIGHTEOUS [EMOTION]
AROUSAL		
EXPRESSION		

This tool can be used in conjunction with a Situation Log:

SITUATION LOG

Today's Date: _____

Today, I was [fill in the particular emotion of interest] when:

What was happening?

Who was present?

What did you say?*

What did you do?*

What did you want?**

What was the outcome?

---

*Consider these as part of the expression of the emotion.
**Consider this as the arousal of the emotion.

The use of these tools will be illustrated with a case study involving a person we'll name Brandon.

Helping Brandon Become
Emotionally Holy

Suppose Brandon comes in for counseling. He is a thirty-three-year-old father with three-year-old twin boys, Jerrod and James. He requests help with getting a handle on his anger around the boys, whose energy and curiosity are becoming more and more wearisome to him. Brandon has never physically harmed the boys, and he wants to make sure this never happens. Brandon, a construction worker, has the reputation of having a short temper. His anger flare-ups primarily occur with his sons. He and his wife, Nikki, do not have heated arguments as much anymore. Brandon and Nikki are relatively new Christians.

Counseling Brandon might begin with learning about Brandon's past experiences with anger: How far back has he struggled with problematic anger? What kinds of situations got him angry in the past? How did he express his anger? Toward whom—or what—did he express his anger? How did his parents or other significant adults in his life handle their anger around him? How did they respond to his anger around them? Have there been any noteworthy changes in his experience of anger—say from his high school years until now? These questions address the social dimension of Brandon's anger; they deal with the expression of his anger and its consequences—and Brandon's counselor should be alert to any patterns that become evident through his answers.

A second line of questions could move the conversation into the present: What happened the last couple of times Brandon was angered by the twins? By his coworkers? What did he do and say in those conversations? What did he want to have happen in those situations (what were his goals)? Brandon might not be able to pinpoint specific goals for the situations, in which case his counselor can suggest he infer from his speech and actions what his desires might have been. These questions presuppose the guiding role of the treasures of the heart (reflected in Brandon's goals).[13]

Following this data-gathering, Brandon's counselor might introduce the Emotion Assessment Grid and the Situation Log as tools to use in the process of learning more about his anger and to begin the process of transforming his experiences with anger. In discussing the Emotion Assessment Grid, the labels for the rows and columns should be clearly defined: "Arousal" refers to *the thinking or desires that fuel* his anger. "Expression" refers to whatever he *does or says* when he is angry. "Unrighteous" means that the arousal or expression violates biblical principles in some way, whereas "righteous" means the arousal or expression *promotes God's will* in the situation. These categories for understanding Brandon's anger tap into the theological dimension of emotionality.

One factor that often makes it a challenge to understand emotions is the wide range of labels that can be used for the broad spectrum of experiences people can have with emotions. This factor can hinder counseling. Consider, for example, a possible lexicon of words associated with the anger spectrum: impatience, frustration, irritation, bitterness, resentment, rage. Some of these words overlap in meaning (frustration and irritation, bitterness and resentment). Some of these words represent opposite ends of intensity in the experience of anger (irritation versus rage). Some of the words represent opposite extremes in the expression of anger (bitterness versus rage). Brandon's counselor needs to be alert to the possible differences in the use of such words. Brandon might not even associate words like *impatience* or *bitterness* with anger, given their less-obvious nature compared to his problem with explosive rage. If this communication obstacle exists, creating a quick lexicon for Brandon might prove valuable.

It might strike Brandon as odd that there is the possibility of "righteous" anger, and he might even think that righteous anger could not be true of him. It will be important to teach Brandon that righteous anger mirrors God's own anger, and yes, it is possible for someone like Brandon to experience righteous anger. It is part what it means to "put on the new self, created after the likeness of God in true righteousness and holiness" (Ephesians 4:24). It will take time, but the growth will occur as he is "renewed in the spirit of [his] mind" (Ephesians 4:23).

This explanation would provide a good transition to filling in the Emotion Assessment Grid with Brandon:

EMOTION ASSESSMENT GRID		
COMPONENTS OF *Anger*	**CHARACTERISTICS OF UNRIGHTEOUS** *Anger*	**CHARACTERISTICS OF RIGHTEOUS** *Anger*
AROUSAL	*When I don't get what I want or think I deserve*	*When God does not get what He deserves (honor, obedience, worship, etc.)*
EXPRESSION	*When I use destructive speech or actions because I am not getting what I want*	*When the energy of anger is used, under control, to promote God's will*

Brandon needs to grasp the significance that righteous anger is righteous because it reflects the concerns of God. As a homework assignment, he would do well to memorize and meditate on James 1:19-20 *while reviewing his Anger Situation Log.* He needs to be absolutely convinced that James was right: "Know this, my beloved brothers: let every person be quick to hear, slow to speak, slow to anger; for the anger of man does not produce the righteousness of God." In what way can Brandon point out from his own experience that his unrighteous anger does not produce the righteousness of God?

Once Brandon is convinced of the dire need to repent of his unrighteous anger, his counselor can begin helping him identify what it is that he desired in the situations he recorded in his log. Sometimes the desires will be obvious. At other times he is likely to scratch his head and admit, "I don't know." At those times, his counselor could suggest he imagine what would have settled Brandon down at that time. This would be an indirect way to infer the ruling desires of his heart.

As Brandon becomes more skilled at spotting unrighteous anger, both internally and externally, he will surely need guidance in being a good father to Jerrod and James. What will it look like for Brandon to "bring them [as three year-old boys] up in the discipline and instruction of the Lord" (Ephesians 6:4)? It seems a different situation log—recording parenting interactions—

would be needed at this stage of counseling. It might be useful for the boys to be brought in for the counselor to observe Brandon's interactions with them in scenarios presented by the counselor. Such firsthand data-gathering will probably be more helpful than Brandon's summaries of situations. Brandon will likely need to learn communication tactics, corrective discipline tactics, and goals for the boys that are derived from Scripture.

Secular psychologists sometimes recommend people who struggle with anger will benefit from physical exercise as a form of stress management. Since anger mobilizes the body to remove an obstacle or threat, recommending physical exercise as part of a counselee's lifestyle can be valuable (as long as it is approved by a physician). This recommendation reflects our psychosomatic makeup. In Brandon's case, however, it might not be as useful if he is physically active on construction sites most days. Physical exercise can help moderate the body's reactivity in the experience of anger, but the heart issues (related to faith and obedience to God) still must be addressed biblically.

Being Emotionally Whole *and* Holy

Emotions have had a long history of neglect in the thinking of the West. They have too often been dismissed as disruptions in otherwise sane living. That point of view is now being altered by psychologists, philosophers, and even some biblical scholars.[14] And well it should, since emotionality is part of God's good design for humanity. Although emotions are just as affected by the Fall as other aspects of our lives, they are also equally transformed in a relationship with Jesus Christ. Christians can become emotionally whole as they become emotionally holy.

The Complex Mind/Body Connection

Laura Hendrickson

In chapters 27 and 28 of *Christ-Centered Biblical Counseling* we address two aspects of human existence that have not always fared well in Christian thinking—emotions and the body. Jeff Forrey has helped us to address some of our misconceptions about emotions—misconceptions that cause us at times to say, "If emotions are so distressing, then why did God create us with feelings?" Emotions often seem more a cursing than a blessing, leading us to say, "Emotions are more harm than good. Suppress them. Ignore them. Don't have them."

Body by God

The body fares little better, perhaps worse, in our mind's eye. "We'd be better off without it. The flesh is evil," we say, not realizing that such thinking smacks of worldly philosophy, not biblical theology.

Our emotions and our bodies are God's idea. "The LORD God formed the man of *dust from the ground* and breathed into his nostrils the breath of life, and the man became a living creature" (Genesis 2:7, emphasis added). We are fearfully and wonderfully made—including our emotionality and physicality.

The interrelationship between body and soul defies our capacity to fully comprehend. The complexity of the mind-body, soul-brain connection is both majestic and deeply troubling to many. When the Biblical Counseling Coalition developed their *Confessional Statement*, one of the areas the three dozen leaders wrestled with the most was crafting a robust statement on biblical counseling and the body/soul. After nearly a dozen drafts, the nuanced statement now reads:

> We believe that biblical counseling should focus on the full range of human nature created in the image of God (Genesis 1:26-28). A comprehensive biblical understanding sees human beings as relational (spiritual and social), rational, volitional, emotional, and physical. Wise counseling takes the whole person seriously in his or her whole life context. It helps people to embrace all of life face-to-face with Christ so they become more like Christ in their relationships, thoughts, motivations, behaviors, and emotions.
>
> We recognize the complexity of the relationship between the body and soul (Genesis 2:7). Because of this, we seek to remain sensitive to physical factors and organic issues that affect people's lives. In our desire to help people comprehensively, we seek to apply God's Word to people's lives amid bodily strengths and weaknesses. We encourage a thorough assessment and sound treatment for any suspected physical problems.[1]

As the Biblical Counseling Coalition's leadership pondered these issues, they turned to the same source we now turn—God's Word. The Creator knows every intricacy of the nature of the human creature.

What Does the Bible Say?

For much of recorded history, much of the world has seen humanity as an angel in a slot machine, a soul incarcerated in a mass from which it hopes one day to be freed forever, a soul entombed in flesh. Not so the biblical view. God gifted us with a physical body perfectly suited to fulfilling our calling to reflect Him, relate to Him and one another, rule as His vice-regents, and rest in Him.

Body and soul are not antithetical. Psalm 63:1 links them inseparably—the soul thirsts and the body longs. In Hebraic thinking, we do not *have* a body, we *are* a body; we are animated bodies. The flesh (*bāśār* in the Old Testament) is our whole life substance organized in corporal form—embodied personalities.

Body (*bāśār* in Hebrew and *sarx* in Greek) represents humanity in a certain type of relationship to God—one of finitude, contingency, neediness, weakness, frailty, and mortality. God is infinite; we are finite. We need Him and what He provides to survive.

In the Garden, Adam and Eve needed the fruit to stay alive. They were perishable, natural creatures, not the Creator. By creation we are connected to the physical world, dependent. Apart from God we are without substantial power; we are impotent.

By making us physical beings, God empowered us to fulfill His Creation Mandate. Genesis 2:5 shows that labor is part of our proper significance and destiny. Genesis 2:15 demonstrates that we are to use our embodied personalities to labor and protect, care and cultivate, guard and expand the Garden. Work transforms our inner being into tangible creations. Work connects us with others in the noble endeavor of leaving behind a better world than we found. Work on planet Earth requires a body—embodied personality.

Our bodies are works of art fashioned by the Father, who fearfully and wonderfully handcrafted us (Psalm 139:13-16). We are works of God's hands, made, shaped, molded, clothed with skin and flesh, and knit together with bones and sinews (Job 10:3-12). We are not to despise our physicality.

The body is purely natural, not supernatural, but this is not bad. Only in the Fall does the natural become unnatural. To "walk after the flesh" does not imply that the body is evil, for ten of the fifteen sins of the flesh listed in Galatians 5:19-21 have nothing to do with sins of sensuality. *Fleshly* means denying our need for God, trying to live in independence from God. To act according to the flesh is to live in limited human strength.

In fact, Paul extended the meaning of "flesh" (*sarx*) beyond any mere reference to physicality. He associated it with our embodied personhood and with any attempt to live apart from connection to Christ and empowerment by the Spirit.

The body includes our brain, neurons, cells, flesh, chemicals, glands, etc., which we can either offer to God as servants of righteousness or offer to sin as servants of unrighteousness. It can be the locus of ingrained righteousness or ingrained evil (Romans 6:11-23; 16:18; Philippians 3:19). When we live *as if* the body is all we have, and, therefore, surrender our members to unrighteousness, then we are fleshly. When we live as if this world is all there is and that our temporal time is all the time we have, then we are worldly. When we, in our bodies, live for God's glory and His coming kingdom, then we are godly.

The Intimate Intertwining of Body/Soul

As noted, the Bible teaches that our human nature is composed of two interconnected dimensions (Genesis 2:7). We are "psychosomatic wholes" with the material and immaterial aspects of our lives intricately interwoven. We are one unified being with a spiritual inner person or heart, and a physical outer person or body.

Our inner being is the part of us that *initiates* our capacities to relate, think, makes choices, act, and feel; while the body is the instrument through which we express those capacities. We interact with God, others, and the world around us through our bodies—our embodied personality. Our speech, behavior, facial expression, and tone of voice reveal to others what's going on inside our heart.

It's important to note that because the brain is an organ of our body, it is not the *responsible source* of our thoughts, feelings, and choices. Scripture teaches that these activities originate in our inner person. But since our brain is the "master controller" (the CEO) of our other bodily functions, it makes sense to think of it as a mediator that translates what's inside of us into physical form. While the Bible is silent about exactly how this happens, its clear teaching is that our heart is the source of what comes out of us, not our brain (Luke 6:45). Ed Welch summarizes the interaction between the inner person and the brain, saying, "It is as if the heart always leaves its footprints on the brain."[2]

The Bible teaches that what is going on in our body affects what goes on in our heart. If we're sleep deprived, sick, in pain, or on medicines that make it harder for us to think clearly, these physical changes will influence our thoughts and emotions. They may even tempt us to make wrong choices.

The prophet Elijah's faith wilted after he confronted the prophets of Baal. He'd been running all day to escape the evil Jezebel. When he finally stopped, he was physically and emotionally exhausted, and very hungry. He asked God to kill him, and then promptly fell asleep. After receiving rest, food, encouragement, and a helper, he was ready to return to the Lord's service (1 Kings 18:21–19:21).

Elijah's body didn't *make* him give up, but it did make the temptation to give up harder to resist. And the test seems to imply that he was given rest and food before God appeared to him because his body needed to be strengthened before he was ready to respond in the right way.

In summary:

- There is much interaction between our body and our inner person. Our body can *influence* our inner person and *vice versa* (Psalm 32:2-4; Proverbs 17:22).

- There is a close interconnection between our inner person and our physical body. They affect each other in many dramatic ways. Our heart can affect our physical health, and our physical health in turn can influence our thoughts, emotions, and choices.

What Does Modern Medicine Say?

Medical science confirms what the Bible teaches about the brain/mind connection. Any doctor can tell you that physical stresses strongly affect heart attitude. People who suffer from pain or illness often struggle with depression and anxiety. Some of this may be due to the discomfort they feel, and some may be a side effect of medication given to treat the condition. Certain diseases of the body can produce the physical symptoms associated with depression (e.g., Parkinson's disease, hypothyroidism, multiple sclerosis) or anxiety (e.g., asthma, arrhythmia, hypothyroidism). Doctors also agree that physical strengthening often improves a sick person's spirits.

Research has shown that psychiatric medicines change the levels of certain chemicals in the brain. This physical support does improve painful feelings. But because the brain controls all the other organs in the body, these drugs can also have powerful unintended effects.

It's also important to understand that some statements we may hear about how psychiatric drugs work are not completely accurate. When television commercials tell you that your painful feelings are caused by an imbalance of chemicals in your brain, they are oversimplifying complicated information. It's true that psychiatric medications change the levels of certain chemicals in your brain, which may make you feel better. But there is no proof that abnormal levels of these chemicals developed all by themselves, thereby causing your emotional pain.

Here's a way to think of the brain's role in our emotions that's consistent with what the Bible teaches: The thoughts and feelings of our heart change our brain's chemical balance. The opposite is also true. Medicines that change our brain's chemical balance can affect the thoughts and feelings of our heart. This view accepts the findings of medical science on the role of the brain, without insisting that our emotional pain comes solely from our body.

The Body/Brain and Psychiatric Medicine

Addressing the brain/soul connection inevitably leads to the important issue of psychotropic medication. And any discussion of the use of psychiatric medicine prompts strong feelings among God's people.

In preparation for this chapter, I spent time surfing blogs and discussion forums to see what Christians are saying these days about this issue. What an eye opener! Although the discussions began pleasantly enough, many ended in angry interchanges.

Those in favor of psychiatric drugs tended to see emotional pain as solely a physical problem. They argued that the use of medicines is rational, necessary in all cases, and compassionate. As the discussion became more heated, some even implied that those who were opposed to their view were ignorant and uncompassionate.

On the other hand, those who disapproved of the use of these drugs were inclined to see emotional problems as strictly spiritual. They found it difficult to believe that using a medication could ever be right. As the dialogue intensified, they came close to accusing their opponents of being weak, unspiritual, or even sinful.

What struck me about these disagreements was that almost nobody was saying, "Maybe medicines aren't always the best choice." They also weren't saying, "Maybe sometimes medications can be helpful." Perhaps Christians take such strong positions on this issue because they feel that certain principles should not be compromised. While zeal for the truth is a good thing, judging the motives of those who disagree with us is not the right response.

A Quest for a Biblical Balance

Sometimes members of the antimedication group can come dangerously close to making a "Job's comforters" kind of mistake. They may not actually be accusing anyone, but it can sound as though they're saying, "You have uncon-fessed sin in your life. Repent and you'll feel better!"

On the other hand, it's easy to understand why members of the promedi-cine group who are on psychiatric drugs want to be sure that everyone under-stands that their troubling emotions are never associated with any sinful life responses. But in their zeal, they can sound as though Romans 3:23, "for all have sinned and fall short of the glory of God," doesn't apply to them. As we'll see, neither extreme position is consistent with the full counsel of Scripture or with the findings of medical science.

I believe we can agree that our bodies play an important role in our emo-tions without insisting that all painful feelings are due to a disease. I also don't think that it's a sin or an admission of weakness to take psychiatric drugs. But taking a medication without considering spiritual issues may leave the most important factor unaddressed. In fact, it's been my experience, through twenty years of psychiatric and biblical counseling practice, that a medicine-only approach doesn't resolve emotional pain completely or permanently in most cases.

The controversy about medicines hinges upon what the Bible and med-ical research say about our emotional problems. Do they really contradict each other, so we have to choose one or the other? Or are they more similar than we may realize? Let's take a careful look at what each one affirms.

Putting It All Together

It is important to realize that every emotion involves a complex interac-tion between body and soul. For example, the Bible teaches that improving the way our body feels can change our emotions for the better. Medical science confirms the Bible's teachings. Whether we're taking arthritis drugs for pain or psychiatric drugs, medications may improve the way we feel. But they won't, by themselves, work the spiritual change that may be needed in our heart.

Remember Elijah's story. Rest and food fortified his body, but they didn't solve his emotional problem. He wanted to give up because he'd decided that his situation was hopeless and his ministry was a lost cause. Elijah's hunger and tiredness didn't do this to him, and food and rest alone couldn't solve it. It took an encounter with God's truth to set Elijah's heart right.

Satan understands the connection between our physical condition and our spiritual struggles very well. That's why he waited until Jesus was weakened by hunger, when He was fasting in the wilderness, before launching a spiritual attack (Matthew 4:1-11). How did Jesus resist Satan? He countered each lie with truth from God's Word, simply stating, "It is written..."

In the same way that food and rest revived Elijah, medications may improve the balance of chemicals in our brains. But by themselves they can't solve complex spiritual problems. We need to hear God speaking truth to our hearts as Elijah did. We also need to actively use God's Word, as Jesus did, when we're struggling.

Martin Luther often struggled against depression and anxiety, and he understood this truth. He urged his followers to fight against depressed and anxious thoughts, "For our adversary, the devil, walks about, seeking not only to devour our souls but also to weaken our bodies with thoughts of the soul."[3] He encouraged his followers to correct their thinking with truths from Scripture.

Charles Spurgeon struggled with depression off and on throughout a long and fruitful ministry. He taught his students that we often experience painful feelings when we're physically weak or under the pressure of circumstances. In his own case, Spurgeon suffered painful gout, kept up a grueling ministry schedule, and struggled with feeling at fault when several people died after someone yelled "Fire!" and panic ensued in a crowded building where he was preaching. But because he understood that suffering is a normal part of the Christian life (see 1 Peter 4:12), he wasn't surprised when he experienced seasons of sadness. Instead, he saw difficult times as opportunities to draw closer to God in faith.

At the same time, Spurgeon recognized the profound mystery of the complex causes of emotional distress. Commenting on Psalm 88, Spurgeon noted, "How low the spirits of good and brave men will sometimes sink. Under the influence of certain disorders everything will wear a somber aspect, and the heart will dive into the profoundest deeps of misery."[4]

We don't have to reject the Bible's teachings about our nature to agree that taking medicines may help us with painful feelings. But we also should understand what we're doing when we take a psychiatric drug. In most cases, we aren't treating an illness. We're simply giving a boost to our bodies by changing the balance of chemicals in our brains. But because the Bible teaches that our emotional reactions come from the heart, this physical improvement can't, by itself, solve our problems.

Mike Emlet summarizes well this balanced perspective:

> We are body-spirit creatures. We should not be surprised that a physical treatment such as medication may be associated with symptomatic and perhaps more substantial change in people's lives. Medication can be an appropriate and even necessary part of someone's care, depending on the specific nature of a person's struggle. Yet, we must admit a great deal of remaining mystery about how psychoactive medications actually work in the human brain. We take care to remain balanced in our assessment of the efficacy of medications. We neither exalt them nor disregard them. Even if we do view medication as a potential piece in a comprehensive ministry approach, we always seek to bring the riches of Christ's redemption to bear upon people's lives. Sinners will always need mercy, grace, forgiveness, and supernatural power to love God and neighbor. Sufferers will always need comfort, hope, and the will to persevere. Ultimately, these blessings are found not in a pill bottle...but in the person of Jesus Christ.[5]

What About Difficult Cases?

Even as we uphold Scripture as a fully sufficient source of answers for every lifestyle problem (2 Peter 1:3), we should remember that there is much that we don't understand. In my years as a biblical counselor, I've sometimes been puzzled when a godly person just can't seem to make full use of Scripture truth to solve her emotional troubles.

I'm comforted to realize that Jesus, in His time on earth, helped different people in different ways. For instance, I can count five distinct ways that He healed blind men. Jesus showed Himself to be the ultimate "heart doctor." He perfectly understood each blind man's spiritual condition, and tailored His actions to meet each one's deeper need. Two men needed to say they believed before their sight was restored (Matthew 9:27-29). Jesus saw faith already present in another, and confirmed it by speaking an immediate healing (Mark 10:52). Two men instantly received their sight by Jesus' touch on their eyes

(Matthew 20:34). Another's vision improved gradually (Mark 8:22-25). And Jesus healed a man's physical *and* spiritual blindness progressively as He spat on his eyes, sent him to wash, and then ordained events to deepen his faith as he testified to others (John 9).

So why are we surprised that the Lord doesn't solve everyone's painful feelings in the same ways today? We're told that one of Martin Luther's faith struggles was settled instantly by reading a single Bible verse. On the other hand, Luther wrote extensively about his lifelong struggle with and against spiritual depression/anxiety. Similarly, in my experience, some counselees grasp right away what God's Word has to say about their problems and recover their emotional balance quickly. But others, no less godly or committed, may toil slowly in counseling for many months.

Some come to me in so deep an emotional hole that it seems best to recommend the physical boost of psychiatric drugs in addition to the ministry of God's Word to restore them. Others come to me already on medications, having already spent many months in counseling, but still grappling with painful feelings. And finally, some people have diseases that require continued medical treatment, as well as biblical counseling, if they are to remain emotionally stable.

Thus, it is dangerous to assume that all emotional struggles can be changed by strictly "spiritual means." For some, spirituality includes embracing physical weakness. When we ignore the importance of the body, we misunderstand what it means to trust God. It is wrong to place extra burdens on those who suffer emotionally by suggesting that all they need to do is surrender to God to make their struggles go away.

It would be equally wrong to suggest that medication is all someone needs. That would be like a pastor entering the cancer ward to talk with a parishioner who was just told that she has cancer. "Well, take your medicine. Do chemo. You'll be fine. See ya' later." No! That pastor would support, comfort, talk with, counsel, and pray for his parishioner.

In *Pilgrim's Progress*, Hopeful crosses the final river easily, while Christian, who has no less faith, struggles desperately to keep his head above water. Spurgeon comments, "I note that some whom I greatly love and esteem, who are, in my judgment, among the very choicest of God's people, nevertheless travel most of the way to heaven by night."[6] I don't know why the Lord deals with one person differently than another, but I know that He is good, and He works everything together for good for His people (Romans 8:28). My confidence as I come alongside suffering counselees is this: Jesus, who healed a number of blind men five different ways, still provides what each of us needs to increase our faith and restore us.

We who love this wise and compassionate Lord should have the same attitude toward one another. Let's stop judging our brothers and sisters' faith by the quantity or difficulty of their trials, the way Job's comforters did. Let's also resist the temptation to offer easy answers, whether they be "Just trust God," or "Just take medicines." Instead, as we seek to be skillful biblical counselors, let's imitate the Lord's gentleness and patience for those whose sufferings we can't fully understand, because only He knows their hearts (Jeremiah 17:10).

A Biblical Counselor's Testimony

What might this brain/mind, body/soul interrelationship look like in real life? Bob Somerville is a NANC-certified biblical counselor (National Association of Nouthetic Counselors) who shares his testimony so that we can get a glimpse of what this body/soul/emotion struggle was like for him.

"Upon returning from a trip to Russia with my wife, traveling and speaking to pastors and their wives, I experienced ever-worsening back pain. The pain became so bad that I could hardly walk. I had to teach my college classes sitting down. At the same time I was endeavoring to counsel a person through a crisis situation requiring hours of intense counseling, which was emotionally draining. I was also carrying an extremely full teaching load and ministering within our local church. Looking back, I can see this combination of events added up to intense physical, emotional, mental, and spiritual challenges converging in one time span. This was taking a greater toll on my body and soul than I could have ever imagined.

"An orthopedic surgeon recommended back surgery to correct the herniated disc causing the back pain and assured me that I would be back to work in a couple of weeks. So the surgery was performed, only to have the disc re-herniate shortly thereafter in another place. Per my doctor's orders, I laid on my back for two months, seeking for it to heal while losing fifty pounds and all muscle mass. The doctor had prescribed heavy pain medication to ease the pain plus medication for the insomnia. Never in my life had I experienced such pain and misery!

"During this whole ordeal I read one book after another to my wife while she lay by my side—books on the cross, the gospel, hope in Christ—that would ordinarily encourage me beyond measure. I was in the Word on a daily basis, seeking to learn what God had for me to learn through this trial. I couldn't teach, nor serve in my church, nor even go about the daily activities of life.

"Finally, after two months of this, my wife realized I had slipped into depression and brought this to my attention. The next day I began to read *Depression: A Stubborn Darkness* by Edward Welch, and by the end of the third chapter I realized I was not just depressed but *severely* depressed. Welch quotes the *Diagnostic and Statistical Manual of Mental Disorders,* which he says is the caretaker of the technical language for depression. It states that if a person experiences five or more out of nine symptoms during the same two-week period and this represents a change from previous functioning, then the person is in a "major depressive episode." I had all nine symptoms. I was in a deep, dark pit, a truly stubborn darkness.

"I sought counsel from the lead biblical counselor in our church, who was encouraging me in all the biblical responses to depression, but still the depression engulfed me to the point that I became nonfunctional. I had no feelings whatsoever, even of being saved—which was the worst feeling of all, not being able to sense God's saving grace. I had constant thoughts of suicide. Everything was black and hopeless. I truly believed that I would never preach or teach again. (I had been a pastor for thirty-five years prior to becoming a professor.)

"I was blessed to have my wife's encouragement as she hardly left my side for months. Together we prayed and sought God's grace to glorify Him through this. I was so thankful for her love, which was constant and strong and continually reminded me of the promises of God."

As you've read Bob's story to this point, how have you pondered the following?

- Diagnosis: How would you diagnose the issues? What principles from chapters 27 and 28 of this book could you apply as you attempt to assess the symptoms?

- Prescription/Cure: What approach to dealing with these physical, emotional, and mental battles would you suggest? What principles from chapters 27 and 28 might guide you as you pondered "curative treatment"?

- Relationship/Care: How would you relate to, care for, and interact with Bob? What primary "lens" would you look through: suffering? Sin? Body/physical? Personal/spiritual? What principles from throughout this book might guide you as you pondered comprehensive and compassionate care?

Bob says, "The depression became so severe that I was taken to the hospital completely out of touch with reality. After receiving a combination of psychotropic drugs in the emergency room that morning, it appeared by that afternoon that I had come back to normalcy. However, within a few days the effect wore off and there was a need for further medication. We sought counsel from a respected biblical counselor/doctor, who advised us that medicines were in order.

"My colleagues concurred. They saw that my condition was not the result of sin that had had sent me into a downward spiral, as Job's comforters had assumed of him, but a matter of response to the pain medication and the impact of what had transpired physically yet was also exacerbated by what was going on with me emotionally. Reluctantly I took the medicine for a six-month period, along with seeking to learn and grow spiritually from the situation. The medicine helped stabilize me so that I could think rationally and apply biblical principles to my situation. My experience has given me a much deeper empathy and understanding for those who suffer in this way than I ever had before.

"While the physical issues—the back problem and the level of serotonin in the brain—were being addressed through physical therapy, rest, and the antidepressant medications, the issues of the soul were being addressed with continued biblical counseling and pursuing God through His Word, biblically based books, and prayer. Our family was very supportive, as well as our church family, ministering to us with calls, cards, meals, and prayers. My recovery was a gradual process that took place over a period of six grueling months.

"I came to the realization that desiring comfort and to be in control were things I had idolized and needed to confess as sin. Suffering was part of God's plan to produce the holiness that He was seeking to work out in my life as He drew me closer to Himself and demonstrated His faithfulness.

"I grew in my awe of the unsearchableness of our humanness. It humbled me to know that I wasn't in control of what was going on in my mind and emotions and that I had to trust in God's good purposes in them, knowing that He would see me through those issues that were out of my control, and that He would do so partly through a medical means.

"I needed to seek only Him and rest in what He has accomplished through His sacrificial death, resurrection, and intercession on my behalf. My entire salvation and sanctification is solely dependent on His grace.

"What praise I offered to God for His amazing grace when I was finally able to go back to teaching and preaching again! My emotions have returned and I have an irrepressible joy over my Savior and a story that I can't keep quiet about. He has allowed me to share this testimony to encourage many, which is just one way that God is using what I went through for His glory."

Toward a Comprehensive Approach to Biblical Counseling

Bob's story is unique. I do not share it as if it neatly wraps up or represents anywhere near all the complexities involved in the body/soul connection. It can, however, open our eyes to something of the interrelationship between our physical, emotional, mental, and relational "worlds." Bob's story illustrates the message of *Christ-Centered Biblical Counseling*. Understanding people, diagnosing the root sources of problems, and prescribing wise "treatment options" requires robust, relational, comprehensive, and compassionate care grounded in our shared redemptive relationship to Christ.

Unity in Truth and Love

Bob Kellemen and Steve Viars

If you were to perform a search on the content of this book, you would find verses from Ephesians 4:1-16 turning up numerous times over the course of twenty-eight chapters by forty authors. Though this was not planned by the editorial team, it is no surprise to us.

The apostle Paul begins Ephesians 4 by laying the foundation for unity—the truth of the gospel that he highlighted throughout Ephesians 1–3. Paul then concludes Ephesians 4:1-16 by exhorting pastors to equip their people to speak and embody gospel truth in love so that the church grows up into Christ, the head of the church.

The Focus of *Christ-Centered Biblical Counseling*

Christ-Centered Biblical Counseling is, of course, about biblical counseling. However, if up to now your picture of biblical counseling has been two people meeting in a corner room in a church, then we hope we've turned that picture upside down for you.

Christ-Centered Biblical Counseling is about one-another ministry, mutual spiritual friendships, discipleship, mentoring, pastoral care, and daily Christian living—lived out together life-on-life in and through the body of Christ. *Christ-Centered Biblical Counseling* is a local church book about how we shepherd one another toward growth in the grace and knowledge of our Lord Jesus Christ so that our lives progressively reflect Christ and increasingly glorify Christ.

Though our forty coauthors represent a wonderful diversity of backgrounds and ministry settings, we all share something in common. We are united in our commitment to equipping the church to speak the truth in love so every member is empowered to change lives with Christ's changeless truth. We are united in our commitment to seeing the church grow up in Christ, "from whom the whole body, joined and held together by every joint with which it is equipped, when each part is working properly, makes the body grow so that it builds itself up in love" (Ephesians 4:16). *Christ-Centered Biblical Counseling* is a practical biblical theology of Christian living together in Christ.

Our Message to You

Perhaps you're a pastor and, upon finishing this book, you're thinking, *Now what?* First, we would say to you, "Don't take a back seat to anyone! You are competent to counsel" (see Romans 15:14). Second, we want to say to you, "Fulfill your calling. Equip your people to speak the truth in love. Shepherd your church toward the place where every member ministers gospel truth to one another in love." The Biblical Counseling Coalition (www .biblicalcounselingcoalition.org) stands ready not only to provide you with online resources, but to link you to the best practice churches, parachurch organizations, schools, and books that can increase your competency in equipping the body of Christ.

Perhaps you're a lay person, a faithful follower of Christ, and you're finishing this book and thinking, *Now what?* First, as we said to pastors, we would say also to you, "Don't take a back seat to anyone!" When Paul penned Romans 15:14, he wrote to "the average Christian" in small house churches dotting the countryside of Rome. He told them that they were competent to counsel. You, too, can speak the truth in love. Second, we would say, "Be equipped." Paul told the believers in Rome that their competency was based upon their being complete in knowledge (biblical content), being full of goodness (growing in Christlike character), and being in community—doing life together as brothers and sisters in Christ (Christian community). Seek to further equip yourself in your church by growing in biblical content, Christlike character, and Christian community.

Perhaps you're a professor and you've finished this book and you're thinking, *Now what?* First, we would say to you with gentleness, humility, and yet with conviction, "Please be sure that the training in counseling that you are providing your students is Christ-centered." When it comes to counseling others, we don't pretend to have arrived or cornered the market.

However, we do believe that truly Christ-centered counseling must seek to promote personal change centered on the person of Christ through the personal ministry of the Word. We believe that Christ-centered counseling should strive to be grace-based and gospel-centered, relationally and theologically robust, grounded in the local church, and relevant to everyday life and ministry. It is our conviction that wise counseling must seek to develop a biblical understanding and application of the classic doctrines addressed throughout this book: theology proper, Christology, pneumatology, Trinitarian theology, bibliology, anthropology, hamartiology, soteriology, eschatology, and ecclesiology. We are convinced that biblical counseling must seek to address the seven ultimate life questions we outlined in the introduction and developed throughout this book:

- Who is God, and how can we know Him?

- Where do we find answers, and what is our source of truth for life?

- How do we understand people biblically?

- What went wrong? What is the condition of fallen human nature?

- How do people change? What difference does the gospel make?

- What difference does our future destiny make in our present reality?

- How do we care like Christ in the body of Christ?

Second, to professors we would say, "Be a good Berean" (see Acts 17:11). Use God's Word to test everything that we have said in *Christ-Centered Biblical Counseling*. We have provided the categories that we each need to examine in order to develop a truly biblical approach to biblical counseling. Ground what you teach your students—future pastors, counselors, educators, missionaries, and Christian leaders—in your study of God's sufficient Word.

Perhaps you're a student and you've finished this book and you're thinking, *Now what?* First, we would say to you, "Look to Christ—the living Word. In Him are hidden all the treasures of wisdom and knowledge." Second, "Look to the written Word. It is God-breathed and useful for teaching, rebuking, correcting, and training in righteousness so that you may be thoroughly equipped." Third, "Engage in and equip the church.

Whatever the present or future place of your vocational work and ministry, use your training to equip God's people for the work of the ministry."

Perhaps you're someone experiencing intense suffering or you're struggling against a besetting sin and you've finishing this book and you're thinking, *Now what?* First, we would say to you, "Don't lose hope! Christ cares and He is in control. Turn to Him, not to a system or a theory." Second, "Find help. Turn to Christ and the body of Christ. Turn to His Word, which is living and active, powerful and effective, sufficient and authoritative, relevant and profound."

To Him Be the Glory

We'll finish where we started: It's all about Him. As Paul discusses unity in the body of Christ, he reminds us of our ultimate focus: "one God and Father of all, who is over all and through all and in all" (Ephesians 4:6). Our initial prayer is also our ongoing prayer: that *Christ-Centered Biblical Counseling* will equip you to equip others also so that we bring Him glory through our individual and corporate growth in Christlikeness.

The Mission, Vision, and Passion Statement of the Biblical Counseling Coalition

Our Mission

The BCC exists to strengthen churches, parachurch organizations, and educational institutions by promoting excellence and unity in biblical counseling as a means to accomplish compassionate outreach and effective discipleship. Our mission is to foster collaborative relationships and to provide robust, relevant biblical resources that equip the body of Christ to change lives with Christ's changeless truth. We pursue this purpose by organizing our thinking around one central question: What does it mean to counsel in the grace and truth of Christ? All that we do flows from our calling to equip people to love God and others in Christ-centered ways.

Our Vision

More than counseling, our vision is for the entire church to speak God's truth in love. Our vision is to unite and advance the biblical counseling movement in Christ-centered cooperation by relating in ways that are loving and wise, pursuing the unity of the Spirit in the bond of peace. We are dedicated to developing the theology and practice of the personal ministry of the Word, whether described as biblical counseling, personal discipleship, one-another ministry, small group ministry, the cure of soul, soul care, spiritual friendship, or spiritual direction. We seek to promote the strengthening of these ministries by ministering to people who offer care, people who are seeking care, and people who train care-givers.

Our Passion

It is our passion to promote personal change centered on the person of Christ through the personal ministry of the Word.

Be Equipped

To fulfill our mission, vision, and passion, the Biblical Counseling Coalition maintains a robust website designed to equip you to change lives with Christ's changeless truth. We invite you to visit us at www.biblical counselingcoalition.org. You will enjoy daily blogs, weekly book reviews, hundreds of free resources, training videos, links to dozens of other equipping websites, and much more.

The Confessional Statement of the Biblical Counseling Coalition

Preamble: Speaking the Truth in Love— a Vision for the Entire Church

We are a fellowship of Christians committed to promoting excellence and unity in biblical counseling. Our goal is to foster collaborative relationships and to provide robust, relevant biblical resources that equip the body of Christ to change lives with Christ's changeless truth. We desire to advance the biblical counseling movement in Christ-centered cooperation by relating in ways that are loving and wise, pursuing the unity of the Spirit in the bond of peace (Ephesians 4:3).

We pursue this purpose by organizing our thinking around one central question: What does it mean to counsel in the grace and truth of Christ? All that we do flows from our calling to equip people to love God and others in Christ-centered ways (Matthew 22:35-40).

More than counseling, our vision is for the entire church to speak the truth in love (Ephesians 4:11-16). We are dedicated to developing the theology and practice of the personal ministry of the Word, whether described as biblical counseling, pastoral counseling, personal discipleship, one-another ministry, small group ministry, cure of souls, soul care, spiritual friendship, or spiritual direction. We seek to promote the strengthening of these ministries in churches, parachurch organizations, and educational institutions by ministering to people who offer care, people who are seeking care, and people who train care-givers.

Introduction:
In Christ Alone

The goal of biblical counseling is spiritual, relational, and personal maturity as evidenced in desires, thoughts, motives, actions, and emotions that increasingly reflect Jesus (Ephesians 4:17–5:2). We believe that such personal change must be centered on the person of Christ. We are convinced that personal ministry centered on Christ and anchored in Scripture offers the only lasting hope and loving help to a fallen and broken world.

We confess that we have not arrived. We comfort and counsel others only as we continue to receive ongoing comfort and counsel from Christ and the body of Christ (2 Corinthians 1:3-11). We admit that we struggle to apply consistently all that we believe. We who counsel live in process, just like those we counsel, so we want to learn and grow in the wisdom and mercies of Christ.

All Christian ministry arises from and is anchored in God's revelation—which is both the written Word (Scripture) and the living Word (Christ). This is true for the personal ministry of the Word (conversational and relational ministry, which our culture calls *counseling*) and for the various public ministries of the Word. In light of this core conviction about Christ-centered, Word-based ministry, we affirm the following central commitments as biblical counselors.

Biblical Counseling Must Be
Anchored in Scripture

We believe that God's Word is authoritative, sufficient, and relevant (Isaiah 55:11; Matthew 4:4; Hebrews 4:12-13). The inspired and inerrant Scriptures, rightly interpreted and carefully applied, offer us God's comprehensive wisdom. We learn to understand who God is, who we are, the problems we face, how people change, and God's provision for that change in the gospel (John 8:31-32; 10:10; 17:17). No other source of knowledge thoroughly equips us to counsel in ways that transform the human heart (Psalm 19:7-14; 2 Timothy 3:16-17; 2 Peter 1:3). Other systems of counseling aim for other goals and assume a different dynamic of change. The wisdom given by God in His Word is distinctive and robust. He comprehensively addresses the sin and suffering of all people in all situations.

Wise counseling is an insightful application of God's all-embracing truth to our complex lives (Romans 15:4; 1 Corinthians 10:6; Philippians 1:9-11). It does not merely collect proof-texts from the Bible. Wise counseling requires ongoing practical theological labor in order to understand Scripture, people, and situations (2 Timothy 2:15). We must continually develop our personal character, case-wise understanding of people, and pastoral skills (Romans 15:14; Colossians 1:28-29).

When we say that Scripture is comprehensive in wisdom, we mean that the Bible makes sense of all things, not that it contains all the information people could ever know about all topics. God's common grace brings many good things to human life. However, common grace cannot save us from our struggles with sin or from the troubles that beset us. Common grace cannot sanctify or cure the soul of all that ails the human condition. We affirm that numerous sources (such as scientific research, organized observations about human behavior, those we counsel, reflection on our own life experience, literature, film, and history) can contribute to our knowledge of people, and many sources can contribute some relief for the troubles of life. However, none can constitute a comprehensive system of counseling principles and practices. When systems of thought and practice claim to prescribe a cure for the human condition, they compete with Christ (Colossians 2:1-15). Scripture alone teaches a perspective and way of looking at life by which we can think biblically about and critically evaluate information and actions from any source (Colossians 2:2-10; 2 Timothy 3:16-17).

Biblical Counseling Must Be Centered on Christ and the Gospel

We believe that wise counseling centers on Jesus Christ—His sinless life, death on the cross, burial, resurrection, present reign, and promised return. Through the gospel, God reveals the depths of sin, the scope of suffering, and the breadth, length, height, and depth of grace. Wise counseling gets to the heart of personal and interpersonal problems by bringing to bear the truth, mercy, and power of Christ's grace (John 1:14). There is no true restoration of the soul and there are no truly God-honoring relationships without understanding the desperate condition we are in without Christ and apart from experiencing the joy of progressive deliverance from that condition through God's mercies.

We point people to a person, Jesus our Redeemer, and not to a program, theory, or experience. We place our trust in the transforming power of the Redeemer as the only hope to change people's hearts, not in any human system of change. People need a personal and dynamic relationship with Jesus, not a system of self-salvation, self-management, or self-actualization (John 14:6). Wise counselors seek to lead struggling, hurting, sinning, and confused people to the hope, resources, strength, and life that are available only in Christ.

Biblical Counseling Must Be Grounded in Sound Theology

We believe that biblical counseling is fundamentally a practical theological discipline because every aspect of life is related to God. God intends that we care for one another in ways that relate human struggles to His person, purposes, promises, and will. Wise counseling arises from a theological way of looking at life—a mind-set, a worldview—that informs how we understand people, problems, and solutions. The best biblical counselors are wise, balanced, caring, experienced practical theologians (Philippians 1:9-11).

Biblical counselors relate the Scriptures relevantly to people's lives (Hebrews 3:12-19). All wise counseling understands particular passages and a person's unique life experience within the context of the Bible's larger storyline: God's creation, our fall into sin, His redemptive plan, and the consummation of all things. Thus we engage in person-specific conversations that flow naturally out of a comprehensive biblical theology of life.

Biblical Counseling Must Be Dependent Upon the Holy Spirit and Prayer

We believe that both genuine change of heart and transformation of lifestyle depend upon the ministry of the Holy Spirit (John 14:15–16:16; 2 Corinthians 3:17-18). Biblical counselors know that it is impossible to speak wisely and lovingly to bring about true and lasting change apart from the decisive, compassionate, and convicting work of the Spirit in the counselor and the counselee. We acknowledge the Holy Spirit as the One who illuminates our understanding of the Word and empowers its application in everyday life.

Wise counselors serve in the truth that God reveals and by the strength that God supplies. By the Spirit's work, God receives glory in all the good that takes place in people's lives. Biblical counselors affirm the absolute necessity of the work of the Holy Spirit to guide and empower the counselor, the counselee, and the counseling relationship. Dependent prayer is essential to the work of biblical counseling (Ephesians 6:18-20). Wise counselors humbly request God's intervention and direction, praise God for His work in people's lives, and intercede for people that they would experience genuine life change to the glory of God (Philippians 4:6).

Biblical Counseling Must Be Directed Toward Sanctification

We believe that wise counseling should be transformative, change-oriented, and grounded in the doctrine of sanctification (2 Corinthians 3:16-18; Philippians 2:12-13). The lifelong change process begins at salvation (justification, regeneration, redemption, reconciliation) and continues until we see Jesus face-to-face (1 John 3:1-3). The aim of wise counseling is intentional and intensive discipleship. The fruit of wise counseling is spiritually mature people who increasingly reflect Christ (relationally, rationally, volitionally, and emotionally) by enjoying and exalting God and by loving others well and wisely (Galatians 5:22–6:10).

Wise counseling seeks to embrace the Bible's teaching regarding God's role and human responsibility in spiritual growth. God's strength and mercy call for our response of faith and obedience. A comprehensive theology of the spiritual life provides the basis for applying relevant biblical methods of spiritual growth. Biblical counseling helps believers to understand what it means to be in Christ (Romans 6:3-14). It equips them to apply the principles of progressive sanctification through renewing their minds and actions based on Scripture with a motive of love for God and others (Romans 12:1-2).

Biblical Counseling Must Be Rooted in the Life of the Church

We believe that we best reflect the Trinity as we live and grow in community (John 17; Ephesians 4). Sanctification is not a self-improvement project, but a process of learning to love and serve God and others. Wise counseling embeds personal change within God's community—the church—with all God's rich resources of corporate and interpersonal means of grace (1 Corinthians 12:12-27). We believe that the church should be both the center and the sender of gospel-centered counseling (Romans 15:14).

By example and exhortation the New Testament commends the personal, face-to-face, one-another ministry of the Word—whether in one-to-one or small group relationships (Hebrews 3:12-19; 10:19-25). God calls the church to mutual wise counseling just as He calls the church to public ministries of the Word in preaching, teaching, worship, and observing the ordinances of baptism and the Lord's Supper. God desires His people to love and serve each other by speaking His truth in love to one another (Ephesians 4:15-16). The primary and fullest expression of counseling ministry is meant to occur in local church communities in which pastors effectively shepherd souls while equipping and overseeing diverse forms of every-member ministry (Ephesians 4:11-14). Other likeminded counseling institutions and organizations are beneficial insofar as they serve alongside the church, encourage Christians to counsel biblically, and purpose to impact the world for Christ.

Biblical Counseling Must Be Founded in Love

We believe that Christ's incarnation is not just the basis for care, but also the model for how we care (John 13:34-35; Hebrews 4:14-16). We seek to enter into a person's story, listening well, expressing thoughtful love, and engaging the person with compassion (1 Thessalonians 2:8). The wise and loving personal ministry of the Word takes many appropriate forms, from caring comfort to loving rebuke, from careful listening to relevant scriptural exploration, all while building trusting, authentic relationships (1 Thessalonians 5:14-15; 1 John 4:7-21).

Wise counseling takes into account all that people experience (desires, thoughts, goals, actions, words, emotions, struggles, situational pressure, physical suffering, abuse, injustice, etc.). All of human experience is the context for understanding how God's Word relates to life. Such awareness not only shapes the content of counseling, but also shapes the way counselors interact so that everything said is constructive, according to the need of the moment, that it may give grace to the hearer (Ephesians 4:29).

Biblical Counseling Must Be Attentive to Heart Issues

We believe that human behavior is tied to thoughts, intentions, and affections of the heart. All our actions arise from hearts that are worshipping either God or something else; therefore, we emphasize the importance of the heart and address the inner person. God fully understands and rightly weighs who we are, what we do, and why we do it. While we cannot completely understand a person's heart (even our own), God's Word reveals and penetrates the heart's core beliefs and intentions (Hebrews 4:12-13).

Wise counseling seeks to address both the inward and outward aspects of human life to bring thorough and lasting change into the image of Christ. The Bible is clear that human behavior is not mechanical, but grows out of a heart that desires, longs, thinks, chooses, and feels in ways that are oriented either toward or against Christ. Wise counsel appropriately focuses on the vertical and the horizontal dimensions, on the inner and the outer person, on observable behavior and underlying issues of the heart (Matthew 23:23-28). Biblical counselors work to help struggling people to learn wisdom; to love God with heart, soul, mind, and strength; to love one's neighbor as oneself; and to endure suffering in hope.

Biblical Counseling Must Be Comprehensive in Understanding

We believe that biblical counseling should focus on the full range of human nature created in the image of God (Genesis 1:26-28). A comprehensive biblical understanding sees human beings as relational (spiritual and social), rational, volitional, emotional, and physical. Wise counseling takes the whole person seriously in his or her whole life context. It helps people to embrace all of life face-to-face with Christ so they become more like Christ in their relationships, thoughts, motivations, behaviors, and emotions.

We recognize the complexity of the relationship between the body and soul (Genesis 2:7). Because of this, we seek to remain sensitive to physical factors and organic issues that affect people's lives. In our desire to help people comprehensively, we seek to apply God's Word to people's lives amid bodily strengths and weaknesses. We encourage a thorough assessment and sound treatment for any suspected physical problems.

We recognize the complexity of the connection between people and their social environment. Thus we seek to remain sensitive to the impact of suffering and of the great variety of significant social-cultural factors (1 Peter 3:8-22). In our desire to help people comprehensively, we seek to apply God's Word to people's lives amid both positive and negative social experiences. We encourage people to seek appropriate practical aid when their problems have a component that involves education, work life, finances, legal matters, criminality (either as a victim or a perpetrator), and other social matters.

Biblical Counseling Must Be Thorough in Care

We believe that God's Word is profitable for dealing thoroughly with the evils we suffer as well as with the sins we commit. Since struggling people usually experience some combination of besetting sin and personal suffering, wise counselors seek to discern the differences and connections between sin and suffering, and to minister appropriately to both (1 Thessalonians 5:14).

Biblical counseling addresses suffering and engages sufferers in many compassionate ways. It offers God's encouragement, comfort, and hope for the hurting (Romans 8:17-18; 2 Corinthians 1:3-8). It encourages mercy ministry (Acts 6:1-7) and seeks to promote justice. Biblical counseling addresses sin and engages sinners in numerous caring ways. It offers God's confrontation of sins, encourages repentance of sins, presents God's gracious forgiveness in Christ, and shares God's powerful path for progressive victory over sin (2 Corinthians 2:5-11; Colossians 3:1-17; 2 Timothy 2:24-26; 1 John 1:8–2:2).

Biblical Counseling Must Be
Practical and Relevant

We believe that a commitment to the sufficiency of God's Word results in counseling that demonstrates the relevancy of God's Word. Biblical counseling offers a practical approach to daily life that is uniquely effective in the real world where people live and relate (1 John 3:11-24). By instruction and example, the Bible teaches foundational methodological principles for wise interaction and intervention (Acts 20:26-37; Galatians 6:1-5; Colossians 1:24–2:1).

Within the Bible's overall guidelines for the personal ministry of the Word, there is room for a variety of practical methods of change, all anchored in applying scriptural truth to people's lives and relationships. The Bible calls us to use wise methods that minister in Christ-centered ways to the unique life situations of specific people (Proverbs 15:23; 25:11). We are to speak what is helpful for building others up according to the need of the moment, that it may benefit those who listen (Ephesians 4:29).

Biblical Counseling Must Be
Oriented Toward Outreach

We believe that Christianity is missionary-minded by its very nature. Biblical counseling should be a powerful evangelistic and apologetic force in our world. We want to bring the good news of Jesus and His Word to the world that only God can redeem. We seek to speak in relevant ways to Christians and non-Christians, to draw them to the Savior and the distinctive wisdom that comes only from His Word (Titus 2:10-15).

We want to present the claims, mercies, hope, and relevance of Christ in a positive, loving, Christlike spirit (1 Peter 3:15). We seek to engage the broad spectrum of counseling models and approaches. We want to affirm what is biblical and wise. Where we believe models and methods fall short of Christ's call, we want to critique clearly and charitably. When interacting with people with whom we differ, we want to communicate in ways that are respectful, firm, gracious, fair-minded, and clear. When we perceive error, we want to humbly point people forward toward the way of truth so that we all become truer, wiser, more loving counselors. We want to listen well to those who disagree with us, and learn from their critiques. Our mission to spread the truth and fame of Jesus Christ includes a desire that all counselors appreciate and embrace the beauty of a Christ-centered and Word-based approach to people, problems, and solutions.

Conclusion: Unity in Truth and Love

We are committed to generating a unified effort among God's people to glorify Christ and multiply disciples through the personal ministry of the Word (Matthew 28:18-20). We trust in Jesus Christ, in whom grace and truth are perfectly joined (John 1:14). We cling to His Word, in which truth and love live in perfect union (Ephesians 4:15; Philippians 1:9; 1 Thessalonians 2:8). We love His church—living and speaking the truth in love, growing up in Him who is the head, and building itself up in love as each part does its work (Ephesians 4:15-16).

We desire to encourage this unity in truth and love through a fresh vision for biblical counseling. When people ask, "What makes biblical counseling truly biblical?" we unite to affirm:

> Biblical counseling occurs whenever and wherever God's people engage in conversations that are anchored in Scripture, centered on Christ and the gospel, grounded in sound theology, dependent upon the Holy Spirit and prayer, directed toward sanctification, rooted in the life of the church, founded in love, attentive to heart issues, comprehensive in understanding, thorough in care, practical and relevant, and oriented toward outreach.

We invite you to join us on this journey of promoting excellence and unity in biblical counseling. Join us as we seek to equip one another to promote personal change centered on the person of Christ through the personal ministry of the Word.

The Doctrinal Statement of the Biblical Counseling Coalition

The following statement summarizes the core doctrinal beliefs of the Biblical Counseling Coalition. It is not an exhaustive statement, but a theological framework concerning our core affirmations regarding the central doctrines of the Christian faith.

About the Bible

We believe that God has given the Bible as His inspired, infallible, inerrant, and living revelatory Word. We affirm the verbal, plenary inspiration of the Bible and are therefore committed to the complete trustworthiness and primacy of Scripture. The Bible is God's relevant, profound, deeply personal communication to us that invites us to intimate fellowship with Him. The Scriptures consist of the sixty-six books of the Old and New Testaments. They are the totally sufficient, authoritative, and normative rule and guide of all Christian life, practice, and doctrine, and are profitable for glorifying God through growth in likeness to Christ which is our life purpose.

The Bible is complete in its revelation of who God is, His person, character, promises, commandments, and will for the salvation of a people for His own possession. The Bible reveals who we are: created in God's image, accountable to God, fallen into sin against God, judged and justly condemned by God, redeemed by Jesus Christ, and transformed by the Holy Spirit. The Bible reveals the meaning of our total life situation in each and all its aspects—all the blessings of this life, the variety of sufferings and hardships, Satan, the influence of other human beings, etc. The Bible also reveals the nature of the Christian life and the ministries of the church, showing the content, the functions, and the goals that express the image of Christ.

About the Triune God

We believe in one God, eternally existing in three equally divine Persons: the Father, the Son, and the Holy Spirit, who know, love, and glorify one another. They are forever equal in nature, attributes, and perfection, yet forever distinct in their relations to one another and distinct in their particular relationships both to the creation and to the actions and processes of redemption. They are equally worthy of our worship, love, and obedience. This One true and living God is infinitely perfect both in His love and in His holiness. The Triune God, in affectionate sovereignty, sustains and rules over all things, providentially bringing about His eternal good purpose to redeem a people for Himself—to the praise of the glory of His grace.

About God the Father

We believe that God, as the Father, reigns over His entire universe with providential care, holy justice, and saving mercy, to His own glory. In His holy love, the Father is all-powerful, all-loving, all-knowing, and all-wise. He is fatherly in attitude toward all men, but Father, indeed, to those who have been made children of God through salvation in Christ.

About God the Son, Jesus Christ

We believe in the deity of our Lord Jesus Christ, the eternal Son of God, Who humbled Himself by taking on the form of a man by means of His virgin birth, becoming forever both fully human without ceasing to be fully God. We affirm that He lived a sinless life of active love and perfect wisdom. He died by crucifixion on the cross, by His shed blood and death making a vicarious, substitutionary atonement for our sins. After three days, He was resurrected bodily from the dead, unto an indestructible life. After appearing to His disciples and instructing them for forty days, He ascended to heaven. He is now seated at the right hand of the Father, interceding for believers, reigning as

King over all creation, and working in and through His church. He will personally return in power and glory to judge the living and the dead, and to raise to immortality those who eagerly await Him, perfecting them in His image.

About God the Holy Spirit

We believe that God the Holy Spirit, sent by the Father and the Son, has come into the world to reveal and glorify Christ, and to convict and draw sinners to Christ. From the moment of spiritual birth, He indwells believers, individually and corporately, as their Helper. By the Spirit's agency, believers are renewed, sanctified, and adopted into God's family. He imparts new life to believers, placing them into the body of Christ, transforming and empowering them for Christlike living, and sealing them until the day of redemption. He is the source of power for all acceptable worship and ministry as He imparts a diversity of enabling gifts that equip God's people for service. He provides the power to understand and apply God's truth in love.

About Humanity—Creation

We believe that God created Adam and Eve in His image, male and female, and declared them "very good," granting them all the capacities of image bearers. God created them to reflect and to enjoy His glory. They were created material and immaterial, physical body and spiritual soul, these qualities united and inseparably interdependent. They were created with a conscience able to discern good and evil, with the capacity to relate, think, choose, and feel in all the fruitfulness of wisdom. They were designed and commissioned to love God and one another, living in holy and devoted fellowship with God, and in loving, complementary relationship with each other. They were designed and commissioned to care for and govern His creation, working in and ruling over all creation as God's faithful servants and stewards.

About Humanity—Fall

We believe that because of voluntary sin against God, Adam and Eve fell from the actively good, sinless, and innocent state in which they were first created. They became self-willed, perverse, and transgressive against God and each other. Immediately they died spiritually and also began to die physically. Consequently, for them and all their progeny, the image of God was distorted and their nature depraved and corrupted in every aspect of their being (spiritually, socially, mentally, volitionally, and emotionally). While human beings are corrupted in every aspect of their being and functioning, because of God's common grace the image of God has not been totally eradicated, and evil is not given full reign. God preserves and enables many common goods. All people have true dignity, a conscience in which clarity coexists with distortion, and many powers of mind, action, and feeling. All humanity is separated and alienated from God and thus spiritually dead—until God's own gracious intervention. The supreme need of all human beings is to be reconciled to God; and the only hope of all human beings is to receive the undeserved grace of God in Christ. God alone can rescue us and restore sinners to Himself.

About Salvation—Redemption

We believe that salvation is the gift of God by grace alone and is received through faith alone in the Lord Jesus Christ. Salvation is wholly conceived, accomplished, and applied by God's sovereign grace. It is not, in whole or in part, conceived or accomplished by human will or works. We believe that salvation refers comprehensively to the entire work of God that redeems His people from the penalty, power, and eventual presence of sin while imputing to His people the righteousness of Jesus Christ and all the benefits of adoption into His family. This salvation overthrows the dominion of darkness and creates a new people who enter Christ's body of light, truth, and love.

We affirm that salvation is only through Christ, for there is no other name given under heaven by which we must be saved. Christ voluntarily took upon Himself the form of a man, was tempted in all points as we are, yet without sin in nature, word, or deed. He honored the Divine Law by His personal obedience, and by His death made a full and vicarious atonement for our sins. Jesus, having risen bodily from the dead, is now enthroned in heaven serving as the suitable, compassionate, all-sufficient Savior and the Mediator for His believer-priests.

We believe that all the blessings of salvation are free gifts of God, and that each is a glorious facet of union with Christ. In Christ, persons once justly condemned are now forgiven and justified because Christ died bearing our sins, because He was raised for our justification, and because God imputes to His people the righteousness of Jesus Christ. In Christ, persons once dead in trespasses and sins are now made spiritually alive in the new birth, receive the Holy Spirit, and receive eternal life. In Christ, persons whose father and master was the devil are now adopted by God the Father into His family, and become citizens and servants in God's kingdom. In Christ, persons who were estranged from God are now reconciled forever. God gives all these gifts, and more, by the Holy Spirit, and we receive all these gifts by faith.

We believe that by His incarnation, life, death, resurrection, and ascension, Jesus Christ acted as our representative and substitute. He did this so that in Him we might become the righteousness of God. On the cross He canceled sin, satisfied by His sacrifice the wrath of God, and, by bearing the full penalty of our sins, reconciled to God all who believe. We believe that by His resurrection, Christ Jesus was vindicated by His Father, broke the power of death, defeated Satan who once had power over it, and brought everlasting life to all His people. We believe that by His ascension, Jesus Christ has been forever exalted as Lord and has prepared a place for us to be with Him. We believe that at His return, Jesus Christ will wipe away all tears, will remove all sin and suffering, will establish forever His kingdom of love, joy and peace, and will perfect His holy bride. We believe that all whom God regenerates are made at once children of God, justified in His sight through faith alone in Christ's atoning work, and brought into His family. We believe that believers are kept by the power of God through faith in a state of grace, and are eternally secure apart from any human works. We believe that we who are Christ's body will see Him face-to-face, and that we will live with Him and with one another forever.

About Sanctification

We believe that sanctification is the process by which believers, each one and all together—as set apart from sin and united in Christ—are increasingly conformed to the image of Christ. Sanctification has past, present, and future aspects. First, believers are "chosen, holy and beloved" in Christ, set apart for God in union with Christ, and are actually made new by regeneration (positional or definitive sanctification). Second, believers begin to mature in their new life, set apart day-by-day through growth in grace into the likeness of Christ. This process (progressive sanctification) takes place by the power of the Holy Spirit, through the Word of God, in the communion of the saints, by the continual use of God's appointed means of growth in grace, each member contributing to the growth of the whole unto maturity in Christ. Third, believers will be set apart from the very presence of sin when sanctification is completed (glorification) at the coming of Christ for the church. Definitive sanctification in the past and glorification in the future provide anchors that sustain hope and bring encouragement amidst the failures and sufferings that make progressive sanctification a long and arduous pilgrimage.

About the Church

We believe that the church, the body of Christ, is composed of all persons living and dead who have been joined to Christ and one another by the power of the Holy Spirit. Every true believer is baptized by the Holy Spirit into the body of Christ and thus united in Christ to one another in unity and love across social, economic, and ethnic lines. We affirm that the local church is God's primary instrument and context for His work today; that every believer should be an active member in a local assembly; and that the Christian community is the context where believers are mutually encouraged, equipped, and empowered to conform to the image of Christ through worship, fellowship, discipleship, stewardship, and ambassadorship (evangelism). The sanctification of an individual is not a personal self-improvement project, but is the formation of a constructive, fruitful member of the body of Christ.

We believe it is every believer's privilege and obligation to be an instrument in the Redeemer's hands. This requires an intentional involvement in the lives of others: learning to speak and to live the truth in love, learning humility, and learning to forgive and to give, so that we all grow in unity and maturity into Christ, who is the head. The true mission of the church is to bring God glory, as believers (individually and corporately) live consistent with the Great Commandment and the Great Commission. We believe that baptism and the

Lord's Supper are ordained by the Lord Jesus Himself. They are our public vows of submission to the once crucified and now resurrected Christ, and anticipations of His return and of the consummation of all things.

About the Eternal State and the Restoration of All Things

We believe in the personal, glorious, and bodily return of our Lord Jesus Christ when His kingdom will be consummated. We believe in the bodily resurrection of both the just and the unjust—the unjust to judgment and eternal conscious punishment in hell, and the just to eternal blessedness in the presence of Him who sits on the throne and of the Lamb, in the new heaven and the new earth, the eternal home of righteousness. On that day, the church will be presented faultless before God by the obedience, suffering, and triumph of Christ; all sin will be purged and its wretched effects forever banished. God will be all in all, His people will be enthralled with Him, and everything will be done to the praise of His glorious grace.

Bibliography of Sources Cited

Adams, Jay E. *The Christian Counselor's Manual*. Grand Rapids: Zondervan, 1973.

———. *Competent to Counsel*. Grand Rapids: Zondervan, 1970.

———. *More Than Redemption: A Theology of Christian Counseling*. Grand Rapids: Zondervan, 1979.

Albert, Octavia. *The House of Bondage or Charlotte Brooks and Other Slaves*. New York: Oxford University Press, 1988.

Alexander, Donald, ed. *Christian Spirituality: Five Views of Sanctification*. Downers Grove, IL: InterVarsity Press, 1988.

Arndt, William, Frederick Danker, and Walter Bauer. *A Greek-English Lexicon of the New Testament and Other Early Christian Literature*. 3d ed. Chicago: University of Chicago Press, 2000.

Arnold, Clinton E. *Ephesians*. Zondervan Exegetical Commentary on the New Testament. Grand Rapids: Zondervan, 2010.

Augustine. *Confessions*. Translated by R.S. Pine-Coffin. London: Penguin Books, 1961.

Austin, J.L. *How to Do Things with Words*. New York: Oxford University Press, 1962/1976.

Barrick, William D. "Isaiah 11:2." In *The Net Bible*. Richardson, TX: Biblical Studies Press, 2003.

Beale, G.K., and D.A. Carson. *Commentary on the New Testament Use of the Old Testament*. Grand Rapids: Baker Academic, 2007.

Berkhof, Louis. *Systematic Theology*. Grand Rapids: Eerdmans, 1996.

Boice, James Montgomery. *The Gospel of John*. Vol. 1, *The Coming of the Light, John 1–4*. Grand Rapids: Baker, 2002.

Bonhoeffer, Dietrich. *Life Together*. New York: Harper & Row, 1954.

Brenton, C.L. *The Septuagint Version: Greek and English*. Grand Rapids: Zondervan, 1970.

Bridges, Jerry. *The Transforming Power of the Gospel*. Colorado Springs: Nav-Press, 2011.

Brooks, Thomas. *Precious Remedies Against Satan's Devices*. Carlisle, PA: Banner of Truth Trust, 1997.

Burge, Gary M. *John*. NIV Application Commentary. Grand Rapids: Zondervan, 2000.

Calvin, John. *The Institutes of the Christian Religion*. In *The Library of Christian Classics*. Edited by John T. McNeil. Philadelphia, Westminster Press, 1559/1960.

Carson, D.A. *The Gospel According to John*. Pillar New Testament Commentary. Grand Rapids: Eerdmans, 1991.

Carson, D.A., and Timothy Keller, eds. *The Gospel as Center: Renewing Our Faith and Reforming Our Ministry Practices*. Wheaton, IL: Crossway, 2012.

Carson, Kevin. "The Well-Planted Church: Vertical Integration and Horizontal Mutuality." D.Min. Dissertation, Westminster Theological Seminary, 2004.

Chandler, Matt. *The Explicit Gospel*. Wheaton, IL: Crossway, 2012.

Chapell, Bryan. *Holiness by Grace: Delighting in the Joy That Is Our Strength*. Redesign edition. Wheaton, IL: Crossway, 2011.

Chapman, Gary. *Now You're Speaking My Language*. Nashville: B&H Publishing, 2007.

Chappuis, Jean-Marc. "Jesus and the Samaritan Woman: The Variable Geometry of Communication." *The Ecumenical Review* 34 (1982): 8-34.

Cole, Graham. *He Who Gives Life: The Doctrine of the Holy Spirit*. Wheaton, IL: Crossway, 2007.

Collins, C. John. *Genesis 1–4*. Phillipsburg, NJ: P&R Publishing, 2006.

Cooper, John W. *Body, Soul, and Life Everlasting*. Updated version. Grand Rapids: Eerdmans, 2000.

Corcoran, Kevin J. *Rethinking Human Nature*. Grand Rapids: Baker, 2006.

Delitzsch, F. *Commentary on the Old Testament.* Vol. VII, *Isaiah.* Grand Rapids: Eerdmans, 1980.

Demarest, Bruce. *The Cross and Salvation: The Doctrine of Salvation.* Wheaton, IL: Crossway Books, 1997.

DeYoung, Kevin. *The Hole in Our Holiness: Filling the Gap Between Gospel Passion and the Pursuit of Godliness.* Wheaton, IL: Crossway, 2012.

DeYoung, Kevin, and Greg Gilbert, *What Is the Mission of the Church?* Wheaton, IL: Crossway, 2011.

Dodson, Jonathan K. *Gospel-Centered Discipleship.* Wheaton, IL: Crossway, 2012.

Edwards, Jonathan. *The "Miscellanies."* Edited by Thomas Schafer. Vol. 13 in *The Works of Jonathan Edwards.* New Haven: Yale University Press, 1994.

———. *Religious Affections.* New Haven, CT: Yale University Press, 2009.

Emlet, Michael. *CrossTalk: Where Life and Scripture Meet.* Greensboro, NC: New Growth Press, 2009.

———. "Listening to Prozac…and to the Scriptures: A Primer on Psychoactive Medications." *The Journal of Biblical Counseling* 26, no. 1 (2012): 11-22.

Ekman, Paul. *Faces Revealed.* 2d ed. New York: Henry Holt, 2007.

Elliott, Matthew A. *Faithful Feelings: Rethinking Emotion in the New Testament.* Grand Rapids: Kregel, 2006.

Equiano, Olaudah. *The Interesting Narrative of the Life of Olaudah Equiano.* New York: The Modern Library, 2004.

Erickson, Millard J. *Christian Theology.* 2d ed. Grand Rapids: Baker, 1998.

Eyrich, Howard, and William Hines, *Curing the Heart: A Model for Biblical Counseling.* Tain, UK: Christian Focus, 2007.

Fee, Gordon. *God's Empowering Presence: The Holy Spirit in the Letters of Paul.* Grand Rapids: Baker Academic, 2009.

———. *New Testament Exegesis.* 3d ed. Louisville, KY: John Knox, 2002.

Ferguson, Sinclair. "The Reformed View." In *Christian Spirituality.* Edited by Donald L. Alexander. Downers Grove, IL: IVP Academic, 1988.

———. *The Holy Spirit.* Downers Grove, IL: InterVarsity Press, 1996.

Fitzpatrick, Elyse. *Idols of the Heart: Learning to Long for God Alone*. Phillipsburg, NJ: P&R Publishing, 2001.

Fox, Michael V. *Proverbs 1–9*. The Anchor Bible. New York: Doubleday, 2000.

Frame, John. *The Doctrine of God*. Phillipsburg, NJ: P&R Publishing, 2002.

———. "In Defense of Something Close to Biblicism: Reflections on *Sola Scriptura* and History in Theological Method." *Westminster Theological Journal* 59:2 (Fall 1997): 269-91.

France, R.T. *The Gospel of Matthew*. New International Commentary on the New Testament. Grand Rapids: Eerdmans, 2007.

Gilbert, Greg. *What Is the Gospel?* Wheaton, IL: Crossway, 2012.

Goleman, Daniel. *Emotional Intelligence: Why It Can Matter More Than IQ*. New York: Bantam Books, 1995.

Greear, J.D. *Gospel: Recovering the Power that Made Christianity Revolutionary*. Nashville: B&H Books, 2011.

Green, Joel B. *Body, Soul, and Human Life*. Grand Rapids: Baker, 2008.

Green, Joel B., and Stuart L. Palmer, eds. *In Search of the Soul: Four Views of the Mind-Body Problem*. Downers Grove, IL: InterVarsity Press, 2005.

Griffiths, Paul E. *What Emotions Really Are*. Chicago: University of Chicago Press, 1997.

Gross, James J. *Handbook of Emotion Regulation*. New York: The Guilford Press, 2007.

Grudem, Wayne. *The Gift of Prophecy*. Wheaton, IL: Crossway, 2000.

———. *Systematic Theology: An Introduction to Biblical Doctrine*. Grand Rapids: Zondervan, 1994.

Harris, R. Laird, Gleason Archer, and Bruce Waltke. *Theological Wordbook of the Old Testament*. Chicago: Moody Press, 1981.

Henderson, John. *Equipped to Counsel: A Training Program in Biblical Counseling—Leader Notebook*. Mustang, OK: Dare 2 Dream Books, 2008.

Hoehner, Harold W. *Ephesians: An Exegetical Commentary*. Grand Rapids: Baker Academic, 2002.

Hoekema, Anthony. *Saved by Grace*. Grand Rapids: Eerdmans, 1994.

Horton, Michael. *The Christian Faith*. Grand Rapids: Zondervan, 2011.

Huggins, Kevin. *Friendship Counseling: Jesus' Model for Speaking Life-Words to Hurting People*. Colorado Springs: NavPress, 2003.

Ironside, H.A. *Addresses on the Gospel of John*. New York: Loizeaux Brothers, 1942.

Johnson, Eric L. *Foundations for Soul Care: A Christian Psychology Proposal*. Downers Grove, IL: IVP Academic, 2007.

Jones, Robert D. *Uprooting Anger: Biblical Help for a Common Problem*. Phillipsburg, NJ: P&R Publishing, 2005.

Jones, Stanton, and Richard Butman. *Modern Psychotherapies: A Comprehensive Christian Appraisal*. Downers Grove, IL: InterVarsity Press, 1991.

Kaiser, Walter C. *Toward an Exegetical Theology: Biblical Exegesis for Preaching & Teaching*. Grand Rapids: Baker, 1981.

Kaiser, Walter C., and Moisés Silva. *Introduction to Biblical Hermeneutics: The Search for Meaning*. Grand Rapids: Zondervan, 2007.

Kellemen, Robert W. *Equipping Counselors for Your Church: The 4E Ministry Training Strategy*. Phillipsburg, NJ: P&R Publishing, 2011.

———. *God's Healing for Life's Losses: How to Find Hope When You're Hurting*. Winona Lake, IN: BMH Books, 2010.

———. *Soul Physicians: A Theology of Soul Care and Spiritual Direction*. Winona Lake, IN: BHM Books, 2007.

———. *Spiritual Friends: A Methodology of Soul Care and Spiritual Direction*. Winona Lake, IN: BHM Books, 2007.

Keller, Timothy. "Contextualization." Unpublished lecture notes, Covenant Theological Seminary, St. Louis, MO: March 2007.

———. "Preaching Christ in a Postmodern World." Unpublished lecture notes, Reformed Theological Seminary, Orlando, FL: January 2000.

Kostenberger, Andreas J. *John*. Baker Exegetical Commentary on the New Testament. Grand Rapids: Baker, 2004.

Lake, Frank. *Clinical Theology*. London: Dartman, Longman, and Todd, 1966.

Lane, Tim, and Paul Tripp. *How People Change*. 2d edition. Greensboro, NC: New Growth Press, 2008.

Lewis, C.S. *Mere Christianity.* New York: Macmillan, 1960.

———. *The Weight of Glory.* San Francisco: Harper, 1960.

Lewis, Michael, Jeannette Haviland-Jones, and Lisa Feldman-Barrett, eds. *Handbook of Emotions.* 3d ed. New York: The Guilford Press, 2010.

Lloyd-Jones, D. Martyn. *Romans: Exposition of Chapter 6—The New Man.* Carlisle, PA: The Banner of Truth Trust, 1972.

Lucas, Dick, and William Philip. *Teaching John: Unlocking the Gospel of John for the Expositor.* Tain, UK: Christian Focus, 2002.

Luther, Martin. *Letters of Spiritual Counsel.* Philadelphia: Westminster, 1955.

———. *Preface to the Epistle to the Romans.* Coromandel East, South Australia: New Creation Publications, 1995.

———. "Sermon on John 18:28." In *What Luther Says.* 3 vols. St. Louis, MO: Concordia, 1953.

———. "The Sermon on the Mount." Vol. 21 of *Luther's Works.* St. Louis, MO: Concordia, 1953.

MacArthur, Jr., John, ed., *Counseling: How to Counsel Biblically.* Nashville: Thomas Nelson, 2005.

MacArthur, Jr., John, and Wayne Mack, *Introduction to Biblical Counseling.* Dallas: Word, 1994.

Maclaren, Alexander. *Expositions of Holy Scripture: Isaiah Chaps. I to XLVIII.* Grand Rapids: Baker, 1982.

Mahaney, C.J., ed., *Why Small Groups?* Gaithersburg, MD: Sovereign Grace Ministries, 1996.

Mayne, Tracy J., and George A. Bonanno, eds. *Emotions.* New York: The Guilford Press, 2001.

Montgomery, Daniel, and Mike Cosper. *Faithmapping.* Wheaton, IL: Crossway, 2013.

Morgan, G. Campbell. *The Gospel According to John.* New York: Revell, 1960.

Morris, Leon. *The Gospel According to St. Luke.* Grand Rapids: Eerdmans, 1982.

Murphy, Nancey. *Bodies and Souls, or Spirited Bodies?* New York: Cambridge University Press, 2006.

Nelson, Jane, Cheryl Erwin, Michael Brock, and Mary Hughes. *Positive Discipline in the Christian Home*. Roseville, CA: Prima Publishing, 2002.

Nolland, John. *The Gospel of Matthew*. New International Greek Testament Commentary. Grand Rapids: Eerdmans, 2005.

O'Brien, Peter T. *The Letter to the Ephesians*. Pillar New Testament Commentary. Grand Rapids: Eerdmans, 1999.

Osborne, Grant R. *The Hermeneutical Spiral: A Comprehensive Introduction to Biblical Interpretation*. Downers Grove, IL: IVP Academic, 2006.

Osborne, Larry. *Sticky Church*. Grand Rapids: Zondervan, 2008.

Oswalt, John. *The Book of Isaiah: Chapters 1–39*. New International Commentary on the Old Testament. Grand Rapids: Eerdmans, 1986.

Owen, John. *The Works of John Owen*. Vol. 1. Ed. William Gould. Edinburgh: The Banner of Truth Trust, 1850–1853/1965.

Parens, Erik, Audrey R. Chapman, and Nancy Press, eds. *Wrestling with Behavioral Genetics*. Baltimore: Johns Hopkins University Press, 2006.

Pascal, Blaise. *The Mind on Fire: A Faith for the Skeptical and Indifferent*. Edited by James Houston. Colorado Springs: Victor Books, 2006.

———. *Pensees*. Edited and translated by Roger Ariew. Indianapolis: Hackett, 2005.

Pettit, Paul, ed. *Foundations of Spiritual Formation: A Community Approach to Becoming Like Christ*. Grand Rapids: Kregel, 2008.

Piasecki, Mellissa, and David Antonuccio. "The DSM Debate: Potential Harms Related to Psychiatric Diagnosis." *Association for the Advancement of Philosophy and Psychiatry Bulletin* 7:2 (2010): 15-17.

Piper, John. *Future Grace*. Sisters, OR: Multnomah, 2005.

———. "God's Glory Is the Goal of Biblical Counseling." *The Journal of Biblical Counseling* 20, no. 2 (2002): 8-21.

———. *This Momentary Marriage*. Wheaton, IL: Crossway, 2009.

———. "Thoughts on the Sufficiency of Scripture: What It Means and What It Doesn't Mean." http://www.desiringgod.org/resource-library/taste-see articles/thoughts-on-the-sufficiency-of-scripture.

Plantinga, Cornelius. *Not the Way It's Supposed to Be: A Breviary of Sin* (Grand Rapids: Eerdmans, 1995.

Powlison, David. "Affirmations & Denials: A Proposed Definition of Biblical Counseling." *The Journal of Biblical Counseling* 19, no. 1 (Fall 2000): 18-25.

———. *Cure of Souls (and the Modern Psychotherapies)*. http://www.ccef.org/cure-souls-and-modern-psychotherapies.

———. "Idols of the Heart and 'Vanity Fair.'" *The Journal of Biblical Counseling* 13, no. 2 (Winter 1995): 35-50.

———. *Seeing with New Eyes*. Phillipsburg, NJ: P&R Publishing, 2003.

———. "The Sufficiency of Scripture to Diagnose and Cure Souls." *The Journal of Biblical Counseling* (Spring 2005): 2-14.

———. "X-ray Questions: Drawing Out the Whys and Wherefores of Human Behavior." *The Journal of Biblical Counseling* 18, no. 1 (Fall 1999), 2-9.

Rainer, Thom, and Eric Geiger. *Simple Church*. Nashville: B&H Publishing, 2006.

Rutter, Michael. *Genes and Behavior*. Malden, MA: Blackwell, 2006.

Ryken, Leland. *Worldly Saints: The Puritans As They Really Were*. Grand Rapids: Zondervan, 1986.

Ryle, J.C. *Holiness*. Moscow, ID: Charles Nolan Publishers, 2001.

Sailhamer, John. *NIV Compact Bible Commentary*. Grand Rapids: Zondervan, 1994.

Schreiner, Thomas R. *40 Questions About Christians and Biblical Law*. Grand Rapids: Kregel, 2010.

———. *Romans*. Baker Exegetical Commentary on the New Testament. Grand Rapids: Baker Academic, 1998.

Singleton, Harry H. III, *Black Theology and Ideology: Deideological Dimensions in the Theology of James H. Cone*. Collegeville, MN: Liturgical Press, 2002.

Solomon, Robert C., ed. *Thinking About Feeling*. New York: Oxford University Press, 2004.

Spurgeon, Charles. "Psalm 88." In *The Treasury of David*. Grand Rapids: Zondervan, 1950.

Stanley, Andy, and Bill Willits, *Creating Community*. Sisters, OR: Multnomah, 2004.

Stanley, Andy, Reggie Joiner, and Lane Jones, *Seven Practices of Effective Ministry*. Sisters, OR: Multnomah, 2004.

Stuart, Douglas. *Exodus*. New American Commentary 2. Nashville: Broadman, 2006.

Stuart, Douglas. *Old Testament Exegesis*. 3d ed. Louisville: John Knox, 2001.

Tan, Siang-Yang. "Holy Spirit, Role in Counseling." In D.G. Benner and P.C. Hill, eds. *Baker Encyclopedia of Psychology and Counseling*. Grand Rapids: Baker, 1999.

Tasker, R.V.G. *John*. The Tyndale New Testament Commentaries. Grand Rapids: Eerdmans, 2002.

———. *John: An Introduction and Commentary*. Leicester, England: Inter-Varsity Press, 1960.

Tchividjian, Tullian. *Jesus + Nothing = Everything*. Wheaton, IL: Crossway, 2011.

ten Boom, Corrie. *The Hiding Place*. Washington Depot, CT: Chosen Books, 1971.

Tripp, Paul. *The Age of Opportunity: A Biblical Guide to Parenting Teens*. Phillipsburg, NJ: P&R Publishing, 1997.

———. *Instruments in the Redeemer's Hands: People in Need of Change Helping People in Need of Change*. Phillipsburg, NJ: P&R Publishing, 2002.

Tripp, Tedd. *Shepherding a Child's Heart*. Wapwallopen, PA: Shepherd Press, 1995.

Vanhoozer, Kevin. *The Drama of Doctrine: A Canonical Linguistic Approach to Christian Doctrine*. Philadelphia: Westminster John Knox Press, 2005.

———. "God's Mighty Speech Acts." In *First Theology: God, Scripture, and Hermeneutics*. Downers Grove, IL: IVP Academic, 2002.

Viars, Steve. *Putting Your Past in Its Place: Moving Forward in Freedom and Forgiveness*. Eugene, OR: Harvest House, 2011.

Ware, A. Charles. "Pastoral Counseling of Multiracial Families." In *Just Don't Marry One*. Edited by George A. Yancey and Sherelyn W. Yancey. Valley Forge, PA: Judson Press, 2002.

Watson, Thomas. *All Things for Good*. Carlisle, PA: The Banner of Truth Trust, 2001.

Welch, Ed. *Addictions: A Banquet in the Grave*. Phillipsburg, NJ: P&R Publishing, 2001.

———. *Blame It on the Brain?: Distinguishing Chemical Imbalances, Brain Disorders, and Disobedience*. Phillipsburg, NJ: P&R Publishing, 1998.

———. *Helping Relationships*. Glenside, PA: Christian Counseling and Educational Foundation, 2011.

———. "Insight into Multiple Personality Disorder." *The Journal of Biblical Counseling* 14, no. 1 (Fall 1995), 18-26.

———. "Who Are We? Needs, Longings, and the Image of God in Man." *The Journal of Biblical Counseling* 13, no. 1 (1994): 25-38.

Westminster Confession of Faith. Glasgow, Scotland: First Presbyterian Publishing, 1646/1976.

Wilkerson, Mike. *Redemption: Freed by Jesus from the Idols We Worship and the Wounds We Carry*. Wheaton, IL: Crossway, 2011.

Wilkins, Michael. *Matthew*. NIV Application Commentary. Grand Rapids: Zondervan, 2004.

Wilson, Jared C. *Gospel Wakefulness*. Wheaton, IL: Crossway, 2011.

Wilson-Kastner, Patricia. *A Lost Tradition*. Washington, DC: University Press of America, 1981.

Wright, Christopher. *Knowing the Holy Spirit Through the Old Testament*. Downers Grove, IL: InterVarsity Press, 2006.

———. *The Mission of God: Unlocking the Bible's Grand Narrative*. Downers Grove, IL: InterVarsity Press, 2006.

Wright, N.T. "How Can the Bible Be Authoritative?" *Vox Evangelica* 21 (1991): 7-32.

Wuest, Ken. *Word Studies in the Greek New Testament*. Vol. 1. Grand Rapids: Eerdmans, 1953.

Yamauchi, Edwin. *Theological Wordbook of the Old Testament*. Vol. 1. Chicago: Moody Press, 1981.

Topical Index

Scripture Index

Author Index

Endnotes

Chapter 1—The Glory of God: The Goal of Biblical Counseling

1. John Owen, *The Works of John Owen*, ed. William Gould (Edinburgh: The Banner of Truth Trust, 1850-1853/1965, Vol. I, lxiii-lxiv.

2. Jonathan Edwards, *The "Miscellanies,"* ed. Thomas Schafer, *The Works of Jonathan Edwards,* Vol. 13 (New Haven: Yale University Press, 1994), 495. Miscellany #448; see also #87, 251-252; #332, 410; #679 (not in the New Haven Volume). Emphasis added.

3. The phrase "When therefore" was used in the NASB prior to the updated edition produced in 1995.

4. Adapted from John Piper, "God's Glory Is the Goal of Biblical Counseling," in *The Journal of Biblical Counseling,* Vol. 20, No. 2, (2002): 8-21.

Chapter 2—The Power of the Redeemer

1. Access Kelli's testimony at the Biblical Counseling Coalition website: http://wwwbiblicalcc.org.

2. For a nuanced, robust, and balanced perspective on biblical counseling and the body, including medication, see chapter 28 of this book.

3. Some commentators would understand this as Isaiah speaking as a forerunner of Jesus, but it is clear from Luke 4:16-21 that it is referring to the Lord.

4. This is the only place in Isaiah where this term is used. The formal title of Messiah is used in Daniel 9:25-26.

5. *Spalagchnizomai* is translated "had compassion" (ESV) or "felt compassion" (NASB).

6. *Spalagchna* is translated "compassion" (ESV) or "heart" along with the word for mercy or compassion so the whole phrase is "heart of compassion" (NASB).

7. The LXX uses the word for "pitiful."

8. The terminology of a "Genesis 3 hangover" comes from part of the Chapel Lecture Series in a message given by Dr. George Zemek at The Master's Seminary.

9. Isaiah 40–48 makes these same promises especially to those who are blind and captivated by idolatry (e.g. 42:7-8). We will see with our New Testament example that this is exactly what was happening in John 4 with the woman at the well.

10. The LXX uses the same word that is used of an apostle in the New Testament—one who was sent with a message.

11. The LXX word here is the same as "gospel" in the New Testament.

12. Many in the biblical counseling movement would see discipleship and counseling as synonymous or almost synonymous terms. Counseling is intense discipleship.

13. *Theological Wordbook of the Old Testament* defines the word bind (*chabash*) as "bandage." "…is often used of 'binding' on a bandage, and thus of medicating and healing the wounded." Edwin Yamauchi, *Theological Wordbook of the Old Testament* (Chicago: Moody Press, 1981), Vol.1, 261.

14. See Romans 6 and Colossians 2 to get a sense of the significance of "union with Christ." For further reading see Grudem's *Systematic Theology* (chapter 43, "Union with Christ"); D. Martyn Lloyd-Jones, *Romans, The New Man, Exposition of Chapter 6:1-23;* Bryan Chapell, *Holiness*

by Grace.

15. Paul Tripp, *Instruments in the Redeemer's Hand* (Phillipsburg, NJ: P&R Publishing, 2002), 101.

16. 2 Corinthians 5:14-21; Ephesians 5:1-2; 1 Peter 1:14-16; 2 Peter 1:4; 1 John 3:2-3.

17. G.K. Beale and D.A. Carson, *Commentary on the New Testament Use of the Old Testament* (Grand Rapids: Baker Academic, 2007), 438.

18. H.A. Ironside, *Addresses on the Gospel of John* (New York: Loizeaux Brothers, 1942), 137.

19. Samaria was not an independent political country during this time. The Samaritans descended from a line of Jewish people who had intermarried with foreigners deported there by the Assyrians ca. 722–721 BC (cf. 2 Kings 17–18). In 400 BC the Samaritans erected their own temple on Mount Gerizim, but it was destroyed by the Hasmonean ruler John Hyrcanus in 400 BC, thus furthering tensions between the Jews and the Samaritans. D.A. Carson, *The Gospel According to John* (Grand Rapids: Eerdmans, 1991), 216.

20. Jean Marc Chappuis, "Jesus and the Samaritan Woman: The Variable Geometry of Communication," *The Ecumenical Review*, 34, no. 1 (1982): 11.

21. Leland Ryken, *Worldly Saints* (Grand Rapids: Zondervan, 1986), 23.

22. Proverbs 18:4; 13:14; Ezekiel 36:24-27; John 2:6; 3:5; 7:37-38.

23. Beale and Carson, 438.

24. Perhaps some of us might read John 4 and think how obvious everything should be for the Samaritan woman, and yet none of that comes out from Jesus in conversation to her. He's loving and patient, but also clear and commanding. R.V.G. Tasker writes, "The Samaritan woman is a timeless figure—not only a typical Samaritan but a typical human being. As she converses with Jesus, it becomes clear that like most men and women she is almost exclusively concerned with the provision of what will satisfy her physical needs, particularly thirst-quenching water which can often be obtained only by the expenditure of much time and energy. The welfare of her soul is not for her a matter of primary concern." R.V.G. Tasker, *The Tyndale New Testament Commentaries: John* (Grand Rapids: Eerdmans, 2002), 75.

25. G. Campbell Morgan, *The Gospel According to John* (New York: Revell, 1960), 75.

26. Kevin D. Huggins, *Friendship Counseling* (Colorado Springs: NavPress, 2003), 123.

27. Augustine, *Confessions*, 21.

28. Blaise Pascal, *Pensees* 10.148.

29. Chappuis, 12.

Chapter 3—The Ministry of the Holy Spirit

1. Jay E. Adams, *The Christian Counselor's Manual* (Grand Rapids: Zondervan, 1973), 6-7.

2. Siang-Yang Tan, "Holy Spirit, Role in Counseling" in D.G. Benner and P.C. Hill, eds., *Baker Encyclopedia of Psychology and Counseling* (Grand Rapids: Baker, 1999), 569.

3. On the term *trialogue* and the implications of seeing all biblical counseling as a trialogue, see Eric L. Johnson, *Foundations for Soul Care: A Christian Psychology Proposal* (Downers Grove, IL: IVP Academic, 2007), 14, 215, 222, 511-12, and Robert W. Kellemen, *Spiritual Friends* (Winona Lake, IN: BHM Books, 2007), 16.

4. One of the best practices among biblical counselors in local churches is to involve advocates from the counselee's community in the process. That too would turn a dialogue into a trialogue. But our focus here is on the addition of a person, namely the Spirit, in the vertical dimension.

5. Paul Tripp, *Instruments in the Redeemer's Hands* (Phillipsburg, NJ: P&R Publishing, 2002), 8-9.

6. In the following, we are influenced by speech-act theory, first made famous in the mid-1900s by J.L. Austin's book *How to Do Things with Words* (New York: Oxford University Press, 1962/1976).

Theologian Kevin Vanhoozer has taken a similar approach to shed light on the Christian doctrine of revelation. He has recognized a rift between those who hold to a traditional doctrine of Scripture, in which revelation is viewed as propositional, verbally inspired, and infallibly authoritative (the classic view), and those who want to see Scripture as a personal revelation of God Himself that can be experienced in a deep way. Put simply, this debate can appear as a dichotomy between revelation as propositional and revelation as personal. Vanhoozer believes we can overcome this apparent dichotomy of personal-propositional revelation by way of speech-act theory. "God's Mighty Speech Acts," *First Theology: God, Scripture, and Hermeneutics* (Downers Grove, IL: IVP Academic, 2002), 148-49. See also Vanhoozer, *The Drama of Doctrine*, 63-68. Eric L. Johnson has applied these insights to Christian psychology and counseling in his *Foundations for Soul Care* (Downers Grove, IL: IVP Academic, 2007).

7. John Calvin, *Institutes*, III.2.xxxiii.

8. Johnson suggests the term "perlocutionary depth" to capture this dynamic. Johnson, *Foundations for Soul Care*, 199.

9. The technical terms used to distinguish these various aspects of how words work are *locution* (the words themselves), *illocution* (the intent) and *perlocution* (the effect or results of the utterance).

10. Ed Welch, *Helping Relationships* (Glenside, PA: Christian Counseling and Educational Foundation, 2011).

11. This is not to suggest that this would be your first movement toward John. You'll usually want to have built a trusting relationship with John first, and ensured that he is adequately grounded in his identity in Christ.

12. Timing is everything. Do this at the wrong time and it will feel forced and mechanical instead of natural and relational.

13. For a discussion of revelation and illumination see Sinclair Ferguson, *The Holy Spirit* (Downers Grove, IL: InterVarsity Press, 1996), 230-33. Ferguson interacts with Wayne Grudem's more charismatic view of the New Testament gift of prophecy. See Wayne Grudem, *The Gift of Prophecy* (Wheaton, IL: Crossway, 2000). While taking a more conservative approach than Grudem, Ferguson nonetheless concludes that "the Spirit must not be quenched, or prophecy despised (1 Thes. 5:19-20). All Spirit-given illumination and insight must be received and welcomed for what it is" (233). The approach we're suggesting here walks the line between what Grudem affirms and what Ferguson affirms.

14. Jay E. Adams, *Competent to Counsel* (Grand Rapids: Zondervan, 1970), 21-22, 24.

15. Tan, "Holy Spirit, Role in Counseling," 569.

16. Douglas K. Stuart, *Exodus*, New American Commentary 2 (Nashville: Broadman, 2006), 649.

17. Michael V. Fox, *Proverbs 1–9*, The Anchor Bible (New York: Doubleday, 2000), 32.

18. It is clear that the first occurrence of "Spirit" in this passage refers to the person of God, because the name of God, YHWH, is there in the Hebrew. Some exegetes see this and similar occurrences in the Old Testament as references to God's Spirit at work, rather than an explicitly Trinitarian reference to the Holy Spirit. For a discussion of these issues, see Graham Cole, *He Who Gives Life* (Wheaton, IL: Crossway, 2007),105-9. The subsequent occurrences of *Spirit* in Isaiah 11:2, however, are sometimes translated "a spirit" (NET, NAB, HCSB), rather than "the Spirit" (ESV, NASB, NIV, NRSV). For our purposes, it would suffice to observe (even if based only on the first reference to the Spirit) that: (1) God Himself empowers the Messiah, (2) this distinguishes Him from other kings, and (3) the results are dramatic. See, for example, Christopher Wright, *Knowing the Holy Spirit Through the Old Testament* (Downers Grove, IL: InterVarsity Press, 2006), 94-96. Yet we would go on to affirm the ESV's choice to capitalize the other occurrences of "Spirit" as well, as Graham Cole affirms when he says, "That Spirit is further characterized in terms of 'wisdom,' 'understanding,' 'counsel,' 'might,' 'knowledge,' and 'fear of the LORD' (v. 2)." *He Who Gives Life*, 133. We find further warrant for this approach below in Gordon Fee's argument that in Paul's use of Isaiah

11:2 language in Ephesians 1:17, he intends to reference the Holy Spirit.

19. Ibid., 30, 37-38.

20. John Oswalt, *The Book of Isaiah: Chapters 1–39*, New International Commentary on the Old Testament (Grand Rapids: Eerdmans, 1986); William D. Barrick, "Isaiah 11:2," The Net Bible (Richardson, TX: Biblical Studies Press, 2003).

21. Oswalt, *The Book of Isaiah*, 277-78.

22. Ibid., 278.

23. Gordon Fee, *God's Empowering Presence* (Grand Rapids: Baker Academic, 2009), 642 fn 30, 31.

24. The ESV translates Ephesians 1:17 with (capital *S*) "Spirit" to show that it is the Holy Spirit Himself whom Paul references here. Gordon Fee argues why this is the correct view of Paul's meaning in this case, and also that Paul's phrase "spiritual wisdom and understanding" in Colossians 1:9 would be more accurately translated "the Spirit's wisdom and understanding/insight," *God's Empowering Presence*, 641-43.

Chapter 4—The Unity of the Trinity

1. "It seems…that Mt. 28:18 is most likely…a reaffirmation of authority after the rejection of Jesus by the Jerusalem authorities which led to his death. Through resurrection God has vindicated Jesus, who is now able to freshly affirm his authority." John Nolland, *The Gospel of Matthew*, New International Greek Testament Commentary (Grand Rapids: Eerdmans, 2005), 1265.

2. Michael Wilkins, *Matthew*, NIV Application Commentary (Grand Rapids: Zondervan, 2004), 951.

3. R.T. France, *The Gospel of Matthew*, New International Commentary on the New Testament (Grand Rapids: Eerdmans, 2007), 1114-5, in notes 27 and 34, is hesitant to make this participle a central element of the Commission because it is commonly used to introduce an imperative in the gospel. Yet at the same time, discipling the "nations" does logically entail moving beyond one's local boundaries.

4. Wilkins, *Matthew,*, 957.

5. According to John 5:26, the Father and the Son each has "life in himself." Although we depend wholly on God for life, God depends on no one for His existence.

6. See also John 8:16-19,26-29; 12:49.

7. See also John 7:14-18; 8:28-29,40; 15:15.

8. See also John 5:30,36; 6:38; 8:55; 9:3-4; 10:32; 14:31; 17:4.

9. To say the Father is "in" the Son and the Son is "in" the Father, and to say the Father and the Son are "one" does not obliterate the personal distinctions within the Trinity. Such expressions point to the unity of being/character and the unity of purpose among the Father and the Son (and also the Spirit). Similarly, to say Jesus is "in" the believer or that believers are "in" Jesus obviously does not obliterate the distinct personhood of anyone; it merely means that believers exhibit the character and live according to the will of Christ, empowered by his Spirit. Christians should reveal Jesus through their character and lifestyles, just as Jesus revealed the Father to people when He was on the earth. For further information on these points, see D.A. Carson, *The Gospel According to John*, Pillar New Testament Commentary (Grand Rapids: Eerdmans, 1991), 394-95; John M. Frame, *The Doctrine of God* (Phillipsburg, NJ: P&R Publishing, 2002), chapters 27-30; and Wayne Grudem, *Systematic Theology* (Grand Rapids: Zondervan, 1994), chapter 14.

10. This is presumably a foreshadowing of what would occur at Pentecost: see Acts 1:1-8; 2:1-33. See the discussions of: D.A. Carson, *The Gospel According to John*, Pillar New Testament Commentary (Grand Rapids: Eerdmans, 1991), 647-55; Andreas J. Kostenberger, *John*, Baker Exegetical Commentary on the New Testament (Grand Rapids: Baker, 2004), 573-76. Gary Burge understands

the matter differently: see Gary M. Burge, *John*, NIV Application Commentary (Grand Rapids: Zondervan, 2000), 559-61.

11. These verses represent one sentence in the original Greek text, consisting of 202 words. Although there are various ways to divide this sentence, there seems to be a progression from person to person in the Trinity and from pronouncement of praise to God to application for the individual believer. For excellent resources on Ephesians see Clinton E. Arnold, *Ephesians*, Zondervan Exegetical Commentary on the New Testament (Grand Rapids: Zondervan, 2010); Harold W. Hoehner, *Ephesians: An Exegetical Commentary* (Grand Rapids: Baker Academic, 2002); Peter T. O'Brien, *The Letter to the Ephesians*, Pillar New Testament Commentary (Grand Rapids: Eerdmans, 1999).

12. In fact, Paul emphasizes the significance of the being together in Christ in Ephesians 3:6, where he writes of believers as "fellow heirs, members of the same body, and partakers of the promise in Christ Jesus through the gospel."

13. Although the English term is used seven times, there are three Greek terms translated here as "one."

14. Paul does not make a distinction here in the text as to whether he is referring to water baptism or Spirit baptism. For other texts that connect baptism and unity, see also 1 Corinthians 12:13; Galatians 3:27-28.

15. Some examples: Be imitators of God (5:1), walk in love as Christ reflecting His sacrifice (5:2), walk in light reflecting the fruit of the Spirit (5:9), walk in wisdom and in the Spirit (5:15-18), live daily as it reflects the work of the Trinity (6:10-20).

Chapter 5—The Grand Narrative of the Bible

1. Matthew 6:34.

2. 1 Corinthians 15:32.

3. 1 Corinthians 7:10-11.

4. Luke 9:23.

5. John 11:25-26; 14:6; Romans 1:16.

6. Genesis 3:1-19.

7. I suspect Reggie was drawing from N.T. Wright, "How Can the Bible Be Authoritative?" *Vox Evangelica* 21 (1991): 7-32.

8. John 3:16-17; 14:6.

9. At this point Reggie could have been thinking of any number of segments in Mike Wilkerson, *Redemption* (Wheaton, IL: Crossway, 2011), 26-33.

10. 1 Peter 1:1-2.

11. Psalm 23:3; Romans 9:22-23; Ephesians 1:6-14.

12. It appears Reggie was drawing from Christopher Wright, *The Mission of God* (Downers Grove, IL: IVP, 2006).

13. Deuteronomy 8:2-3; 1 Peter 2:1-3.

14. 2 Peter 1:3-4.

15. David Powlison talks about this idea in *Seeing with New Eyes* (Phillipsburg, NJ: P&R Publishing, 2003), 9-10.

16. Genesis 1:1.

17. Though Reggie doesn't say so directly, I think he had Colossians 1:15-16 in mind, and was drawing some of his conclusions about creation from John Calvin, *Institutes* (1536), I. v. 8; I. vi. 2; I. xiv. 20.

18. Isaiah 54:5; Ezekiel 16:6-15; Hosea 1:2-11.

19. Ephesians 5:22-33.

20. Reggie was probably alluding to Ephesians 5:22-33 as well as John Piper, *This Momentary Marriage* (Wheaton, IL: Crossway, 2009), 75.

21. Genesis 3:1-16.

22. Genesis 3:15.

23. Joel 2:28-32.

24. 1 Peter 3:15-18.

25. 1 Peter 2:20-25.

Chapter 6—The Sufficiency of Scripture

1. Louis Berkof, *Systematic Theology* (Grand Rapids: Eerdmans, 1996), 167.

2. Westminster Confession of Faith (Glasgow, Scotland: First Presbyterian Publishing, 1646/1976), 24.

3. Wayne Grudem, *Systematic Theology* (Grand Rapids: Zondervan, 1994), 127.

4. John Piper "Thoughts on the Sufficiency of Scripture: What It Means and What It Doesn't Mean." http://www.desiringgod.org/resource-library/taste-see-articles/thoughts-on-the-sufficiency -of-scripture (February 9, 2005).

5. John Frame, "In Defense of Something Close to Biblicism: Reflections on *Sola Scriptura* and History in Theological Method," *Westminster Theological Journal*, 59:2 (Fall 1997), 275.

6. David Powlison, *Cure of Souls (and the Modern Psychotherapies)*. http://www.ccef.org/cure-souls- and-modern-psychotherapies (April 10, 2010).

7. Mellissa Piasecki and David Antonuccio, "The DSM Debate: Potential Harms Related to Psychiatric Diagnosis," *Association for the Advancement of Philosophy and Psychiatry Bulletin* 7:2 (2010): 15-17.

Chapter 7—The Spiritual Anatomy of the Soul

1. For an extensive theology of biblical counseling regarding the comprehensive nature of human nature, see Robert W. Kellemen, *Soul Physicians* (Winona Lake, IN: BMH Books, 2007).

2. Jonathan Edwards, *Religious Affections* (New Haven, CT: Yale University Press, 2009).

3. See chapter 28 of this book for a comprehensive approach to understanding biblical counseling and the body.

4. Ed Welch, "Who Are We? Needs, Longings, and the Image of God in Man," *Journal of Biblical Counseling*, 13, no. 1 (1994): 31.

5. C.S. Lewis, *The Weight of Glory* (San Francisco: Harper, 1960), 45-46.

6. John Piper, *Future Grace* (Sisters, OR: Multnomah, 2005), 330.

Chapter 8—The Influences on the Human Heart

1. In this chapter we address in broad strokes the possible role of the body on people's psychological makeup. For additional in-depth insights on biblical counseling and the body, we refer you to chapter 28. For a comprehensive view of the nature of human nature and the interaction of the inner and outer person (embodied personality) with the world, we recommend chapter 7.

2. Several different words are used in Scripture for the inner, nonmaterial dimension of human experience: for example, *heart* (Deuteronomy 6:5), *spirit, soul* (Deuteronomy 6:5; Joshua 22:5; Matthew 10:28), *mind* (Romans 8:5-8; 12:2), and *conscience* (Romans 2:15). These words have

overlapping meanings. Even though they might have different connotations in different contexts, they are used in enough parallel constructions to indicate they all point to the same basic reality.

3. An article in a local paper spoke of pedophiles as victims who suffer because of their genetic makeup. Another article speaks of a man charged with the stabbing to death of six people who claims that he did it because he has a "killer gene" (*North County Times*, March 16, 2012; Section A, page 2).

4. I am indebted to Dr. Laura Hendrickson, who patiently and graciously helped me to gain a biblically informed understanding of physical/medical issues in counseling.

5. For a biblical counseling book that provides a relevant, relational, and robust biblical balance on the impact of the past, we recommend: Steve Viars, *Putting Your Past in Its Place* (Eugene, OR: Harvest House, 2011).

6. *Congenital* means "existing since birth"—although not usually genetic in origin.

7. Not all evangelicals understand these texts to refer to a substantial "soul/spirit" distinct from the physical body. Readers can gain a survey of the various positions in Joel B. Green and Stuart L. Palmer, eds., *In Search of the Soul* (Downers Grove, IL: InterVarsity Press, 2005). More detailed analyses are found in Joel B. Green, *Body, Soul, and Human Life* (Grand Rapids: Baker, 2008); John W. Cooper, *Body, Soul, and Life Everlasting*, updated version (Grand Rapids: Eerdmans, 2000); Kevin J. Corcoran, *Rethinking Human Nature* (Grand Rapids: Baker, 2006); and Nancey Murphy, *Bodies and Souls, or Spirited Bodies?* (New York: Cambridge University Press, 2006).

8. "Sufficient cause" means any factor that produces an effect by its presence.

9. This was a topic on the *CBS This Morning Saturday* program, March 10, 2012, with guest Dr. Ian Smith. Dr. Smith clarified that the gene in question coded for oxytocin, a hormone that in women is correlated with bonding behaviors. Women in one study that had a modified form of the gene (resulting in less oxytocin) were also more prone to divorce and an unwillingness to commit to long-term relationships. However, mere correlation cannot specify causation (since other unidentified variables can be involved); at most we can only say that less oxytocin might be a condition that makes a lack of bonding behavior more likely. But this is far from saying "less oxytocin *causes* divorce" or from saying "divorce might be in some women's genes," as the program host said.

10. Even when a claim of correspondence can be made (that is, people with a certain genetic makeup are prone to a certain behavior pattern), there will be individuals with that genetic makeup who do not exhibit the behavior pattern. Therefore, the genetic makeup is not the sufficient cause of the behavior pattern. *People* make choices for which they are accountable to God. For more information on the effect of genes on behavior patterns or personality traits, see: Erik Parens, Audrey R. Chapman, and Nancy Press, eds., *Wrestling with Behavioral Genetics* (Baltimore: Johns Hopkins University Press, 2006); Michael Rutter, *Genes and Behavior* (Malden, MA: Blackwell Publishing, 2006).

11. I (Jeff) know a former pastor who has a daughter with Down syndrome. She could not understand as much of her father's preaching as the rest of the congregation, but she had such a sweet spirit and love for the Lord, it was hard to see her congenital "defect" as any kind of barrier for her growing closer to her Savior.

12. "Why is it that a lame man does not annoy us in the way a lame mind does? Is it not because a lame man recognizes that we are walking straight, while a lame mind assumes we are all limping? Were it not for this distinction, we would feel sorry for him rather than angry." Blaise Pascal, *The Mind on Fire* (Colorado Springs: Victor Books, 2006), 77.

Chapter 9—The Problem of Sin

1. For a further examination of the influences on the human heart, including nature/nurture, we recommend chapter 8 of this book.

2. Cornelius Plantinga, *Not the Way It's Supposed to Be* (Grand Rapids: Eerdmans, 1995), 123.

3. Question 14 in the 1674 Westminster Shorter Catechism, http://www.westminstershortercate chism.net/.

4. Millard J. Erickson, *Christian Theology*, 2d ed. (Grand Rapids: Baker, 1998), 596. See also Wayne A. Grudem, *Systematic Theology* (Grand Rapids: Zondervan, 1994), 1254.

5. Erickson, *Christian Theology*, 595-96.

6. Along these lines, Michael Emlet, *CrossTalk* (Greensboro, NC: New Growth, 2009), suggests that we can view people simultaneously as sinners, saints, and sufferers.

7. See Edward Welch, *Blame It on the Brain?* (Phillipsburg, NJ: P&R Publishing, 1998).

8. For an understanding of biblical counseling for sufferers, we recommend chapter 26 of this book.

9. Erickson, *Christian Theology*, 518.

10. Louis Berkhof, *Systematic Theology* (Grand Rapids: Eerdmans, 1996), 227.

11. David Powlison, *Seeing with New Eyes* (Phillipsburg, NJ: P&R Publishing, 2003), 208.

12. This is an enjoyable piece you can look for on youtube.com.

13. Welch, *Blame It on the Brain?*, 169.

14. Robert D. Jones, *Uprooting Anger* (Phillipsburg, NJ: P&R Publishing, 2005), chapters 3-4.

15. A Penitential Order: Rite One," *The Book of Common Prayer*, http://www.bcponline.org/HE/penord1.html.

16. Grudem, *Systematic Theology*, 493. Similarly, John Sailhamer writes, "The disobedience of our first parents is not so much an act of great wickedness or a great transgression as it is an act of great folly. They had all the 'good' they needed, but they wanted more—they wanted to be like God." *NIV Compact Bible Commentary* (Grand Rapids: Zondervan, 1994), 15-16.

17. Edward Welch, *Addictions* (Phillipsburg, NJ: P&R Publishing, 2001), 33.

18. Powlison, *Seeing with New Eyes*, 206.

19. David Powlison, "Affirmations & Denials: A Proposed Definition of Biblical Counseling," *The Journal of Biblical Counseling* (Fall 2000), 24.

20. Ed Welch, "Insight into Multiple Personality Disorder," *The Journal of Biblical Counseling*, 14, no. 1 (Fall 1995): 21.

21. Paul Tripp, *Instruments in the Redeemer's Hands* (Phillipsburg, NJ: P&R Publishing, 2002).

22. Plantinga, *Not the Way It's Supposed to Be*, 199.

Chapter 10—The Centrality of the Gospel

1. Here is a sampling of some recently published works: Jerry Bridges, *The Transforming Power of the Gospel* (Colorado Springs: NavPress, 2011); D.A. Carson and Timothy Keller, eds. *The Gospel as Center* (Wheaton, IL: Crossway, 2012); Kevin DeYoung, *The Hole in Our Holiness* (Wheaton, IL: Crossway, 2012); Matt Chandler, *The Explicit Gospel* (Wheaton, IL: Crossway, 2012); Jonathan K. Dodson, *Gospel-Centered Discipleship* (Wheaton, IL: Crossway, 2012); Greg Gilbert, *What Is the Gospel?* (Wheaton, IL: Crossway, 2012); J.D. Greear, *Gospel* (Nashville: B&H Books, 2011); Tullian Tchividjian, *Jesus + Nothing = Everything* (Wheaton, IL: Crossway, 2011); Jared C. Wilson, *Gospel Wakefulness* (Wheaton, IL: Crossway, 2011).

2. A comprehensive view of the gospel presented in Daniel Montgomery and Mike Cosper, *Faith-mapping* (Wheaton, IL: Crossway, 2013), adapted from Tim Keller's unpublished but widely utilized course "Preaching Christ in a Postmodern World" (Orlando, FL: Reformed Theological Seminary, January 2000), 82-83.

3. Kevin DeYoung and Greg Gilbert, *What Is the Mission of the Church?* (Wheaton, IL: Crossway, 2011), 119-22.

4. Michael Horton, *The Christian Faith* (Grand Rapids: Zondervan, 2011), 267-68.

5. Psalm 16:11; Matthew 11:28-30; John 15:9; 2 Corinthians 3:18; 4:6.

Chapter 11—The Gospel in Balance

1. Mark Dever has a simple yet complete presentation of the main points of the gospel on his *9 Marks* website (http://www.9marks.org/what-are-the-9marks/the-gospel). It reads, "The good news is that: 1) The one and only God who is holy made us in His image to know Him (Genesis 1:26-28); 2) But we sinned and cut ourselves off from Him (Genesis 3; Romans 3:23); 3) In His great love, God became a man in Jesus, lived a perfect life, and died on the cross, thus fulfilling the law Himself and taking on Himself the punishment for the sins of all those who would ever turn from their sin and trust in Him (John 1:14; Hebrews 7:26; Romans 3:21-26; 5:12-21); 4) He rose again from the dead, showing that God accepted Christ's sacrifice and that God's wrath against us had been exhausted (Acts 2:24; Romans 4:25); 5) He now calls us to repent of our sins and trust in Christ alone for our forgiveness (Acts 17:30; John 1:12); 6) If we repent of our sins and trust in Christ, we are born again into a new life, an eternal life with God (John 3:16); 7) He is gathering one new people to Himself among all those who submit to Christ as Lord (Matthew 16:15-19; Ephesians 2:11-19)." A definition found on *The Gospel Coalition* Website (http://thegospelco-alition.org/about/who) under their Confessional Statement reads, "The Gospel: We believe that the gospel is the good news of Jesus Christ—God's very wisdom. Utter folly to the world, even though it is the power of God to those who are being saved, this good news is Christological, centering on the cross and resurrection: the gospel is not proclaimed if Christ is not proclaimed, and the authentic Christ has not been proclaimed if his death and resurrection are not central (the message is that Christ died for our sins...[and] was raised). This good news is biblical (his death and resurrection are according to the Scriptures), theological, and salvific (Christ died for our sins, to reconcile us to God), historical (if the saving events did not happen, our faith is worthless, we are still in our sins, and we are to be pitied more than all others), apostolic (the message was entrusted to and transmitted by the apostles, who were witnesses of these saving events), and intensely personal (where it is received, believed, and held firmly, individual persons are saved)."

2. Jerry Bridges, *The Transforming Power of the Gospel* (Colorado Springs: NavPress, 2012). Bridges says, "The Puritans understood the concept of dependent responsibility. They used to say (and this is not an exact quote but captures their attitude), 'Work as if it all depends on you, yet pray as if it all depends on God.' They labored diligently to become more like Christ, but they also prayed diligently because they knew they were dependent on the Holy Spirit to make their labor effective" (107).

3. Kevin DeYoung, http://thegospelcoalition.org/blogs/kevindeyoung/2011/08/16/glorying-in-ini dactives-and-insisting-on-imperatives.

4. See Donald L. Alexander, ed., *Christian Spirituality* (Downers Grove, IL: InterVarsity Press, 1988). This overemphasis on position is very similar to the Lutheran view of sanctification. Gerhrd O. Forde says, "Sanctification is thus simply *the art of getting used to justification*. It is not something added to justification" (13, emphasis in original).

5. In *The Cross and Salvation* Bruce Demarest writes, "Keswick authorities aver that one becomes a 'spiritual Christian' by a post conversion, crisis experience of unconditional surrender or complete abandonment to Christ. The Christian receives the fullness of the Spirit not by protracted spiritual effort and struggle, but simply by a decision of the will to dethrone self and enthrone Christ—hence the slogan, 'Let go and let God!'...In a chapter entitled 'Victory Without Trying,' Trumbull argued that the secret to the victorious Christian life is for the Christian to make an unconditioned and absolute surrender to God in faith...[Trumbull said,] 'Any victory that you have to get by trying for it is counterfeit...'" (John S. Feinberg, gen. ed., Wheaton, IL: Crossway Books, 1997, 397-98.)

6. Kevin DeYoung, http://thegospelcoalition.org/blogs/kevindeyoung/2011/06/14/gospel-driven -effort.

7. Bruce Demarest, *The Cross and Salvation*, John S. Feinberg, ed. (Wheaton, IL: Crossway Books,

1997), 423. Demarest says, "It should be evident that Christians' serious regard for God's law does not constitute *legalism*. The plague of legalism seeks mechanical compliance with the letter of the law while violating its inner spirit. Legalism strives to obey in order to acquire merit. Christian believers have been set free in Jesus Christ from compulsive legalism. They fulfill the law of Christ by the power of the Spirit out of heart gratitude to God. Likewise, respect for God's law as interpreted by Jesus and his apostles avoids the error of *antinomianism*. The latter claims that Christ released Christians from the task of ordering their lives according to God's law. In mind and action, Christians owe grateful loyalty to God and his law revealed for our highest good. Saints avoid the twin pitfalls of legalism and antinomianism by imitating Jesus Christ (1 Corinthians 11:1; Philippians 2:5; 1 Peter 2:21), the interpreter *par excellence* of God's law."

8. Thomas R. Schreiner, *40 Questions about Christians and Biblical Law* (Grand Rapids: Kregel, 2010), 140-41.

9. Thomas R. Schreiner, *Romans*, Baker Exegetical Commentary on the New Testament, vol. 6 (Grand Rapids: Baker Academic, 1998), 701.

10. John Charles Ryle, *Holiness* (Moscow, ID: Charles Nolan Publishers, 2001), 57-58. Ryle says, " I fear it is sometimes forgotten that God has married together justification and sanctification...tell me not of your justification unless you have also some marks of sanctification...Well says Rutherford, 'the way that crieth down duties and sanctification is not the way of grace. Believing and doing are blood-friends.' I would say it with all reverence, but say it I must—I sometimes fear if Christ were on earth now, there are not a few who would think His preaching *legal*; and if Paul were writing his epistles, there are those who would think he had better not write the latter part of most of them as he did. But let us remember that the Lord Jesus *did* speak the Sermon on the Mount, and that the Epistles to the Ephesians contain six chapters and not four."

11. Sinclair Ferguson, *Christian Spirituality*, edited by Donald L. Alexander (Downers Grove, IL: IVP Academic, 1988), 51.

Chapter 12—The Pursuit of Holiness

1. Anthony Hoekema, *Saved by Grace* (Grand Rapids: Eerdmans, 1994), 192.

2. Study guide adapted from Tim Keller, *Galatians: Living in Line with the Truth of the Gospel* (New York: Redeemer Presbyterian Church, 2010). Modified by The Village Church with permission.

3. See also chapter 13 of this book for an in-depth biblical examination of our battle against Satan.

4. Thomas Chalmers, *The Expulsive Power of a New Affection*, http://www.monergism.com/Chalmers,%20Thomas%20%20The%20Exlpulsive%20Power%20of%20a%20New%20Af.pdf.

5. See also chapter 19 of this book for an in-depth biblical presentation of spiritual formation and spiritual disciplines.

6. Thomas Watson, *All Things for Good* (Carlisle, PA: The Banner of Truth Trust, 2001), 35.

Chapter 13—The Weapons of Our Warfare

1. Ken Wuest, *Word Studies in the Greek New Testament*, vol. 1 (Grand Rapids: Eerdmans, 1953), 141.

2. The following material is developed from Robert W. Kellemen, "The Battle for Our Soul," chapter 7 in *Soul Physicians* (Winona Lake, IN: BMH Books, 2007), 103-15.

3. Thomas Brooks, *Precious Remedies Against Satan's Devices* (Carlisle, PA: Banner of Truth Trust, 1997), 29.

4. Martin Luther, "Sermon on John 18:28," in *What Luther Says*, vol. 1 (St Louis, MO: Concordia, 1953), # 983, 333-34.

5. Martin Luther, "The Sermon on the Mount," in *Luther's Works*, vol. 21 (St Louis, MO: Concordia, 1953), 42.

6. Elyse Fitzpatrick, *Idols of the Heart* (Phillipsburg, NJ: P&R Publishing, 2001), 116.

Chapter 14—The Hope of Eternity

1. Corrie ten Boom, *The Hiding Place* (Washington Depot, CT: Chosen Books, 1971), 181.
2. Ibid., 191.

Chapter 15—The Biblical Counseling Ministry of the Local Church

1. James MacDonald, "Foreword," in *Equipping Counselors for Your Church* (Phillipsburg, NJ: P&R, 2011), 11.
2. Robert W. Kellemen, *Equipping Counselors for Your Church* (Phillipsburg, NJ: P&R, 2011), 31.
3. See chapter 17 of this book for a robust development of the personal, private, and public ministry of the Word.
4. Reading material includes, but is not limited to, books such as Paul Tripp, *Instruments in the Redeemer's Hands* (Phillipsburg, NJ: P&R Publishing, 2012); Tedd Tripp, *Shepherding a Child's Heart* (Wapwallopen, PA: Shepherd Press, 1995); John MacArthur, Jr. and Wayne Mack, *Introduction to Biblical Counseling* (Dallas, TX: Word, 1994); Jay Adams, *Competent to Counsel* (Grand Rapids: Zondervan, 1970); and Paul Tripp, *Age of Opportunity* (Phillipsburg, NJ: P&R Publishing, 1997).

Chapter 16—The Health of the Church and Biblical Counseling

1. For a comprehensive examination of equipping biblical counselors, see Robert W. Kellemen, *Equipping Counselors for Your Church* (Phillipsburg, NJ: P&R Publishing, 2011).

Chapter 17—The Personal, Private, and Public Ministry of the Word

1. William Arndt, Frederick Danker, and Walter Bauer, *A Greek-English Lexicon of the New Testament and Other Early Christian Literature*, 3d ed. (Chicago: University of Chicago Press, 2000), 10.
2. Common examples might include: Overemphasis of spiritual warfare, "Deal with your demon of lust, your bondage to Satan." Some teach an instant sanctification, "You just need revival"—although you could interchange several terms here such as "renewal" or "rededication" or "to be saved again." Others point to a better prayer life, "You need to pray for deliverance," or "You just need to give this to God and pray through." Some suggest it is a Spirit issue: "You just need to yield to the Spirit and totally surrender. Once you have the Spirit's anointing, you won't have this problem anymore."
3. Resources for understanding how to ascertain the meaning of the biblical text include Walter C. Kaiser, *Toward an Exegetical Theology* (Grand Rapids: Baker, 1981); Walter C. Kaiser and Moisés Silva, *Introduction to Biblical Hermeneutics* (Grand Rapids: Zondervan, 2007); Gordon D. Fee, *New Testament Exegesis*, 3d ed. (Louisville, KY: John Knox, 2002); Douglas Stuart, *Old Testament Exegesis*, 3d ed. (Louisville: John Knox, 2001); Grant R. Osborne, *The Hermeneutical Spiral* (Downers Grove, IL: IVP Academic, 2006).
4. "Meaning is fixed and unchanging." Kaiser, *Introduction to Biblical Hermeneutics*, 42.
5. Kaiser, *Toward an Exegetical Theology*, 31-40.
6. Ibid., 43.
7. Paul regularly considered his own motivation and behavior as a minister of the Word. In Corinth he calls God as his witness to testify to his God-honoring motives (2 Corinthians 5:11-15). He gives testimony of his love and care for those to whom he ministered (Philippians 2:14-18; 1 Thessalonians 2:1-12; 2 Timothy 3:10-4:8). He mentions several times his emotional response

of tears for those to whom he ministered (Acts 20:19,31; 2 Corinthians 2:4; Philippians 3:18).

8. I initially heard the term *self-counsel* from David Powlison as a D.Min. student at Westminster. This is my definition of the concept as I wrote in Kevin Carson, "The Well-Planted Church: Vertical Integration and Horizontal Mutuality" (D.Min. Dissertation, Westminster Theological Seminary, 2004), 225.

9. For *self-counsel*, see also David Powlison, "The Sufficiency of Scripture to Diagnose and Cure Souls," *The Journal of Biblical Counseling* (Spring 2005), 2-13; David Powlison, "X-ray Questions: Drawing Out the Whys and Wherefores of Human Behavior," *Journal of Biblical Counseling* 18, no. 1 (Fall 1999): 2-8.

10. Paul Tripp, *Instruments in the Redeemer's Hands* (Phillipsburg, NJ: P&R Publishing, 2002), 231. This book is helpful in many aspects, including for counseling homework ideas that we can use for ourselves as well—see Appendix 5, "Homework and the Four Phases of Counseling," 329-48.

11. Paul writes, "…work out your own salvation with fear and trembling" (Philippians 2:12).

12. This is what Tripp refers to as entry gates in *Instruments in the Redeemer's Hands*, 126-31.

13. I first heard Randy Patton ask this question in regard to a counseling situation from the Sermon on the Mount (Matthew 7:24-27).

Chapter 18—The Transformational Tie Between Small Group Ministry and Biblical Counseling

1. Larry Osborne, *Sticky Church* (Grand Rapids: Zondervan, 2008), 71.

Chapter 19—The Goal and Focus of Spiritual Formation

1. Martin Luther, *Preface to the Epistle to the Romans* (Coromandel East, South Australia: New Creation Publications, 1995), 5-6.

Chapter 20—The Importance of Multiculturalism in Biblical Counseling

1. Figures obtained from our own calculations using the 1998 National Congregations Study directed by Mark Chaves.

2. Statement based on personal conversation on March 29, 2012 with Hosea Baxter.

3. Harry H. Singleton III, *Black Theology and Ideology: Deideological Dimensions in the Theology of James H. Cone* (Collegeville, MN: Liturgical Press, 2002), 31.

4. A. Charles Ware, "Pastoral Counseling of Multiracial Families," in *Just Don't Marry One*, eds. George A. Yancey and Sherelyn W. Yancey (Valley Forge, PA: Judson Press, 2002), 28.

5. Westminster Confession of Faith, Chapter I, Sec. vii.

6. Timothy Keller, "Contextualization," unpublished lecture notes (St. Louis, MO: Covenant Theological Seminary, March 2007).

Chapter 21—The Nature of the Biblical Counseling Relationship

1. For an in-depth examination of the relationship between biblical counseling and small group ministry, we recommend chapter 18 of this book.

Chapter 22—The Central Elements of the Biblical Counseling Process

1. Jay E. Adams, *The Christian Counselor's Manual* (Phillipsburg, NJ: P&R Publishing, 1973). John MacArthur, Jr. and Wayne Mack, eds., *Counseling: How to Counsel Biblically* (Nashville: Thomas Nelson, 2005). Paul Tripp, *Instruments in the Redeemer's Hands* (Phillipsburg, NJ: P&R Publishing, 2002).

Chapter 23—The Diagnoses and Treatment of Idols of the Heart

1. "Idols of the heart" is a phrase used often by the Puritans and re-introduced to the modern biblical counseling world, in part, by David Powlison in his "Idols of the Heart and 'Vanity Fair,'" in *The Journal of Biblical Counseling*, 13, no. 2 (Winter 1995). See also Howard Eyrich and William Hines, *Curing the Heart* (Tain, UK: Christian Focus, 2007); and Elyse Fitzpatrick, *Idols of the Heart* (Phillipsburg, NJ: P&R Publishing, 2001).

2. John Calvin, *Institutes of the Christian Religion*, ed. John T. McNeil, 2 vols, Library of Christian Classics (Philadelphia: Westminster, 1960), 1:108.

3. Blaise Pascal, *Pascal's Pensees* (Bibliolife, 2008), pensee #425.

Chapter 25—The Power of Forgiveness

1. C.S. Lewis, *Mere Christianity* (New York: Macmillan, 1960), 104.

Chapter 26—The Ministry of Soul Care for People Who Suffer

1. The use of sinner, sufferer, saint as a way of looking at counselees is commonly used by the Christian Counseling Education Foundation (CCEF).

2. Frank Lake, *Clinical Theology* (London: Dartman, Longman, and Todd, 1966), 21.

3. For an in-depth development of the process of biblical soul care through sustaining and healing, see Robert W. Kellemen, *Spiritual Friends* (Winona Lake, IN: BMH Books, 2007).

4. Octavia Albert, *The House of Bondage* (New York: Oxford University Press, 1988), 2.

5. Ibid., 15.

6. Ibid., 28-29.

7. Olaudah Equiano, *The Interesting Narrative of the Life of Olaudah Equiano* (New York: The Modern Library, 2004), 25.

8. Ibid., 41-42.

9. Ibid., 30.

10. Albert, *The House of Bondage*, 27.

11. Robert W. Kellemen, *Soul Physicians* (Winona Lake, IN: BMH Books, 2007), 15.

12. Patricia Wilson-Kastner, *A Lost Tradition* (Washington, DC: University Press of America, 1981), 19.

13. Ibid., 27.

14. Ibid., 28.

15. Ibid., 26-27.

16. Ibid., 28.

17. Ibid.

Chapter 27—The Biblical Understanding and Treatment of Emotions

1. Representative efforts to understand emotions include Tracy J. Mayne and George A. Bonanno, eds., *Emotions* (New York: The Guilford Press, 2001); Michael Lewis, Jeannette Haviland-Jones, and Lisa Feldman-Barrett, eds., *Handbook of Emotions*, 3d ed. (New York: The Guilford Press, 2010); Robert C, Solomon, ed., *Thinking About Feeling* (New York: Oxford University Press, 2004); Paul E. Griffiths, *What Emotions Really Are* (Chicago: University of Chicago Press, 1997).

2. At a popular level, emotional highjacking was described in Daniel Goleman, *Emotional Intelligence* (New York: Bantam Books, 1995). A more technical summary of emotion regulation research can be found in James J. Gross, *Handbook of Emotion Regulation* (New York: The Guilford Press, 2007).

3. This "suppression of the truth" refers to non-Christians' *active* attempts to dismiss or ignore the reality of God's existence and our accountability to Him. The suppression is sometimes overt and sometimes covert. Either way, the results are "exchanging the truth for a lie," "worshipping the creation rather than the Creator." The resulting "futile thinking" yields ungodly behaviors and attitudes. It can also result in the *misinterpretation* of data by psychologists and philosophers. All of life is lived in the presence of God—and *in response to God.* See Psalms 19; 139; Romans 1:18-32; 2:14-15.

4. The feelings can vary in intensity, and this variance can result from two factors. (1) More intense feelings are associated with values that are centrally important to the person; less intense feelings are associated with less crucial values. (2) As a function of the body's functioning, feelings can become less intense or motivating with alterations in physiology, which might occur with diseases, exhaustion, or habituation. *Habituation* results from increased exposure to situations; as the situations become more familiar and comfortable, they are less arousing.

5. This is an important caution for counselors in their attempts to understand the data they receive from talking to and observing counselees (see Proverbs 14:10,13).

6. Paul Ekman, *Faces Revealed,* 2d ed. (New York: Henry Holt, 2007).

7. This clearly contrasts the repeated evaluation by God recorded in Genesis 1: Seven times He says that what He had done throughout the creation week "was good."

8. C. John Collins, *Genesis 1-4* (Phillipsburg, NJ: P&R Publishing, 2006).

9. In Paul's vocabulary, it is important to note: (1) "Mind" does not mean "morally neutral thinking ability." It is more like the English word *mind-set;* it describes an orientation or predisposition to think in certain ways, either in line with God's Word or against it. (2) Consequently, it is functionally equivalent in meaning to the older Hebrew term translated "heart." Paul alternates his use of "heart" and "mind" (for example, see Romans 1:21-28; 2:28-29; 8:5-8; 10:8-10; 12:2; Ephesians 4:18,23; Philippians 4:7).

10. Jane Nelson, Cheryl Erwin, Michael Brock, Mary Hughes, *Positive Discipline in the Christian Home* (Roseville, CA: Prima Publishing, 2002), 158.

11. Gary Chapman, *Now You're Speaking My Language* (Nashville: B&H Publishing, 2007), 84.

12. See also 1 Peter 3:13-16.

13. Notice that God has not been mentioned yet. I typically try to give ample opportunity early in counseling for the counselee to initiate discussion of a relationship with God or God's role in the counselee's struggles—especially with immature believers who are not used to thinking theologically. This strategy can help facilitate building rapport early in counseling.

14. Matthew A. Elliott, *Faithful Feelings* (Grand Rapids: Kregel, 2006).

Chapter 28—The Complex Mind/Body Connection

1. Biblical Counseling Coalition, *Confessional Statement,* http://biblicalcounselingcoalition.org/about/confessional-statement/.

2. Ed Welch, *Blame It on the Brain* (Phillipsburg, NJ: P&R Publishing, 1998), 48.

3. Martin Luther, *Letters of Spiritual Counsel* (Philadelphia, PA: Westminster Press, 1955), 99.

4. Charles Spurgeon, "Psalm 88" in *Treasury of David* (Grand Rapids: Zondervan, 1950), 4.3.

5. Mike Emlet, "Listening to Prozac…and to the Scriptures: A Primer on Psychoactive Medications," *Journal of Biblical Counseling* 26, no. 1 (2012), 21.

6. Charles Spurgeon, Quoted in http://www.bulletininserts.org/spurdepr.html, accessed on 8/15/09.